DAYBREAK

DAYBREAK
UNDOING THE IMPERIAL PRESIDENCY AND FORMING A MORE PERFECT UNION

DAVID SWANSON

SEVEN STORIES PRESS
NEW YORK

A Seven Stories Press First Edition

Seven Stories Press
140 Watts Street
New York, NY 10013
www.sevenstories.com

In Canada: Publishers Group Canada, 559 College Street, Suite 402, Toronto, ON M6G 1A9

In the UK: Turnaround Publisher Services Ltd., Unit 3, Olympia Trading Estate, Coburg Road, Wood Green, London N22 6TZ

In Australia: Palgrave Macmillan, 15–19 Claremont Street, South Yarra, VIC 3141

College professors may order examination copies of Seven Stories Press titles for a free six-month trial period. To order, visit http://www.sevenstories.com/textbook or send a fax on school letterhead to (212) 226-1411.

Library of Congress Cataloging-in-Publication Data

Swanson, David, 1969 Dec. 1-
 Daybreak : undoing the imperial Presidency and forming a more perfect union / by David Swanson.
   p. cm.
 Includes index.
 ISBN 978-1-58322-888-3 (pbk.)
 1. Presidents--United States. 2. Executive power--United States. I. Title.
 JK516.S86 2009
 352.230973--dc22

                                2009023856

Book design by Jon Gilbert

Printed in the USA

9 8 7 6 5 4 3 2

CONTENTS

V. Citizen Power

ANOTHER PATRIOT FROM VIRGINIA

Let me tell you about David Swanson, and America.

Our story begins on a Saturday night in New England, in the seventh year of the Bush-Cheney interregnum. David and I had just finished speaking at a church in the college town of Keene, New Hampshire. We had rallied one more crowd in one more corner of the republic to the cause of impeaching Bush and Cheney for high crimes and misdemeanors. There we were in the backseat of another car driven by another volunteer patriot, late as ever and racing on to the state capital in Concord for the last rally of the night.

Everyone in the car was talking, everyone was enthusiastic about the serious work of renewing our country's connection to its Constitution and holding to account the men who had broken that bond. But David was doing something else. His computer was open, his wireless card was plugged in, and he was online, typing in another update to the website he had so long and meticulously maintained to promote the impeachment cause.

I had been campaigning on these constitutional issues for the better part of two years, having written a condemnatory biography of Dick Cheney and then a manual of citizenship in times of crisis, *The Genius of Impeachment*, which took as its purpose convincing cautious citizens that impeachment was an American sacrament. I had delivered hundreds of speeches, written scores of articles, recorded dozens of radio interviews. But nothing I had done could or would compare with David Swanson's contribution. I was a campaigner for the Constitution. David was the campaign.

From the moment when the British media release revealed the details of the Downing Street Memos, which confirmed that the Bush-Cheney administration had actively lied in order to make the "case" for invading and occupying Iraq, David became the driving force in the movement to hold the president and vice president to account for the highest of crimes. With the AfterDowningStreet.org website as a platform, he cajoled, prodded, and pressured a genuine movement into being.

The work was rewarding, especially when David began to recognize the level of grassroots support for the most fundamental of American precepts: No man, not even the president of the United States, can stand above the law or dismiss the dictates of the Constitution. The people got it, as revealed by polls and the anecdotal experiences of hundreds of rallies, marches, and pickets.

Unfortunately, the politicians and the press refused, for the most part, to be moved. And that frustrated David, turning him from a mild-mannered, good-natured organizer into a raging prophet who channeled the fury of the Founders at another King George. David warned, correctly, and at times fiercely, that the republic was not merely endangered by the wrongdoing of Bush and Cheney. It was threatened as well by supposedly liberal Democrats and supposedly enlightened journalists who chose to play politics rather than apply the remedies established by James Madison and George Mason for lawless executives.

By the conventional measures of American political life, David Swanson failed as a campaigner for impeachment—as did I. George Bush and Dick Cheney finished their tenures without being held to account. The rule of law was not respected. The Constitution was disregarded—not by the people, but by the politicians who had sworn an oath to support and defend it against all enemies foreign and domestic.

But by the broad measures of history, David's work will be counted as a success. That's because David's work was always about more than impeaching Bush and Cheney. It was about renewing respect for our founding document and for a system of checks and balances that was ordained with the purpose of constraining the war-making whims and crude assaults on liberty by presidents and vice presidents, who diminish not merely their administrations but the republic.

In time, America will be reacquainted with her better angels and this country will return to its rule-of-law roots, not for reasons of nostalgia but for the purpose of perfecting the ongoing experiment that was begun in 1776 but has yet to realize its promise. When that happens, David Swanson will be recognized as the citizen who, like good Tom Paine, held up a lamp in the darkness and cried, "We have it in our power to begin the world over again."

This book is the outline for that project, written in the pamphleteering style of Paine by a man who is the true heir of the most radical—and thus the most American—of our Founders.

David Swanson is a worthy heir to Paine—and he is a neighbor of Paine's friend, Tom Jefferson.

A resident for many years of Charlottesville, the city where the Founder created his great university, David well recalls that Jefferson ended his days with a July 4th declaration—not unlike the one he had penned fifty years earlier—that eschewed the cheap sentimentality of holiday nostalgia in favor of a call to action. To be an American, Jefferson explained, requires a radical faith.

Addressing the anniversary of his revolutionary declaration, the enlightened, if imperfect, Founder said, "May it be to the world, what I believe it will be—to some parts sooner, to others later, but finally to all—the signal of arousing men to burst the chains under which monkish ignorance and superstition had persuaded them to bind themselves, and to assume the blessings and security of self-government."

Americans are still struggling to assume the blessings and security of self-government. We will know them fully only when the presidency has been brought back within the confines of the Constitution, when the system of checks and balances has been restored, when the people recognize that they have the power—and the responsibility—to hold even the most powerful to account.

If Tom Jefferson were with us today, he would be saying that we still must burst the chains of monkish ignorance and superstition and break the bindings that strangle our liberty.

But Jefferson—like Paine—is gone. So it falls to another from Virginia to sound the signal for a rising on behalf of the republic and our own freedom.

That man is David Swanson, and this remarkable book is his—and America's—call to arms.

JOHN NICHOLS
June 21, 2009

"The only kinds of fights worth fighting are those you are going to lose, because somebody has to fight them and lose and lose and lose until someday, somebody who believes as you do wins. In order for somebody to win an important, major fight 100 years hence, a lot of other people have got to be willing—for the sheer fun and joy of it—to go right ahead and fight, knowing you're going to lose. You mustn't feel like a martyr. You've got to enjoy it."

—I. F. STONE

"I leave Sisyphus at the foot of the mountain! One always finds one's burden again. But Sisyphus teaches the higher fidelity that negates the gods and raises rocks. He too concludes that all is well. The universe henceforth without a master seems to him neither sterile nor futile. Each atom of that stone, each mineral flake of that night-filled mountain, in itself forms a world. The struggle itself toward the heights is enough to fill a man's heart. One must imagine Sisyphus happy."

—ALBERT CAMUS

"Some men look at constitutions with sanctimonious reverence, and deem them, like the Ark of the Covenant, too sacred to be touched. They ascribe to the men of the preceding age a wisdom more than human, and suppose what they did to be beyond amendment. . . . [L]aws and institutions must go hand in hand with the progress of the human mind. As that becomes more developed, more enlightened, as new discoveries are made, new truths disclosed, and manners and opinions change with the change of circumstances, institutions must advance also, and keep pace with the times. We might as well require a man to wear still the coat which fitted him when a boy as civilized society to remain ever under the regimen of their barbarous ancestors."

—THOMAS JEFFERSON

"A republic, if you can keep it."

—BENJAMIN FRANKLIN

INTRODUCTION

The Constitution of the United States begins with this familiar preamble, of which we the people are the authors:

> We the People of the United States, in Order to form a more perfect Union, establish Justice, insure domestic Tranquility, provide for the common defence, promote the general Welfare, and secure the Blessings of Liberty to ourselves and our Posterity, do ordain and establish this Constitution for the United States of America.[1]

Not bad, but hardly a match for the eloquence of our modern statesmen. When told in 2008 that two-thirds of the people of the United States thought the Iraq War was "not worth it," Vice President Dick Cheney replied with this familiar expression of contempt:

"So?"[2]

The Constitution, outdated and longwinded though it may be when compared with Cheney's chillingly concise statement, begins with the idea that in a democracy, power lies with the people. The Tenth Amendment concludes the Bill of Rights by stipulating that any powers not given in the Constitution to the various branches of the federal government remain with the people or their state governments.[3] But what happens when the people, not to mention their supposed representatives in Congress, forget that they should care about being in charge?

If the last several years are any indication, not a whole lot of good.

It may be a surprise to many, but the Constitution gives the vast bulk of power in the federal government to the Congress, and relatively little to the executive and judicial branches. (You might have to read that last sentence a few times. It doesn't contain a typo.) The Congress is intended to represent the people. It is given so much power that it is sub-

1

divided into two houses, and one of the two is called the "House of Representatives."

About 58 percent of the words in the Constitution (excluding the amendments, and deleting words altered by amendments) are found in Article I, which is devoted to the Congress, the legislative branch. This compares to 18 percent for the executive branch and 7 percent for the judicial branch. The three branches are presented, in that order, in the first three articles of the Constitution. Each article is broken into sections, and—with the exception of a section on how to elect the president, which was later altered by amendment—the single longest section is Article I, Section 8, which lists various powers of the Congress.

According to the Constitution, Congress has the exclusive power to enact laws, as well as complete control over the raising and spending of money. No one can write a law without Congress. No one can raise or spend a dime of federal money without Congress. No one can declare war, fund and oversee the military, or regulate international and interstate trade, without Congress. Congress handles immigration, bankruptcies, the printing and valuing of money, the postal system, and copyrights. Congress has the power to "constitute tribunals inferior to the Supreme Court," and "to define and punish piracies and felonies committed on the high seas, and offenses against the law of nations."

The various powers that the framers of the Constitution thought a government would need were almost entirely given to the Congress, which was then also granted the exclusive right to create any laws needed to carry into execution any other powers vested by the Constitution in "the Government of the United States, or in any Department or Officer thereof."

Of course, Congress is less popular than roadkill these days (although slightly more popular than the record low it hit in the polls in 2008), but that's not because it's too powerful. While Congress has always tended to be unpopular, it is better liked when it wields more power.[4] The problem now is that Congress, more than ever, fails to take on its responsibilities, and even more egregiously, fails to represent the will of the people.[5] We spent the eight Bush-Cheney years watching a gang of 535 go along with the crimes and abuses of two. It may strike us as being much easier to change the two than to change the 535. At least the two are term-limited, whereas members of Congress seem to almost never leave. If we could just elect good presidents and vice presidents, we'd be better off hanging onto a Congress that obediently takes orders, right? Well, yes, that might begin to make sense if the two people to whom we were planning to hand what Michael Goldfarb, who was later deputy communications director for presidential candidate John McCain, approvingly called "near dictatorial power,"[6] were anything other than homo sapiens. If we could count on each future president and vice president belonging to a very different species that was capable of always foregoing opportunities to abuse power, then we'd be fine. But even then, we wouldn't have much of a democracy.

Just a few weeks before the 2008 elections, vice presidential candidate Joe Biden told a group of supporters,

> There are going to be a lot of you who want to go, "Whoa, wait a minute, yo, whoa, whoa, I don't know about that decision." Because if you think the decision is sound when they're made, which I believe you will when they're made, they're not likely to be as popular as they are sound, because if they're popular they're probably not sound.[7]

The comments Biden had made in the previous breath, about the likelihood of President Obama being tested with a military crisis in his first six months, made big news, but this equally distressing comment was mostly overlooked. It is simply accepted wisdom in our democratic republic that self-governance is a bad idea, that we should elect people who despise us and advise us to despise ourselves. If an idea is popular it's probably a bad one—so said our new vice president shortly before the election, reinforcing the very denial of self-governance that had allowed the Bush-Cheney disaster.

It seems to me that whether or not we can change this way of thinking will determine the direction of our country to a far greater extent than the choice of what people we elect to office. We hope that we can expect our leaders to listen to our voices. In fact, you'll notice that Biden contradicts his own assertion that sound ideas will be unpopular ones by telling his listeners that they (the populace) will find his ideas to be sound. Biden is not so much telling people to despise themselves as suggesting that they are an in-the-know group who can afford to despise the greater masses of riff-raff.

I recall working on a campaign with ACORN (The Association of Community Organizations for Reform Now) in New Orleans several years ago to create a higher citywide minimum wage.[8] We placed the question on the ballot, and a strong majority voted for it. The US Chamber of Commerce and various hotel and restaurant industry groups opposed our efforts. But one of their spokesmen told the media that they had decided not to bother trying to influence the vote, since it would be easier for them to overturn the vote in court. Well, they immediately took the question to court and lost. And I recall one of their spokesmen telling the media that the disgraceful decision of the judge who had upheld the law was only to be expected from someone trying to please her constituents.

That was the ultimate criticism, it seemed. She had been trying to please people. When the Louisiana Supreme Court overruled the local court on appeal, and wages were kept down, the decision was depicted as wise and just because it was above the fray and divorced from popular interests. It was a sound decision rather than a popular one. But that is exactly the kind of thinking that damages a democratic nation and can ultimately turn it into a very different kind of state.[9]

Popular rule is not mob rule. It is the foundation of a functioning democracy. When our elected officials and representatives keep promising to disregard our voices whenever they feel like it, we should be concerned.

How did we get from "We the People" to "So?" The ABC News reporter who received that answer followed up with, "You don't care what the American people think?" to which Cheney replied, "No, I think you cannot be blown off course by the fluctuations in the public opinion polls." Polls are consistently denounced by politicians of all stripes, even though polls are nothing other than (if imperfect and sometimes dishonest) attempts to measure the will of the people.

The proper political role of the public, in what seems to be a prevailing view, is to participate in elections and then shut up and go shopping until the next election season begins. And, with Congress deferring to the president on all important matters, the only elections that can really change anything come four years apart.

This gets right to the heart of what is ailing our democratic republic. There is a lack of engagement between citizens and representatives in between elections and apart from elections. There is a deficiency in outrage over the fact that the majority opinion very often runs counter to the decisions made by our so-called representatives. We don't think of them as representatives, but as people who, if we're really lucky, will stick with the positions they held a year or two or five ago and not be influenced by polls, or phone calls, or e-mails, or visits, or sit-ins, or letters to editors, or books. As a result, our government is run as an enormous taxpayer-funded duel between two endless public relations (PR) campaigns headed by the leaders of the two major parties. From 2001 to 2008, according to a string of disgruntled former cabinet members and top officials, as well as many other press reports, the Republican White House made nearly every decision with electoral PR in mind. John Dilulio, the first director of Bush's White House Office of Faith-Based and Community Initiatives, summed it up:

> There is no precedent in any modern White House for what is going on in this one: a complete lack of a policy apparatus. What you've got is everything—and I mean everything—being run by the political arm. It's the reign of the Mayberry Machiavellis.[10]

These six short quotations from Dick Cheney provide a glimpse of what happens when we trust that the American people need to be deceived as the means to a higher end:

> I'm often asked why I left politics and went to Halliburton and I explain that I reached the point where I was mean-spirited, short-tempered and intolerant of those who disagreed with me and they said, "Hell, you'd make a great CEO," so I went to Texas and joined the private sector.... Oil remains fundamentally a government business. While many regions of the world offer great oil opportunities, the Middle East, with two-thirds of the world's oil and the lowest cost, is still where the prize ultimately lies.[11] (1999)

Conservation may be a sign of personal virtue but it is not a sufficient basis for a sound, comprehensive energy policy.[12] (2001)

His regime has had high-level contacts with al-Qaeda going back a decade and has provided training to al-Qaeda terrorists.[13] (2002)

We know he's been absolutely devoted to trying to acquire nuclear weapons, and we believe he has, in fact, reconstituted nuclear weapons.[14] (2003)

My belief is we will, in fact, be greeted as liberators.[15] (2003)

I think they're in the last throes, if you will, of the insurgency.[16] (2005)

We seem to be getting away from the fundamentals upon which this country was started. For one, the only way for the majority of a people to rule a nation is through laws. To fail to adhere to the Constitution (including the now much-violated Bill of Rights) without amending it, is not to outgrow an old document. Rather, it is to lose something very, very precious: the rule of law. By allowing that, we enable the rule of tyrants. And we've come quite close.

Our government has often strayed from adherence to the Constitution and other lesser laws, but never before in as drastic a manner as during the years 2001 to 2008. We are in unprecedented territory, far closer than ever before to losing our republic, and losing it in much the way that Rome lost hers. Even if you believe that the president should possess certain powers that the Constitution does not give him, your only safe course is to amend the Constitution to include those changes. Allowing presidents to simply seize new powers confers on them the right to seize any other new powers as well, including powers that you do not want them to hold. If you cannot think of any powers that you wouldn't want a president to hold, even a president whose politics you opposed, then you are probably not thinking hard enough.

John Adams, who would later become the second president of the

United States, wrote some words in the Constitution of Massachusetts that have been quoted approvingly by the US Supreme Court and every state supreme court in the United States. He described a separation of powers among three branches of government and said that this would be created "to the end it may be a government of laws and not of men."[17] Thomas Paine, in his "Common Sense" pamphlets, which helped launch the American war for independence, wrote that "so far as we approve of monarchy . . . in America THE LAW IS KING. For as in absolute governments the King is law, so in free countries the law ought to be King; and there ought to be no other." (Emphases in original.)[18]

For as long as the United States of America has had presidents, presidents have assumed greater power than was probably intended by the authors of the Constitution, and certainly greater power than is healthy for our democracy. This has been especially true during wars and similar crises. But rarely have those powers been relinquished when the crises have ended. And rarely have powers claimed by one president not been maintained by his successors, resulting in an ever-expanding accumulation of power over the years.

Only slightly more frequently do the American people protest this trend. We have been trained to think of the president as our government, and of Congress and the courts as impediments to efficiency. We hear thousands of times a year on our televisions that bipartisanship is preferable to debate (and debate is modeled for us as angry name-calling and screaming rather than attempts to persuade and understand). We hear that legislation is created by the White House and voted on out of loyalty or opposition to the White House, that keeping the workings of our government secret from us is necessary to protect us, that allowing presidents to seize unconstitutional powers and even violate laws is the only way to keep us safe, and that we all—not just members of the military—must obey our "commander-in-chief."

During the eight Bush-Cheney years we saw the president far more blatantly and frequently than ever before assume the power to legislate, to create secret laws, to rewrite brand new laws with "signing statements," and to create "legal opinions" permitting the violation of long-standing laws. We watched the power to make and end wars, little used by Congress in the previous sixty years, move fully into the Oval Office, as a president secretly misspent funds to begin a war, misled Congress and the public to justify a war, declared war with Congress's "authorization" but in violation of the terms of that authorization, and even created a treaty stipulating three more years of war without ever having sought the consent of the Senate. We saw the power to spend money further removed from Capitol Hill, not just through the explosion of the military budget, war budgets, and secret budgets, but also through the giving and loaning of trillions of dollars by the executive branch as part of an economic "bailout." We saw our public policy created in private meetings by participants whose names we were not even permitted to know. We saw the vice president assume more powers than the nation's founders ever imagined the president possessing. And we saw very little pushback from the courts, and almost none from Congress.

The US government has been fundamentally changed.

The danger of further abandoning the rule of law is in fact nothing other than the danger of recreating a monarchy. When Cheney asked "So?" in response to a report that his policies were opposed by the real sovereigns of this nation, he was not speaking as just any arrogant holder of power. Cheney was speaking as the man who had led the efforts to intentionally deceive the people and their representatives in Congress into an illegal, disastrous, bloody, and costly war that was still happening and from which he himself had shamelessly profited.[19]

We now imagine that when Cheney moved from the vice president's house to his new home next door to Central Intelligence Agency (CIA) headquarters, and when Bush moved from the White House back to Texas, that we were rid of them, and that in being rid of them we have been rid of the imperial presidency. But we cannot make the mistake of pretending that the last eight years never happened, of letting dangerous changes to the law and cuts into the Constitution and our rights go unchecked. Some of the policies of the Cheney-Bush years will certainly change "under" Obama, as the common phrase puts it. But changing policies will not deny future presidents or vice presidents the powers that were seized by Bush and Cheney. In fact, in the early months of Obama's presidency he committed to ceasing some of Bush's crimes and abuses, but claimed the power to continue others, opposed holding his predecessors accountable, worked hard to keep Bush and

Cheney's crimes secret, and aggressively sought to maintain and expand presidential power. While a signing statement by President Obama giving himself the power to fire whistleblowers, for example, is not as offensive as one by Bush giving himself the power to torture, the two are equally unconstitutional, and the repetition of the same abuse by two presidents establishes it as a tool available to future ones—unless we act. And act we must. What is at stake here is how and whether our democratic republic survives.

Undoing the imperial presidency is not just a matter of documenting the abuses of one or two or a handful of men (and Condoleezza Rice) or even of punishing them to deter others (although that certainly would be a step in the right direction). Cheney and Bush could never have done what they did without the active support of hundreds of thousands and the passive acceptance of millions who knew better. When we elected Jimmy Carter we saw policy changes, but our failure to prosecute President Nixon helped produce the Cheney-Bush catastrophe. Accountability is not about looking backward. It's about looking forward.

Undoing the damage is probably going to be the work of many years. While we can't erase the harm already done, we can reconstitute a nation of laws and a democratic system of government to ensure it doesn't happen again. While we cannot bring back the dead or undo irreparable destruction of the environment, of cities, and of cultures devastated by the maladministration of the eight Bush-Cheney years, we can, if we choose, make reparations to the people of Iraq and Afghanistan and the neglected victims of Hurricane Katrina along the Gulf Coast, the mistreated first responders to 9/11, the veterans of the Bush-Cheney wars and their families, and all the others. And we can chart a very different course for our country and its influence on the world.

We must reestablish a nation of laws by enforcing them, and we must go beyond that by rewriting our laws to improve upon them, including by amending our Constitution. These steps must be taken in that order.

Forming a more perfect union will require major changes outside our government as well, beginning with the replacement of our current media system with something more democratic. We will need a revolution of values in our own habits of thought and action, which will include some changes we may not at first find appealing. It will not be easy, but it will be well worth the effort. We can, if we choose, do more than keep our republic. We can do more than bandage the wounds. We can create a better place than what any one of us can now imagine, a country capable of cooperating with other countries as one among equals, a country able once again, at long last, to lead by example instead of coercing by bloodshed.

While this book focuses on the presidential abuses and the congressional spinelessness of the Bush-Cheney years, plus the first few months of the Obama presidency, the trends described began more than eight years ago. And if we the people do not step into our appropriate democratic roles, they will continue for years to come. This book focuses on how we should view our own roles, how we should understand the structure of our government, what changes we should seek to make, and how we can begin to go about it.

To make the right kind of changes, we must evaluate the damage done in recent years, as well as problems that have grown over the past decades. We must chart a course that creates accountability for wrongdoing, that preserves and protects the rights we have or are supposed to have, and that institutes a new establishment of rights to face the new century.

Finally, this book explains how we can successfully make these demands of our government, and where and how we must mobilize for social change. At heart, the aim of this book is to encourage the American people to take actions that are absolutely necessary. Now.

I.

PRESIDENTIAL POWER GRAB
Damage Done and Repairs Needed

1. POWER OF LAW

From 2001 to 2008, Americans witnessed an unprecedented phenomenon in US politics. Here was a president who violated numerous laws that predated his presidency, including laws banning torture[1] and laws banning warrantless spying.[2] Here was a Congress (the 107th through 110th Congresses, from 2001 to 2008) that repeatedly re-criminalized some of the president's crimes through new legislation, including bills banning torture and bills forbidding the spending of funds to make use of information gathered in violation of the Fourth Amendment.[3] Here was a president who signed those bills into law and then posted "signing statements" on his website announcing his right and his intention to violate those new laws along with the old ones. And here was an administration that proceeded to do just that, while the Congress responded with new proposals to re-criminalize the crimes yet again.

Article II of the Constitution requires that the president "take care that the laws be faithfully executed." And, as we all learned in elementary school, the Constitution also sets forth the manner in which a bill can become a law. In fact, elementary schools (not to mention high schools, colleges, and US Park Service tour guides) continue to teach this today as if it were still accurate.

Article I, Section 7 of the Constitution says,

> . . . every bill which shall have passed the House of Representatives and the Senate, shall, before it become a law, be presented to the President of the United States; if he approve he shall sign it, but if not he shall return it, with his objections to that House in which it shall have originated, who shall enter the objections at large on their journal, and proceed to reconsider it. If after

such reconsideration two thirds of that House shall agree to pass the bill, it shall be sent, together with the objections, to the other House, by which it shall likewise be reconsidered, and if approved by two thirds of that House, it shall become a law.

The reality has now become this: every bill which shall have passed the House of Representatives and the Senate, shall, before it become a law, be presented to the President of the United States; he shall sign the bill in the presence of select members of the House of Representatives, Senate, and the media; during the next convenient holiday weekend he shall quietly rewrite the law with a signing statement. Congress can neither override a signing statement nor challenge it in court; but courts can cite signing statements in their opinions as though they have the force of law, which they do.

Signing statements are not new. My neighbor here in Charlottesville, Virginia, James Monroe, wrote the first one. But, until Bush-Cheney, signing statements were very rarely used to alter the meaning or intention of the law. President Andrew Jackson once controversially used a signing statement to alter a bill funding road construction, and Reagan used a signing statement in such a manner on the Deficit Reduction Act of 1984. He announced his intention and proceeded to violate the law. But a series of court rulings and a vote by the House Judiciary Committee to eliminate funds for the Office of the Attorney General brought Reagan into compliance. Most early signing statements did not rewrite the laws. Even when Reagan brought signing statements into more common usage, it was not for the purpose of directing members of his administration to violate new laws. Rather, his goal was to make his views part of the legal history of a law, in hopes of influencing future decisions by the Supreme Court, which has in fact cited signing statements in its rulings.[4]

Bush Sr. and Clinton also went beyond mere expression of opinion in at least some instances. Bush Sr. objected to a provision of the National and Community Services Act of 1990 and refused to enforce it, but submitted legislation that was subsequently passed by Congress, thus legally remedying what he considered a problem. Clinton argued that he had the right to violate a law if he believed the Supreme Court would agree with him, but that he must obey the law, even if he thought the law unconstitutional, if he did not believe the Supreme Court would back him up.[5]

All in all, 322 pre–George W. Bush signing statements addressed, by one count, some 600 provisions of law. Rivaling that grand total of his forty-two predecessors, Bush Jr.'s 161 signing statements challenged over 1,100 provisions of law in 160 acts of Congress.[6] And, although written in especially coded language, Bush Jr.'s signing statements again and again effectively announced his intention to violate those sections of those laws.[7] His attorneys openly argued before a congressional committee that the president has the inherent right to violate any law until the Supreme Court specifically rules in favor of it.[8] When they had serious disagreements with bills, Reagan, Bush Sr., and Clinton vetoed them. In contrast, during the first five-and-a-half years of his presidency, Bush Jr. never vetoed a bill, preferring to sign legislation into law and then quietly rewrite important sections of it with signing statements. During the 110th Congress, Bush began to use the veto, reserving the signing statement for bills containing some elements he particularly wanted to see become law.

Signing statements are no easier to read than the bills they alter. When Congress said "Stop the illegal spying," and Bush said "I'd like to see you make me," it looked like this:

CONGRESS: None of the funds provided in this Act shall be available for integration of foreign intelligence information unless the information has been lawfully collected and processed during the conduct of authorized foreign intelligence activities: Provided, That information pertaining to United States persons shall only be handled in accordance with protections provided in the Fourth Amendment of the United States Constitution as implemented through Executive Order No. 12333.

BUSH: Also, the executive branch shall construe section 8124, relating to integration of foreign intelligence information, in a manner consistent with the President's constitutional authority as Commander in Chief, including for the conduct of intelligence operations, and to supervise the unitary executive branch.

In almost every signing statement, Bush claims the power of a fictional being that Cheney's lawyers invented, building on ideas developed in the Reagan administration: the "unitary executive." This creature does not exist in the Constitution, but is worthy of notice because he claims absolute power, a substance said to corrupt absolutely.

One instance of Bush's signing-statementing torture made the news in at least a minor way thanks to the reporting of Charlie Savage at the *Boston Globe*, and also thanks to the heavily covered lobbying competition prior to passage of the bill. Senator John McCain had lobbied successfully for a provision to redundantly re-ban torture.[9] Vice President Dick Cheney had lobbied unsuccessfully against it (although McCain had granted Cheney a loophole for the CIA). Over New Year's weekend in 2006, the White House quietly posted a signing statement on its website, and the *Boston Globe* reported on it. Senator John McCain, having won a very public contest, said little about Bush's quiet reversal of the outcome. McCain later transformed himself from a leading opponent of torture into a cheerleader for its use.[10]

Of course it wouldn't be as serious a concern if Bush had merely claimed the right to torture and engage in warrantless spying, but ceased to actually do so until it was made legal. In the case of unconstitutional spying, Congress passed a bill that Bush signed into law in 2008 retroactively granting civil immunity to telecom companies that had violated the law at the president's request.[11] Congress disgraced itself even further by doing so without being informed of the details of the crimes it was thereby pardoning. But leading members of Congress of both parties had known some level of information about both the torture and the spying years before any members of the public found out, and that complicity may have contributed to Congress's reluctance to investigate or impeach. In fact, Democratic Congresswoman Jane Harman was blackmailed by White House Counsel Alberto Gonzales into pressuring the *New York Times* to delay reporting on the spying for a year.[12] However, the fact that Congress granted immunity to Bush's accomplices doesn't change the fact that, beginning prior to September 11, 2001, Bush engaged in the crime of warrantless spying for years, in secret. At first he lied about it, but then he claimed the right to spy through signing statements.

The offense is not the signing statement itself so much as the claim to possess the right to violate laws. This is not something that should be allowed to pass unnoticed. Defenders of Bush's signing statements have claimed they are no more harmful than press releases. But the Government Accountability Office in 2007 studied a sample of obscure Bush signing statements and found that, as with the famous ones, in a significant percentage of cases the Bush administration had already begun violating the laws that Bush instructed the government to violate.[13]

Congress might have ignored this behavior even more fully than it has if not for the reporting of Charlie Savage at the *Boston Globe*, who blew this story open with the April 30, 2006 article that began,

> President Bush has quietly claimed the authority to disobey more than 750 laws enacted since he took office, asserting that he has the power to set aside any statute passed by Congress when it conflicts with his interpretation of the Constitution. Among the laws Bush said he can ignore are military rules and regulations, affirmative-action provisions, requirements that Congress be told about immigration services problems, 'whistle-blower' protections for nuclear regulatory officials, and safeguards against political interference in federally funded research.
>
> ... Legal scholars say the scope and aggression of Bush's assertions that he can bypass laws represent a concerted effort to expand his power at the expense of Congress, upsetting the balance between the branches of government. The Constitution is clear in assigning to Congress the power to write the laws and to the president a duty "to take care that the laws be faithfully executed." Bush, however, has repeatedly declared that he does not need to "execute" a law he believes is unconstitutional.[14]

Even after the *Boston Globe* ran this story, most other corporate media outlets in the United States continued to ignore it. This story alone generated congressional hearings, proposed legislation, and initiated studies by groups including the American Bar Association.

The media was failing over and over again to report a constant assault. Four times Bush used signing statements to overturn a ban on using US troops to combat rebels in Colombia. Twice Bush brushed aside the creation of an Inspector General in Iraq to report directly to Congress, requiring instead that he or she report to the executive branch. At least nine times, Bush rejected affirmative action requirements (despite the Supreme Court's having already ruled on the issue). Several times Bush signed into law and then tossed out requirements that information be provided to Congress, including information on spying programs.

Now Congress often repeats itself, especially in funding bills that it passes on an annual basis. But why, one must wonder, did it repeatedly pass measures that were then repeatedly annulled through signing statements? Was Congress hoping that Bush would allow it to create a law if it passed a second time or a third time? Once you've passed a bill and the president has thrown it out, if you aren't going to impeach him, why not spend less time passing that provision again and more time golfing or reading?

One reason may be theater. The Democratic leadership in the House sought public credit and support for including yet another ban on torture in a "supplemental spending bill" for the occupation of Iraq in 2007, a bill that primarily provided money for war, some of which was no doubt used for torture. (A small minimum-wage increase, the 110th Congress's most loudly claimed success, was also used as lipstick on this economy-draining, grandchildren-impoverishing pig of a war bill.) In November of 2003, Bush had thrown out, with a signing statement, limitations on the use of troops in Iraq who were not rested and ready—limitations that had been passed by Congress in the National Defense Authorization Act that year. Yet the Democrats made similar limitations a central focus of their 2007 war supplemental. However, in a move that seemed to advertise their awareness of Bush's disregard for the law, congressional leaders stipulated that Bush could waive those limitations by publicly signing a waiver. This, they presumably thought, would make a better spectacle than an incomprehensible signing statement posted on a website on a Friday night and ignored by the media.

What else did Bush undo unconstitutionally? He threw out a requirement to report to Congress when money from regular appropriations is diverted to secret operations—such as black sites. (So now the president can torture and pay for it.) He eliminated a requirement to make background checks of civilian contractors (including mercenaries) in Iraq. He erased a ban on using said contractors to perform security, law enforcement, intelligence, and criminal justice functions. And, in a somewhat well-known case, Bush signing-statemented away a requirement to report back to Congress on the use of PATRIOT Act authority to secretly search and seize. In this case and others, Bush quietly signing statemented away provisions that he himself had negotiated with Congress to include in order to win passage of the legislation.

John Dean, former legal counsel to President Richard Nixon, had this to say in his column from April 2000 titled "Why It Is a Bad Day For The Constitution Whenever Attorney General Alberto Gonzales Testifies":

> As readers will recall, in early 2006, Congress reauthorized the controversial USA PATRIOT Act. Previously, [Republican Senator Arlen Specter], as chairman of the Judiciary Committee, had negotiated with [Attorney General Alberto] Gonzales in good faith over reauthorization. They agreed that Specter would approve reauthorization—but only on condition that there would be more stringent oversight of the law's application by Congress. Yet on March 6, 2006, after Congress reauthorized the Act, Bush issued a signing statement that boldly betrayed that agreement.
>
> So at the January 18th hearing, Senator Specter asked the Attorney General to explain the betrayal of their agreement. He pointed out that the agreement was that Congress would have "additional safeguards on oversight." And he noted that, nevertheless, the President's signing statement "reserved what he calls his right to disregard those oversight provisions." He then asked Gonzales, "In a context where the chairman of the committee and the attorney general negotiate an arrangement, is it appropriate for the president to put a signing statement which negates the oversight which had been bargained for, which has been bargained for?"

Gonzales simply cited the legal proposition that "a signing statement cannot give to the President any authority that he doesn't already have under the Constitution." But Specter responded adeptly that "if [the President] thinks those provisions inappropriately take away his constitutional authority and the Act's unconstitutional, then he ought to veto it. Or at least not to bargain it away." Gonzales had little to say in response, except to reiterate that the President wanted the Act reauthorized, and had the power not to honor the deal Gonzales had made.

This kind of practice might be common on used car lots, but should not be common in our government.[15]

Well, at least that's the worst of it, right? Illegal spying, torture, and so on? Bush didn't use signing statements to pull any other fast ones, did he?

Well, only if we overlook his elimination of a requirement that government scientists transmit findings to Congress uncensored. Only if we pay no attention to his blocking the creation of an educational research institute to report directly to Congress on the state of our schools (Bush chose to have it report to his Department of Education—all governmental departments being thought of as somehow belonging to the executive branch). And only if we overlook those numerous times Bush tossed out requirements not to punish whistleblowers. Who knows what crimes went unreported, crimes that could still be reported in years to come.

Bush's revisionist approach was not limited to domestic bills either. In December of 2006, Bush signed an agreement on nuclear weapons approved by Congress following long negotiations with the White House and with India. Then Bush issued a signing statement announcing his lack of commitment to nine major sections of the agreement, including those aimed at countering nuclear proliferation.[16] Congress may not have noticed, but India seemed to. Indian Prime Minister Manmohan Singh issued a similar statement explaining which parts of the agreement he would feel free to ignore, agreeing with Bush on the elimination of congressional oversight and accepting Bush's signing statement as part of the treaty.

Is this starting to look troubling?

To a very limited and sporadic extent, the media picked up on Bush's little game. When, for Christmas 2006, Bush used a signing statement to bestow upon himself the right to read anyone's private mail, the story was fairly well-reported. Senator Russ Feingold wrote Bush a letter asking: "[H]as your administration authorized any government agency to read Americans' first-class mail without obtaining a search warrant, complying with the applicable court order requirements of the Foreign Intelligence Surveillance Act, or satisfying Postal Service regulations?"[17] As far as I know, Bush never replied.

The Congressional Research Service, the widely respected nonpartisan research office working on behalf of Congress, its members, and committees, called Bush's use of signing statements "an integral part" of his "comprehensive strategy to strengthen and expand executive power," adding that the "broad and persistent nature of the claims of executive authority forwarded by President Bush appear designed to inure Congress, as well as others, to the belief that the president in fact possesses expansive and exclusive powers upon which the other branches may not intrude."[18]

The American Bar Association "opposes, as contrary to the rule of law and our constitutional system of separation of powers, the misuse of presidential signing statements."[19]

The bipartisan Constitution Project's Coalition to Defend Checks and Balances stated, "We are former government officials and judges, scholars, and other Americans who are deeply concerned about the risk of permanent and unchecked presidential power, and the accompanying failure of Congress to exercise its responsibility as a separate and independent branch of government." Associated attorneys released a report called "Presidential Signing Statements: Will Congress Pick Up the Gauntlet?"[20]

Republican Senator Arlen Specter called Bush's signing statements "a very blatant encroachment" on Congress's power to legislate. Democratic Senator Patrick Leahy called them "a grave threat to our constitutional system of checks and balances."[21]

As Savage pointed out in his original *Boston Globe* article and followed up on in additional articles and in his book, *Takeover: The Return of the Imperial Presidency and the Subversion of American Democracy*, Bush's signing statements radically challenge the powers of both the legislative and the judicial branches of government. While Bush's Deputy Attorney General claimed that the president could violate a law until the Supreme Court ruled otherwise, in reality Bush used signing statements to announce his intention to violate measures on which the Supreme Court had already clearly ruled, and to instruct members of the executive branch to act contrary to the relevant rulings of the Supreme Court as well as the laws passed by Congress and signed by the president.

On the day of the State of the Union Address in January 2008, apparently hoping nobody would notice, Bush posted a signing statement on the White House website announcing his intention to violate major sections of the Defense Authorization bill that he had just signed into law, including a section creating a commission to probe contractor fraud in Iraq and Afghanistan, a section protecting whistle-blowing by contractors, a section requiring US intelligence agencies to reply to congressional requests for documents, a section banning the spending of any funds on permanent US military bases in Iraq, and a section banning the spending of any funds to gain US control over Iraq's oil. In October 2008, Congress yet again barred the spending of any funds to gain US control over Iraq's oil, and Bush yet again threw that out with another signing statement. Now, why in the world would a president reluctantly waging defensive wars to eliminate weapons of mass destruction and spread democracy need to illegally claim the right to spend our money to gain control of Iraqi oil?

As Savage noted, many of Bush's signing statements were related to military operations kept so secret that it was impossible to know whether Bush was following the law or not. It later became widely known that Bush's Office of Legal Counsel was issuing secret interpretations of law that functioned as laws themselves within the Bush administration, but with the advantage over signing statements that nobody could find them anywhere on the White House website. One of these "interpretations," delivered as legal advice, purported to give the president the right to secretly cancel any executive order, whether ordered by himself or a previous president. The Foreign Intelligence Surveillance Act (FISA) Court's interpretations of law (as distinct from the details of specific cases) were kept secret as well. Dozens of National Security Presidential Directives issued by Bush were kept secret. (In this case, Clinton had done the same.) Bush also illegally kept dozens of Transportation Security Administration regulations secret. And Congress passed classified annexes to intelligence authorization bills.[22] There is, of course, no way for citizens to know how to obey laws or to check up on whether the government is obeying laws if there is no way to find out what the laws are.[23] Clearly placing the legislative power in the hands of one person is made even more horrifying by allowing that one person to keep his decisions secret from the public.

Although the general pattern of secret lawmaking was known well before Bush and Cheney left office, more details emerged in 2009. First, in February, *Newsweek*'s Michael Isikoff reported the existence of e-mails, sent between the White House and the lawyers at the Justice Department, that drafted "legal opinions" claiming that the illegal would henceforth be legal. If it could be proven that the White House had demanded that its crimes be legalized, then the defense of claiming to have followed legal advice would be even weaker than it had appeared. Second, in March the government revealed, in response to a lawsuit, that the CIA had destroyed ninety-two videotapes of torture, not just the two previously admitted to. Third, that same day the Obama administration made public seven previously secret "legal" opinions that Bush Justice Department lawyers Jay Bybee, John Yoo, Patrick Philbin, and Robert Delahunty had written in 2001 and 2002. We'd already seen a number of their memos, including some pretending to legalize torture, and we were familiar with numerous crimes defended in these latest documents. Now here in black and white was more of the laughably twisted reasoning that had been meant to secretly legalize illegal actions, including the use of the military domestically, the suspension of habeas corpus and the First and Fourth Amendments, the suspension of treaties, rendition, the detention of American citizens without charge or trial or access to legal counsel, and the pseudo-trials of detainees by military commissions as a substitute for due process. This last argument was made as, in effect, a preemptive signing statement to a bill not yet passed by Congress. Four more Office of Legal Council (OLC) opinions, more commonly known as torture memos, were made public in response to an American Civil Liberties Union (ACLU) lawsuit in April 2009. One of these, an August

1, 2002, memo signed by Jay Bybee, openly explained that torture methods the CIA had asked permission to use would henceforth be "legal."

Even when the secret memos were not known, many of the crimes they purported to authorize were. In June 2008, Congressman Dennis Kucinich introduced, along with thirty-four other articles, an article of impeachment titled "Announcing the Intent to Violate Laws with Signing Statements, and Violating Those Laws."[24] Impeachment was the response the Constitution called for and still calls for. Impeachment is possible even after an official leaves office.[25] Bush Jr.'s signing statements are announcements of intent to violate laws. Passing a new law requiring that presidents obey laws would make no sense. And there is an almost comical weakness as well in the idea of passing a new law to ban signing statements.

When the House Judiciary Committee held a six-hour hearing on Bush and Cheney's impeachable offenses on July 25, 2008, former Deputy Attorney General under Ronald Reagan, Bruce Fein, whose logic is usually flawless and whose testimony was largely devoted to demanding immediate impeachment, suggested passing a bill banning the use of funds for any activities authorized by a signing statement. Congressman Keith Ellison asked why the president couldn't just use a signing statement on that bill. Fein had no answer.[26]

In my opinion, in addition to impeaching Bush as soon as possible (even if it's decades from now), Congress should, for what it may be worth, pass a bill simply banning the use of signing statements to alter laws. The funding approach is an unnecessary complication that fails to cover all possible signing statements. Of course, this bill could be signing statemented or ignored, but it wouldn't be if the threat of impeachment had been reestablished.

We could also consider a constitutional amendment, but there is good reason to be reluctant about proceeding with that. No reasonable interpreter of the current Constitution could ever have imagined that the president had the right to rewrite laws with signing statements. If we amend the Constitution to clarify that point, we could be seen as suggesting that any bizarre outrage against the basic principles of a government of laws is permissible until explicitly forbidden in detail by constitutional amendment. And the Constitution already includes the power of impeachment.

As a candidate for the presidency, Obama committed to not using signing statements to reverse laws. In a questionnaire published by the *Boston Globe* on December 20, 2007, Obama said,

> Signing statements have been used by presidents of both parties, dating back to Andrew Jackson. While it is legitimate for a president to issue a signing statement to clarify his understanding of ambiguous provisions of statutes and to explain his view of how he intends to faithfully execute the law, it is a clear abuse of power to use such statements as a license to evade laws that the president does not like or as an end-run around provisions designed to foster accountability. I will not use signing statements to nullify or undermine congressional instructions as enacted into law. The fact that President Bush has issued signing statements to challenge over 1100 laws—more than any president in history—is a clear abuse of this prerogative.[27]

On February 17, 2009, President Obama published what some authorities considered his first signing statement in the Federal Register, commenting on HR 1, the "American Recovery and Reinvestment Act of 2009." He wrote the statement in plain English and did not declare the right to violate the law. His statement appeared to be exactly what Bush's lawyers claimed his were, a press release. But, unlike Bush, Obama did not post his first signing statement on his website, and—as far as I know—he didn't send it to any press. So what was the point? One point may have been to simply establish that there would still be signing statements. Another may have been to make part of the formal law these seemingly innocuous and admirable phrases:

> My Administration will initiate new, far-reaching measures to help ensure that every dollar spent in this historic legislation is spent wisely and for its intended purpose. The Federal Government will be held to new standards of transparency and accountability. The legislation includes no earmarks. An over-

sight board will be charged with monitoring our progress as part of an unprecedented effort to root out waste and inefficiency. This board will be advised by experts—not just Government experts, not just politicians, but also citizens with years of expertise in management, economics, and accounting.[28]

While nothing is said here that Obama did not also say publicly, he has hereby (if we allow this interpretation of signing statements to stand) made part of the law his right to use the hundreds of billions of dollars appropriated in this bill in "new" and "far-reaching" ways that he "initiates," as well as the understanding that an "oversight board" created by the executive branch—rather than Congress—will oversee the activities of the executive branch, or as Obama calls it "the Federal Government."

On March 9, 2009, Obama published a "Memorandum for the Heads of Executive Departments and Agencies on the Subject of Presidential Signing Statements" in which he defended the practice of signing statements, but promised not to abuse it. The memo read, in part, "executive branch departments and agencies are directed to seek the advice of the Attorney General before relying on signing statements issued prior to the date of this memorandum as the basis for disregarding, or otherwise refusing to comply with, any provision of a statute,"[29] suggesting that Bush's signing statements permitting the violation of laws would be reviewed on a case-by-case basis as needed. There was no indication of how the public would learn of such reviews. But unless we learn of such reviews we will have yet another form of secret law, and even if we do learn of such reviews, we will still have legislating done by the executive branch.

Some commentators exclaimed that by so reviewing Bush's signing statements, Obama had finally agreed to "look backwards." I disagree. Obama's "look forward" idea, a phrase he used repeatedly to oppose investigating or prosecuting past crimes, was always all about undoing bad policies and creating new ones. It was not about holding anyone accountable for their crimes or limiting the power of the president.

In November 2008, Obama said that he was preparing a list of about 200 executive orders issued by Bush that he, Obama, would simply reverse.[30] By March 2009, that list had not been published, and the memo regarding signing statements suggested that they would not be included in the list if it was ever published. The most constitutional move that President Obama could make would be to toss out every signing statement that authorized violating laws, and every executive order, memo, determination, finding, directive, proclamation, or other royal decree that his predecessor did not have the constitutional right to issue. Instead, at least in the early months of his presidency, Obama reversed a handful of Bush's orders because of "policy differences." Some of these were potentially wonderful and lifesaving reversals, such as abandoning the use of torture. But they all involved the maintenance of dangerous monarchical power. Congress should give the president explicit and limited rule-making powers. All rules should be publicly available. And Congress should be understood to have the power to overrule them. Outside of those restrictions, a president should not be permitted to make decrees carrying the force of law.

The danger of leaving in place the signing statement power as established by Bush became clearer to many in the days and weeks following Obama's announcement of his policy. Just two days after publishing the policy memo, President Obama published what some considered his second and many considered his first signing statement, HR 1105, on the Omnibus Appropriations Act of 2009. This signing statement closely resembled Bush's and openly declared Obama's intention to violate dozens of sections of the law he was signing into law, including sections providing for the spending of funds, sections related to the creation of international treaties, and sections restricting retaliation against whistle-blowers. Later that month, on March 30, 2009, Obama issued yet another signing statement, this one on HR 146, the "Omnibus Public Land Management Act of 2009," announcing his intention to violate requirements in the law related to the appointment of a government commission that manages historical and economic issues along the Erie Canal.

Obama, like Bush, argues in his signing statements that the sections of law he intends to violate are unconstitutional. The problem is not that either one of these presidents was necessarily always wrong or that such questions can ever be decided to everyone's satisfaction. The problem is that the Constitution requires the president to veto a bill or to sign and execute it. The time to argue against the constitutionality of a provision is before a bill is passed or upon vetoing it. Such an argument can even be made upon signing a bill, but not accompanied by a declaration of the right to violate the law. This leaves us with presidents able to rewrite laws, and nothing could be more unconstitutional.

In March 2009 the often relatively progressive Democratic senator from Wisconsin, Russ Feingold, joined with Republican Senators John McCain and Paul Ryan to reintroduce legislation that would effectively give presidents an unconstitutional line-item veto for spending bills. Unwilling to ban or simply stop including wasteful earmarks (sections added to unrelated bills to fund pet projects with public dollars) these senators were proposing to give presidents the power to undo congressional decisions. Rather than rejecting an item with a signing statement, a president could legally "rescind" it, requiring both houses to vote again on that item alone. The same result could be achieved by requiring each house to vote on such items individually to begin with, but that wouldn't transfer power to the president and therefore wouldn't look as much like a reform to Washington insiders. This was a move in the wrong direction.

With members of Congress and even much of the public unwilling to oppose a president of one party or the other, and presidents of both parties having now engaged in the signing statement abuse, as with other abuses discussed below, the big question is whether we, the people, can adjust our priorities and become sufficiently engaged to undo an imperial power. Even if you like the way one president or the other has abused this power, it is very unlikely that you will approve of how future presidents abuse the power and expand upon it, which is what they can be counted on to do if we do not resist.

2. POWER OF WAR

Scaling back a war is not the same thing as ending one. Ending a war and starting a different one is not the same thing as making peace. Ending current wars while leaving the power to make war solely in the hands of the president is not the same thing as putting the dogs of war on appropriate chains.

The invasions of Afghanistan and Iraq, the strikes into Pakistan, Syria and other nations, the support for military action in Iran, and the assistance in Israel's bombing of Lebanon and Palestine: these are not wholly new phenomena in US history, and ending the current occupations in Afghanistan and Iraq will not end this frightening pattern unless further steps are taken.

"Regime change," the US policy of overthrowing foreign governments, has a long history dating back to the overthrow of the queen of Hawaii. A list of such regime change operations—excluding those that the United States only assisted in, and excluding a much longer list of invasions that did not change regimes—includes actions in Cuba, Puerto Rico, the Philippines, Nicaragua, Honduras, Iran, Guatemala, Vietnam, Chile, Grenada, Panama, and Afghanistan, as well as Hawaii and Iraq.[31] Whether this policy will end in Iraq under the first US president raised in Hawaii will depend on how well we understand it and what we do about it. Virtually none of those responsible for this list of regime change operations (and some names and families come up again and again through this history) have ever been held accountable for their actions in any way. Virtually all of these operations have resulted in massive suffering and blowback against the United States.

Lies in support of wars of aggression also have a long history in the United States.[32] They have been present in every case, and they have been supported by major media outlets in every case. In 1812, taking over Canada was going to be a cakewalk. In 1846, Mexico had supposedly attacked the United States, whereas the opposite was true. Ending slavery was a belated excuse for the Civil War already underway (much like spreading democracy to Iraq), and it is entirely possible that slavery would have ended fairly swiftly had the South been allowed to secede in peace. The rest of the Western hemisphere ended slavery without war, and repealing the Fugitive Slave Law would likely have sped slavery's demise in the US South.[33] In 1898, lies about the Spanish that would have made Fox News proud (including lies about the *Maine*, a ship that was actually blown up from within) helped launch a US war to liberate Cuba. But the US occupied Cuba instead of liberating it, then occupied the Philippines for good measure, slaughtering people there by the thousands for years.

In 1916, Woodrow Wilson was reelected president on the slogan "He Kept Us Out of War." He proceeded to set up an early version of the White House Iraq Group known as the Committee on Public Information whose mission it was to make Americans hate Germans. The lies (including misinformation about the content of the *Lusitania*, another ship that launched a thousand faces, and which was in fact carrying weapons) were so effective that they shaped the settlement at the end of the First World War, contributing to the rise of Nazism and the Second World War. The United States entered that second war following an unprovoked attack by the Japanese—unless the threats we had sent the Japanese and the devastating economic sanctions we had imposed on them count as provocation—and ignoring the fact that the US Navy had, nine days before Pearl Harbor, been given orders to shoot down Japanese planes and blow up Japanese boats it encountered. The lies about the Cold War, the Gulf of Tonkin, and the mythical babies taken out of incubators prior to the first Gulf War are still familiar to most Americans.

Bush Jr.'s Iraq lies were unique because the truth was obtainable immediately, not years or generations later. We knew, far more than in most past wars, that we were being fed lies. If we want to strip the presidency of the power to lie us into wars, we cannot allow any of Bush Jr.'s lies to pass; we cannot leave in place a system of government that lacks adequate checks on lying warmakers; and we must as a people finally learn to withstand the siren call of waving flags and war music that has coaxed us into so many wars against so many other nations whose leaders have, in many cases, also lied their own people into war.

In the case of Iraq, it's possible to show that Bush, Cheney, and their associates knew that the claims they were making with great certainty and much repetition were false or highly dubious. This is true of the claims about attempted purchases of uranium, about the aluminum tubes, about the chemical and biological weapons, about the unmanned aerial vehicles, about Iraq's capacity to attack us within forty-five minutes, about the ties to al-Qaeda, about the failures of the inspectors, and about the ludicrous notion that Saddam Hussein's Iraq was an imminent threat to the United States. Many have collected quite voluminous evidence of this.[34] It's also worth noticing that the president's power to classify great quantities of information and the lack of any penalty for his illegally declassifying misleading sections of documents facilitated the fraud.

But the whole idea ought never to have looked credible to anyone. (My friend Jonathan Schwarz publicly bet a war supporter $1,000 that no "WMD" would be found in Iraq, and collected.) It was openly and publicly known that Dick Cheney and several other top members of the Bush administration had wished to invade Iraq for years. (In fact, it was also known that Cheney and Donald Rumsfeld had made false claims about Soviet weaponry in the 1970s as part of a CIA project called Team B.) They had made their goals public through a think tank called the Project for a New American Century (PNAC). They had stated that their mission would be difficult, "absent some catastrophic and catalyzing event—like a new Pearl Harbor."[35] Making clear that it simply did not care whether Iraq had weapons, that the point of occupying Iraq was something else entirely, PNAC wrote in 2000, "Indeed, the United States has for decades sought to play a more permanent role in Gulf regional security. While the unresolved conflict with Iraq provides the immediate justification, the need for a substantial American force presence in the Gulf transcends the issue of the regime of Saddam Hussein."[36]

On October 27, 2004, Russ Baker reported on an interview he'd conducted with author and journalist Mickey Herskowitz, who had worked with George W. Bush in 1999, having been engaged to write his "autobiography." Baker wrote, "According to Herskowitz, George W. Bush's beliefs on Iraq were based in part on a notion dating back to the Reagan White House—ascribed in part to now–Vice President Dick Cheney, Chairman of the House Republican Policy Committee under Reagan.

'Start a small war. Pick a country where there is justification you can jump on, go ahead and invade.'" While this did not come out until 2004, Bush hadn't exactly kept his views secret. Baker reported,

> In December 1999, some six months after his talks with Herskowitz, Bush surprised veteran political chroniclers, including the *Boston Globe*'s David Nyhan, with his blunt pronouncements about Saddam at a six-way New Hampshire primary event that got little notice: "It was a gaffe-free evening for the rookie front-runner, till he was asked about Saddam's weapons stash," wrote Nyhan. "'I'd take 'em out,' [Bush] grinned cavalierly, 'take out the weapons of mass destruction... I'm surprised he's still there,' said Bush of the despot who remains in power after losing the Gulf War to Bush Jr.'s father... It remains to be seen if that offhand declaration of war was just Texas talk, a sort of locker room braggadocio, or whether it was Bush's first big clinker."[37]

Nine days after the necessary catastrophic event arrived on September 11, 2001, PNAC urged Bush to remove Saddam Hussein from power, even if no evidence could be found to tie him to 9/11.[38] Saddam Hussein and al-Qaeda were known enemies. It wouldn't have made any sense for them to have worked together. Their closest tie was that they had both worked in the past with the United States. Iraq was known to have destroyed its weapons and to be struggling and suffering under sanctions and bombing raids imposed by the United States.[39]

"We are able to keep his arms from him. His military forces have not been rebuilt," said Condoleezza Rice on CNN on July 29, 2001, shortly before warning us about "mushroom clouds."

"Saddam Hussein has not developed any significant capability with respect to weapons of mass destruction. He is unable to project conventional power against his neighbors," said Colin Powell on February 24, 2001, not long before switching his tune and ultimately holding up a vial of anthrax and threatening us with Winnebagos of death.

Not only was it very well understood that Iraq had no weapons, but there was no evidence that Iraq had any way of using its alleged weapons in the United States. And then there was the biggest insanity of the whole pile, namely the notion that Iraq would willingly commit national suicide by attacking the owners of the world's most powerful military. In fact, in October 2002, the CIA told Bush that Saddam Hussein was unlikely to attack the United States unless the United States attacked him first. This was just prior to Bush's speech on October 7 in Cincinnati, Ohio, warning of the dire threat from Iraq.[40] According to news reports, on at least four earlier occasions, beginning in the spring of 2002, Bush was informed during his morning intelligence briefing that US intelligence agencies believed it was unlikely that Iraq was an imminent threat to the United States.[41]

US intelligence agencies produced a National Intelligence Estimate on October 1, 2002, but kept it classified. On October 4, they published an unclassified shortened version often referred to as the "white paper." The longer version, which was eventually declassified, contained all sorts of dissensions and qualifications that were simply omitted from the white paper. Not only were whole paragraphs left out, but single words were carefully changed or deleted to erase all disagreement and uncertainty. Among the bits left out was, of course, the conclusion that Saddam Hussein was unlikely to attack first. Vincent Bugliosi, in his book *The Prosecution of George W. Bush for Murder*, examines in detail the editing job that was done and demonstrates that the only possible purpose was to mislead the nation into war.

Bush even wanted to provoke Saddam Hussein into attacking Americans. On January 31, 2003, prior to the full-scale invasion of Iraq in March, Bush met with British Prime Minister Tony Blair in the White House. After their meeting, they spoke to the media and claimed not to have decided on war, to be working hard to achieve peace, and to be worried about the imminent threat from Iraq to the American people. They claimed that Iraq possessed weapons of mass destruction and had links to al-Qaeda, and—Bush implied, but avoided explicitly stating—to the attacks of September 11, 2001. They also claimed to have UN authorization for launching an attack on Iraq.[42]

Behind closed doors, however, other words were spoken. Blair advisor David Manning took notes that day. The memo is available online.[43] The accuracy of what it says has never been challenged by Bush or Blair.

According to Manning, Bush proposed to Blair a number of possible ways in which they might be able to create an excuse to launch a war against Iraq. One of Bush's proposals was "flying U2 reconnaissance aircraft with fighter cover over Iraq, painted in UN colours [sic]. If Saddam fired on them," Bush argued, "he would be in breach" of UN resolutions. In other words, Bush wanted to falsely paint US planes with UN colors and try to get Iraq to shoot at them. This is what he really thought about the horrible, evil threat of Saddam Hussein: he wanted to provoke him.

Bush understood that the United Nations had not passed a resolution that would have legalized an attack on Iraq. The memo claims, "[Bush said] the US would put its full weight behind efforts to get another resolution and would 'twist arms' and 'even threaten.' But he had to say that if ultimately we failed, military action would follow anyway." In other words, going to the United Nations was not actually an attempt to avoid war, but an attempt to gain legal cover for a war that would be launched regardless of whether that project succeeded. And Bush wasn't kidding about twisting arms; that very same day the National Security Agency (NSA) launched a plan to bug the phones and e-mails of UN Security Council members.[44]

At this time, a month and a half before the invasion of Iraq, and for months prior, the US military was already engaging in hugely escalated bombing runs over Iraq and redeploying troops, including to newly constructed bases in the Middle East, all in preparation for an invasion of Iraq, and all with money that had not been appropriated for these purposes. The reporters who questioned Bush and Blair on January 31, 2003, did not know about or ask about those activities, and since the revelation of this memo, not one reporter who was so blatantly lied to that day has gone back and asked a question or written a single word about it.

That Bush was interested in provoking Iraq is confirmed by extensive covert operations called DB/Anabasis reported by Michael Isikoff and David Corn in their book *Hubris*:

> Over an intense forty-five day period beginning in late 2001, [two CIA operatives] cooked up an audacious plan. . . . It called for installing a small army of paramilitary CIA officers on the ground inside Iraq; for elaborate schemes to penetrate Saddam's

regime; recruiting disgruntled military officers with buckets of cash; for feeding the regime disinformation . . . for disrupting the regime's finances . . . for sabotage that included blowing up railroad lines. . . . It also envisioned staging a phony incident that could be used to start a war. A small group of Iraqi exiles would be flown into Iraq by helicopter to seize an isolated military base near the Saudi border. They then would take to the airwaves and announce a coup was under way. If Saddam responded by flying troops south, his aircraft would be shot down by US fighter planes patrolling the no-fly zones established by UN edict after the first Persian Gulf War. A clash of this sort could be used to initiate a full-scale war. On February 16, 2002, President Bush signed covert findings authorizing the various elements of Anabasis. The leaders of the congressional intelligence committees—including Porter Goss, a Republican, and Senator Bob Graham, a Democrat—were briefed. "The idea was to create an incident in which Saddam lashes out" [said CIA operative John McGuire]. If all went as planned, "you'd have a premise for war: we've been invited in."[45]

A similar story came out about Dick Cheney with regard to Iran in 2008. Journalist Seymour Hersh reported at a journalism conference in 2008 that at a 2008 meeting in the vice president's office, soon after an incident in the Strait of Hormuz in which a US carrier almost shot at a few small Iranian speedboats, "There were a dozen ideas proffered about how to trigger a war. The one that interested me the most was why don't we build—we in our shipyard—build four or five boats that look like Iranian PT boats. Put Navy Seals on them with a lot of arms. And next time one of our boats goes to the Straits of Hormuz, start a shoot-up. Might cost some lives. And it was rejected because you can't have Americans killing Americans. That's the kind of—that's the level of stuff we're talking about. Provocation. But that was rejected."[46]

Do these sound like accounts of the behavior of men worthy of imperial powers? What about this: After the invasion of Iraq, with no weapons or ties to 9/11 having been found, Diane Sawyer asked Bush on camera about the claims he had made about "weapons of mass destruction," and he replied: "What's the difference? The possibility that [Saddam] could acquire weapons, if he were to acquire weapons, he would be the danger."[47]

Yes, what's the difference? No big deal. Just a million human beings killed and four million displaced.[48]

When Bush joked about his hunt for "weapons of mass destruction" at the 2004 White House Correspondents Dinner, members of the media as well as prominent members of Congress, like Nancy Pelosi, laughed along with him.[49]

In August 2008, journalist Ron Suskind reported that the Iraqi government's intelligence chief had secretly told the British and Americans prior to the invasion that there were no nuclear, biological, or chemical weapons in Iraq.[50] National Public Radio (NPR) reported denials from the White House and from then–CIA head George Tenet that failed as denials and actually admitted the truth of the account:

> We have called key players in Ron Suskind's account . . . George Tenet says the Iraqi failed to persuade, and a White House spokesman adds that any information the Iraqi may have provided was, quote, "immaterial."[51]

In 2006, we had learned that in 2002 Iraq's foreign minister had also told the CIA that Iraq had no "weapons of mass destruction."[52] Also in 2006, we learned that prior to the war, the CIA had sent thirty relatives of Iraqi scientists to Iraq to ask them what WMD Iraq had, and they uniformly reported it had nothing.[53]

Of course, it was already, prior to the invasion, public knowledge (for those who cared to look) that Saddam Hussein's son-in-law, Hussein Kamel, had told the British and the Americans the very same thing.[54] It was thus very odd to observe Colin Powell telling the United Nations about all the weapons that Kamel reported Iraq had possessed before destroying them, and neglecting to mention that he'd said they'd destroyed them.[55] This was one of many reasons the world media did not report Powell's little show in the same way the American media did. While American editors saw an upstanding general who would never lie, foreign editors saw the representative of a nation hell-bent on war presenting a combination of obvious lies and fantastic tales that strained the imagination, all meant to suggest that an impoverished war-and-sanctions-damaged nation was creating large supplies of state-of-the-art weaponry. Later, during the occupation, we were asked to believe that only Iranians, not Iraqis, could produce basic roadside bombs!

Powell, or whoever told him what to say, actually went so far as to fabricate dialogue. Powell provided this translation of an intercepted conversation between Iraqi army officers:

> "They're inspecting the ammunition you have, yes."
> "Yes."
> "For the possibility there are forbidden ammo."
> "For the possibility there is by chance forbidden ammo?"
> "Yes."
> "And we sent you a message yesterday to clean out all of the areas, the scrap areas, the abandoned areas. Make sure there is nothing there."

The incriminating phrases "clean all of the areas" and "Make sure there is nothing there" simply do not appear in the official State Department translation of the exchange.[56]

Much of the rest of Powell's presentation consisted of claims that his own staff had warned him UN inspectors would not even find plausible.[57] Powell delivered his platter of baloney to the United Nations with CIA director George Tenet seated behind him, but Alan Foley, the head of the CIA's Weapons Intelligence Non-Proliferation and Arms Control Center (WINPAC), didn't believe the hype. In their book *The Italian Letter*, Peter Eiser and Knut Royce reported on what Foley actually believed and what he instructed analysts to say, which were two very different things. According to Eiser and Royce,

> There were strong indications that Foley all along was toeing a line he did not believe. Several days after Bush's [2003] State of the Union speech, Foley briefed student officers at the National Defense University at Fort McNair in Washington, DC. After the briefing, Melvin Goodman, who had retired from the CIA and

was then on the university's faculty, brought Foley into the secure communications area of the Fort McNair compound. Goodman thanked Foley for addressing the students and asked him what weapons of mass destruction he believed would be found after the invasion. "Not much, if anything," Goodman recalled that Foley responded.[58]

He told his subordinates something different:

One day in December 2002, Foley called his senior production managers to his office. He had a clear message for the men and women who controlled the output of the center's analysts: "If the president wants to go to war, our job is to find the intelligence to allow him to do so." The directive was not quite an order to cook the books, but it was a strong suggestion that cherry-picking and slanting not only would be tolerated, but might even be rewarded.[59]

Blogger and reporter Jonathan Schwarz, who has followed these matters as closely as anyone and blogged about them at AfterDowningStreet.org and on his own blog TinyRevolution.com, has pointed out that this incident was reported, although without identifying Foley by name, in at least two other books: *Pretext for War* by James Bamford, and *Blowing My Cover: My Life As a CIA Spy* by Lindsay Moran.[60] Why is it always books doing the news reporting these days?

Of course the most extreme claims about the threat from Iraq, during the lead-up to the war, were made by Dick Cheney, but you've probably heard them, and I've quoted a few of them above. It's important to bear in mind the well-informed and sensible reasons Cheney had provided, on camera, in 1994, for why they had NOT gone into Baghdad during the first Gulf War:

Because if we'd gone to Baghdad we would have been all alone. There wouldn't have been anybody else with us. There would have been a US occupation of Iraq. None of the Arab forces that were willing to fight with us in Kuwait were willing to invade

Iraq. Once you got to Iraq and took it over, took down Saddam Hussein's government, then what are you going to put in its place? That's a very volatile part of the world, and if you take down the central government of Iraq, you could very easily end up seeing pieces of Iraq fly off: part of it, the Syrians would like to have to the west, part of it—eastern Iraq—the Iranians would like to claim, they fought over it for eight years. In the north you've got the Kurds, and if the Kurds spin loose and join with the Kurds in Turkey, then you threaten the territorial integrity of Turkey. It's a quagmire if you go that far and try to take over Iraq. The other thing was casualties. Everyone was impressed with the fact we were able to do our job with as few casualties as we had. But for the 146 Americans killed in action, and for their families, it wasn't a cheap war. And the question for the president, in terms of whether or not we went on to Baghdad, took additional casualties in an effort to get Saddam Hussein, was how many additional dead Americans is Saddam worth? Our judgment was, not very many, and I think we got it right.[61]

Ten years later? They feigned ignorance, pretending none of these concerns expressed by antiwar groups were legitimate.

When Bush promised to fire anyone in the White House involved in leaking the identity of Valerie Plame Wilson, and then didn't do so, the media left it alone, but some of us noticed anyway.[62]

When Bush claimed in his 2007 State of the Union speech to have prevented four terrorist plots, the claims, just like many other such claims before and since, turned out to be fictional.[63]

When Bush claimed he hadn't been warned about Hurricane Katrina, someone leaked video of him being warned of exactly what might, and did, happen.[64]

When Bush swore he wouldn't spy without a warrant, James Risen showed otherwise with his book *State of War*, and Bush readily confessed to the crime.[65]

When Bush said the United States never tortures, the torture victims stepped forward by the dozens and told their stories.[66]

In August 2008, Ron Suskind reported that in 2003 the White House (quite possibly led by Dick Cheney) had instructed subordinates to forge a letter that might be used to claim there had been some connection between Saddam Hussein and al-Qaeda.[67] Surely that, too, was just an honest mistake. It appears that the United States also paid the same person to forge letters smearing vocal opponents of the invasion.[68]

It's not as if all this fibbing amounted to violating any laws, right?

Well, actually . . .

Since 1973, presidents who have launched wars without the authorization of Congress have done so, not just in violation of the Constitution, but also in violation of the War Powers Act, a law written in reaction to President Richard Nixon's abuses of power and passed over his veto. The law allows a president to send armed forces into action abroad only with the authorization of Congress, unless the United States is actually under attack or serious threat. The president is required to notify Congress within forty-eight hours if he commits armed forces to action abroad, and forces cannot be kept in action for more than sixty days without an authorization from Congress. This law is actually weaker than the constitutional requirement and should be strengthened, but it is a law that Bush (and Congress) violated.

One way in which Bush Jr. outdid his predecessors in martial criminality was by persuading Congress to issue a vague and general authorization to "use force" at any point in the future when the president believed certain conditions had been met. By so doing the Congress, as well as the president, violated the Constitution and the War Powers Act. The Iraq War was not launched with any specific and timely authorization from Congress. That is the first of many reasons the war is widely considered illegal.[69] Congress's authorization allowing the president to determine whether to go to war was an unconstitutional delegation of the power to declare war. My friend John Bonifaz led a legal suit on behalf of soldiers and members of Congress aimed at preventing the war on those grounds, and the courts avoided it rather than ruling on the merits.[70]

In defense of Congress, its resolution did require that if the president decided to use force (as if there were any doubt that he would!) he must submit a report to Congress explaining how this use of force met certain criteria. The explanation was not required to be credible or truthful, of course, and it was neither, asserting as it did familiar claims about "weapons of mass destruction" and ties to al-Qaeda.[71] (In an added bit of arrogance, Bush cited as sources for his claims his own prior speeches and the laughable presentation his own secretary of state had made to the United Nations.) The fact that Bush used Congress's "Authorization to Use Force" without actually complying with its terms is a second reason the Iraq War is illegal.[72] Of course, Bush signed that authorization and asserted in the accompanying signing statement that he did not actually need any authorization at all. But we've already established the illegality of signing statements.

The claims that Bush made in that report to Congress, as well as a long list of claims that he and his subordinates made publicly and directly to Congress, orally and in writing, established a false case for war. Bush, Cheney, Rice, Rumsfeld, et alia, violated the federal anti-con-spiracy statute, 18 USC-371, which makes it a felony "to commit any offense against the United States, or to defraud the United States, or any agency thereof in any manner or for any purpose," and the False State-ments Accountability Act of 1996, 18 USC-1001, which makes it a felony to issue knowingly and willfully false statements to the United States Congress.[73] That the Iraq War was based on lies is a third reason that it is widely deemed illegal.[74]

Bush unsuccessfully sought a resolution from the United Nations to make his war on Iraq legal under international law. The single biggest day of protest around the world in the history of the world, including a massive demonstration in New York City, on February 15, 2003, played a role in persuading the United Nations to refuse to authorize the inva-sion.[75] On March 6, 2003, this exchange took place between a reporter and President Bush at the White House:

> Q: Thank you, Mr. President. As you said, the Security Council faces a vote next week on a resolution implicitly authorizing an attack on Iraq. Will you call for a vote on that resolution, even if you aren't sure you have the vote?
>
> THE PRESIDENT: Well, first, I don't think—it basically says that he's in defiance of 1441. That's what the resolution says. And it's

hard to believe anybody is saying he isn't in defiance of 1441, because 1441 said he must disarm. And, yes, we'll call for a vote.

Q: No matter what?

THE PRESIDENT: No matter what the whip count is, we're calling for the vote. We want to see people stand up and say what their opinion is about Saddam Hussein and the utility of the United Nations Security Council. And so, you bet. It's time for people to show their cards, to let the world know where they stand when it comes to Saddam.[76]

The United States did not call for the vote, because it became clear that it would fail. Under Article VI of the US Constitution, any treaty to which the United States is a party is the law of the land. The United States is a party to the United Nations Charter. Under the UN Charter, any war not fought in actual self-defense and not authorized by the UN Security Council as an exception to that rule is illegal. That the Iraq War is blatantly illegal under the UN Charter is a fourth, and perhaps the most influential, reason that it is considered an illegal war.[77]

It is also illegal, under international treaties to which the United States is party, to invade another nation for the purpose of controlling its resources.[78] That the Iraq War had this basis is a fifth powerful reason that it is considered an illegal war. This issue has been widely misunderstood since 2002, when many of us took to the streets with "No Blood for Oil" posters. An editorial cartoon that came out in June 2008, around the time Congressman Dennis Kucinich introduced his articles of impeachment, showed a Democratic donkey shouting before the war that it was just about cheap oil, and complaining years later that there wasn't any cheap oil. But Kucinich was just about the only Democrat in Congress who had joined with peace activists in arguing that the war was for control of the oil, plus profits for oil companies, as well as permanent bases, profit from "reconstruction," and political advantage at home (most of which, above all the profits for oil companies, came to pass). The rest of the Democratic Party had either agreed with Bush, Cheney, and other Republicans, or had taken no clear position on what the war was for, adamantly denouncing in the strongest terms the suggestion that it had anything to do with oil. Nobody at all ever thought the war was for "cheap oil." The notion that corporate thugs like Bush and Cheney would slaughter our young men and women and the people of Iraq in order to save us money at the gas pump is only topped in insanity by the notion that peace activists would have suspected Bush and Cheney of such a thing.

In terms of violations of international law, it doesn't stop there. The Nuremberg tribunal in 1945 concluded that, "To initiate a war of aggression . . . is not only an international crime; it is the supreme international crime differing only from other war crimes in that it contains within itself the accumulated evil of the whole."[79] The current occupation of Iraq has seen the United States target civilians, journalists, hospitals, and ambulances; use antipersonnel weapons including cluster bombs in densely settled urban areas; use white phosphorous as a weapon; use depleted uranium weapons; employ a new version of napalm found in Mark 77 firebombs; engage in collective punishment of Iraqi civilian populations, including by blocking roads, cutting electricity and water, destroying fuel stations, planting bombs in farm fields, demolishing houses, and plowing down orchards; detain people without charge or legal process without the rights of prisoners of war; imprison children; torture; and murder. The various war crimes that accumulate into the evil of the whole, including those turned into prominent scandals, such as the Abu Ghraib prison photos or massacres of civilians by Blackwater mercenaries, are a sixth reason that the Iraq War is considered illegal.[80]

The seventh reason to view the Iraq War, along with the "global war on terror" of which it is supposedly a part, as illegal is the endless plague of crimes and abuses of power that surround the war and are supposedly justified by it. The criminal waste and fraud in contracting is part of this.[81] The planning of the war has gone on in illegal secrecy.[82] The lies used to launch the war involved the illegal selective leaking of classified information; and whistleblowers exposing those lies have been illegally punished, including by exposing the identity of an undercover agent. Investigations of those abuses have been criminally obstructed.[83] Mercenaries and other contractors in Iraq have been permitted to operate in a lawless zone, subject neither to Iraqi law nor to US military justice.[84] People, including children, in Iraq, Afghanistan, and around the world, including in the United States, have been detained without charge or due process, tortured, rendered to other nations to be tortured, imprisoned in secret prisons with no access to legal counsel, and murdered.[85] Bush and Cheney threatened a similar war against Iran, made similar lies about Iran, and funded terrorist activities within Iran.[86] Bush violated the Posse Comitatus Act at home,[87] as well as engaging in warrantless spying and various illegal assertions of power. Bush and Cheney used the war to try to justify all of the above actions.

An eighth reason the ongoing occupation of Iraq is illegal is that, while the United Nations did not and could not have legalized the invasion, it did, after the fact, condone the occupation until December 31, 2008. When that UN fig leaf expired it was replaced with a treaty negotiated by President Bush and Iraqi President Nouri al-Maliki. The US Senate was never consulted, and the Iraqi Parliament only approved the treaty on condition that the Iraqi people be permitted to vote it up or down sometime before the end of July 2009. A treaty authorizing three years of war has dubious legal standing to begin with, and this is aggravated by the unconstitutional failure to gain Senate ratification. If the Iraqi people are denied their vote or vote the treaty down, additional levels of illegitimacy will be added. If the Iraqi people approve the treaty it will likely be because of the commitments to withdraw occupation forces from all localities by July 2009 and to withdraw from the nation completely by the end of 2011, two commitments the US military has made clear it plans to violate.

One horrible result of the war in Iraq is that for years it has made the war in Afghanistan look good by comparison, or disappear entirely, as the media has focused only on Iraq. On September 14, 2001, Congresswoman Barbara Lee spoke, in tears, on the floor of the House of Representatives. She, alone, would vote No on letting the president decide on going to war in Afghanistan. She, alone, would refuse to authorize the president to use powers the Constitution does not give him, and trust him to use those powers wisely. In April 2009, the House voted on a budget that included funds for a major expansion of the war in Afghanistan. This time Congressman Dennis Kucinich stood alone in voting No in opposition to war. An expansion of the occupation of Afghanistan will increase US casualties there and possibly gain it greater media attention.

We are now a nation that regularly bombs civilians, detains the innocent, and tortures suspects—sometimes to death.[88] We're threatening to attack Iran, and nobody in Washington is questioning the legality of aggressive war, because that would mean questioning the invasions of Iraq and Afghanistan. Opinion of the United States around the world has plummeted to the point where we are seen as the most dangerous "rogue state."[89] And this began with Afghanistan, where we have killed and destroyed in great measure, but done very little to either apprehend the criminals we were supposedly there to find, or to benefit the innocent people whose country we have made a more dangerous, more impoverished place to live. Our own puppet president of Afghanistan has been pushing the US media to cover his demand that the US cease using air strikes against the people of Afghanistan.[90]

When self-defense is not on the line, anything other than war—no matter how damaging or costly or humiliating—is preferable to war, because war causes far more suffering than anything else ever invented. The wars we are fighting are not wars of defense or even wars between two militaries. They are wars of a powerful military against the guerilla resistance of occupied populations. No one "wins" these wars any more than you can "win" a hurricane. They are unmitigated disasters, and our own intelligence services tell us our occupations have become recruiting tools for terrorists.[91] International terrorist incidents increased in 2004, and then the US government ceased reporting the statistic.[92] It is time to rethink our strategy.

The Constitution very clearly puts the president in charge of the military, a fact that found its way through the brain of George W. Bush and exited his mouth as "I'm the commander guy."[93] And yet, this does not put the president in charge of war, or in charge of rules for prisoners of war, or in charge of funding and creating the military, or of making rules to govern and regulate the military, because the Constitution gives those powers to Congress, along with the power to raise and support armies as needed for wars. The Constitution bans the appropriation of any money for that use for longer than two years. This means that during a lengthy war Congress must decide again at least every two years to keep fighting it, and therefore the "commander guy" does not have the power to begin or end wars, but only the power to serve as the commander of the military determining how a war is fought.

No president is ever intended to be the commander of anything other than the military. I've been on radio shows to which listeners call in and say things like "I just don't believe we should question our commander in chief in the time of war." Well, unless you are serving in the military, the president is not your commander in anything. The president is not the commander of Congress, of the courts, of the executive branch, or of the people. He is in charge of the executive branch and is supposed to run it in accordance with the law.

The king of the country is supposed to be the Constitution. Any war by the United States is illegal if Congress has not declared war or if Congress has declared a war over. This was the clear intention of the authors of the Constitution, including the primary author, our fourth president, a man too short to be elected to anything in the twenty-first century, James Madison. These were his words:

> Of all the enemies of true liberty, war is, perhaps, the most to be dreaded. . . . In war, the discretionary power of the executive is extended; its influence in dealing out offices, honors and emoluments is multiplied; and all the means of seducing the minds are added to those of subduing the force, of the people. . . . No nation can preserve its freedom in the midst of continual warfare. War is in fact the true nurse of executive aggrandizement. In war, a physical force is to be created; and it is the executive will which is to direct it. In war, the public treasuries are to be unlocked; and it is the executive hand which is to dispense them. In war, the honors and emoluments of office are to be multiplied; and it is the executive patronage under which they are to be enjoyed; and it is the executive brow they are to encircle. The strongest passions and most dangerous weaknesses of the human breast, ambition, avarice, vanity, the honorable or venal love of fame, are all in conspiracy against the desire and duty of peace.[94]

The question arises, of course: Why did James Madison hate his country and love the terrorists? It's a question we should also ask about our sixteenth president, Abraham Lincoln, or rather about his behavior as a Congressman prior to becoming a president. In February 2007, Alaska Congressman Don Young attempted on the floor of the House to quote Abraham Lincoln's opinion on opposition to presidents' war plans. Young failed rather dramatically.

He misquoted Lincoln:

> Congressmen who willfully take actions during wartime that damage morale and undermine the military are saboteurs and should be arrested, exiled, or hanged.[95]

That was close. You can see how Young could have made the mistake. Here's what Lincoln actually said:

> Allow the President to invade a neighboring nation, whenever he shall deem it necessary to repel an invasion, and you allow him to do so, whenever he may choose to say he deems it necessary for such purpose—and you allow him to make war at pleasure. Study to see if you can fix any limit to his power in this respect, after you have given him so much as you propose. If, today, he should choose to say he thinks it necessary to invade Canada, to prevent the British from invading us, how could you stop him? You may say to him, "I see no probability of the British invading us" but he will say to you "be silent; I see it, if you don't." The provision of the Constitution giving the war-making power to Congress, was dictated, as I understand it, by the following reasons: Kings had always been involving and impoverishing their people in wars, pretending generally, if not always, that the good of the people was the object. This, our Convention understood to be the most oppressive of all Kingly oppressions; and they resolved to so frame the Constitution that no one man should hold the power of bringing this oppression upon us.[96]

Lincoln wrote those words while America was at war with Mexico, under the presidency of James Polk, and while Lincoln was a member of Congress, on the floor of which he spoke in the same vein. But Lincoln did more than talk about the fraud that had been used to launch that illegal and imperialistic war. He introduced a resolution demanding that Polk provide proof of his supposed justification for the war. Polk claimed to have launched that war only after American blood had been shed on American soil. Lincoln's resolution required Polk to identify the spot where that blood had been shed.

"Let him answer fully, fairly, and candidly," Lincoln said of the wartime President. "Let him answer with facts and not with arguments. Let him attempt no evasion, no equivocation." Lincoln accused the president on the floor of the House of sounding like the "half-insane mumbling of a fever dream," a comment that would never be permitted under the rules of Congress today.[97]

When President Polk did not answer, Lincoln and John Quincy Adams sought a formal investigation of the president's prewar intelligence claims, and of his use of secret funds to launch his fraudulent and illegal war. Under this pressure, Polk announced that he would not seek reelection. Lincoln, Adams, and their allies in Congress then passed a resolution honoring the service of Major General Zachary Taylor "in a war unnecessarily and unconstitutionally begun by the President of the United States."[98]

Back to more recent history, unconstitutional wars—in particular wars lacking any congressional declaration of war—have become the norm by now, with Democrats launching at least as many as Republicans. Nonetheless, George W. Bush managed in this area, as in many, to outdo his predecessors. For one thing, he repeatedly declared in signing statements that Congress cannot in any way regulate the military. Never mind that the Constitution says precisely the opposite, that Congress and only Congress has the power "to make Rules for the Government and Regulation of the land and naval Forces."

Yes, the Constitution also makes the president the "Commander in Chief of the Army and Navy of the United States, and of the Militia of the several States, when called into the actual Service of the United States." But the Constitution sought to avoid a standing army existing in peacetime, and intended to place the president in charge of the army in time of war, while leaving it entirely in the hands of Congress to determine when such times should be.

We now have a permanent national military in a time that has been rather vaguely but dangerously designated by former President Bush as an eternal war against a state of mind (terror) or a tactic (terrorism), a war that by definition can never be won, lost, or ended. So, what can we do? The Obama administration early on stopped saying "global war on terror" and began saying "overseas contingency operations," but this change in vocabulary did not, at least immediately, seem to lead to behavior that reflected an altered understanding of war powers.

Three proposals have been floated recently related to the War Powers Act, one of them awful, the other two commendable. The first comes from a bipartisan commission of elder statesmen including Ed Meese, Warren Christopher, James Baker, and Lee Hamilton—what blogger and professor David Michael Green calls, "The Center-Right Dinosaur Club."[99] The proposal that came out of this latest commission in July 2008 was, predictably, to repeal the War Powers Act and replace it with an act requiring that the president "consult" with Congress prior to launching a war.[100] This role of consultant is exactly the role current congressional leaders want, a role once played with more grace by court jesters. But it is a recipe for legislating in place the aggrandizement of the executive against which James Madison warned.

The second proposal seeks instead to remedy this problem. It comes from Larry Sabato's 2007 book *A More Perfect Constitution*. Sabato recommends a constitutional amendment that would add to the War Powers Act the requirement that congressional authorizations of war include time limits, after which Congress must vote again to extend the war or end it.[101] While I agree time limits would be ideal, I think the same solution should be pursued first through legislation. I would add that those time limits should be no longer than twelve months.

The third proposal comes from a white paper published by the Center for Constitutional Rights (CCR) in April 2009 called "Restore. Protect. Expand. Amend the War Powers Resolution." Because it is so difficult to end wars once begun, CCR proposed eliminating the permission that the War Powers Act currently and unconstitutionally grants for a president to wage war for sixty to ninety days before gaining congressional approval, arguing that the only exception should be for the short-term use of force to repel (not retaliate for) sudden attacks on US territories, troops, or citizens. (The inclusion of troops here seems to weaken the reform and provide an easy way to provoke or pretend an excuse for war, so I would limit it to territories and citizens.) CCR also proposes adding an adequate enforcement mechanism to deal with occasions on which presidents violate the law. A new law would prohibit the use of funds for actions violating the law, allow for judicial oversight in cases of conflict between Congress and the president, and explicitly make a violation of this law an impeachable offense.[102]

Of course, when Congress does authorize military action, it must be in accordance with the UN Charter and international law, and it must not be treated as the supposed authorization to engage in abuses of power and violations of rights.

We also need a reform, perhaps called "The Cheney-Halliburton Act," that would make war profiteering by any war-maker a major felony. This would apply to employees of the federal government or anyone who had within the past decade been an employee of the federal government, especially the President and Vice President themselves.

I'm very much in favor of another reform that might truly prevent aggressive wars. When soldiers are sent into war, they and their friends and family do not play any significant role in the war-making decision. Yet their lives are put at risk on the basis of claims made by people themselves taking no risk at all, claims of a sort that have through the course of history proven almost universally false. The United States is not supposed to have a lower class that suffers and dies and an upper class that decides when others should suffer and die. There is a simple way around this. We should require that, in any war, the military-aged children and grandchildren of the president, the vice president, all cabinet officials, and all Congress members serve on the front lines in the most dangerous combat positions—no exceptions.

Oh, how cruel and awful! But how much more cruel and awful to send other families' children to die—families not cheered, saluted, funded, or celebrated, families whose only relationship to the war is blood, trauma, and heartache. The purpose of this proposed law is not to kill, but to save lives. I think it would render wars obsolete. If it did not, it would at least inspire basic rights and benefits for veterans.

Of course, much of our military activity is not categorized as war, and yet it does great damage to our nation at great financial expense, and increases the likelihood of wars. We spend over $130 billion a year to maintain US military bases in foreign lands. We should give up having our nation's flag flying over other nations' soil, and in exchange we'll end up safer, freer, and more prosperous.

Some of our military activity is conducted now by private mercenaries unaccountable to any laws or even to the military. This project of privatizing war-making as measured in blood, dollars, impact on the military, and US relations around the world, has proven disastrous. It has also helped to blur the growing use of US military force on American soil. We should strictly prohibit the use of mercenaries or any armed contractors, as well as the use of any military force on American soil, except when directly engaged in defensive war against a foreign nation.

While legislation to make these changes may sound like an uphill fight, we can begin the process that takes us there by repealing a bunch of bad bills without which we were getting along quite well several years ago. We should start by repealing the Detainee Treatment Act of 2005 and the Military Commissions Act of 2006, both of which—among other problems—seek to provide retroactive immunity for crimes. The same goes for the 2008 FISA "Modernization" Act and the 2007 Protect America Act. In fact, the original Foreign Intelligence Surveillance Act should be completely repealed. While violating FISA constitutes a troubling lawlessness, the law itself provides a rubber stamp rather than serious judicial oversight. The PATRIOT Act is an assault on our Bill of Rights as well, and should be repealed as were the measures facilitating martial law in the John Warner National Defense Authorization Act for Fiscal Year 2007 (repealed in 2008). The Homeland Security Act of 2002 should also be repealed.[103]

The pressure on President Obama to escalate and launch illegal wars is intense. The Project for a New American Century had been shut down for months and had taken down its website, but it was put back up immediately following the 2008 elections. If we can hold President Obama to his commitments to respect the Constitution and the limitations of the Presidency, our lobbying of Congress—and the existence of Congress!—will have some purpose at last. These commitments would prevent President Obama not only from launching major new wars, but also from engaging in isolated strikes of the sort Bush launched against Pakistan, Syria, and other nations—strikes that the American public and most or all of the Congress have sometimes learned about years after the fact.

Obama expressed support for such strikes as a candidate and quickly began launching them as president. Immediately upon taking office he began launching military strikes into Pakistan, and proposed increased funding for unmanned drones with which to engage in this sort of warfare. By February 2009, Obama had announced he would send an additional 17,000 troops to Afghanistan. He had also announced that he would end the occupation of Iraq in nineteen months rather than the sixteen months he'd promised, leaving as many as 50,000 troops behind after "ending" the occupation. These troops would be labeled "non-combat" troops, even while the purposes listed for their continued presence included combat activities. The idea of fully ending the occupation of Iraq, removing all troops, mercenaries, and contractors, and relinquishing control over bases, oil, and the Iraqi government was still not being discussed, even though the United States had elected a president who had given countless speeches declaring that he would "end the war in Iraq."

Shutting down the empire, rather than slowing it down, is going to require punishing past imperialism but also making major changes to the structure of our government. An updated US Constitution might state that:

> ➤ No more than 25 percent of discretionary US government spending in any given year can be devoted to military expenses of any sort, including wars, including debt and interest payments for past military expenses and wars, and including care for veterans.

> ➤ All military veterans must be provided with free comprehensive health care and education.

> ➤ The United States is forbidden to maintain a military presence in any foreign nation, to engage in any war of aggression, to employ mercenaries, or to make use of military force on

American soil except when actually engaged in a defensive war against a foreign nation.

➤ The executive cannot begin a war without authorization and funding from Congress, and Congress cannot provide those for longer than one year at a time.

➤ A congressional vote to end a war is not subject to presidential veto.

➤ During war, the children and grandchildren of the president, vice president, all cabinet officers, and every member of Congress, who are of military age, must serve in the most dangerous combat positions.

➤ A president, vice president, or member of Congress who profits financially from any war and is convicted of doing so in a court of law shall be imprisoned for a minimum of ten years, and there shall be no statute of limitations on this crime.

3. POWER OF MONEY

The Constitution gives Congress tight control over the raising and spending of public money, and gives the House in particular the power to initiate any bills that raise money. Unless Congress has appropriated money for a particular purpose, not a dime can be spent. And any dimes that are spent following congressional appropriation must be reported publicly. These congressional prerogatives are commonly known as "the power of the purse." That phrase is often used to describe not simply the power to determine how money is spent, but the technique of using that power to restrain illegal activities by the president.

The power of the purse has been weakened by the creation of secretive branches of government, including the NSA, CIA, and so on, with secret budgets (the total of which is now believed to be about $60 billion), as well as by the massive military budget (about $600 billion) over which Congress technically has oversight but which in reality knows far less than it should. In addition, the Bush-Cheney White House kept secret the activities of numerous departments previously quite open to congressional and public view, held secret policy meetings, refused Freedom of Information Act (FOIA) requests, and established secret laws. Purse power was further weakened to the point of nonexistence by Bush through the simple technique of ignoring it and making clear his intention to ignore it, as well as by bestowing upon himself the right to secretly move money from any authorized public budget to a secret budget.

Under federal statutory law, as well as under the Constitution, it is illegal to use government funds for anything other than what Congress appropriates them for.[104] In most cases, activities that are in violation of other laws, and activities engaged in without the knowledge of Congress, are also activities for which Congress has never appropriated funding. The warrantless spying programs would fall into this category (although some members of Congress did know some of what was going on), as would the efforts of the White House Iraq Group to defraud the nation into an illegal war, White House efforts to punish whistleblowers, Karl Rove's work on Republican party strategy out of the White House, etc. When Bush deployed troops to prepare for the Iraq invasion and in fact engaged in unpublicized bombing campaigns prior to the invasion, even while telling the public and the Congress that he hoped to avoid war, he was misspending funding that had been appropriated for Afghanistan and elsewhere. Congress obligingly ignored that matter and eagerly appropriated massive amounts of funding for the invasion of Iraq and the short little skirmish of a war that was supposed to follow. When Bush, Cheney, and gang began building permanent US military bases in Iraq, they were misspending funding that had not been appropriated for that purpose. Congress let that slide and funded the ongoing construction and occupation. Eventually, however, Congress specifically banned the spending of any funds on permanent bases, and did so in legislation signed into law by Bush. But the construction of the bases never stopped. Bush just called them "enduring" rather than "permanent." In other cases, such as warrantless spying, Congress sought to enforce its will through the power of the purse, and the White House ignored such spending bans. Of course, bans on the use of funds for illegal projects ought to go without saying, and so it is not exactly shocking that such bans, once made explicit, have gone ignored, given the access the White House has to unaccounted-for money with which to circumvent the wishes of Congress.

One of the reasons the power of the purse was less than powerful during the Bush-Cheney era was House Speaker Nancy Pelosi's repeated assurance that Congress would not impeach the president no matter what he did. That was a very dangerous promise to make, given the almost unfathomable pile of cash sloshing around in the Pentagon and available for spending on anything at all, legal or otherwise, at the whim of the "commander in chief." The Pentagon cash is augmented by the enormous secret budget that is also stuffed in the president's wallet available for secret operations, including secret prisons in foreign lands. As noted above, Bush used a signing statement to give himself the right to secretly transfer funds from any authorized program to any secret operation, including brand new secret operations of his own invention. Or rather, Bush's signing statement erased a requirement that he notify Congress when he was so transferring funds. Such transfers should, of course, be banned entirely, not legitimized with a requirement to notify Congress.

In 2007, Congress required, and Bush signed a law stipulating, that the amount of money in the US intelligence budget be made known. But it's unclear what that's worth, with Bush having decreed that the president can secretly transfer secret amounts into secret, possibly "intelligence," programs. You might wonder, in these cash-strapped times, where any serious money exists that a president could potentially transfer into secret programs. But if you wondered that you would be forgetting about the existence of the United States military, which has more money than the rest of the world's militaries combined, 220 times the money of Iran's military, more money than the total budget of most countries, more than half of every dollar of US income tax, 483 times the loot raked in by Wal-Mart, vastly more cash than was used in the Cold War competition with the Soviet Union—and not a legitimate enemy anywhere in sight.[105]

The misspending of funds to begin the Iraq War in the fall of 2002 is a particularly disturbing abuse of power, because Bush, Cheney, and gang were pretending to be seeking a diplomatic solution to their phony crisis right up until the invasion in March 2003. Congressman John Conyers included this abuse in the list of crimes his staff documented in his 2006 book, *George W. Bush versus the U.S. Constitution*, on Bush and Cheney's impeachable offenses.[106] It also became one of Congressman Dennis Kucinich's thirty-five articles of impeachment introduced against Bush in June 2008.[107] His piece charged that Bush had "illegally misspent funds to begin a war in secret prior to any congressional authorization," and went on to say,

> The president used over $2 billion in the summer of 2002 to prepare for the invasion of Iraq. First reported in Bob Woodward's book, *Plan of Attack*, and later confirmed by the Congressional Research Service, Bush took money appropriated by Congress for Afghanistan and other programs

and—with no congressional notification—used it to build air-fields in Qatar and to make other preparations for the invasion of Iraq. This constituted a violation of Article I, Section 9 of the US Constitution, as well as a violation of the War Powers Act of 1973.

This sort of behavior also telegraphed an important message to Congress. If Congress ever chose to stop funding a war, Bush would find a way to fund it anyway—as long as Congress kept up its commitment never to impeach him. On September 10, 2007, General David Petraeus testified before the House Armed Services Committee, where Congressman Brad Sherman asked Petraeus what he would do if Congress stopped funding the occupation of Iraq and Bush illegally ordered him to keep it going. Petraeus' answer, that he'd have to ask his lawyer, was less interesting than Sherman's question, which demonstrated awareness of how Bush would react to a cutoff of funds.[108]

Of course, the power of the purse needs its own reforms. It's very hard to manage a purse with secret compartments. We need to force Congress to ban secret budgets. After all, the Constitution says that a "regular Statement and Account of the Receipts and Expenditures of all public Money shall be published from time to time." It doesn't say some public money, but all public money. And all money belonging to our government is public money.

The power of the purse has been used, over the past fifty years, and especially over the past eight years, to create the destructive power of the military industrial complex rather than prevent it. We need to consider creative ways to restrain that power. One idea would be to limit the percentage of federal spending each year that can be devoted to the military (including all the hidden military spending in every department, and including "emergency" spending on wars). I think setting a maximum of 10 percent would be appropriate, but I'd be thrilled to get it down to 25 percent. We should all be aware of how much of our tax money goes to the military. One way to inform the public what is happening would be to require that the amount of income tax one is sending to the military be calculated and entered on a separate line on federal tax forms. Everyone would still be required to pay both their military and their nonmilitary taxes, but at least they would be made aware of where their money goes.[109]

Toward the end of the Bush-Cheney regime, a new sort of monetary abuse gained prominence, involving the unconstitutional borrowing and spending or loaning of military levels of money on something other than the military. This new abuse went by the name "bailouts," though many of us preferred the term "Paulson's Plunder" in honor of then Secretary of the Treasury Henry Paulson. There had been bailouts before, sometimes involving other members of the Bush family, but never on this scale. Look at some of the figures. In November 2008, CNBC published a list that added up to over four trillion:

> $900 billion for (TAF) Term Auction Facility
> $99.2 billion for Commercial Banks
> $56.7 billion for Investment Banks
> $76.5 billion for Loans to buy ABCP
> $112.5 billion for AIG
> $29.5 billion for Bear Stearns
> $225 billion for (TSLF) Term Securities Lending Facility
> $613 billion for Swap Lines
> $540 billion for (MMIFF) Money Market Investor Funding Facility
> $257 billion for Commercial Paper Funding Facility
> $700 billion for (TARP) Treasury Asset Relief Program
> $25 billion for Automakers
> $300 billion for (FHA) Federal Housing Administration
> $350 billion for Fannie Mae/Freddie Mac
> Rough total: $4,284,500,000,000—Four trillion and growing very fast!

Within another week, on November 24, 2008, Bloomberg News placed the total at $7.4 trillion, with only $700 billion of it authorized by Congress. The next day Bloomberg had its total at $7.6 trillion before the Federal Reserve announced another $800 billion, bumping the overall total to $8.4 trillion. The public had never condoned such a thing. As an alternative, every member of the public could have been given about $27,000.[110] Is there any doubt that the public would have preferred that, or any doubt that such a move would have benefitted the economy? I asked author and former government policy analyst Richard Cook this question, and he wrote to me in an e-mail, "More than benefitted—it would have revolutionized the economy by a grassroots stimulus unprecedented in history. Instead the government decided to turn the nation over entirely to the creditor class and condemn the people to long-term debt slavery."

On November 10, 2008, Bloomberg.com published an article that began, "The Federal Reserve is refusing to identify the recipients of almost $2 trillion of emergency loans from American taxpayers or the troubled assets the central bank is accepting as collateral."[111]

The portions of Paulson's Plunder approved by Congress on condition of very minimal oversight were proceeding without any oversight. The power to borrow and spend or loan a fortune the size of many nations' budgets (probably larger than any nation's GDP except the United States') had been given to the executive branch, along with the power to do it in secret. And new plunders were underway without any involvement of Congress whatsoever, except perhaps of particular members who had been and would again be corporate tax lawyers. The power of taxation, remember, constitutionally belongs in the Congress, and in particular, in the House of Representatives. The Treasury Department has no legal authority to alter tax law. The bill passed by Congress authorizing the $700 billion plunder, we were told, banned the use of any money for bonuses, severance pay, dividends, or acquisitions of other institutions—in fact, for anything other than making loans. Yet the money was openly used for all of those things because, in reality, the law was merely a suggestion.

But the secrecy of the Federal Reserve regarding the recipients of $2 trillion in loans was in such blatant violation of the law that, while Congress was happy to look the other way, Bloomberg.com filed a lawsuit. The violation of the Constitution inherent in moving the power of the purse from Capitol Hill to the Treasury Department was something only Congress could have opposed, but Congress, in which many leading members of both parties owned large amounts of stock in AIG and other companies involved, supported it.

The public overwhelmingly opposed the so-called bailout vote in Congress and succeeded in defeating it in the House on the first go-round. But the influence of campaign contributions, party discipline, and media manipulation won out over democracy. The bill was passed first in the Senate and then in the House, despite the Constitutional requirement that all bills to raise money begin in the House. While this bill did not raise money in the old-fashioned way, by taxation, it did so in the new traditional way, by borrowing. Passage in the always less democratic Senate was used to pressure the House to pass the bill as well.

As presidential candidates, both Obama and McCain supported the bill and urged passage. (There were rumors of possible opposition from McCain, but it never materialized.) The first half of the $700 billion was doled out while Bush was president, and the second half would be forked over during Obama's presidency. Obama effectively maintained Bush's policy on Wall Street bailouts through the first months of his presidency, despite continued public opposition (a poll by Zogby found that 6 percent of Americans favored bailing out bankers[112]), as well as opposition by numerous economic experts who argued that giving or loaning more money to the people responsible for reckless speculation would not solve the problem of oversized and under-regulated banks or the problem of our gutted and forgotten nonmilitary real economy. In fact, rather than making the money received in the bailouts available to people, banks actually raised some rates and fees in order to squeeze more out of those of us not being bailed out.[113]

Early in Obama's presidency, Congress also passed a $787 billion stimulus bill (which Democrats unnecessarily allowed Republicans to water down with tax cuts unlikely to stimulate anything) that, unlike the "bailout," sent money to people who actually needed it. But while the bill may have been relatively benevolent, it provided for little congressional oversight, and protections for whistleblowers were stripped out of the final version. It was also criticized by Paul Krugman and other more progressive economists as being too small and doing too little for infrastructure.

There was one other bit of good news at the dawn of the Obama era. Congressman Barney Frank (D-MA), chairman of the House Financial Services Committee and one of the leaders responsible for pushing

Paulson's Plunder through Congress, was struck by a strange fit of remorse, or perhaps recognition of reality, and blurted out in public that unless all domestic programs were to be cut, the military budget would have to be. Frank proposed cuts of 25 percent to the budgets for the military and wars. A few weeks later, again on November 10, 2008, the *Boston Globe* reported that "A senior Pentagon advisory group, in a series of bluntly worded briefings, is warning President-elect Barack Obama that the Defense Department's current budget is 'not sustainable,' and he must scale back or eliminate some of the military's most prized weapons programs."[114]

This is, of course, good news, but notice to whom the Pentagon's advice is directed; it's not to Congress. And were it directed to Congress, it might not be effective, since Congress has been known in the past to give the Pentagon money it did not want, or at least more money than it asked for.

In the ordinary course of things in Washington, DC, and on television, there are two separate conversations. In one conversation, everything that the government spends money on (schools, transportation, police, and so on) must be trimmed back to save money. In the other conversation, the expenses of wars and the military must be unquestioned. In February 2009, Congressman Frank went on ABC television and combined the two. After a right winger proposed more tax cuts to "stimulate" the economy and denounced any spending programs as not being "stimulus," Frank pointed out that the largest spending program we've seen is the war on Iraq. Host George Stephanopoulos clearly felt the force of some galactic wind about to suck him into a different dimension, because he jumped in and said, "That is a whole 'nother show." But Frank faced the taboo head-on, saying,

> No it isn't. That's the problem. The problem is that we look at spending and say oh don't spend on highways, don't spend on health care, but let's build Cold War weapons to defeat the Soviet Union when we don't need them, let's have hundreds and hundreds of billions of dollars going to the military without a check. Unless everything is on the table then you're going to have a disproportionate hit in some places.[115]

In late February 2009, before President Obama proposed what he wanted to see in the next year's budget, during the preparation of which the president required everyone working on it to sign non-disclosure agreements, Congressman Frank announced a detailed plan to cut 25 percent from wars and the military. He calculated a savings of hundreds of billions per year from scaling back and ending the occupation of Iraq over the coming four years, even while escalating the occupation of Afghanistan. (He was clearly supporting what he took to be Obama's program.) And, borrowing calculations from the Institute for Policy Studies, Frank proposed saving $60 billion per year by "eliminating wasteful weapons systems, reducing the number of active nuclear warheads and tightening procurement processes to reduce waste, fraud and abuse." The US corporate media completely ignored this, and a couple of days later Obama proposed a larger military budget than the year before as well as $205 billion for wars through fiscal year 2010.

Obama did, in his first weeks in office, support a ban on space weapons and propose reducing US and Russian nuclear weapons to 1,000 each. He also proposed doubling the relatively tiny amount of funding the United States devotes to foreign aid. But seriously challenging the military-industrial-congressional complex was not on the agenda.

Of course, it was likely that most Democrats in Congress would do what the president told them to do. In fact, just as Congresswoman Barbara Lee had voted alone against the authorization to attack Afghanistan, Congressman Dennis Kucinich was the only member of Congress who voted no on a 2010 budget bill in April 2009 in opposition to funding an escalation in Afghanistan. Meanwhile, the corporate and progressive media almost universally reported on the military's proposed 2010 budget as if it were smaller than the year before. And the same Congress members who had been claiming that government spending couldn't stimulate an economy began screaming that cutting military spending would wreck the economy. In reality, while some weapons systems (and therefore jobs) faced proposed cuts, others were slated for expansion, and the overall budget was larger than ever before. While True Majority, an activist group that seeks to shift funding from the military to human needs, e-mailed its members asking them to support a military budget with cuts in it, never mentioning that this was a larger budget overall, the financial news source *Jane's* ran the headline "US Defence Stocks Surged on Gates' Budget Proposal." Most media outlets and even activist groups appeared unready to recognize what the business analysts did: militarism was on the rise in the post-Bush world.

Congress is in dire need of reforms that will be discussed in this book, but substituting the president for Congress is not a safe or democratic solution. The power of the purse must be returned to Congress; Congress must be made accountable to the American people. Violations of this power by presidents or their subordinates must result in jail time, Congress must break up monopolies and regulate the financial "industry," and budgets for public money must reflect new priorities and stop wasteful spending where it is most prevalent—in budgets for war, weapons, and banker bailouts.[116]

4. POWER OF JUDICIARY

We have already seen that Bush and Cheney bestowed upon the presidency the power to write laws and to violate laws when the president is actually only supposed to have the power to enforce laws. So, let's talk now about law enforcement. Bush and Cheney did make good use of the government's law enforcement agencies, including the Department of Justice—but they used them for illegal and partisan purposes. They used the NSA and the FBI to illegally spy. They used the CIA and the military to illegally detain, torture, and murder. And they established a new court system for "enemy combatants" that was separate from the judicial branch of our government, and that had not been created by Congress.

You can call the executive power "unitary" as Dick Cheney did with some irony, as a vice president sharing heartily in the supposedly unitary power. You could call the executive power multitudinous, or beauteous, or miraculous. But no matter what you call it, you can't change the fact that it indisputably does not include rendition power or torture power or any of the other criminal powers seized by Bush and Cheney. (Rendition began with President Bill Clinton, but was greatly expanded by Bush, which is what presidents tend to do with powers they've been handed by their predecessors. In fact, Obama announced that he would continue rendition but not use it for torture—he would not use "extraordinary rendition." Once used openly by multiple presidents and left unchallenged, rendition, like other abuses, becomes ordinary.)

The power to decide to kidnap people, disappear them, hang them by their wrists, electroshock their genitals, and hide them away from the world indefinitely simply does not exist in the Constitution. It did exist until 1865, when the Thirteenth Amendment banned slavery. But it existed as a personal, nongovernmental power for any president of the land of the free who happened to own a bunch of human beings (the same power any Congress member or private citizen had). It never existed at all as part of the executive power of the president in his official capacity, as something on which he might openly or secretly spend public funds. To do so would have been, and still is, in violation of the Fourth through Eighth Amendments, which were ratified as the heart of the Bill of Rights (for non-slaves) in 1791.

Bush and his Attorney General Alberto Gonzales abused the Justice Department for political ends. The routine hiring and firing of career employees was, by the department's own admission, illegally based on loyalty to the Republican Party. The Department of Justice even fired nine US Attorneys (top federal prosecutors) in December 2006 for apparently partisan reasons. The department's own Inspector General called the process "arbitrary" and "fundamentally flawed," and said that it "raised doubts about the integrity of Department prosecution decisions."[117]

Some of the fired prosecutors had been investigating Republicans. Others had been refusing to prosecute particular targeted Democrats or to pursue the prosecution of nonexistent crimes that were part of Republican talking points, primarily the crime of "voter fraud." (While election fraud, meaning the wholesale manipulation of vote counts, does occur, instances of lone individuals misrepresenting themselves in order to illegally cast a single vote are few and far between—almost nonexistent, though we've been told they occur in epidemic volume.)

Given this level of corruption in the Justice Department, it was not surprising that when, in 2007 and 2008, Congress asked it to enforce subpoenas and contempt citations against its own employees and partisan allies, the Justice Department refused. It was slightly more surprising when in February 2009 the new Justice Department refused to enforce some of the same subpoenas then reissued by Congress. Obama's White House supported former Bush aide Karl Rove's claim of "executive privilege" and negotiated partial compliance by Rove with a subpoena from the House Judiciary Committee, openly arguing that this was appropriate in order to maintain presidential power.[118]

The complete corruption of the Department of Justice meant that the Bush White House could engage in any criminal behavior it chose without fear of prosecution. In fact, Bush engaged in illegal partisan activities in the White House as well as the Department of Justice. He routinely used federal resources for partisan politics by orchestrating partisan political events during work hours at federal government facilities involving federal government employees in violation of the Hatch Act, which bars federal officials from partisan political activity while on the job. Bush's top adviser Karl Rove worked on electoral politics out of the White House at taxpayer expense and led an "asset deployment" team that influenced the use of government resources for the purpose of electing President Bush and other Republican politicians. Among these resources were cabinet secretaries, who were deployed to key media markets to promote the Republican electoral agenda. The White House Office of Political Affairs, headed by Rove, presented its partisan political information during meetings held by other government departments. Up through the 2008 election of Obama, Democrats in Congress favored eliminating the White House Office of Political Affairs. After the election, they went silent.

The Cheney-Bush gang found plenty of other laws to violate as well. Prior to the attacks of September 11, 2001, not just after, President Bush authorized the NSA to violate the Fourth Amendment and the Foreign Intelligence Service Act of 1978 (FISA) by spying on Americans without court warrants to do so, and without even the very easily and retroactively obtained warrants of the FISA Court.[119] For five years, Bush lied to the public and most of Congress about this. Some key members of Congress of both parties were informed and remained criminally silent. Bush repeatedly made clear his awareness of the law and falsely claimed to be abiding by it. For example, at a White House press conference on April 20, 2004, Bush said:

> Now, by the way, any time you hear the United States government talking about wiretap, it requires—a wiretap requires a court order. Nothing has changed, by the way. When we're talking about chasing down terrorists, we're talking about getting a court order before we do so.

The *New York Times* finally broke the story in 2005, having sat on it for over a year because it might have influenced voters in the 2004 election. What a disaster it would have been for voters to be influenced by knowledge of what their government was actually doing! The *New York Times* only published the story when it did because the reporter, James Risen, was about to tell it in his book *State of War*. From that point forward, Bush shifted from denying he was engaged in warrantless spying to insisting that he had every right to engage in warrantless spying, and that questioning that fact amounted to putting Americans' lives in danger. In a radio address on December 17, 2005, Bush said,

> I have reauthorized this program more than thirty times since the September II attacks, and I intend to do so for as long as our nation faces a continuing threat from al-Qaeda and related groups. The NSA's activities under this authorization are thoroughly reviewed by the Justice Department and NSA's top legal officials, including NSA's general counsel and inspector general.

Bush falsely implied in the above statement that the program had begun after the September II attacks. And he falsely implied that he was obeying the law by indicating that lawyers working for him had obligingly approved of his crime. Yet even this pretense of legality was not entirely accurate. On March 10, 2004, Attorney General John Ashcroft had refused to authorize the entire warrantless spying program or some aspect thereof, summoning the strength to lift his head from a hospital bed to do so when White House Counsel (later to become Attorney General) Alberto Gonzales and Bush's chief of staff Andrew Card Jr. had tried to take advantage of Ashcroft's condition.[120] Top members of the Justice Department threatened mass resignation until the programs were altered in some unknown way. Perhaps Bush, Card, and Gonzales had proposed eavesdropping on Americans domestically without any pretense of focusing on foreign communications, or eavesdropping on Congress or courts or political enemies or reporters. Perhaps they wanted to plant bugs in church confessionals. Who knows. It was something that even Ashcroft in his hospital bed couldn't bring himself to approve, but that his successor Gonzales favored.

At a December 19, 2005 press conference Bush claimed the right to violate the law in as explicit a manner as we have heard from a president since former President Nixon had claimed that anything a president did was legal. Bush's mangling of the English language does not prevent the clear understanding that he was claiming the right to use the FISA court when he chose, and to ignore it when he saw fit:

> We use FISA still—you're referring to the FISA court in your question—of course, we use FISAs. But FISA is for long-term monitoring. What is needed in order to protect the American people is the ability to move quickly to detect. Now, having suggested this idea, I then, obviously, went to the question, is it legal to do so? I am—I swore to uphold the laws. Do I have the legal authority to do this? And the answer is, absolutely. As I mentioned in my remarks, the legal authority is derived from the Constitution, as well as the authorization of force by the United States Congress.[121]

Remember that Authorization to Use Military Force, by which Congress had unconstitutionally transferred the power to declare war to the White House? Nowhere in it was there any authorization to violate FISA or the Fourth Amendment; in fact, Congress has no power to authorize the violation of the Fourth Amendment, and FISA explicitly establishes itself and two chapters of the federal criminal code as the "exclusive means by which electronic surveillance . . . and the interception of domestic wire, oral, and electronic communications may be conducted." At a December 19, 2005 press briefing, Attorney General Gonzales admitted that the nature of the surveillance being done was so far removed from what FISA could approve (or perhaps from what the public would ever tolerate) that FISA could not even be amended to allow it. He said, "We have had discussions with Congress in the past—certain members of Congress—as to whether or not FISA could be amended to allow us to adequately deal with this kind of threat, and we were advised that that would be difficult, if not impossible."[122]

In fact, contrary to claims made by Bush, Cheney, and the gang, the spying programs they established illegally spied on domestic communications within the United States, not just communications to or from individuals outside the country. Mark Klein, a retired AT&T communications technician, submitted an affidavit in support of a lawsuit against AT&T filed by the Electronic Frontier Foundation. Klein testi-fied in 2006 that in 2003 he had connected a "splitter" that sent a copy of all Internet traffic and phone calls to a secure room that was operated by the NSA in the San Francisco office of AT&T. Klein testified that he had been told by a coworker that similar rooms were being constructed in other cities, including Seattle, San Jose, Los Angeles, and San Diego.[123]

Bush violated the Stored Communications Act of 1986 and the Telecommunications Act of 1996 by creating a huge database drawn from the private telephone calls and e-mails of American citizens and provided, at the Bush administration's request, by major telecommuni-cations companies, including AT&T, Verizon, and Bell South.[124] In 2007 we learned that in early 2001, prior to the September 11 attacks, Joseph Nacchio, the CEO of Qwest, had rejected as illegal a request from the NSA to turn over customer records of phone calls, e-mails and other Internet activity.[125]

On August 17, 2006, the United States District Court in Detroit ruled in *ACLU v. NSA* that the Bush-Cheney spying programs violated the Fourth Amendment and FISA. In July 2007, the Sixth Circuit Court of Appeals dismissed the case without ruling on its merits. In fact, the appeals court ruled only that the plaintiffs had no standing to sue because they couldn't be certain they'd been spied upon, and they couldn't be certain they'd been spied upon because the spying had been done in secret. Thus did all three branches of government become com-plicit in the removal of the Fourth Amendment from our Constitution.

We don't, of course, know the full extent or nature of the spying, but we know that Bush knowingly violated FISA on a grand scale, and that FISA carries a potential penalty of five years in prison for each violation.

And we have had hints at the things we don't know. In 2007 we learned that Director of National Intelligence Mike McConnell had written to Senator Arlen Specter admitting that an executive order from Bush in 2001 had authorized a series of secret surveillance activities that included undisclosed activities beyond the warrantless surveillance of e-mails and phone calls that Bush had confirmed in December 2005.[126]

On July 1, 2007, I broke the story on my *After Downing Street* blog that for the first time one of the operators who had engaged in uncon-stitutional spying at the NSA was willing to talk about it.[127] Adrienne

Kinne had eavesdropped on phone calls to the United States from soldiers, aid workers, and journalists in Iraq. And she revealed evidence of more crimes than just the spying. Kinne described an incident just prior to the invasion of Iraq in which a fax had come into her office at Fort Gordon in Georgia that purported to provide information on the location of Iraqi weapons of mass destruction. The fax came from the Iraqi National Congress, a group opposed to Saddam Hussein and favoring an invasion. The fax contained types of information that required that it be translated and transmitted to President Bush within fifteen minutes. But Kinne had been eavesdropping on two nongovernmental aid workers driving in Iraq who were panicked and trying to find safety before the bombs dropped. She focused on trying to protect them, and was reprimanded for the delay in translating the fax. She then challenged her officer in charge, Warrant Officer John Berry, on the credibility of the fax, and he told her that it was not her place or his to challenge such things. None of the other twenty or so people in the unit questioned anything, Kinne said. She dated this incident to the period just before the official invasion of Iraq, or possibly just after. She said that because the US engaged in so much bombing prior to the official invasion, she could not recall for sure. As far as I know, *Wired* is the only media outlet that followed up on this particular part of Kinne's story.

Many of the people Kinne spied on, including Americans, were journalists. Some were staying at a hotel in Baghdad that later showed up on a list of targets. Kinne said she expressed concerns to her officer in charge, letting him know that the military should be made aware of the situation, or that the journalists should be warned to move to another location. Kinne said that Berry brushed her off. He was, she said, "completely behind the invasion of Iraq. He told us repeatedly that we needed to bomb those barbarians back to kingdom come." Berry was later promoted to Chief Warrant Officer. As far as I know, *Wired* and *Democracy Now!* were the only media outlets that followed up on this part of the story, and it took *Democracy Now!* until May 13, 2008, to do so.

On May 19, 2008, I broke the story of the second NSA operator willing to discuss what he'd done.[128] David Murfee Faulk, who had also been stationed at Fort Gordon, said that in May 2004 he found an extremely large text file containing grid coordinates for alleged chemical weapons sites in Iraq. Faulk said he showed it to his supervisor, who had been surprised. But the supervisor was not surprised that the file existed, only that it had not been deleted. The supervisor said he had believed all such files had been deleted. He claimed that US Special Forces had gone to the locations and found nothing. That's what usually happens, Faulk's supervisor told him, when you get a tip from the Israelis. "Four out of five times it's complete and total bullshit."

I asked veteran CIA analyst Ray McGovern what he made of this, and he told me in an e-mail that there was "no such thing as a 'friendly' intelligence service. Reporting from liaison services always needs to be taken with utmost reserve. That goes in spades for what comes from the Israelis, the more so since they have unique, yes, unique, access to the White House and Pentagon, and are thus able to circumvent the intelligence bureaucracy set up to vet and evaluate raw intelligence and prevent unverified and/or tendentious 'intelligence' from reaching senior officials, lest they be misled."

As far as I know, no other media outlet has ever, to this day, followed up on this aspect of Faulk's story. But on October 9, 2008, ABC News ran a story on both Kinne and Faulk.[129] ABC called the story "exclusive" despite being years behind the curve, ignored the evidence related to the war, and focused on the fact that Faulk and others had listened in on "phone sex" between US soldiers and their spouses. While Kinne had tried to get Congress to pay attention to her since before I'd first reported her story, the first sign of interest came from a handful of senators and House members just after the ABC "exclusive," and vanished again as the story quickly faded from view.

On June 9, 2008, Congressman Kucinich introduced thirty-five articles of impeachment against Bush, including two covering the unconstitutional spying.[130] During the presidential election primaries, Obama defeated Senator Hillary Clinton, aided in some measure by his unequivocal promise to oppose and to filibuster against any bill that would grant immunity to the telecom companies for their illegal spying. When a bill came before the House and Senate in July 2008 granting civil immunity to the telecoms, Obama's supporters gathered on his website, creating the largest self-organized group of Obama activists, with the goal of pushing Obama to keep his word. Instead he voted for the bill, stating,

> [The FISA bill] also firmly reestablishes basic judicial oversight
> over all domestic surveillance in the future. It does, however,
> grant retroactive immunity, and I will work in the Senate to
> remove this provision so that we can seek full accountability for
> past offenses.[131]

Not only should that "modernization" act be repealed, but the original Foreign Intelligence Surveillance Act should be completely
repealed as well. While violating FISA constitutes a troubling lawlessness, the law itself provides a rubber stamp rather than serious judicial
oversight. FISA and the PATRIOT Act should be repealed as violations
of our Bill of Rights, and replaced with strict laws in defense of our
rights. But violators of even the unconstitutionally loose standards of
FISA must be prosecuted and imprisoned if rewriting laws is to have
any meaning. In addition, we must compel Congress to compel the
Obama administration to make public everything it knows about the
crimes of Bush and Cheney in this and other areas. We must not fall into
the foolish trap of believing that because we don't know all the details,
we don't know crimes have been committed. Prosecutions should proceed without delay. But the full story should still be exposed, and simply
having elected a new president will not accomplish that. In November
2008, President-elect Obama scheduled a meeting with outgoing Vice
President Dick Cheney to discuss secret programs that Cheney wanted
to see continued. We don't know what was discussed there. But by May
2009, President Obama had announced that he would continue to claim
the power of indefinite detention without charge.

On the rare occasions during the Cheney-Bush era that I appeared
on corporate cable news shows and was asked what the president could
possibly have done wrong, I always said he's spied without warrants,
detained without charges, tortured, and murdered. Sometimes I continued with a longer list, but I always started with those same ten words.
Obviously I considered the spying without warrants to be the least of
it.[132] The other abuses were more severe and equally impeachable and
prosecutable.

Between 2000 and 2008, the United States became (at least more
directly and openly than in the past) a country whose government kid-

naps people, Americans and others, at home and abroad; locks them up without charge or due process, and without access to the outside world; and tortures them or sends them to foreign allies to be tortured. The Fifth Amendment has been shredded without a word, while the Geneva Conventions—which, under Article VI of the Constitution, are the law of the land—were explicitly rejected by a decree from "The Decider" on February 7, 2002. Such decrees were typically signed by Bush when his subordinates got nervous about covering their asses, not when the crimes began. By February of 2002, the Bush administration was already shipping people from Afghanistan and around the world to prisons in Afghanistan and at Guantánamo Bay, Cuba. The rounding up of Muslims in the United States had begun immediately after September 11, 2001. So had the practice of "ghosting" prisoners: in violation of US law and the Geneva Conventions, Bush instructed the Department of Justice and the US Department of Defense (DOD) to refuse to provide the identities or locations of detainees, despite requests from their attorneys, Congress, and the Red Cross. Bush claimed the right to detain foreigners and US citizens alike indefinitely, without charge or access to counsel. Several US citizens were held in solitary confinement in military brigs for months or years. At least 2,500 of those subjected to the Bush system of injustice were children under eighteen. That's how many children the United States told the United Nations it was holding as "enemy combatants" in May 2008, not counting children who had by then reached the age of eighteen while imprisoned.

Early in the move to what Cheney called "the dark side," the Bush gang chose to ask foreign allies to do its torturing. We, our US government, "renditioned" people to secret prisons in nations known to practice torture. Much of this was handled by the CIA, which has no legal authority to be involved in law enforcement—if that's even what this can be called. Torture and aiding or abetting torture is all illegal under US law and the Convention Against Torture (CAT), the International Covenant on Civil and Political Rights (ICCPR), the Geneva Conventions, the US Bill of Rights, and the Universal Declaration of Human Rights.

Once fully immersed in the dark side, our public employees and their contractors did more of the torturing themselves. Bush explicitly authorized it, and it became standard procedure at Guantánamo, Abu Ghraib Prison, other US detention sites in Iraq, and at Bagram Air Base in Afghanistan. Bush's lawyers, in this case, did not simply claim that Bush had the right to break the law. Instead they claimed that torture was not torture, redefining torture as the inflicting of pain akin to that accompanying "serious physical injury, such as organ failure, impairment of bodily function, or even death."[133] They went on to claim, however, that the president indeed had the right to engage in torture, even as thus redefined. John Yoo of the Office of Legal Counsel famously claimed in 2006 that the president had the right to crush a child's testicles.[134] Somehow that image doesn't strike me as a worthy replacement for the Statue of Liberty.

Bush's lawyers were wise to claim that he had the right to engage in torture even with torture having been redefined as indistinguishable from murder, because US military autopsy reports showed that dozens of prisoners had been tortured to death.[135] In his 2003 State of the Union address, Bush announced,

> To date we have arrested or otherwise dealt with many key commanders of al-Qaeda.... All told, more than 3,000 suspected terrorists have been arrested in many countries.... And many others have met a different fate. Let's put it this way: They are no longer a problem to the United States and our friends and allies.... We've got the terrorists on the run. We're keeping them on the run. One by one the terrorists are learning the meaning of American justice.[136]

The new meaning of American justice was the absence of a judicial system, and one by one American states, counties, and cities were learning it as well. The government unconstitutionally spied on peace activists, infiltrated organizations, charged Quakers with "terrorism," detained independent reporters without charges during major events, and even tortured. The Republican National Convention in Minneapolis / St. Paul in the summer of 2008 left behind allegations of all of these activities as well as videotape of police in riot gear randomly arresting peaceful citizens.

By declaring hundreds of detainees at Guantánamo Bay and elsewhere to be "enemy combatants" not subject to US law and not even subject to military law, but nonetheless potentially liable to the death penalty, Bush violated laws and the Constitution. He also replaced the judicial branch of our government with something of his own creation: military commissions, a justice system stripped of all justice.

Unlike the legislative branch, the judicial branch appeared to take offense at its proposed replacement.

The judicial branch of our government did in cases stand up for the rule of law against the incredible abuses of the Bush-Cheney White House, as evidenced in the Supreme Court cases *Rasul v. Bush*, *Hamdan v. Rumsfeld*, *Hamdi v. Rumsfeld*, and *Boumediene v. Bush*. In the 2004 *Rasul* case, the Supreme Court ruled that detainees at Guantánamo could challenge their detentions in US courts, detentions that had been imposed on them purely by the decree of the president. The *Hamdi* decision the same year came to the same conclusion, but only as applied to US citizens. In 2005, Congress gave Bush the Detainee Treatment Act, including the "McCain Amendment," purporting to legalize presidential detentions and pseudo-trials and to provide legal protection to those involved in these crimes.

In the June 2006 *Hamdan* case the Supreme Court ruled that the president did not have the right to substitute "military commissions" for court trials, and was in fact bound by Common Article 3 of the Geneva Conventions as well as the War Crimes Act of 1996. In October 2006, Congress gave the president the Military Commissions Act, including Section 7(e), which purported to allow the president to do what he wanted, justice be damned, and tossed out the right of habeas corpus. In the June 2008 *Boumediene* case the Supreme Court ruled that prisoners at Guantánamo had the right of habeas corpus, and that the denial of that right by the Military Commissions Act was unconstitutional. None of these rulings were unanimous, and the justices ruling against limitations on presidential power tended, ominously, to be the younger ones. The Bush Justice Department fought prisoners' habeas petitions, and in April 2009 the Obama Justice Department placed a help wanted ad for lawyers who could do the same.

In December 2007, the *Boston Globe* asked candidate Obama, "Does the president have inherent powers under the Constitution to conduct surveillance for national security purposes without judicial warrants, regardless of federal statutes?" Obama replied, "The Supreme Court has never held that the president has such powers. As president, I will follow existing law, and when it comes to US citizens and residents, I will only authorize surveillance for national security purposes consistent with FISA and other federal statutes."[137] But, as noted, Obama then voted for a bill granting immunity to telecom companies. He claimed at the time that he would work to remove that immunity and that the bill provided judicial oversight. Instead, during his first months as president, Obama's Justice Department renewed and expanded upon Bush's claims of "state secrets" in attempts to have court cases dismissed that sought accountability for warrantless spying and torture. Obama used the "state secrets" excuse to argue not only for keeping information out of court, but for dismissing cases entirely. His administration argued that under the PATRIOT Act the government had "sovereign immunity" and could not be sued for illegal spying unless it intentionally made public what it found. The new Justice Department also argued that a president should be able to declare anything classified and deny any court, even in closed session, the right to review it. These were all innovations that expanded presidential powers of secrecy and immunity. That they were used to cover up the crimes of the previous administration, and that the new administration promised not to commit some of the same crimes, was good news, but the ability of future presidents to engage in such abuses undetected was being enhanced, not restrained. And the effort was quite aggressive; Obama's White House even threatened to cut off intelligence sharing with the British government if it exposed past crimes.

The *Boston Globe* asked further questions:

> Q: Does the Constitution permit a president to detain US citizens without charges as unlawful enemy combatants?
>
> A: No. I reject the Bush administration's claim that the President has plenary authority under the Constitution to detain US citizens without charges as unlawful enemy combatants.

Q: If Congress prohibits a specific interrogation technique, can the president instruct his subordinates to employ that technique despite the statute?

A: No. The President is not above the law, and not entitled to use techniques that Congress has specifically banned as torture. We must send a message to the world that America is a nation of laws, and a nation that stands against torture. As President I will abide by statutory prohibitions for all US Government personnel and contractors.

Q: Is there any executive power the Bush administration has claimed or exercised that you think is unconstitutional?

A: I reject the view that the President may do whatever he deems necessary to protect national security, and that he may torture people in defiance of congressional enactments. I reject the use of signing statements to make extreme and implausible claims of presidential authority.

Some further points:

➤ The detention of American citizens, without access to counsel, fair procedure, or pursuant to judicial authorization, as enemy combatants is unconstitutional.

➤ Warrantless surveillance of American citizens, in defiance of FISA, is unlawful and unconstitutional.

➤ The violation of international treaties that have been ratified by the Senate, specifically the Geneva Conventions, was illegal (as the Supreme Court held) and a bad idea.

➤ The creation of military commissions without congressional authorization was unlawful (as the Supreme Court held at least in part, ruling that combat status review tribunals are no substitute for habeas corpus) and a bad idea.[138]

These were encouraging answers from candidate Obama, especially regarding US citizens. But what about the other 95 percent of the people in the world? During the first weeks of his presidency, Obama made it clear that, at least for them, the rule of law would be optional. He would maintain the power to kidnap people and ship them across borders, as well as the power to detain people without charge indefinitely. While committing to not torturing, to closing secret CIA prisons, and to eventually closing the Guantánamo prison, Obama claimed the continued power of rendition and the power to detain people indefinitely outside any rule of law. He would simply do so in prisons other than the one at Guantánamo. Obama's Justice Department appealed a ruling that would have given prisoners at Bagram air base in Afghanistan the right to habeas corpus.

Fixing this mess will require that Congress repeal all legislation that has facilitated its creation, including the Detainee Treatment Act of 2005 and the Military Commissions Act of 2006.

I'm grateful for the steps that have been taken, and I'm all in favor of Obama not torturing anyone. However, I oppose accepting the pretense that one president can order torture legal and the next order it illegal. If we accept that, then what is to prevent a future president declaring it legal again? Just after the election of 2008, a large coalition of well-intended organizations called The Constitution Project released a report recommending solutions to a wide range of Bush-Cheney crimes and abuses.[39] But most of the recommendations were addressed to President Obama, not to Congress. The policy positions were good ones, the understanding of power and deterrence weak.

Repealing and passing legislation will not be enough. Remember that when Congress redundantly re-banned torture, Bush used a signing statement to claim the right to torture anyway. Any future president will be aware of the privilege to ignore the law unless Bush, Cheney, and gang are prosecuted. Following the 2008 elections, groups like the ACLU, Human Rights First, People for the American Way, and many others published proposals to cease committing the crimes involved in detention and torture, but did not prominently propose prosecuting anyone guilty of the crimes. (By February 2009, most such groups were supporting prosecution but more loudly urging the creation of commissions, hearings, or investigations by Congress or a special body.) By April, the ACLU was strongly in favor of appointing a special prosecutor.

Senator Russ Feingold also prepared a list of recommendations to the new president, but failed to include the one piece of advice I would have offered: remember that Congress makes the laws. Senator Dianne Feinstein, who was expected to become, and did become, the new chair of the Intelligence Committee, planned to "introduce legislation that would require America's intelligence agencies to follow the Army field manual in interrogations; to prohibit the use of contractors in interrogations; to grant the International Committee of the Red Cross access to detainees; and to close the Guantánamo Bay detention facility within one year," according to her spokesman, Phil LaVelle. "If President Obama accomplishes these goals through executive action, then we won't need to pursue them legislatively as well." Obama so ordered, and Congress did not have to be troubled to act. Feinstein appeared to have difficulty thinking more than four years into the future.

If we were thinking ahead we would demand that Congress pass all appropriate legislation, whether or not the current president engages in the same abuses as others. We would work to amend the Constitution as needed to render possible future abuses unconstitutional. And we would give strength and meaning to existing laws by enforcing them. In February 2009, as Congress members and media pundits debated whether to turn a blind eye or set up a "truth commission" to mull over the past eight years, I drafted a short statement that over 180 human rights groups signed onto, including the Center for Constitutional Rights, the National Lawyers Guild, the Society of American Law Teachers, etc. The statement read in its entirety:[140]

> We urge Attorney General Eric Holder to appoint a non-partisan independent Special Counsel to immediately commence a prosecutorial investigation into the most serious alleged crimes of former President George W. Bush, former Vice President Richard B. Cheney, the attorneys formerly employed by the Department of Justice whose memos sought to justify torture, and other former top officials of the Bush administration.
>
> Our laws, and treaties that under Article VI of our Constitution are the supreme law of the land, require the prosecution of crimes that strong evidence suggests these individuals have

committed. Both the former president and the former vice president have confessed to authorizing a torture procedure that is illegal under our law and treaty obligations. The former president has confessed to violating the Foreign Intelligence Surveillance Act.

We see no need for these prosecutions to be extraordinarily lengthy or costly, and no need to wait for the recommendations of a panel or "truth" commission when substantial evidence of the crimes is already in the public domain. We believe the most effective investigation can be conducted by a prosecutor, and we believe such an investigation should begin immediately.

5. POWER OF TREATY AND APPOINTMENT

Constitutionally, the president has the power to make treaties if he gets the advice and consent of the Senate and two-thirds of the senators present concur. Just prior to leaving office, President Clinton had signed a treaty creating an International Criminal Court. The Senate had not yet ratified it and was not expected immediately to do so. (Clinton himself opposed ratification in what might be considered the first signing statement of the Bush era.)[141] But the matter was set aside, because the brand new president immediately "unsigned" the treaty. This display of arrogance will be remembered if Bush's political career eventually ends where it should, with his conviction as a defendant in the court he opposed.

Bush's tenure as president ended with the negotiation of a treaty with Iraq without obtaining the consent of the US Senate. While the invasion of Iraq had been illegal, the United Nations had pathetically given its blessing to the occupation, and that fig leaf was set to expire on December 31, 2008. It was considered likely that an extension of the UN authorization could be obtained, but Bush preferred to try to negotiate a treaty with his own puppet, the government of Iraq. Bush didn't call it a treaty, but rather a Status of Forces Agreement (SOFA). Such things had long existed as part of the post–World War II US empire of bases around the world. They had just never before been used quite so blatantly as substitutes for treaties. The proposed Iraq SOFA did not just allow troops to live in bases, it granted US troops the authority to fight. In other words, it violated Congress's right to declare war, as well as the Senate's right to approve treaties.

Bush had, through the course of his presidency, negotiated other treaties without Senate approval and called them SOFAs. These included treaties in 2008 to place "missile defense" bases in Poland and the Czech Republic. The Czech people were overwhelmingly opposed to this treaty, and the US corporate media reported on the possible rejection of the treaty—referring to it often as "a SOFA treaty"—by the Czech Parliament, without ever mentioning the failure of the US Senate to assert its constitutional right to a say in the matter. This problem of an empire of bases created by unconstitutional treaties predated Bush, but his actions in Iraq took it to another level.

Clearly Congress needs to have, and be compelled to use, the power to reject treaties and also to define what counts as a treaty. Presidents have made numerous agreements with other nations, without the approval of the Senate, and called those agreements something other than treaties, often referring to them as "executive agreements." The website of the US Senate explains,

> In addition to treaties, which may not enter into force and become binding on the United States without the advice and consent of the Senate, there are other types of international agreements concluded by the executive branch and not submitted to the Senate. These are classified in the United States as executive agreements, not as treaties, a distinction that has only domestic significance. International law regards each mode of international agreement as binding, whatever its designation under domestic law. The difficulty in obtaining a two-thirds vote was one of the motivating forces behind the vast increase in executive agreements after World War II. In 1952, for instance, the United States signed 14 treaties and 291 executive agreements. This was a larger number of executive agreements than had been reached during the entire century of 1789 to 1889. Executive agreements continue to grow at a rapid rate. The United States is currently a party to nearly nine hundred treaties and more than five thousand executive agreements.[142]

While the Senate comments on this state of affairs on its website, it may not actually do anything about it. Certainly there was no great outcry from the US Senate over Bush negotiating a treaty with the prime minister of Iraq, Nouri al-Maliki. Resistance to the treaty came primarily from the Iraqi Parliament, under pressure from the Iraqi people. In the United States the House passed an amendment to the 2009 Defense Authorization Act in May 2008, authored by Congress-woman Barbara Lee, requiring that any agreement providing security for Iraq be approved by Congress; however, the Senate removed that language from the bill. Lee introduced a resolution to the same effect that picked up thirteen cosponsors, as did senator and future vice president Joe Biden who picked up four.

Bush's goal was clearly to create a permanent US military presence in Iraq, while the goal of the Iraqi Parliament was to set a firm date for complete US withdrawal. The two sides also differed on whether to finally make US mercenaries and soldiers subject to Iraqi law—and on a long list of other issues. Americans learned about the details of the negotiations primarily from bloggers who obtained the Arabic versions of the treaty from Iraqi newspapers and translated them. Majorities in both nations wanted the occupation to end and wanted to know what was happening, but only the Iraqi government was representing its constituents, and only the Iraqi media was reporting the news. By these key measures, Iraq already had a better democracy in place than the United States. According to the US argument that we were imposing democracy on Iraq, that ought to have been grounds for immediate US withdrawal and a request for the occupation of the United States by Iraqis.

On Thanksgiving Day 2008, the Iraqi Parliament approved the treaty. It had been radically altered from Bush's original approach and required complete withdrawal by the end of 2011. But that meant three more years of hell for the people of Iraq. And Bush had already made clear that he would "interpret" the treaty however he saw fit. Many of the members of Parliament only voted for the treaty on condition that the Iraqi people be allowed to approve or reject it in a public referendum sometime before the end of July 2009. So, here was a country whose people would vote on the most significant factor in determining its future, whose representative government insisted on the right to approve or reject treaties, and whose media had covered the ongoing negotiations. On the other hand we had the United States, a nation that allowed one man to make all important decisions; whose people never got to vote on anything more important than whether to elect a new president who wanted Robert Gates as Secretary of "Defense," or his opponent, who preferred Robert Gates for that job; and whose media barely noticed the news buried under celebrity gossip. And we bomb them to promote democracy?

The Senate's power to advise and consent to treaties was voluntarily restricted by the Senate during the presidencies of both Clinton and Bush Jr. by means of something called "fast track." This policy allows a president to present a completed economic treaty, also known as a trade agreement, to the Senate, and to insist on a speedy vote, yea or nay, with no amendments allowed. I could imagine someone making an argument in support of this unconstitutional transfer of power if it hadn't produced such devastatingly awful corporate-written treaties. It is up to us to insist that our representatives in Congress insist on their proper role in government.

A new and improved US Constitution might make clear that:

➤ Congress shall have the authority to approve treaties and appointments, and the same authority to approve or reject the termination of any treaties.

➤ Congress shall have the authority and obligation to legislate the definition of a treaty, distinguishing treaties from other agreements not requiring congressional approval.

➤ Congress shall be required to exercise its authority in these matters.

The Constitution, as it is, already makes all treaties the supreme law of the land. But the Constitution doesn't compel presidents to obey them. Only we can do that.

On November 10, 2008, President-elect Obama, still serving as a senator, met with President Bush at the White House. There were no reports that Obama made any mention of the Senate's authority to approve or reject any treaty with Iraq. President-elect Obama's transition website expressed his strong support for the SOFA and his hope that it would be "subject to congressional review to ensure it has bipartisan support here at home." As a candidate Obama had favored congressional "approval," so "review" was already a softer demand.

Obama made no mention of the constitutional requirement of Senate authorization or the reasons for it, although Senator Biden had sponsored a bill (with a grand total of four cosponsors) requesting that Bush follow the Constitution on this one. I got the impression that Obama would just as soon let Bush get the credit for ending the occupation in order to avoid getting the blame for the "defeat." There were no reports in the early months of Obama's presidency that he planned to hold Bush accountable for his treaty violations in any way. That job may fall to the International Criminal Court.

Once president, Obama and the military he commanded maintained an ambiguous relationship to the treaty with Iraq, never challenging its legitimacy, but openly claiming the right to violate its requirements that all troops withdraw from cities and towns by the end of June 2009 and leave the country by the end of 2011. While peace groups in the United States had refused to challenge the precedent established by Bush of a president making a treaty alone because they liked the withdrawal requirement, the withdrawal clauses were being treated as optional but the power of a president to make treaties alone was being accepted and re-enforced. Obama's March 11, 2009, signing statement proclaimed:

> Certain provisions of the bill, in titles I and IV of Division B, title IV of Division E, and title VII of Division H, would unduly interfere with my constitutional authority in the area of foreign affairs by effectively directing the Executive on how to proceed or not proceed in negotiations or discussions with international organizations and foreign governments. I will not treat these provisions as limiting my ability to negotiate and enter into agreements with foreign nations.

The president's "constitutional authority in the area of foreign affairs" is not actually in the Constitution.

In January 2009, Congresswoman Barbara Lee introduced a resolution proposing that the Iraq treaty be considered merely advisory because it was never approved by Congress. By the end of February she had only six cosponsors, and I and others were unable to persuade most peace and justice organizations to get behind it. The problem was that the treaty contained some good requirements (withdrawal from localities by summer 2009, complete withdrawal from Iraq by the end of 2011, rule of law for mercenaries) and most people assumed that anything the Senate would approve would be worse. In fact, there was such enthusiasm for the 2011 deadline for complete withdrawal that many overlooked the requirement to withdraw from cities and the requirement that Iraqis be permitted to vote in the summer of 2009, even though a negative vote would result in withdrawal either immediately or by summer 2010 (since the treaty claimed to require a year to be ended). Many overlooked as well the fact that most Americans thought their country had just elected a president promising to end the occupation in sixteen months, not thirty-six. And virtually no one stopped to consider the larger matter of precedent. If a president could create such a treaty single-handedly, then why couldn't another president create a new one to extend it, or create a similar one for a neighboring nation? And how could anyone enforce a president's commitment to his own creation? In fact, talk of a similar arrangement with Afghanistan surfaced in early 2009, and US generals made clear from the start that they would not comply with the better terms of the Iraq agreement. Perhaps what we need is more dialogue between peace activists and Native Americans, who have a few stories to tell about putting trust in treaties.

Very similar to its current power over treaties is the power the Senate has, according to the Constitution, to provide advice and consent to appointments of ambassadors, ministers, consuls, judges of the Supreme Court, and all other officers of the United States. The Senate can choose to vest sole appointment power for inferior offices in the president, the courts, or the heads of departments. During a recess of the Senate, the president can fill any vacancy with an appointee whose term will expire at the end of the next congressional session.

Here, too, is a power that Bush Jr. managed to abuse more egregiously than any of his predecessors. A vacancy in the office of US ambassador to the United Nations did not happen during a recess of the Senate, but one did happen while the Senate was in session. Bush nominated a new ambassador, and the Senate rejected him, in part because he had provided the Senate false information related to his involvement in past crimes and abuses of the White House. In fact, the Senate rejected him twice. So, Bush appointed the same person, John Bolton, during the next recess.

Even when the Senate does exercise its authority, it often does so as a formality, with most of its members acting on the assumption that they must approve all presidential appointees except in the most egregious circumstances. And you had to be pretty far gone toward criminality, incompetence, or both to count as egregious during the Bush-Cheney era. Harriet Miers was a Bush nominee to the Supreme Court who met the test. A majority of Senators made clear their opposition, and Bush withdrew his nomination. But Bush quickly nominated someone who appeared at least as likely to make a terrible Supreme Court Justice in Samuel Alito, whom the Senate promptly confirmed. When Senator Russ Feingold disappointed many Americans by voting to confirm John Ashcroft as attorney general, Feingold said that he thought he was supposed to give the president the benefit of the doubt and that he wanted to do Republicans a favor so that they might return the favor someday. (Read that twice and let me know if you laugh or cry, because I can't decide which to do.)

In March of 2001, the *Progressive* reported,

> "Now if he doesn't do what he said, we will have learned a lesson," Feingold said of Ashcroft. "I will have to revisit my views on cabinet appointments, just as I had to revisit my views on judicial appointments."[143]

Let's hope so! If senators were to take their power to reject unsuitable nominees seriously, the people would be free to base their votes for president a lot less on fear of how disastrous each presidential candidate's Supreme Court nominees might be. This is critical, because four of the younger of the nine justices (John Roberts, Samuel Alito, Antonin Scalia, and Clarence Thomas) have expressed support for the idea that a president has as much right as the Supreme Court to interpret the Constitution, meaning that presidents are not bound by Supreme Court rulings.

In the short term, the Senate should exercise its authority more courageously and more often, insisting on the right to approve or reject a greater number of appointments. In the long term, the Constitution should be amended to state that the president cannot make recess appointments of individuals previously rejected by the Congress. (This might be nicknamed the John Bolton Amendment.)

At the end of his term, Bush began converting deputy level appointees into career service employees to prevent their replacement by new appointees, as well as firing or forcing into resignation whistleblowers and other federal employees deemed insufficiently loyal to the Bush agenda. These moves could and should also be reversed by Congress.

6. POWER OF EXECUTIVE

Executing the laws, the proper responsibility of the president, involves a lot more than prosecuting criminals. This does not include the role of "The Decider," as Bush called himself. (As we know, that role belongs to Congress.) The Constitution says of the president: "[H]e shall take care that the laws be faithfully executed." This means that he or she need not simply refrain from violating laws, but must, in contemporary lingo, proactively take care that the laws are acted upon faithfully. The faithfulness is clearly to the laws, as written, not to the president's interpretation, gut, indigestion, insecurity, conversations with God, or sadistic urge, none of which are mentioned. And a president cannot take care that the laws be faithfully executed while taking record-setting vacations.[144]

"There are a lot of lessons we want to learn out of this process in terms of what works. I think we are in fact on our way to getting on top of the whole Katrina exercise."[145] Thus spake Dick Cheney in 2005 after Hurricane Katrina had been allowed to kill and destroy on a massive scale. As former Congresswoman Elizabeth Holtzman has argued,[146] the "take care" clause of the Constitution gave the president a duty not to ignore the warnings prior to Katrina, a duty not to staff vital agencies with incompetent cronies, a duty not to ignore the disaster as people drowned and lost their homes. An article of impeachment introduced by Congressman Dennis Kucinich in June 2008 noted that there existed "decades of foreknowledge of the dangers of storms to New Orleans and specific forewarning in the days prior to the storm."[147] Nonetheless, "The President failed to prepare for predictable and predicted disasters, failed to respond to an immediate need of which he was informed, and has subsequently failed to rebuild the section of our nation that was destroyed."

As Kevin Wehr has noted, Bush's unconstitutional negligence extended to the threat of global warming, and included even the retrograde action of intentionally hiding, disguising, and distorting scientific evidence of

89

the problem.[148] Another case of Bush-Cheney negligence: the fact that Bush was warned in detail of a looming foreclosure crisis for American homeowners and chose to ignore all advice to prevent it. A truly horrifying example of negligence was Bush's failure to provide adequate body and vehicle armor to troops in Iraq, all while dumping hundreds of billions of dollars into the pockets of war profiteers.[149] Similar negligence can be found everywhere you look in the Bush-Cheney copresidency.

Let's focus on one particular bout of negligence. As Dennis Kucinich describes in his articles of impeachment, Bush allowed 9/11 to happen, then failed to provide adequate care to rescue workers. He failed to make any serious effort to prevent the attacks despite being repeatedly warned, displayed no concern for the victims or the safety of those responding to the disaster at the World Trade Center, and focused from the start on exploiting this catastrophe to expand presidential power, launch wars of empire, and benefit politically from the fear-driven upside-down spin the corporate media cooperatively put on the events. Rather than being blamed for allowing the attacks, Bush was widely praised in the media for talking tough afterwards, and his popularity soared.

The flip side of negligence during Bush's presidency was micromanagement. While the Constitution allows the president to request reports from department heads, Bush and Cheney did not allow department heads to function without approval of every move. To examine one case of many, Bush and Cheney ran the Environmental Protection Agency (EPA) out of the White House, contrary to the wishes of Congress, contrary to the mission of the agency, and in violation of various laws.[150] And then he laughed about it. On July 10, 2008, the British newspaper the *Telegraph* reported on a G8 summit in Japan:

> The American leader, who has been condemned throughout his presidency for failing to tackle climate change, ended a private meeting with the words: "Goodbye from the world's biggest polluter." He then punched the air while grinning widely, as the rest of those present, including Gordon Brown and Nicolas Sarkozy, looked on in shock. Mr. Bush, whose second and final term ends at the end of the year, then left the meeting at the Windsor Hotel in Hokkaido where the leaders of the world's

richest nations had been discussing new targets to cut carbon emissions.[151]

In July 2008, former Environmental Protection Agency (EPA) official Jason Burnett blew the whistle on Dick Cheney, reporting that Cheney's office had pushed successfully to have "any discussion of the human health consequences of climate change" removed from testimony that Julie Gerberding, director of the Center for Disease Control, had presented to Congress in 2007. In fact, under administrator Stephen Johnson, the EPA consistently took its orders from Cheney and Bush and pressured scientists to make their findings conform to White House demands.[152]

In August 2003, the Bush administration denied a petition to regulate CO_2 emissions from motor vehicles by deciding that CO_2 was not a pollutant under the Clean Air Act. In April 2007, the US Supreme Court overruled that determination. The EPA then conducted an extensive investigation involving sixty to seventy staff who concluded that "CO_2 emissions endanger both human health and welfare." These findings were submitted to the White House, after which work on the required regulations was effectively delayed for the remainder of the Cheney-Bush presidency. The EPA under President Obama accepted the scientists' conclusion.

Stephen Johnson's EPA set ozone pollution limits at unhealthy levels after rejecting the conclusions of its own scientists, and then weakened those limits further after a late-night intervention by Bush on the eve of announcing the new standards. And Johnson and the EPA stonewalled Congress, refusing to produce subpoenaed documents, leading top senators and Congress members to pathetically ask Johnson to resign, which of course he did not do, as he was merely following orders from Cheney and Bush—whom Congress had promised never to impeach.

Asking Dick Cheney to protect our environment was like asking a serpent to guard a cage of mice. But, of course, nobody ever really asked him. Stephen Johnson had been approved to serve as the administrator of an agency in an open and democratic government, not to obey secret orders to mislead the Congress and the people, and not to reverse the legal actions of his staff. If Cheney and Bush are never held accountable, and Johnson is never held accountable, and those EPA employees who failed to blow the whistle are never held accountable, their faces will need to be carved onto a strip-mined mountain as a giant monument to our species' attempted suicide. That, I would argue, might make an even more appropriate memorial to eight years of disaster than the George W. Bush Sewage Treatment Plant proposed by the good people of San Francisco.

Much of this sort of failure to properly execute the laws was facilitated by equally unconstitutional secrecy. Dick Cheney had explained the need for secrecy in 1979 thus:

> It's really a matter of trade-offs. There is no question that to the extent that you involve a number of people in the consultative process before you make a decision, you raise the level of noise in the system. You enhance the possibility of premature disclosures and leaks. You also take more time, cut down in efficiency.

Unfortunately for Cheney's noiseless efficiency, there is no right to secrecy in the Constitution, no right to mislead Congress or the people, no right to operate under secret laws, no right to run the military in such secrecy that announcements in signing statements of intent to violate laws cannot even be checked, because nobody knows whether the laws are being followed. There is no right to make secret plans for the continuity of power in the event of deaths, leaving Congress, the people, and the Constitution out of the process.[153] There is no right to secretly manufacture illegal chemical and biological weapons even while invading other nations on the pretense that they have done the same. And nowhere in the Constitution is there any right to what we call "the intelligence community."

Along with banning secret budgets and all secret funding, as discussed above, we need to ban secret laws, which run counter to the very idea of law. And we need to ban secret agencies in which the identities of employees and the work they do is kept secret. The CIA, the NSA, and the whole web of secret agencies, departments, and offices—including those illegally maintained by the military—that we pay to spy on people, do much else besides: things that they could not do if required to be open and transparent. They manufacture bogus "intelligence" to justify what would otherwise be unpopular policies. They lie about what intelligence they have provided to the president, even when the information provided was accurate. They spy on us in violation of our constitutional rights. They engineer military coups in other nations. They assassinate. They kidnap people and disappear them into secret prisons. They torture, hire contractors to torture, and encourage other nations to torture. They form alliances with dictators and criminals. They sell weapons and provide weapons to terrorists. They fund terrorists. And they create enemies for the United States around the world.

Open and legitimate departments of the government should still engage in spying, in accordance with the law. The Federal Bureau of Investigation (FBI) spies. Police spy. The problem is not the spying, when conducted legally (and I am not suggesting that the FBI and police have always been on the right side of the law; in fact, the FBI has grossly abused power in recent years, including through the use of national security letters). The problem is all the other activities that grow like fungus on any powerful organization permitted to act in dark shadows with no oversight. Potential terrorists do not discover that the United States is trying to spy on them when someone reports in the press on the constitutional abuses of the latest secret spying program. They already know that the United States is trying to spy on them. The best leads prior to September 11, 2001, which might have preempted those attacks had they not been ignored, were obtained by FBI agents in Minneapolis who were openly identified as FBI agents and whose job descriptions were publicly available. The strongest internal resistance, which was also ignored, to the cooked "intelligence" used to justify attacking Iraq came from employees of the Departments of State and Energy. The most accurate assessment of Iraqi weaponry came from United Nations inspectors. And the most tragically on-target predictions of how Iraqis would react to a foreign occupation came from people who had lived in Iraq, spoke and read Arabic, and/or had studied history. Our government employs many different experts, but none of them historians.

We have grown so used to the presence of a secret government in Washington that it's hard for us to imagine eliminating it. We like to think that for all the harm it may do, it performs useful functions that nobody else could manage. But there is no evidence that this is the case. Claims of success, as far as I have seen, are usually vague or bogus, and in many cases the work could have been performed by above-board government departments.

Some of us sometimes like to imagine that the secrecy of agencies like the CIA provides us, the people of the United States, with a sort of excuse. How can we be responsible for someone being tortured to death if we don't even know exactly which contractor did it and we were never asked to approve the decision in the first place?

Don't believe that excuse for an instant. We the people permit these agencies to exist, and we are responsible for every ounce of suffering they inflict on the world, as is the president.

During a press conference in his first week as president-elect, Barack Obama was asked a very general question about our "intelligence" services, and whether, "anything that you've heard [has] given you pause about anything you've talked about on the campaign trail?" He replied, "Well, Candy, as you know, if there was something I'd heard, I couldn't tell you . . . Our intelligence process can always improve. I think it has gotten better. And, you know, beyond that I don't think I should comment on the nature of the intelligence briefings." I saw the video clip of this on a progressive website that was praising Obama for having declined to answer a "stupid question." That's not what I would call a progressive attitude.

Eugene Jarecki argues in *The American Way of War* for replacing the National Security Act of 1947 with something very different because of the imperial presidential powers that act created. This law unified the military under a single cabinet member, created the CIA, created the National Security Council and the National Security Advisor, and created the Air Force. Not only the secretive CIA, but each of these other bodies, according to Jarecki's analysis, has expanded presidential power to set policy, to make war, and to act without consulting Congress.[54]

Legislating an appropriately transparent government will also require reforming the executive privilege and the state secrets privilege. For the most part these serve as excuses for the executive branch to deny information to the other two branches, information that is no threat at all to national security. In fact, the abuse of these excuses has become a threat to national security. But it would not make sense to just eliminate these "privileges," because there could someday conceivably really be a legitimate secret. An appropriate solution might be for the executive branch, whenever it asserts these privileges, to be compelled to present its case in closed session and abide by the decision of the Congress or the congressional committee or the courts as to whether the information can be kept secret or not. The presentation should be mandatory, denying a spineless legislative or judicial branch the possibility of volunteering to forego it. These reforms may, in the end, require a constitutional amendment, but there is no reason not to begin with legislation.

A parallel power to "state secrets" is "executive privilege." The Constitution does not contain any reference to either. In 1974 in *The United States v. Nixon*, the Supreme Court ruled that a president may claim executive privilege, at least when the exposure of information would jeopardize national security, but may not claim the privilege in general without proof of any national security risk. So, when Bush instructed former staffers to assert "executive privilege" rather than comply with subpoenas to testify about their roles in the so-called Justice Department's partisan hiring and firing, one was obliged to conclude that Bush and Cheney equated "national security" with the ability of the Republican party to lie, cheat, and steal.

Now, if Congress or the courts were to ask for documents or testimony that actually could endanger the nation, there is no reason that the president could not make the information available in closed session, after which Congress or the Supreme Court could decide whether there was a legitimate need to keep it secret or whether it should be made public over the wishes of the White House. It is much more difficult to imagine Congress or the Supreme Court jeopardizing national security in order to inform the people than it is to imagine the president jeopardizing national security by falsely claiming a need for secrecy in the name of "national security." After all, Bush and Cheney kept the National Intelligence Estimate on Iraq classified while releasing a misleading summary, and the damage to our actual national security has been severe.

Presidential candidate Barack Obama told the *Boston Globe* in December 2007,

I believe the Administration's use of executive authority to over-classify information is a bad idea. We need to restore the balance between the necessarily secret and the necessity of openness in our democracy—which is why I have called for a National Declassification Center.[155]

In the early months of the Obama presidency, our new president did declassify a small number of the many documents that had been kept secret. Still secret were numerous memos related to Bush-Cheney abuses of power that had been identified in law suits but not released,[156] as well as numerous White House e-mails which the National Security Archive and Citizens for Responsibility and Ethics in Washington had sued to obtain. The new US Justice Department, run by Attorney General Eric Holder, opposed releasing the e-mails and urged a federal appeals court to dismiss a lawsuit against Boeing subsidiary Jeppesen DataPlan for its role in the extraordinary rendition program. *Mohamed et al. v. Jeppesen* had been brought on behalf of five men who were kidnapped and secretly transferred to US-run prisons or foreign intelligence agencies overseas where they were tortured. The Bush administration had asserted the "state secrets" privilege, claiming the case would somehow undermine national security, and Holder's department agreed. In April 2009, the court disagreed and said the case could proceed.

Holder's Justice Department also used a "state secrets" claim to try to block a lawsuit, *Al Haramain Islamic Foundation v. Obama*, over Bush's warrantless spying, and broke new ground by claiming in a brief filed in that case that only a president can decide on the use of any classified information in court (even in a closed court), a power that would allow presidents to give themselves immunity by simply classifying evidence of their crimes. The brief defied a ruling already made by the court and effectively threatened to seize from the judge's chambers documents he already had.

Britain's High Court of Justice ruled that evidence in the UK civil case of Binyam Mohamed, one of the plaintiffs in the Jeppesen case, had to remain secret because of US threats to cut off intelligence sharing. Britain's *Telegraph* newspaper reported that "Mohamed's genitals were sliced with a scalpel and other torture methods so extreme that waterboarding, the controversial technique of simulated drowning, 'is very far down the list of things they did.'"[157] Britain's *Daily Mail* reported that Mohamed "was identified as a terrorist after confessing he had visited a 'joke' website on how to build a nuclear weapon.... [He] admitted to having read the 'instructions' after allegedly being beaten, hung up by his wrists for a week and having a gun held to his head in a Pakistani jail."[158]

Numerous civil rights groups asked Holder not to block cases like this one with "state secrets" claims. But in April 2009, the new Justice Department under Attorney General Eric Holder sought to have a suit brought by the Electronic Frontier Foundation (EFF), called *Jewel v. NSA*, tossed out on the grounds of both "state secrets" and a brand new claim that the PATRIOT Act provided "sovereign immunity" against lawsuits for illegal spying unless the information obtained was intentionally made public. Blogger Glenn Greenwald pointed out that the brief filed by the new Justice Department read exactly as if it had been written by the previous one, making similar claims about executive power and secrecy.[159]

Surprisingly and encouragingly, it was in this context that some members of Congress in March 2009 indicated a willingness to take action. In a remarkable show of their continuing desire for Congress to exist as a functioning part of our government, and willingness to challenge a president of the same political party, leading Democrats in the House and Senate re-introduced the State Secrets Protection Act, which would require court (but not congressional) review of any "state secrets" claims. Senator Russ Feingold (D-WI) also requested a classified briefing to have one of Obama's "state secrets" claims explained to him. Of course, if he was given an explanation he was forbidden from sharing it with us. Either the claims secretly make sense but we can't know it, or they are as outrageous as they appear.

While these contests should continue in the courts, ultimately we must make Congress accountable to us and persuade it to assert its powers: its power to reject appointments, its power to oversee government operations, and its power to impeach any civil officer guilty of treason, bribery, or other high crimes and misdemeanors. If those powers continue to be neglected, they will cease to exist even as they become more badly needed.

7. POWER OF PARDON

The Constitution says that the president "shall have Power to Grant Reprieves and Pardons for Offenses against the United States, except in Cases of Impeachment . . ." This power has often been abused, with presidents now being routinely expected to hand out a stack of pardons on their very last day in office, pardons that they know the public will disapprove of. We saw Ford pardon Nixon, Bush Sr. pardon Iran-Contra criminals, Clinton pardon a campaign donor, and Bush Jr. commute the sentence of a top White House staff person convicted of obstruction of justice for blocking the investigation of a crime apparently committed by Bush.[160]

In the case of Bush, there was concern that he might pardon members of his own government for crimes he instructed them to commit, possibly even pardoning himself of the same crimes. When Cheney's chief of staff I. Lewis "Scooter" Libby was convicted of obstruction of justice for blocking a criminal investigation that appeared to be headed toward Cheney and Bush, Bush commuted his sentence. There was widespread expectation that he would also pardon the crime and was simply waiting for his last day in office. And, in fact, in the autumn of 2008, former White House Press Secretary Scott McLellan toured the country selling his book and telling anyone who would listen that Bush had authorized the leaking of the classified undercover identity of a CIA agent, the crime of which Libby was convicted of obstructing the investigation.[161]

Libby was sentenced following a conviction on one count of obstruction of justice, two counts of perjury, and one count of making false statements to federal investigators. These crimes were committed during an investigation by Special Counsel Patrick Fitzgerald of the "outing" of covert CIA operative Valerie Plame. President Bush and Vice President Cheney were directly implicated in the investigation through evidence that included a handwritten note by Vice President

Cheney. Bush's commutation of Libby's sentence directly interfered with the Special Counsel's ongoing investigation of Plame's "outing" and therefore constituted obstruction of justice. And Bush was arguably protecting himself from prosecution, which constituted an impeachable abuse of presidential power.

In the end, pressure from Congress, led by Rep. Jerrold Nadler, and pressure from the public against Bush pardoning crimes that he himself had authorized proved either successful or unnecessary. Bush did not issue the pardons. But many in the media claimed that he could and urged him to do so. Even people in Congress, including Nadler and Senator Feingold, claimed that he could issue the pardons if he so chose.

Can a president pardon his underlings of crimes he authorizes, and even pardon himself? Well, the Constitution doesn't say that he can't. Former consigliere generale Alberto Gonzales claimed that the Constitution says that the right to habeas corpus cannot be taken away (except in certain circumstances), but does not assert that anyone ever has the right to habeas corpus in the first place. By that logic, a president can self-pardon, and the Bill of Rights provides no rights at all, the president being free to do almost anything imaginable, including, as Bush's legal advisor John Yoo once asserted, crushing a child's testicles—or, we can then assume, Congress's (should it develop any).[162]

The Supreme Court has never limited the president's pardon power, and yet common sense would suggest that there should be limits. In September 2008, Lawrence R. Velvel, Dean of Massachusetts School of Law, wrote,

> The idea that a President has an absolute, unfettered ability to grant pardons does not strike me as persuasive. Could a President order the mass murder of 5,000 people [or hundreds of times that many, say in Iraq] and then allow the perpetrators and he himself to escape all punishment by pardoning them and himself? The idea is preposterous and would mark the end of a government of laws. Were such a pardon permissible, the law is at an end and we might as well all move to Canada—or, as I believe Lincoln said, to Russia, where they take their tyranny straight, without the base alloy of hypocrisy.[163]

At the Constitutional Convention, James Madison and George Mason both argued that impeachment would be the response if a president ever pardoned someone for a crime he himself was involved in (as Bush effectively did for Libby). The idea of a president pardoning himself for a crime he had committed was so patently abusive that I am certain Madison and Mason would have declined to include an explicit ban of it had anyone suggested the idea. Madison wrote in "Federalist No. 10" that "No man is allowed to be a judge in his own cause, because his interest would certainly bias his judgment, and, not improbably, corrupt his integrity.[164]

A careful analysis, I believe, would lead to the conclusion that Congress is completely within its rights to legislate a ban preventing the presidential pardon power from being distorted to include the power to self-pardon the president, or to pardon any staff or contractors of the executive branch, including the vice president, for crimes authorized by the president. Another course that Congress could take would be to introduce and support legislation creating a constitutional amendment to restrict self-pardons and pardons of subordinates for crimes ordered by the president.

One way to get a feel for how a congressional hearing on this topic might go is to read the transcripts of the last ones. The House Committee on Government Reform, chaired by Republican Dan Burton, held a hearing on February 8 and March 1, 2001, on the topic of Clinton's pardon of campaign contributor Marc Rich, a hearing that apparently dragged on for many, many hours. One noteworthy witness was Scooter Libby himself, in his capacity as lawyer for Marc Rich, a man alleged— among other things—to have traded with enemy nations, a practice long engaged in by Libby's boss in the White House, Dick Cheney. The Senate held a similar hearing, but I haven't read it. And the House Judiciary Committee's Subcommittee on the Constitution, chaired by Republican James Sensenbrenner, held a hearing on February 28, 2001, on the general topic of presidential pardon power.

What you can learn from reading these transcripts is that corrupt pardons are nothing new. But pardons of the sort that some feared Bush would make, and indeed the commutation of Libby's sentence, were so new as to not yet have been even contemplated by most observers.

Toward the end of the Constitution Subcommittee hearing, the topic did arise of a president issuing a pardon from which he would benefit indirectly through bribery from the person pardoned. On this topic, the strongest comments in favor of holding the president to the rule of law came from Jerrold Nadler, the man who, during the 110th Congress, was the chair of that same subcommittee.

The Government Reform transcript makes clear that the Washington bureaucracy has all variety of concern over the process of issuing pardons, over requests coming a certain number of years after sentences have been served, over input being received from prosecutors, and so forth. Congressman Bob Barr goes so far as to suggest that pardons issued by Clinton are invalid because he didn't follow proper procedures, and because he speedily pardoned a long list of people without properly explaining himself to the public.

During the Constitution Subcommittee hearings, two legislative solutions were considered, but both were widely criticized as unconstitutional. The proposal that received more support was one to ban pardons during the last four months of a president's term. For presidents to lose the right to pardon during the last four months of a term in office would mean that all pardoning would have to take place prior to an election, which might provide a limited check on abuses, even if the president was a lame duck.[165] Of course, this restriction could be made by constitutional amendment if not by legislation.

The Constitution might also be amended to stipulate that the existing ban on ex post facto laws include laws that grant retroactive immunity from prosecution—such as the Detainee Treatment Act, the Military Commissions Act, and the FISA Amendments Act. This would prevent Congress from abusing the pardon power on behalf of the president, but would deny the Congress a power that might prove legitimately useful in other circumstances.

There was discussion during Bush's last months of the legality of blanket pardons as well, with some former judges and other pundits asserting that a blanket pardon that did not specify the names of the people being pardoned would not be constitutional. But President Washington had pardoned participants in the Whiskey Rebellion, Lincoln and Johnson had pardoned participants on the Confederate side in the Civil War, and Carter had pardoned Vietnam War resisters. A blanket pardon might be appropriate and legitimate in years to come. What can never be legitimate is a pardon of oneself or of subordinates guilty of crimes authorized by oneself. As we go about correcting abuses it is important that we employ the proper corrections, and not just anything that works at the moment. While we should be encouraged and gain faith in our government from the fact that Bush did not attempt this sort of pardon except in the case of Libby's commutation, the public consensus that he could have done so had he wanted to cannot be allowed to stand. We must alter that understanding, even if amending the Constitution is the only way to do so, or we are putting our nation in serious danger.

8. THE CHENEY BRANCH

Aside from the vestiges of royalty, the ceremonial hoo-ha, the fawning over the first family, and so forth, why do we need an executive at all, rather than simply a Congress? I don't think speed and efficiency is a persuasive answer. In most situations, though probably not all, Congress can act with plenty of speed, and would be even faster without vetoes. I think the ability to act in secret is even less persuasive as a justification for an executive, since I don't want my government acting in secret. Were Congress cleaned up and made truly representative in ways discussed later in this book, couldn't we do much better without the bother of a president? Under the Articles of Confederation, prior to the Constitution, Congress governed the nation without employing an executive. And "strength" is certainly not a good justification, since one person is no stronger than 500 people, although an idealized superhero version of that one person might be.

Without a president, we would be able to rid ourselves of what Dana Nelson in *Bad for Democracy* calls presidentialism, the debilitating public obsession with the president as a symbol of democracy and presidential elections as the essence of democracy, a delusion that gets in the way of putting democracy into action in our lives every day; of viewing ourselves as in charge; of taking local and national action to engage our neighbors, influence elected officials, and make changes directly; of organizing to pressure every member of Congress to do what we want, rather than what our president or our presidential candidate tells us to want. Without a president, disagreement, debate, and compromise would become our idea of democracy, rather than unilateral efficiency supported by loyal obedience.[166]

Of course, there may be some uses for a president. As long as the globe is cursed with wars and there is an infinitesimally small possibility of some other nation committing suicide by attacking this one, the president is available to serve as commander in chief whenever the Department of Defense actually has to do some defending. More importantly, the president also serves as a useful check on Congress. If the presidential election process were cleaned up, as will be discussed later in this book, a president truly elected by the nation would be an appropriate person to push back against abuses by Congress. As James Madison wrote, "Ambition must be made to counteract ambition."

Another reason to have a president is one that has been understood throughout American history, including by the founders of our governmental system. Executing the laws is a different job from creating them, and by placing that job in the hands of a single person, rather than a council or a triumvirate, we establish exactly who can be held accountable for the performance of the executive branch. The president can be held accountable for the crimes or abuses of any of his or her subordinates—or at least he could be if Congress would do its job.

Perhaps even more relevant, considering the last administration, is not the question of the president's powers, but those of the vice president. What was once a position to stand as back-up should the president die or become unable to serve is now, it would seem, a branch of government all of its own. On June 22, 2007, *Time* magazine ran an article with the headline "The Cheney Branch of Government," that began thus:

> On the same day that the CIA announced it will soon release hundreds of pages of once-classified documents that detail some of the agency's most closely guarded—and controversial—secrets of old, it was revealed that Vice President Dick Cheney has been resisting even his own Executive Branch's efforts to find out what kind of secret material his office has been stashing away over the last four years. Cheney's office, according to a story first reported by the *Chicago Tribune*, has resisted attempts by a tiny federal agency to compile information—in accordance with an executive order signed by George Bush himself—on the classified documents being held by the Vice President's operation. Cheney's office argued that the Vice President's office, because it has both executive and legislative

branch duties, is exempt from the order. Cheney's dustup with the normally non-controversial National Archives and Records Administration is the latest reminder that Cheney believes he can play by his own rules. And it probably secures for Cheney a place alongside Richard Nixon in the Washington pantheon of secret-keepers.[167]

Actually, Nixon doesn't even come close. Nixon never kept as much of our government secret as Bush-Cheney did, and when push came to shove, he gave up some of his secrets and left town. Nixon's former legal counsel John Dean agrees that the Cheney-Bush gang far surpassed Nixonian levels of secrecy and abuse of power.[168] Not to mention lawyerly deviousness. Cheney claimed privileges supposedly belonging to the executive branch when it suited him. For example, he refused to comply with subpoenas because "the president and the vice president are constitutional officers and don't appear before the Congress." At other times, Cheney claimed to be part of Congress in order to avoid complying with rules governing the executive branch. Hence the conclusion that if Cheney belonged to any branch it had to be the hitherto unheard of Dick Cheney Branch, which perhaps existed in Cheney's well-known "undisclosed location." Speaking of which, the fact that there's not a snowball's chance in hell that Vice President Joe Biden will reveal the nature of the bunker Cheney created at the vice presidential residence makes a nice analogy for how power accumulates from one ruler to the next. It's much easier to create and pass down than it is to refuse. Still, the first few months of the Obama-Biden administration gave every indication that Biden would not exercise the sort of power that Cheney had.

All in all, Dick Cheney dramatically enlarged the powers of the vice presidency, claiming for it authority that rightfully belongs to other sections of the government, or to no section of government at all. These powers will lie around like a loaded weapon on the vice presidential estate and in the White House. These powers may be abused by any new duumvirate in the near or distant future.

In the Constitution the vice president is given the succession to power should the president be removed from office, but he or she is also made the president of the Senate and given the power to break a tie there. Had Dick Cheney gone out of his way to comply with the rules governing both the executive and the legislative branches, probably nobody would have complained (although some of us might have fainted from shock). There wasn't any actual conflict between the vice president's two roles of breaking ties and sitting around until the president died. Cheney didn't need to keep his executive activities secret in order to properly preside over the Senate. He simply latched onto an excuse, regardless of how nonsensical, and proceeded to do as he chose.

The legislative duties of the vice president were also expanded under Cheney from hanging around in case he needed to break a tie vote to participating in Republican caucus meetings, often bringing presidential advisor Karl Rove with him. Senator Patrick Leahy said he believed this new involvement was meant to encourage Republicans to put party loyalty ahead of institutional loyalty.[169] In addition to this legislative power, executive branch duties of the vice president in the case of Cheney expanded to include presidential power.

The executive branch role of the vice president has become more widely recognized than the legislative. So it is easy to suppose that the best way to eliminate the Cheney branch would be to eliminate the vice president's legislative duties or give precedence in cases of conflict to the rules governing the executive branch. We could amend the Constitution to require the vice president to comply with all laws and rules applying to both branches, and to give priority to rules governing the executive branch should some actual conflict arise.

I think there might be a better solution than that one.

When vice presidential candidate Sarah Palin declared that the vice president was in charge of the Senate, she was mocked and ridiculed. Of course she also foresaw a large role for herself on a President McCain team, but it's possible that her widely criticized comment about the Senate actually came closer to an appropriate description of the proper and desirable role of a vice president. It might be more useful to restrict the veep to his or her legislative role than to focus on the executive role or permit the combination of the two. Glenn Harlan Reynolds proposes that Congress solve the Cheney Branch dilemma by prohibiting the vice president from exercising any executive power.[170] This would keep the spare president untainted by involvement in abuses committed by the president, whereas the current system makes it difficult to impeach either the president or vice president without impeaching the other one as well.

The framers of the Constitution intentionally chose to have a single executive—not a pair, not a triumvirate, not a council. The main reason for this choice was in order to better control the executive and to be able to hold him responsible for everything done by himself and his subordinates, including the vice president—although the role of the vice president was generally considered to be that of waiting around in case the president died. Presidents and vice presidents did not originally run for election as a ticket from a party.

On December 20, 2005, on board Air Force Two, Cheney spoke to reporters about his creative notions of presidential power. "The President of the United States," Cheney said, "needs to have his constitutional powers unimpaired, if you will, in terms of the conduct of national security policy. That's my personal view."[71] So much for checks and balances. Unimpaired, if we will.

Cheney did not defend the secrecy of his energy task force on the grounds that it was about national security. He defended it on the grounds that the president can get more honest advice, presumably on any topic at all, if that advice is given secretly: "My belief [is] that the President is entitled to and needs to have unfiltered advice in formulating policy, that he ought to be able to seek the opinion of anybody he wants to, and that he should not have to reveal, for example, to a member of Congress who he talked to that morning."

Of course, Congress had never asked to know who the president had talked to on some random morning. Congress wanted to know who the vice president had talked to in a meeting setting energy and military, and therefore financial and foreign relations, policies for the United States, for the next decade at minimum. But the vice president claimed that people are more honest behind closed doors and that the president needed honest advice—even though common sense might suggest that people are more honest in the light of day, and Cheney had carefully badgered "intelligence" analysts to secretly give the president dishonest advice about Iraq.

But that wasn't all Cheney had to say. He also implied that even if the president's claims might have been unjustified in normal times (perhaps some moment in the past with Russian nukes or Japanese planes aimed at the United States), the incredible dangers of today called for breaking the rules: "I believe in a strong, robust executive authority. And I think the world we live in demands it. And to some extent that we have an obligation as an administration to pass on the offices we hold to our successors in as good a shape as we found them." Now there's slick for you. We have to seize unconstitutional powers because the world is dangerous right now, and we have to pass those powers on to future presidents because . . . well, because I say we have that obligation.

Still cruising along on Air Force Two, Cheney was asked about the secret illegal warrantless spying programs that he and his sidekick had created. I will preface his answer with an oldie but goodie, straight from the father of the modern signing statement, former attorney general for President Ronald Reagan, Ed Meese: *US News* had asked in 1985, "You criticize the Miranda ruling, which gives suspects the right to have a lawyer present before police questioning. Shouldn't people, who may be innocent, have such protection?" Meese replied: "Suspects who are innocent of a crime should. But the thing is, you don't have many suspects who are innocent of a crime. That's contradictory. If a person is innocent of a crime, then he is not a suspect." How's that for an attitude to discover lurking in the brain of the top law enforcement officer in the country? Here's what Cheney said: "It's important that you be clear that we're talking about individuals who are al-Qaeda or have an association with al-Qaeda, who we have reason to believe are part of that terrorist network. . . . It's not just random conversations. If you're calling Aunt Sadie in Paris, we're probably not really interested. . . . [O]ur obligation and responsibility given our job is to do everything in our power to defeat the terrorists. And that's exactly what we're doing."

Cheney was out to "defeat the terrorists," and so, in all areas of governing, we were supposed to take his word that everything they were doing in secret was being done exactly right. Well, illegal spying and wiretapping was not all that Dick Cheney was doing. After having served as secretary of "defense" and having given Halliburton, now a well-known corporation, the contract to draw up a plan calling for giving more contracts to companies like Halliburton, Cheney revolved out the revolving door to spend five years as Halliburton's chief executive, during which period the company illegally conducted major oil and construction business with Iran, Iraq, and Indonesia and illegally sold nuclear technology to Libya. Cheney left his Halliburton job, taking a $33.7 million parting gift, to return to government as vice president, in which position he directed the Pentagon to grant no-bid contracts worth many billions of dollars to Halliburton. For at least two years as vice president, Cheney received hundreds of thousands of dollars from Halliburton in "deferred compensation." Did Cheney do anything improper? Of course, but he doesn't think you'll mind. He continued his defense of illegal spying thus:

> But if there's anything improper or inappropriate in that, my guess is that the vast majority of the American people support that, support what we're doing. They believe we ought to be doing it, and so if there's a backlash pending, I think the backlash is going to be against those who are suggesting somehow that we shouldn't take these steps in order to protect the country.

The backlash of the 2006 and 2008 elections proved Cheney wrong, but not wrong enough. We need a much larger and more sustained backlash against lying us into illegal wars, torturing human beings, recklessly exacerbating global warming, bribing and distorting the news media to mislead us, punishing whistleblowers, and profiting financially from the suffering inflicted on others.[172] During the Cheney-Bush reign, the Pentagon and other departments displayed not only the traditional photo portraits of the president and the head of the department, but also a third: that of Dick Cheney. We need to take that picture down, and not replace it with Joe Biden's or anyone else's.

Early indications were that Biden agreed with me. But today's vice president and tomorrow's will know in the back of their heads how Bush and Cheney achieved greater secrecy and less accountability by running some of their seamier activities out of Cheney's office. If Obama and Biden do not abuse that power, the team that follows them might, unless we stop electing teams and return to electing presidents, and unless we hold Bush and Cheney accountable. While many of the abuses committed by Cheney and Bush were crimes, others were noncriminal abuses of power, otherwise known as "high crimes and misdemeanors" or impeachable offenses. We may be able to substitute for Congress by prosecuting Bush and Cheney in court, but if Congress does not reclaim some of its rightful power, we will fail to restrain future presidents and vice presidents.

II.

CONGRESSIONAL COLLAPSE

9. VOLUNTARY IMPOTENCE

I'm taking up the conduct of Congress second, after my preceding look at the president, primarily in order to make my argument comprehensible to contemporary Americans. But the US Constitution does something else, something that is potentially bewildering: it speaks first of Congress, and it speaks much more of Congress than of anything else, including the other two branches of government combined. We should attempt gradually to return to an understanding of our government in those terms, the way it was meant to be understood.

As I've discussed, if we are to achieve democratic representation, peace, justice, or any of the goals of the Preamble, two things are necessary. We must shift power away from the White House and back to Congress, and we must reform Congress. These two tasks are interrelated. The corrupt nature of the current Congress has led to its abandonment of power, its choice not to take control, its voluntary impotence. We should never forget that Bush and Cheney could not have done anything they did without the consent of Congress. Congress had the power to stop every crime and chose not to. And by choosing not to enough times, Congress has lost the powers it once had.

Following the 2008 elections, in which—as has become the norm—most incumbents won, I heard from people in various parts of the country saying, in one way or another: "Well, my Congress member is still a no-good useless bum, but now I can lobby President Obama—hurray!" But can an entire nation of hundreds of millions of people lobby one man, the same man who so clearly ignored his own supporters on telecom immunity and on appointing a special prosecutor for Bush and Cheney (the top demands on his campaign and transition websites respectively); a man who opposed the overwhelming majority of us in backing the banker bailout; a man empowered for four years, not two; a man who could lose favor with your entire town or county or state or region and still be returned to office for a second four-year term?

I'm not saying it's impossible and that public pressure has never influenced a president. But there is a disturbing habit of thought with some dedicated and active Americans that maintains that lobbying a president amounts to putting your faith in the people, whereas lobbying Congress amounts to naively believing that a government can work. As I see it, creating public pressure always involves people, but thinking clearly about where to apply that pressure involves a greater likelihood of succeeding. I've often encouraged activist groups to protest on Capitol Hill rather than in front of the White House, not because I want them to stop being aware that the president is deciding everything, but because I believe that by acting as if Congress can decide something we make that reality more likely. And if we succeed by that means, we also deny future presidents the ability to easily undo what we have done.

In the early days of the new Obama administration there was a great deal of opposition to lobbying Obama or Congress at all. The idea was to leave Obama alone, stay out of the way, "give him a chance." This was put forward as a reason not to lobby the government at all. But the way you give elected officials the best chance of being good leaders to a democratic nation is to tell them what you want. That's your part of the bargain you make when you elect them. At first I was encouraged by the fact that a group of activists were planning a twenty-day sit-in outside Obama's Chicago house in January 2009.[1] Then I read their list of demands; they were demands that should have been put to Congress.

The three major forces that contribute to Congress members' failure to represent their constituents are money, media, and party. (For presidents you have to add the corrupting influence of near-absolute power.) Unlike the so-called executive branch, Congress members, especially senators, tend to spend half their time raising money. They work three-day weeks at best. They defer to the opinions of the very few people who control the corporate media, since media coverage is worth huge amounts of money and is exactly what they raise most of their money for. And they take orders from their party leaders (and above all the president, if he is in their party) who can bestow upon them or withhold all variety of favors, including money. I'll discuss all of these problems and what can be done about them later in this book. But first, I think it's important that we examine Congress' recent performance from a sufficiently close angle to understand why the official explanations for that performance are not credible, why something is indeed rotten on Capitol Hill.

For much of the Bush-Cheney copresidency, a majority Republican Congress refused to lead, challenge, or conduct oversight. (The Democrats had a 51–49 majority in the Senate for much of the first two years, including at the time of the 77–23 vote to allow the invasion of Iraq, but otherwise the Republicans controlled both houses from 2001 through 2006.) The Congress was virtually a twig on the executive branch. Lindsey Graham, a Republican senator from South Carolina, explained that:

> The Congress was intimidated after 9/11. People were afraid to get in the way of a strong executive who was talking about suppressing a vicious enemy, and we were AWOL for a while, and I'll take the blame for that. We should have been more aggressive after 9/11 in working with the executive to find a collaboration, and I think the fact that we weren't probably hurt the country. I wish I had spoken out sooner and louder.[2]

By November 2006, the American people had finally had enough of the rubber-stamp Congress. We elected thirty-one new Democrats in the House and six in the Senate. We told exit pollsters that we were primarily motivated by our opposition to the war and to Bush and Cheney. We were, as we would in 2008, voting for change. These were stunning victories (considering the near invincibility of incumbents in today's system) and both houses of the legislature were given Democratic majorities. Members of the US media were in almost universal agreement on their interpretation of the 2006 elections as votes against the war and the president. CNN reported on November 8, 2006:

> After a sweeping Democratic takeover of the House of Representatives in Tuesday's midterm election, and with control of the Senate hanging in the balance, exit polls indicated views of President Bush and the war in Iraq were key to the outcome.

According to CNN senior political analyst Bill Schneider, voters were angry and wanted change—and the old adage that "all politics is local" did not apply this year. Schneider said as he interviewed voters across the country, "A lot of voters said, 'I'm going to vote Democratic.' They didn't even know the name of the Democrat, but they said, 'I'm going to vote Democratic because I don't like Bush, I don't like the war, I want to make a statement.'" According to exit polls, 57 percent of all voters disapprove of the war in Iraq and 58 percent disapprove of Bush's job performance.

As the new Congress got underway in January 2007, new Democratic Caucus Chair Rahm Emanuel (later chosen as White House chief of staff by President-elect Obama) let slip to the *Washington Post* what party leaders thought of the reasons they'd been elected:

> For the rest of the year, Emanuel says, the leadership hopes to stress energy independence (with fuel-saving efficiency standards for appliances and cars) and a move toward better health care for children. And here's what Emanuel doesn't want to do: fall into the political trap of chasing overambitious or potentially unpopular measures. Ask about universal health care, and he shakes his head ... Reform of Social Security and other entitlements? Too big, too woolly, too risky ... The country is angry, and it will only get more so as the problems in Iraq deepen. Don't look to Emanuel's Democrats for solutions on Iraq. It's Bush's war, and as it splinters the structure of GOP power, the Democrats are waiting to pick up the pieces.[3]

In other words, the Democrats' thinking immediately after the 2006 elections was all about how they could win the 2008 elections. Knowing that Republicans would never satisfy the public's demands for peace and fundamental change, and knowing that third-party or independent candidates suffered from major disadvantages in terms of funding, organization, and media, the Democrats saw more advantage in keeping the problems of 2006 around in order to run against them again (and in order, no doubt, to please major funders, including weapons makers, telecoms, and others involved in ongoing governmental crimes) than they did in addressing the problems they'd been elected to solve. Emanuel himself had already directed Democratic funding to pro-war candidates in the 2006 primaries and general elections, a strategy that may have cost the Democrats some additional seats but which certainly helped to limit the range of debate and defend against attacks by the pro-war media.[4] Rather than ending the war or impeaching Bush and Cheney, the Democratic leadership (and most Democrats, who chose to be led) opted to keep all three unpopular items (Bush, Cheney, and the war) around for two more years in order to campaign against them again.

While the 110th Congress did see a weak and compromised bill on fuel standards and other energy policies signed into law, and did accomplish a handful of other useful tasks, it did not provide a single child with better health care or accomplish many of the goals it set, much less others that it should have set. But that wasn't necessarily the point. Emanuel had never said they would make those things happen, only that they would "stress" them. And they stressed children's health care by passing a bill and getting it vetoed and complaining about the veto. At the same time, Congress gave up the power of oversight, losing the ability to compel the White House to respond to requests, FOIA requests, or subpoenas. While the systemic reasons for this behavior were not new and the conduct not unprecedented, it was during this Congress that the first branch of our government took the last major step away from its proper role, effectively devolving into a debate society or a collection of court jesters, rather than a functioning branch of government. Not too long ago, the president was understood to influence the government (the legislature) through what Teddy Roosevelt called a "bully pulpit." Now Congress is understood to, at most, influence the governing of the White House through its futile rhetorical pursuits.

Would I prefer to have seen members of Congress ignore the concerns and opinions of likely voters in the next election? That hardly seems like a good way to support our democracy! Well, I'll tell you what I would prefer. I would prefer for individual representatives to listen to their constituents rather than the leaders of their parties (even when those leaders include the president). I would prefer for campaigns to be publicly funded, with no advantages given to the two major parties, no possibility for wealthy candidates to buy their way in, and no financial influence for corporate and wealthy interests. I would prefer our American media challenge official lies, include multiple points of view, report ugly truths, and educate citizens about their roles rather than disempowering and excluding them. I would prefer to see everyone registered to vote, smaller districts, elections held on weekends, publicly counted paper ballots, a nonpartisan end to gerrymandering, the strengthening of institutions of international law (to the extent that Congress might refuse to violate a law even in the face of a public outcry), and a wide array of additional systemic changes that I will discuss through the course of this book. If representative democracy were developed and perfected to a substantial extent, and our representatives still believed that they were best off pretending to try to end wars rather than actually ending them, then I would indeed ask those representatives to risk an election defeat in order to save lives. But I doubt very much that such a dilemma can be created (or that, if it were, any representatives would listen to me). I am convinced that it is possible to structure a representative government so that representatives do not have to choose between losing their jobs and killing people.

War is an extreme example that seems to pull together the worst of every ailment from which our republic suffers. But there are many other issues on which majority public opinion consistently diverges from majority opinion inside Congress. A majority of Americans have long opposed the influence of corporations in Washington, supported a serious effort to slow global warming, backed major investment in public education and jobs, and favored creating single-payer health coverage with choice of doctors and the elimination of private health insurance. If it were up to the public, we'd have long since created a decent minimum wage, established public financing of elections, and freed up space for more honest voices on our airwaves.[5] During the 110th Congress, polls found a majority of Americans favoring the use of the power of the purse to bring the war to an end, and favoring impeachment proceedings for Bush and Cheney.[6] Polls vary, and some found less support for these positions, but public opinion follows media coverage to a great degree, so anything close to majority support for something not even being discussed in the media is usually an indication of potential for strong majority support should the topic be placed, as House Speaker Nancy Pelosi would put it, "on the table."

Majority opinion can, of course, be misinformed. When the United States invaded Iraq, I wanted Congress to prevent what a majority of Americans supported. But a majority also believed blatant falsehoods about that war and the supposed justifications for it. And polling showed that those who believed the lies were far more likely to support the war, and that those who watched certain news channels were far more likely to believe the lies.[7] It was not just the president and vice president, but also many members of Congress, of both parties, who joined with the media in promoting those falsehoods. There is no way to excuse the pro-war votes of so many members of Congress. They had a responsibility to question the lies, educate the public, and oppose foreign wars of aggression.

But the solution does not involve asking representatives to be smarter than their constituents. We are given evidence all the time of what goes wrong when representatives claim such superiority. We all had those very same responsibilities to question and resist. The solution involves, in large part, reforming our system of communications so that never again can a majority of Americans swallow such destructive and obvious falsehoods. Americans have, in fact, proven much more resistant to manipulation by lies about the supposed need to attack Iran, but I think that resistance is superficial and that the danger remains of our government dragging us to war again, in one country or another, not kicking and screaming, but applauding and howling for blood.

As the 110th Congress pretended to govern, global warming advanced, those lacking life's necessities continued to suffer, and over 1,200 US troops died in Iraq under the Congress elected to bring them home alive. Justice delayed was, as it always is, justice denied. There were, as some of us knew and said in November 2006, only two major things the 110th Congress would be able to do. The first thing that Congress could have done was to simply stop funding the occupation of Iraq. The second thing it could have done was to impeach Bush and Cheney. It chose to do neither. The result was very little in the way of good laws placed on the books, some outrageously unconstitutional laws placed on the books, some useful measures erased by signing statements, some other useful measures erased by vetoes, the effective elimination of congressional oversight of the executive branch and all those portions of the government commonly believed to be part of the executive branch, enough hot air to lift the Capitol dome, and a record low approval rating for Congress.[8] I'll discuss below not just how these two things (stopping the funding and impeachment) were possible, but also what effects they might have had and what the lasting impact may be of Congress's failure to take these steps.

Before we can figure out the solutions, we need to understand exactly how Congress collapsed and why congressional leaders claim it didn't. The two main excuses for the failures of the 110th Congress were the president's veto power and the power of Republican senators to threaten a filibuster. Those excuses were removed (or nearly so) by the 2008 elections, which put a Democrat in the White House, enlarged the Democrats' majority in the House of Representatives, and gave the Democrats fifty-seven senators plus two independents caucusing with them. Democrats could have, had they chosen to, reached the filibuster-proof majority of sixty senators through a number of means, including President Obama appointing Republican senators from states with Democratic governors to his cabinet. Or, with only fifty-one votes, they could have changed the rules to lower the threshold for stopping a filibuster. Instead, in the early months of the 111th Congress we saw bills significantly altered and appointments delayed in order to avoid filibusters, an incredibly anti-democratic procedure. The filibuster allows a group of multi-millionaires elected by 11.2 percent of the American public (forty-one senators from the twenty-one smallest states) to undo the work of the Senate and the House. In April of 2009, Republican Senator Arlen Specter became a Democrat, giving the Democrats a filibuster-proof majority if all sixty refused to join a filibuster.

In looking at the 110th Congress, however, the important point to remember is that Congress could have accomplished its two most pressing tasks (defunding the war and impeaching the president) without overcoming any filibuster or any veto.

Not so very far back in history, Congress used to use the powers it had to negotiate for its demands. When president Nixon nominated

Elliot Richardson for attorney general, the Senate refused to confirm him unless he first committed to naming a special prosecutor to investigate Watergate. When Bush nominated Michael Mukasey for the same job, necessitated by the departure of Alberto Gonzales under a dark cloud of criminal activities, former Congresswoman Liz Holtzman recommended a similar approach and was ignored. The Senate demanded nothing, Mukasey testified at his confirmation hearing that the president has the right to violate laws, and the Senate made him the top law enforcement officer in the land.

> SENATOR PATRICK LEAHY: Can a president authorize illegal conduct? Can the president—can a president put somebody above the law by authorizing illegal conduct?
>
> MICHAEL MUKASEY: The only way for me to respond to that in the abstract is to say that if by illegal you mean contrary to a statute, but within the authority of the president to defend the country, the president is not putting somebody above the law; the president is putting somebody within the law.[9]

Jonathan Mahler asked Democratic Senator Carl Levin how Congress might ever retake the power it was giving to the White House, and Levin replied: "We need a Democrat in the White House."

In school we learn about the "separation of powers" and "checks and balances" (already misleading terms because Congress is supposed to have much more power than the other branches, not aspire to being "co-equal"). A glance at the list of ways in which each branch is supposed to check the others reveals that one branch, the Congress, has lost its checking ability.

The president still has all of these checking powers:

1. The veto.
2. The vice president's tie-breaking vote in the Senate.
3. Recess appointments.
4. Calling Congress into session in emergencies and determining adjournments when the two houses cannot agree.

And the president has these powers to check the judicial branch:

1. Appointing judges.
2. Pardoning convicts.

The executive branch also has a check on itself. The vice president and the cabinet, thanks to the Twenty-fifth Amendment, can vote that the president is unable to discharge his duties. Similarly, the Congress can impeach or simply expel one of its own.

The judicial branch has an important check on Congress and the president in that it can rule laws to be unconstitutional. Courts also must approve warrants prior to government spying (or so we thought). The chief justice of the Supreme Court also serves as president of the Senate during a presidential impeachment, although that power depends on the House of Representatives first impeaching.

The legislative branch, in contrast, has lost the following checking powers:

1. Overriding a veto, rendered meaningless by the new presidential powers of signing statements and secret laws.
2. Approving and rejecting appointments and treaties.
3. Approving or rejecting a new vice president, which depends on removing the current one.
4. Defunding.
5. FOIA, subpoena, and contempt.
6. Impeachment.

Impeachment is not just the power on which the other intra-governmental powers of the legislative branch depend. It is the central power through which the framers of the Constitution expected the legislative branch to be able to hold the other two branches in check. Congress also has the power, by the Twenty-fifth Amendment, to remove the president from office with a two-thirds vote in both houses determining that he is unable to discharge his duties.

But who enforces all of these checks of one branch of the government on another? If the Supreme Court rules an action by the president unconstitutional (such as denying prisoners habeas corpus), but the president keeps doing it, or acts with such secrecy that nobody knows whether he's doing it or not, then what happens? If the Supreme Court, on the contrary, rules in favor of blatantly unconstitutional actions, who can stop them?

If Congress repeatedly passes unconstitutional laws, even overriding vetoes to do so, what can be done about it? Well, the Supreme Court can check Congress, but ultimately the people must do so through the power of elections (or recall) or, stepping outside the formal structure of government, nonviolent direct action. And it is ultimately the Congress, compelled by the people, that must enforce checks by itself or another branch on either of the other two branches. Those checks often require compliance by the other branches, and that compliance is compelled by the threat of impeachment, which always hovers in the background. Or at least it used to.

10. WE WON'T IMPEACH YOU NO MATTER WHAT

Impeachment is not an incidental afterthought in our system of government. It's mentioned in six places in the US Constitution,[10] and is one of very few procedures spelled out in any detail. Impeachment is the first power given to the House, and the only power given as part of the definition of the House. The power of impeachment was given to the House for the same reason that the power to originate bills for the spending of money was given to the House: because it was to be the body closest to the people. The creators of the Constitution, James Madison, George Mason, and Thomas Jefferson, believed that impeachment would need to be used quite often and that nothing else in the Constitution would be more important for preserving the republic by holding in check the executive and judicial branches. Having fought a bloody war to remove a king, the last thing the founders wanted was to install new kings for four-year periods, something Jefferson dreaded and referred to as "elected despotism." And they had no illusions about being able to elect human beings who would not abuse their power. The founders' focus was on denying any one person enough power to do much damage. "No point is of more importance than that the right of impeachment should be continued. Shall any man be above Justice? Above all shall that man be above it, who can commit the most extensive injustice?" Mason asked on July 20, 1787.[11]

Impeachment has, in fact, been used far more routinely through American history than most people realize. The history of impeachment is very well told by John Nichols in his book, *The Genius of Impeachment: The Founders' Cure for Royalism.*[12] Impeachment proceedings have been initiated in the House sixty-two times, and seventeen people have been impeached. Thirteen of those have been federal judges, one a secretary of war, one a senator, and two presidents. Seven individuals have subsequently been convicted in a trial in the US Senate, all of them federal judges. On September 17, 2008, the House Judiciary Committee began impeachment proceedings against US District Judge Thomas Porteous of Louisiana. On January 13, 2009, the full House voted to direct the Judiciary Committee to proceed.

But that's not the half of it. Impeachment often achieves its purpose of preserving our democratic rights short of actually arriving at a majority House vote for impeachment. Richard Nixon was never impeached, but he rightly resigned from the presidency. Harry Truman was never impeached, but he ceased the abuses of power for which Congress members were pushing to impeach him and which the Supreme Court rapidly ruled against (during "wartime" to boot). Attorney General Alberto Gonzales was never impeached, but there was a major push in Congress to impeach him. Prior to summer recess 2007, there were thirty-two Congress members who had cosponsored a resolution calling for impeachment hearings to begin. Many more pledged to sign on when Congress returned in the fall, but before that occurred, Gonzales announced his resignation.

Our Constitution was written as Edmund Burke was leading the impeachment of Warren Hastings in England—an effort that did not achieve impeachment but did restore democratic checks on power. American colonies, too, impeached governors and justices. In recent years, the British Parliament saw an active effort to impeach Prime Minister Tony Blair, which weakened his power. Impeachments went on in nations all over the world during the Cheney-Bush era, and a threat of impeachment led Pakistan's President Pervez Musharraf to resign.

While only two US presidents, Bill Clinton and Andrew Johnson, have been impeached, and neither one of them was convicted in the Senate, articles of impeachment have also been filed in the House against presidents Tyler, Cleveland, Hoover, Truman, Nixon, Reagan, Bush Sr., and Bush Jr. That's a total of ten out of forty-three presidents, or 23 percent. Some of these cases involved serious threats of impeachment, and others involved one or a dozen defenders of our rights in Congress going up against congressional leaders intent on ignoring them.

While there was much fuss from Democrats that impeachment would negatively impact the 2008 elections, impeachment has actually been a path to electoral success throughout US history. After the Whigs attempted to impeach Tyler, they picked up seven seats, and Tyler left politics. Weeks after he lobbied for Johnson's impeachment, Grant was nominated for president. Lincoln had pushed toward the impeachment of Polk without introducing actual articles before he was elected president. Keith Ellison, who introduced a resolution to impeach Bush and Cheney into the Minnesota state legislature, was elected to Congress in 2006, where he did very little to support impeachment. After the Republicans pursued impeachment of Truman and won what they wanted (and the nation needed) from the Supreme Court, they won in the next elections. After Nixon resigned, the Democrats won the White House and picked up four seats in the Senate and forty-nine (yes, forty-nine!) in the House.

Even during and following the unpopular impeachment of Clinton (an impeachment the public was overwhelmingly opposed to), the Republicans held onto majorities in both houses and lost very few seats. They also had the pleasure of watching Al Gore campaign for president while pretending he'd never met the extremely popular Bill Clinton and picking the unpopular Joe Lieberman, a critic of Clinton, as his running mate. On the other hand, when Democrats chose not to pursue impeachment of Reagan for Iran-Contra, so that they could win the next elections, they lost the next elections. When the movements were begun to impeach Johnson, Truman, Nixon, and Clinton, those presidents were never again going to face an election, so it would have made no sense to propose waiting and voting them out of office. The same was true of Bush Jr., of course, but that didn't stop the current crop of Democrats from making that proposal.[13]

Now, I was of the opinion that reestablishing the rule of law was more important than the outcome of the next presidential election, but I was also of the opinion—for the reasons listed above—that the Democrats had at least as good a shot at winning the White House in 2008 if they impeached as if they did not. Voters appreciate efforts to push for a cause. Cowardice and impotence are not very popular.

The Democrats (and some Republicans) tried to impeach Nixon, and the people elected Carter. The Democrats refused to impeach Reagan, and the people elected Bush Sr. The Republicans (and a few Democrats) impeached Clinton, and Bush Jr. moved into the White House.

Proposals to impeach Bush were almost always greeted by Congress members with horrified shouts of "But we wouldn't want a President Cheney!" The greatest insurance against impeachment as president had become serving with an unpopular and frightening vice president. Never mind that the vice president was already running the country or that activists were proposing to impeach Cheney first. (This is another argument for denying vice presidents any role in the executive branch. They should be uninvolved and available for a clean break and fresh start.)

Among those who understood that you could impeach Cheney first, some rather creatively expressed concerns about whoever would replace him, or about a President Pelosi. (Speaker of the House Nancy Pelosi would have only become president had Bush and Cheney been simultaneously removed from office by surprise, denying them the possibility to resign and nominate replacements.) But, in fact, both houses of Congress would have had to approve any replacement, and this whole conversation betrayed a horrible lack of understanding on the part of impeachment advocates and opponents alike. The big question is what precedent is laid down for the future, not who sits in the Oval Office for a period of months.

The Clinton impeachment was an absurd bad-faith witch hunt that made a mockery of our entire system of government. That, of course, was not what disturbed Congress members. Many of them live to make a mockery of our entire system of government. What disturbed them were a number of false beliefs, including the following: that they hadn't gotten anything else done while impeaching Clinton because it had taken several months, that the public had opposed the Clinton impeachment because the public opposed all impeachments, that the public's fondest wish was for comity[14] and bipartisanship even if it meant going along with whatever Cheney wanted, and that voters had horribly punished Republicans and thrown them out of power during and following the Clinton impeachment. These were and are widespread beliefs, but they are all false.

Yet, while Congress stuck its head in the sand, a movement did develop on the ground. In March 2006, the *Wall Street Journal* did—for one day—what most media outlets never did: cover the movement to impeach Bush and Cheney.[15] While most polling companies refused to ever poll on the question, even for cold hard cash, Zogby had released a poll in November 2005 that we at After Downing Street and Democrats.com had commissioned.[16] *The Wall Street Journal* led off with a graphic showing the results of that poll and those of a 1998 poll on impeaching Clinton. The same pollster had done both polls and asked almost identical questions. Both polls were conducted among "likely voters." The results showed that 27 percent favored impeachment for Clinton and 51 percent for Bush. That would have been an impressive gap even without the contrasting media attention. The impeachment of Clinton had been promoted in saturation coverage night-and-day for months, with newspapers editorializing in support of it. The impeachment of Bush was absolutely unheard of and unmentionable in US corporate media.

The Wall Street Journal did print that one article, but, tellingly, the article was written exactly as if the reporter had not seen the graphic at the top and was unaware of the poll results. In fact, she was perfectly well aware of them, but chose to disregard them. "Democratic Party leaders," she wrote, were "keeping their distance from impeachment talk. They remember how the effort boomeranged on Republicans in the 1998 midterm elections." Of course, that boomerang was minimal (the Republicans lost five seats and held the majority), but look at those poll results again. The voters did not want Clinton impeached, and did want Bush impeached. So why in the world would voter opposition to the former suggest that there would be voter opposition to the latter?

An impeachment of Bush and/or Cheney for an indisputable offense (refusing subpoenas, refusing to enforce contempt citations, rewriting laws with signing statements, openly violating the Foreign Intelligence Surveillance Act, and so on) could have taken one day, with a Senate trial adding a second day to the process. President Andrew Johnson was impeached three days after the offense. Senator William Blount was impeached four days after the offense. The Senate expelled Blount the day after he was impeached. Judge Halsted Ritter's Senate trial took eleven days. Judge John Pickering's trial took nine days. Judge James Peck's trial took three days. Judge West Humphreys' trial took one day.

The House began impeachment procedures for Bill Clinton on October 8, 1998, and impeached him on December 19th. Clinton's Senate trial lasted from January 14, 1999, to February 12, 1999. The whole farce happened in four months. The House Judiciary Committee began impeachment hearings on Nixon on May 9, 1974, and passed the first of three articles of impeachment on July 27. Nixon resigned on August 8. There was plenty of time to impeach Cheney and Bush.

Impeachment did not go without representation entirely, but due to the sad state of Congress, its fate was as follows: on the last day of the 109th Congress in 2006, and the last day of her service, having lost an election, Congresswoman Cynthia McKinney introduced articles of impeachment against the president.[7] There was no way that any other members could cosponsor.

In April 2007, Congressman Dennis Kucinich introduced three articles of impeachment against the vice president. The resolution became H. Res. 333, and Kucinich reintroduced it on November 6, 2007, as H. Res. 799, in order to force a vote on the floor of the House.[8] Twenty-seven Congress members cosponsored. The full House voted to send the resolution to committee, but that was understood as a way to kill it.

In June 2008, Kucinich introduced thirty-five articles of impeachment against Bush.[9] The resolution became H. Res. 1258 and gained seven cosponsors. Kucinich read the articles for six hours on the floor of the House, forced the clerk to reread the whole thing, and forced a vote, which sent the resolution to committee.

On July 15, 2008, Kucinich introduced a single article of impeachment against Bush. The resolution became H. Res. 1345 and gained two cosponsors. Kucinich forced a vote on the floor, sending it to committee but also resulting in Pelosi instructing Representative Conyers to hold a hearing on impeachable offenses, which he did on July 25, 2008.

While not introducing his own articles of impeachment, Congressman Robert Wexler sought to advance the cause in January 2008 by publishing a letter to Chairman John Conyers urging him to begin impeachment hearings on Dick Cheney, and asking other members of the Judiciary Committee to sign the letter. Twenty members of Congress signed on, including five members of the committee. In March 2008, House Judiciary Committee Chairman John Conyers promised that he would pursue impeachment or some similar process after the November elections.[20] He did not do so.

Not all crimes rise to the level of impeachable offenses, and not all impeachable offenses are crimes at all. Impeachable offenses are significant abuses of power. Nonetheless, it is useful to compile lists of the crimes Bush and Cheney appear to have committed. John Conyers did this in two lengthy reports, one released in 2005 and the other in 2009.[21] Former federal prosecutor Elizabeth de la Vega, author of *United States v. George W. Bush et al.*, has compiled a list of the crimes involved in Kucinich's thirty-five articles of impeachment.[22] Many fine authors have compiled their own lists of impeachable offenses and drafted their own articles of impeachment.[23]

These lists are important because some of the deterrent value of impeachment could still be achieved by impeaching even after the offenders are out of office. Their "legacies" could be damaged and they could be barred from ever again holding public office, and could be denied pensions and benefits. In 1797 the Senate tried Senator William Blount in an impeachment trial despite having already expelled him. He was not convicted, but the reason for not convicting him was not that he was out of office. In 1876 the House impeached and the Senate tried Secretary of War William Worth Belknap, who had resigned prior to the impeachment. The Senate ruled by a vote of 37–29 that it had jurisdiction despite the resignation.[24]

Bush and Cheney can and should still be impeached. Other guilty parties should be impeached as well. A likely success would be the impeachment of Jay Bybee. Bybee was assistant attorney general for Bush and Cheney, in which role he authored, co-authored and approved memos purporting to legalize torture. Before that became known, however, Bush nominated him, and the Senate confirmed him, to become a judge on the Ninth Circuit Court of Appeals, where he sits to this day holding the power to undo the legal rulings of honest men and women. Bybee's memos were reversed by Bush's own Justice Department. In April 2009, Bybee faced a likely indictment for his crimes in a Spanish court. And there were only two ways he could be held accountable in the United States: criminal prosecution or impeachment. A movement driven by all the organizations that had backed the impeachment of

Bush and Cheney grew rapidly to demand Bybee's impeachment. They were supported by the *New York Times*, which called for his impeachment after having never even reported on the impeachment movement; Congressman Jerrold Nadler and Senator Russ Feingold, who proposed his impeachment after having refused to support impeaching Bush or Cheney for years; Common Cause, Think Progress, People for the American Way, and other organizations joining in for the first time; and Nancy Pelosi, who refused to take this one "off the table."

A Zogby poll in 2006 had found that Americans' top answer for how to restore trust in government was impeachment.[25] Trust has not yet been restored.

11. OVERLOOKING OVERSIGHT

I have no idea that I'm going to be subpoenaed, and obviously, we'd sit down and look at it at the time, but probably [I would] not [comply], in the sense that the president and the vice president are constitutional officers and don't appear before the Congress.

—Dick Cheney, 2006.[26]

As the 110th Congress opened, it was clear that the leadership would try to avoid impeachment, and, as a substitute, attempt to conduct investigations into impeachable offenses. The problem was that with a commitment made not to impeach, members of the executive branch and anyone else it wanted to protect could not be compelled by the Justice Department to appear and testify or to produce subpoenaed materials. Congress could only compel witnesses to appear if it sent its own police to lock them up, something it was as reluctant to do as it was to begin impeachment. This does not mean that there could not be any hearings. There were, in fact, lots of them. But each hearing fell into one of two patterns. Either witnesses refused to appear (or appeared and said "I do not recall" in response to any uncomfortable questions), or the hearings relied on friendly witnesses and did not produce significant new information. Some of the hearings of this latter type did review already public evidence of clear impeachable offenses, but once the hearings had been held, there was no second step to take, and the world ended up looking just about the way it had before the hearing had begun. Some of the hearings with which subpoenaed witnesses refused to cooperate produced new impeachable offenses in the form of refusal to cooperate with Congress, but those offenses, like the underlying ones being investigated, were not addressed through impeachment. Many hearings went largely ignored by the media and thus were not even able to serve an educational purpose.

By the end of the 110th Congress, House Judiciary Committee Chairman John Conyers would claim to have held forty-five public hearings on impeachable offenses.[27] But there were many hearings that did not happen or were held in the absence of key elements. These included hearings on the firings of US Attorneys. Conyers subpoenaed information from the Justice Department, which did not produce it.[28] There was also to be a July 2007 hearing on the same subject with former White House counsel Harriet Miers and former White House chief of staff Joshua Bolten, both of whom refused to appear. There was to be a May 2008 hearing on the same subject with Karl Rove, who refused to appear when subpoenaed. There was to be a December 2007 hearing on someone who was an alleged victim of gang rape while employed by Halliburton; the Department of Justice did not comply with a subpoena. There was a July 2008 hearing scheduled on the outing of an undercover CIA agent, but again the Justice Department did not comply with a subpoena. And then there were the hearings that reviewed crimes and abuses but did not result in any further action. These included committee and subcommittee hearings on signing statements, spying, air pollution at "ground zero" in New York, punishment of whistleblowers, and various other topics.[29]

Other committees had the same experience that the House Judiciary Committee had. The Senate Judiciary Committee subpoenaed Karl Rove's e-mails in May 2007, but did not receive them. The same committee scheduled a July 2007 hearing with Joshua Bolten and materials he was required to produce. The White House did not produce them, and he did not appear. The same month the committee scheduled a hearing with White House political director Sara Taylor, but got no documents and one witness who would not answer questions. In August the committee was stood up by Karl Rove. White House Deputy Political Director J. Scott Jennings showed up when subpoenaed, but refused to answer questions. The committee also subpoenaed legal analysis and other documents concerning the NSA warrantless wiretapping program from the White House, Dick Cheney, DOJ, and NSC. If the documents were not produced, testimony was required from Joshua Bolten, Alberto Gonzales, Cheney chief of staff David Addington, and National Security Counsel executive director V. Philip Lago. Nothing was produced and nobody showed. The committee subpoenaed a copy of opinions of the Justice Department Office of Legal Counsel in order to reveal the secret laws under which Bush was running the government. The laws remained secret.

The House Oversight and Government Reform Committee, under the chairmanship of Henry Waxman, was extremely active during the 110th Congress, holding endless hearings, releasing reports, and sending countless polite requests, insistent demands, and subpoenas. Plenty of corruption was revealed, including in military contracting and in hearings featuring friendly witnesses, but the corruption remained after the hearings were over. Other hearings never occurred. Then Secretary of State Condoleezza Rice repeatedly refused to comply with a subpoena, explaining that she was "not inclined to." When the committee subpoenaed Lt. General Kensinger in the matter of the apparent murder of US soldier and former football star Pat Tillman, he dodged it for months. When the Department of State would not turn over materials related to corruption in Iraq, Congress passed a resolution condemning this refusal, but the refusal remained in place. The committee subpoenaed the White House Office of Management and Budget to produce materials about White House influence over the EPA on climate policy, and was refused. The Administrator of the EPA also refused to appear, as did Attorney General Mukasey, in the matter of outing a CIA agent. Dr. Kaye Whitley, the director of the Defense Department's Sexual Assault Prevention and Response Office, refused to appear and testify on the topic of sexual assault in the military.

These and many other hearings were held or attempted, but some topics were not even attempted. Chief among them was the topic that had been at the front of Conyers' push toward impeachment in 2005: the lies that had taken us into war. Jonathan Schwarz and I published an article detailing the hearings we most wanted to see held, and the Democrats held none of them.[30] They steered completely clear of the war lies, with the new House Intelligence Committee Chairman Silvestre Reyes saying he would leave it up to the Senate Intelligence Committee, where, as the ranking member in recent years, the new Chairman Jay Rockefeller had screamed bloody murder over the Republican chairman's refusal to investigate. As chairman, however,

Rockefeller did nothing for a year and a half and then quietly released a report in 2008 with nothing significant or new in it—the "Report on Whether Public Statements Regarding Iraq by U.S. Government Officials Were Substantiated by Intelligence Information." The conclusion was a tentative, qualified, and complicated "No," a conclusion long since reached by a majority of Americans, and a conclusion based on information that was virtually all already public.[31]

But, even steering clear of the lies that had taken us to war, there was an overabundance of crimes and abuses, swindles, rackets, forgeries, briberies, and potentially treasonous acts to look into. And a number of committees and subcommittees began doing so, especially the House Committee on Oversight and Government Reform chaired by Henry Waxman, the House Judiciary Committee chaired by John Conyers, and the Senate Judiciary Committee chaired by Patrick Leahy.

In his first month as chairman, Conyers held a hearing on signing statements that perfectly laid out the most quintessentially impeachable offense with evidence that was simply indisputable. But then nothing happened. The hearing was held, the evidence exhibited. And that was that. Congress would not impeach, the Justice Department would not prosecute, and the White House would not reform. And very few people had learned anything. So hearings became ends in themselves. And when, a year and a half later, Conyers told a hearing packed with supporters of impeachment that he had held forty-five hearings, some of us were not as grateful as might have seemed appropriate. While hearings brought out some new information, and some offenders, like Gonzales, ended up resigning from office, for the most part hearings had become talk for the sake of talk. They fit into the role of consultants that Lee Hamilton envisions for Congress.

The other type of hearings that were held, or in some cases not held, during the 110th Congress involved the White House refusing to turn over documents, witnesses refusing to appear, and witnesses appearing but refusing to answer questions. congressional committees requested documents and witnesses and were turned down. They sent Freedom of Information Act (FOIA) requests and were turned down. In fact, the White House effectively closed the office that handled those requests (by shifting the funding from the National Archives to the Department of Justice), even after Bush had signed the Open Government Act into law on New Year's Eve 2007, requiring that FOIA requests be answered.[32] Democrats had seen FOIA and other requests ignored by the same White House prior to 2007. Now that they were in the majority, they could also send subpoenas.[33] It took until April 2007 for them to begin doing so. Cheney-Bush Inc. immediately began refusing to comply with the subpoenas.[34] It took until the following February (2008) for either branch of Congress to hold anyone in contempt for refusing to comply with subpoenas. Sadly, enforcement of the type of contempt citations that the House chose to issue fell to the "Justice Department," which of course refused at the instruction of the president. It took until July 2008 to get a court ruling requiring the witnesses to obey the subpoenas, but the Bush administration appealed the ruling, further dragging out the process, even as the Democrats—ever hopeful of avoiding any actual confrontation—were beginning to grin and quietly chant from sunrise to sundown, "An Election Is Coming! An Election Is Coming!"

Much needed oversight from Congress was dying, and it's not hard to see why. Not only had the House unilaterally disarmed by refusing to ever impeach the president no matter what,[35] but both the House and the Senate were refusing to make use of a contempt procedure that did not depend on the Justice Department, a procedure known as inherent contempt.[36]

"Contempt" refers to the process of compelling a witness to testify who has refused to do so and punishing the refusal by, for example, locking him in jail until he agrees to testify. "Inherent" simply refers to the idea that Congress can enforce its own contempt citations, as it did up until the early twentieth century, by locking them up. Congress eventually began asking the Justice Department (part of the executive branch) or the courts (part of the judicial branch) to enforce its contempt citations. This procedure seems to work just as well as the other except in cases in which the Justice Department has an interest in allowing a witness to not comply. In at least those cases, if not all, Congress ought logically to enforce its own contempt citations, a power that it never lost and which has never been challenged, merely forgotten. Believe it or not, Congress has always had—and used to actually use— the power to lock people in jail until they agreed to answer questions. Congress did this over eighty-five times between 1795 and 1934.

Reviving a procedure not used since 1934 might sound radical if we do not understand why it fell out of practice. Congress members actually believed that by establishing a legal statute of contempt and asking the Justice Department to enforce, they would strengthen the process and eliminate the need for inherent contempt within Congress. And perhaps they had, until the occasion arose when the Justice Department had a conflict of interest. Bush and Cheney revived claims of presidential power unheard of since Abraham Lincoln, their Justice Department acted out of strict loyalty to the president rather than the law, and Congress behaved as if nothing significant had changed. Congress members had to ask the Justice Department to compel its own employees to appear as witnesses under strong suspicion of wrongdoing. In June of 2008, fifty-six members of Congress even asked Attorney General Mukasey to appoint a special counsel to prosecute the crimes of Bush, Cheney, and their coconspirators.

Congress didn't need to turn to the Justice Department, but they were afraid to use their own power of inherent contempt simply because Congress had not used it since 1934, or because they falsely believed that a committee could not act without the full House, or because they thought Fox News would call them names, or because they preferred to leave the matter to the courts even if that process took years to complete.

In August 2007, a group of Congressman Henry Waxman's constituents met with him and urged him to make use of inherent contempt.[37] Waxman was the chair of the House Committee on Oversight and Government Responsibility that issued so many rejected subpoenas discussed above. His constituents were obliged to explain to him what inherent contempt was, as he clearly had no idea. While the 110th Congress had probably seen more requests, subpoenas, and contempt citations ignored than all previous Congresses combined, Waxman had certainly endured more such insult than all other committee chairs combined in the 110th Congress. Waxman had single-handedly destroyed whole forests with the flood of letters and requests and subpoenas he'd sent down Pennsylvania Avenue, and yet he was apparently unaware of a procedure commonly used by Congress through most of this nation's history that would actually compel people to show up and answer questions and produce documents.

Through the months of the 110th Congress, a vague sort of awareness of inherent contempt crept into the minds of certain committee members and party leaders, almost entirely as a result of thousands of citizens demanding that they immediately make use of it. Quasi-grassroots groups afraid to demand impeachment took up the cry for inherent contempt, but pro-impeachment groups did not pay sufficient attention to it, their eyes set on a bigger and better prize.

In the spring of 2008, Congresswoman Zoe Lofgren wrote the following dismissive letter to her constituents who were demanding inherent contempt:

> Thank you for contacting me about Karl Rove's failure to appear before the Judiciary Committee. I appreciate that you took the time to share your thoughts with me. The Judiciary Committee is taking Karl Rove's failure to testify very seriously, and we are currently considering all options—including contempt proceedings—to compel him to answer important questions regarding the firing of several US attorneys. Some have suggested that Congress implement "inherent contempt" as if that is a viable option. The jail cell in the basement of the Capitol doesn't exist and the Sergeant at Arms is an over sixty-year-old executive. Congress is not a police force, and we will likely need to continue to utilize the courts and system of justice to pursue these matters. Again, thanks for being in touch. Please do not hesitate to let me know if I may ever be of assistance to you or your family.

Congresswoman Lofgren was either very poorly informed or she chose to pretend to be. The age of the Sergeant at Arms is not a decisive factor in the question of whether the Congress will engage in what for most of its history was understood as "inherent self-protection." There is a Sergeant at Arms for the House and one for the Senate, there are deputies, and there is an entire Capitol police force. The House can hold a prisoner until the end of a two-year Congress, and the Senate can hold someone indefinitely.

But what about the jail? When inherent contempt began to be discussed in 2007, having not been used in some seventy-five years, the *Politico* (never a publication overly careful with facts) reported that the jail had been razed in 1929. Congresswoman Lofgren, on the other hand, maintained that "the jail cell in the basement of the Capitol" didn't exist. She seemed to take no position on whether such a thing ever did. Both of these replies wildly missed the mark. The House or the Senate or, in fact, any committee thereof, has the power, according to tradition and to rulings of the US Supreme Court, to instruct the Sergeant at Arms of the House or Senate to imprison anyone being charged with contempt of Congress or being thereby punished for contempt of Congress. The difficulty of finding a place to imprison them has been easily solved in a variety of ways and could be solved again quite quickly.

During the latter part of the nineteenth century and the early part of the twentieth, the common jail of the District of Columbia was routinely used by the Sergeants at Arms of the House and Senate. While the jail did not belong to Congress, an arrangement was made to use it, housing the occasional "contumacious witness" in the same building with the general DC prison population.[38] In 1872 a congressional committee discussed the problem of the DC jail not being controlled by Congress, but apparently concluded that the Sergeant at Arms could keep control of a prisoner in that jail. Congress has not always made use of outside jails. In 1868 Congress set aside rooms in the US Capitol to be used as "guard rooms" for holding a particular prisoner.

The US Capitol and the House and Senate office buildings are full of rooms that could easily be transformed into guard rooms, and are in fact full of guard rooms already. And DC is chock full of jails, several of them quite close to the Capitol. In fact, the Capitol Police make extensive and frequent use of them under an ongoing understanding with the custodians of the jails. The Capitol Police also hold people in a building very near the Senate office buildings.

Inherent contempt is available to the House or the Senate or any committee thereof, whether or not preceded by a subpoena, and can be used with witnesses who agree to appear but, as in the case of Alberto Gonzales, decline to directly answer questions. While the House Judiciary Committee's vote in 2008 to hold Rove in contempt was what had excited the activist groups, the Senate Judiciary Committee had already voted for the same thing in December 2007. It simply never followed through, choosing to defer to the full Senate, which chose to shut its eyes, cover its ears, and hum.

Many members of Congress and most members of the public simply believe that subpoenas and contempt citations cannot be directly enforced by Congress. The idea that they could doesn't even occur to people, simply because Congress hasn't done it for a while. When it comes to power sharing among different bodies, the rule is: Use it or lose it.

The power of inherent contempt that I am proposing Congress must use or lose is not the sort of power the Bush-Cheney White House claimed, and to some extent the early Obama White House maintained, to randomly kidnap, detain, disappear, torture, and murder (President Obama foreswore torture, disappearing, and murder, but not the other crimes). Everything Congress does when holding (literally holding) someone in contempt must be open and public. Congress must not randomly, even if publicly, arrest someone for an offense unrelated to contempt of Congress—or for no offense at all. It must allow communication with legal counsel and family. It must treat everyone humanely. It must not abuse its power, and if it does, such abuses must be checked by the judicial branch. The purpose of Congress detaining prisoners must be to compel them to produce information believed to be of potentially vital importance to the governance of our nation.

If a crucial power goes unused for seventy-five years and those who should be using it have to be informed that it exists, we have probably reached the point at which it would make sense to amend the Constitution to include that power in explicit terms. We need a new constitutional amendment giving Congress the power of inherent contempt.

When Congresswoman Lofgren wrote that her committee was contemplating "contempt proceedings" she meant that—in fulfillment of the popular "definition" of insanity—Congress would consider doing with Karl Rove what it had long been doing with Harriet Miers and Joshua Bolten: that is, waiting for the executive branch of our government to go through some sort of magical conversion and begin prosecuting its own most loyal criminals. Rove, like Condoleezza Rice and others before him, had said that he wouldn't testify before Congress because he simply didn't have to. Numerous others had refused to appear or turn over documents by claiming "executive privilege."

Throughout the 110th Congress one of the tactics used to avoid impeachment was to propose doing investigations and "seeing where they lead." One place they quickly led was to new impeachable offenses. After all, the House Judiciary Committee had passed an article of impeachment against President Richard Nixon for refusing to comply with subpoenas. Cheney announced in 2006 that he would "probably not" comply if subpoenaed, and he followed through on that commitment. A variety of branches of the administration refused to comply, at the president's instruction, and Bush went so far as to openly obstruct justice by instructing former staffers not to comply.

A second reason why "Let's do investigations!" drove some of us crazy is that an impeachment hearing is supposed to itself be an investigation. Evidence against Nixon came out as part of the impeachment process. The precedent established by Congress is that if a hearing is an impeachment hearing, claims of "executive privilege" cannot be made. The executive can comply, or be impeached for not complying. And, of course, impeachment hearings would have garnered much more media and informed many more people what was happening than did all the dozens of non-impeachment hearings on impeachable offenses.

A third problem with the investigations strategy was that a majority of the public already knew about proven impeachable offenses.[39] Impeachment could begin and end in a morning. Had they refused subpoenas and contempt citations? Yes. No ifs, ands, or buts.[40] Had they claimed the power to violate laws? The signing statements were posted on the White House website.[41] Had Bush authorized spying programs knowing they violated the law and the Bill of Rights? He was on videotape confessing to it.[42] Was Bush criminally negligent during Hurricane Katrina? He was on videotape being warned of the danger, and on videotape claiming he was never warned.[43] Did Bush and Cheney mislead us into war? The evidence was overwhelming. Did they threaten an aggressive war on Iran? Yes, on videotape.[44] Did they unlawfully detain and torture? The Supreme Court said so in at least three cases,[45] and the documentary, photographic, and first-hand witness evidence was voluminous, including memos claiming to legalize torture. (Of course even more evidence has continued to emerge, including televised interviews of Bush and Cheney admitting to authorizing torture,[46] numerous additional accounts from victims and participants, and a report from the International Committee of the Red Cross.[47])

By July 25, 2008, the 110th Congress had neared its chronological end as well as the reductio ad absurdum of its claim to exist. It was soon to break for the summer, with plans to only work two more weeks in Washington for the rest of the year. On this day, a Friday, House Judiciary Committee Chairman John Conyers chose, at the instruction of Nancy Pelosi, to hold a hearing on all the various impeachable offenses of Bush and Cheney, but to insist that it was not an impeachment hearing.[48] In Conyers' opening statement he bragged about all the other non-impeachment hearings he'd held, including the unofficial hearings he'd held during the previous Congress when the Democrats were in the minority. He didn't distinguish between the two, and he was right not to. I had worked closely with Conyers' staff in 2005 when he had been pushing toward impeachment. We'd organized unofficial hearings on the *Downing Street Minutes*, relegated to the basement of the Capitol. Now he was including that as one of his accomplishments, because he saw the holding of hearings as an end in itself.

On July 25, 2008, Conyers listed impeachable offenses in his opening remarks, including the politicization of the Justice Department; signing statements; detention; rendition; "possible" manipulation of intelligence; retaliation against whistleblowers, including the outing of Valerie Plame; and excessive secrecy. "Some say we've done too little too late," Conyers said, before protesting that he'd held hearings on the *Downing Street Memo* and the 2004 Ohio election results before becoming chairman, and that as chairman he had held "more than forty-five separate public hearings on these matters." To what end? "We've sent subpoenas and pursued criminal contempt." With what outcome?

Some have proposed, as a sort of substitute spine for an invertebrate Congress, the strengthening of Congress's power to create a special independent investigation. Congress may, in fact, want to pass legislation establishing its right to employ a special legal counsel to investigate possible crimes. Such a special counsel would need to not be subject to control by either of the other branches of government involved (Nixon fired the special prosecutor investigating him), and would ideally not be given unlimited funding, time, and field of play (the independent counsel investigating Clinton dug through anything he could, failing for years to find any crimes, and finally billed tax payers approximately $5 million per episode of oral sex about which Clinton lied).

But there is a danger here of the same sort of slow weakening of Congress that we've seen with the power of contempt. Congress always had the power of contempt, then passed a law to establish that power but make it dependent on other branches of government, and then forgot that it ever had the power in a completely independent form. Congress has always had the power to fund impeachment investigations. If Congress is not investigating a potential impeachment, it has no business doing the work of prosecutors, but if it is pursuing impeachable offenses, then it has every right to hire skilled investigators without passing any legislation to establish that right and weaken it. So, the question of whether Congress should try to legislate procedures for special prosecutors, I think, boils down to whether the impeachment process has been so thoroughly erased from the Constitution that a poor substitute needs to be developed.

With colleagues at Democrats.com, I collected a list of the subpoenas (at least two dozen, probably more-subpoenas are not always made public) issued by the 110th Congress through investigations, and laughed at by the Bush-Cheney Justice Department.[49] But by the time Obama had been elected president, a lot of people were in a mood to "look forward." However, come January 2009 there would be a brand new Justice Department. And justice departments don't do "looking forward." Punishing crimes is always about looking backwards, even though the purpose is to deter future crimes. Plus, back during the Pennsylvania primary, President-to-be Barack Obama had promised a *Philadelphia Daily News* reporter that his Justice Department would look into the crimes of his predecessor.[50] And reporters like Seymour Hersh claimed that all sorts of insiders wanted to spill their guts come January 20 if anyone was going to be willing to listen.[51]

So Congress members must have been chomping at the bit to reissue their subpoenas and finally see them enforced, right?

Well, it turned out that Chairman Henry Waxman of the Oversight and Government Reform Committee decided to move to the Energy and Commerce Committee, apparently taking the position that there was no longer any great need for oversight, and—despite having his requests and subpoenas laughed at—considered his work complete. His replacement, Chairman Edolphus Towns, displayed no interest in re-issuing Waxman's subpoenas or contempt citations. If his committee and others were to reissue and enforce all the outstanding subpoenas, either to their original recipients or to their replacements, I suspect much more could be learned about how Bush and Cheney governed than any independent commission would produce.

While the attitude of Waxman and others boded very ill for the prospect of restoring powers to Congress during the tenure of a poten-tially relatively law-abiding president, it told us something even more damning as well. If the Democrats did not reissue all of their subpoenas and contempt citations, they would be admitting that they had only been pretending to care about justice for the previous two years. It had been about changing the occupant of the White House, not about enforcing the law.

In September 2008, Congresswoman Tammy Baldwin introduced a resolution urging the next president (instead of Congress) to pursue accountability for the crimes of his predecessor.[52] Not a single colleague co-sponsored. Baldwin suggested she would re-introduce the resolution in the 111th Congress, and was expected to do so in expanded form in April or May. Also in April, 2009, Congress members Barbara Lee and Robert Wexler were expected (by those of us confidentially informed by their staff) to introduce a bill to create a House select committee to make recommendations on undoing imperial abuses.

When a bill does not have the support of the leaders of either big party, that bill tends to become little more than birdcage lining, even if it has 100 cosponsors. And if the parties don't want to impeach or con-duct serious oversight, then very few party members will challenge that line. The Republican leaders in Congress during Clinton's presidency persuaded many of their members to put party ahead of constituents and even ahead of legality and simple decency, and they continued to do so during the Bush-Cheney years. The Democratic leaders in Con-gress during the last two years of Bush-Cheney were just as ruthless and manipulative as any Republican leaders, negotiating and threatening progressive Democrats to cast regressive votes including to fund wars.

During the floor debate over "Paulson's Plunder" (the "bailout" bill) in October 2008, Democratic Congressman Brad Sherman said on the floor of the House that a few Congress members had been told by the Bush administration that there would be martial law in America if they did not pass the bill.[53] Sherman should be praised for the unusual burst of courage or forgetfulness that it took to say something his party had not asked him to say. But did he demand to know which individuals had made that statement? Did he haul them into Congress for questioning? Did he connect it with the fact that the US Army had just, for the first time, illegally begun stationing troops on US soil to confront US citizens? (On September 30, 2008, the *Army Times* reported on the US Army deploying the 3rd Infantry Division's 1st Combat Brigade Team (BCT) on US soil for "civil unrest" and "crowd control" duties. As an apparent response to public outcry led by the American Freedom Campaign and other groups, the Army later removed crowd control from the BCT's duties, but did not deny that it would be deployed on US soil to handle emergencies.)

Congressman Sherman was clearly reprimanded by party bigwigs, because later that month (October 2008) he put out a statement trying to backtrack without actually retracting what he'd said.[54] I exchanged e-mails with his press secretary but never got a straight answer. This is one example of thousands of areas where oversight might have made sense, but never even became a topic of conversation.[55]

Once the new Justice Department was in place in late January of 2009, Conyers subpoenaed Rove again. He did not comply, and the new Justice Department did not compel him to. In mid-February 2009, Conyers subpoenaed Rove yet again to appear on February 23, and again he did not comply. The Justice Department did not compel Rove to appear because of interference from the White House—the Obama White House. White House counsel Gregory B. Craig said, "The president is very sympathetic to those who want to find out what happened. But he is also mindful as president of the United States not to do anything that would undermine or weaken the institution of the presidency. So, for that reason, he is urging both sides of this to settle."[56]

Think about that statement. Here was a new president, just elected in a show of massive opposition to the policies of the outgoing president, a new president who had promised to undo many of the crimes and abuses of his predecessor, and now he was going to avoid doing anything that might weaken the presidency? Wouldn't removing the power of aggressive war without congressional declaration weaken the presidency? Wouldn't ending warrantless spying weaken the presidency? And think about how this is framed. The president is asking an individual suspected of gross abuses of power and the primary branch of our government to "settle" as if they are two equal and bickering parties. The proper role of the executive is of course to execute the will of Congress, not to tell Congress to negotiate with Karl Rove until he's happy with a pre-arranged list of questions. On March 4, 2009, an agreement was announced that would see Rove and Harriet Miers testify in private, without being sworn in, but with transcripts that could later be made public (following the last interview and a period of time in which everyone's lawyer could review the transcripts). As part of the deal, a court case seeking to compel their compliance was dropped.[57]

In January 2009 Conyers released the lengthy report that his committee staff had spent the previous two years writing.[58] At the same time, Conyers both urged creation of a special counsel to prosecute and introduced a bill to create a year-and-a-half investigative commission. He also recommended extending statutes of limitations to ten years, but did not introduce any bill to do so. Senator Patrick Leahy, Chair of the Senate Judiciary Committee, also spoke out very publicly for a "truth and reconciliation" commission. Several other prominent senators and Congress members joined the chorus. Since leaving office, Bush and Cheney had both confessed on television to authorizing procedures that are legally considered torture;[59] former Department of Justice attorney John Yoo had published an op-ed in the *Wall Street Journal* admitting that Bush had authorized torture;[60] and Bush's own top official overseeing military commissions in Guantánamo had refused to try a prisoner because, in her words, the United States had tortured him.[61] The number one question voted for by visitors to Obama's transition website was whether his attorney general would appoint a special prosecutor. The topic of prosecution was in the news in February, March, and April 2009 in a way that impeachment never had been; the pressure was building, and Congress was offering itself as a relief valve.

A *USA Today* Gallup Poll from February 2009 on torture found that 38 percent of Americans wanted criminal investigations, 24 percent wanted an independent panel, and 34 percent wanted neither.[62] A congressional truth and reconciliation commission was a very odd idea. We didn't need to put thousands of people on trial, just the top several. Our ordinary justice system was completely up to the task. But the commission, or independent panel, was a way for investigations to substitute for prosecution just as they had already substituted for impeachment. Sufficient evidence for prosecutions was already known. A commission of half Republicans and half Democrats, with no willingness to use inherent contempt, would never produce the kind of new evidence that an independent criminal prosecutor would. People look back fondly to the Nixon hearings, forgetting that he was being threatened with impeachment, and forgetting the miserable failures of commissions that investigated the Kennedy assassination, Iran-Contra, 9/11, and other crimes. A commission might offer immunity as a way to motivate witnesses. And the delay of the whole process would only strengthen calls to "move forward." But Congress had by now come to see holding hearings as its essential function, completely apart from whether those hearings would serve a substantive purpose. It was just what Congress did.

This is not to suggest that there was not still mountains of evidence known to exist, but not yet made public (not to mention what Rumsfeld would have called the unknown unknowns—the evidence of crimes we hadn't even heard of). Nor am I suggesting that some members of Congress didn't want to use hearings and commissions toward good ends, including making prosecutions even harder to reasonably avoid. But failing to simply enforce the law amounted to buying into the idea that there was something special and legitimately extra-judicial about the behavior of our elected officials and their staff during a "war on terror." Delaying justice was likely to amount, yet again, to denying it, and to establishing for future presidents that the penalty for open criminality would be moderately critical hearings.

While this debate was going on in early 2009 over whether to hold a "truth commission" or do nothing (those were the two main positions in the media), more evidence of crimes came dribbling out through law-suits filed by the ACLU and through the choice of Obama's White House to release selected Bush memos. Over the past eight years more evidence had come from journalists, bloggers, and lawsuits than from hearings, and that appeared likely to remain true. President Obama had the option of releasing a great many more documents known to exist, but whether he would do so quickly, slowly, or never, I couldn't predict, although I could predict that no congressional committee and probably no congressionally established commission would try to force him to.

Some members of Congress, including Nancy Pelosi, who had always opposed impeachment, came out in support of prosecution, speaking as if the crimes they'd never before recognized were universally known. I suspected that Pelosi's interest was in avoiding the sort of independent truth commission that Senator Leahy described as looking into the complicity of Democrats as well as Republicans in the horrors of the years from 2001 to 2008. Others who appeared to have that same interest, such as new Senate Intelligence Committee Chairwoman Diane Feinstein, proposed closed-door classified hearings as a substitute for a public commission or a commission that would publish its results.

While activists were appreciative of any gestures in the direction of governmental accountability, many were wary of panels or commissions that might end up delaying or substituting for law enforcement. In claiming "state secrets" to block a civil suit against an airplane company involved in rendition and torture (Mohamed v. Jeppesen), the Department of Justice argued that there were lots of good alternatives to enforcing the law, such as congressional oversight, foreign relations, inspector general investigations, and reports. On February 10, 2009, the Atlantic reported that a "senior administration official" also argued for alternative avenues to hold Bush officials accountable, rather than law enforcement, such as a "truth commission idea, a DOJ truth commission, or even investigations run by the Justice Department."[63]

Senator Leahy himself argued against prosecution on the grounds that it would be horrible if such a prosecution failed, and he character-ized prosecutions as "vengeance."[64] But by April, 2009, he admitted that his Senate colleagues were not supporting his "truth commission" idea. He blamed Republican senators, of course, but there was no significant support from Democrats. Nor was there major support in the House for Conyers' similar proposal. It had twenty-nine cosponsors, including one Republican. Word that these commissions were not finding support was, understandably, taken as bad news by many. But I'm not sure it was bad news.

The idea of truth and reconciliation in this context had never included reconciliation with Iraqis, Afghanis, Pakistanis, Palestinians, torture victims, spying victims, victims of political prosecutions, or anyone other than the commission members themselves. Real reconciliation was years away from even being comprehensible to, much less supported by, the US Senate.

There were and are very useful things that Congress or an outside commission could do, but most of them have nothing to do with punishing or deterring crimes, or reconciling victims and abusers. The only thing that can deter future crimes of the sort that have been committed is criminal prosecution. Any commission begun before a special prosecutor is appointed would risk serving as a substitute for what is most needed, and risk having its requests and subpoenas ignored as Congress's have been. But once a prosecutorial investigation is begun, Congress will be able to take up related issues without creating a substitute for prosecution and with better public understanding that there are advantages to complying with subpoenas and other legal obligations.

A commission dedicated to truth would have a hard time ignoring ongoing criminal investigations in Spain and Britain, and likely indictments there and elsewhere. The reconciliation would almost inevitably develop into opposition to international law, which is exactly the offense we most need to correct and deter.

A nonpartisan commission would be a bipartisan commission, with half of the members named by each of the two parties into which our government is now more fundamentally divided than it is into three institutional branches. Both parties would favor a commission designed to cover up congressional complicity in crimes. And if there is some hope that a congressional committee might be motivated to restore constitutional powers to Congress, an outside commission would not be as likely to have that interest.

A commission unable to compel witnesses could be designed to bribe them with immunity for their crimes. But unless there are prosecutions and the serious threat of prosecutions, that immunity is not a valuable bribe. And the granting of immunity is not justified by the circumstances. Our justice system is not overrun by too many defendants to be processed. It is simply refusing to prosecute a small number of individuals against whom there is extremely powerful evidence and for whom trials could potentially be very, very swift.

While we will never have the complete "truth" about anything and should not encourage the false belief that we lack probable cause to prosecute, obtaining more information about crimes and abuses is certainly desirable. But more information is likely to be obtained by a criminal prosecution than anything else. And more information is likely to quickly be made public by demanding the release of memos, e-mails, minutes, reports from the DOJ's Office of Professional Responsibility, reports from the CIA, reports from the Senate Armed Services Committee, and so on than from any hearing or panel or commission. If Congress wants the truth about the treatment of prisoners, it should demand their release and listen to them. If it wants whistleblowers to speak, it should legislate protections for them. If it wants new stories to break, it should bust the media monopolies.

The sort of discussion most needed from Congress is not a weak substitute for a criminal investigation, but rather a study of how to restore constitutional powers to Congress that have been usurped by presidents. A committee or panel or commission could most profitably examine treaty power, appointment power, pardon power, power of the purse, power of war, and power to legislate, signing statements, secret laws, secret agencies, secret budgets, state secrets claims, executive privilege claims, vice presidential powers, the power of impeachment, the power of subpoena, and the practice of inherent contempt. The most effective way to do this, and probably the only possible way to do it, would be with a House-only select committee. Not only is the Senate hopeless, but a proper list of democratizing reforms would include, as discussed below, proposing the elimination of the Senate.

A public airing of the crimes and abuses, if it did not interfere with criminal proceedings, if it enforced (or persuaded the Justice Department to enforce) its demands, and if it was covered by the media, would certainly be useful. It would be less useful, however, if it repeated the endless public airings of the past two years in hearings that have been largely ignored by the media, or if it refused to call the crimes crimes, or if it reinforced the loss by Congress of the power of subpoena. Again the best and probably the only possible way to make this happen would be with a House select committee, subsequent to the beginning of a criminal investigation.

Existing committees and subcommittees can also hold closed and open hearings without delay, and with the possible advantage of Democrats holding majorities over the Republicans on every committee. Some were planning to do so. Committees could, if they chose, reissue all of their subpoenas that were refused over the previous two years. Enforcing those subpoenas, into which much thought and work was poured, would reveal more than any bipartisan commission would be likely to.

In March and April 2009, the movement was rapidly and impressively building to demand a special prosecutor, to prosecute locally and abroad as well, and to legislate reforms through Congress. The State Secrets Protection Act, a resolution challenging an unconstitutional treaty with Iraq, a bill to restrict the abuse of National Security letters, and other good bills expected just after the April recess marked a trend in the necessary direction. The possibility of impeaching torture memo author and now federal judge Jay Bybee was even under discussion in the halls of Congress. By impeaching Bybee, Congress could restore its primary power, the one that gives teeth to the others.

In the meantime, members of Congress could urge the new attorney general Eric Holder to appoint a special prosecutor. While Congress members John Conyers, Jerrold Nadler, and Nancy Pelosi and Senators Carl Levin, Sheldon Whitehouse, Jack Reed, Russ Feingold, and Charles Schumer expressed some support for the idea, none of them—much less the fifty-six Democrats who had written to Michael Mukasey—had publicly written to Holder to make this request by April 2009. Then, on April 28, 2009, Conyers, Nadler, and fourteen other Democratic members of the House Judiciary Committee finally sent a similar letter to Holder.[65] Day was beginning to break.

12. EMBARRASSING EXCUSES

Throughout the 110th Congress a myth was spread very successfully by the Congress and the media that Congress could only end the occupation of Iraq by passing a bill. This would have required the support of sixty-seven senators to override a veto, and sixty senators just to invoke cloture and break a Republican filibuster. But this was a stalling tactic. It simply was not true that Congress had to pass a bill at all. In order to end the legal funding of the occupation, Congress simply had to stop passing bills to fund it. The Democrats had a large majority in the House and a narrow one in the Senate. But if your goal is stopping a bill, rather than passing one, you only have to succeed in one house or the other.

It is possible for a majority of members of the House to force a bill to the floor over the wishes of the Speaker. To do this, 218 Congress members would have had to take the highly unusual step of signing a discharge petition. Even if a lot of Republicans did that, it is highly unlikely that many Democrats would have opposed their party leadership and the will of the public to force a funding bill to the floor for a very unpopular war. Pelosi persuaded a lot of Democrats to vote for the war and could have used the same techniques to persuade a smaller number not to oppose her effort to end it, had she wanted to end it.

Any proposal to fund the war in the Senate that might have been brought by Republicans or pro-war Democrats could have been blocked by forty-one senators, and the Democrats had fifty-one. While not all bills can be filibustered (appropriations bills can be, budget reconciliation bills cannot), you can hardly claim you need sixty votes to get past a filibuster without admitting that with only forty-one you could launch your own filibuster, and that with fifty-one you could defeat any bill at all. In addition, Senate Majority Leader Harry Reid alone could have refused to bring a bill to the floor, and any other senator could have put a secret hold on a bill.

What's more, the Democrats could have brought to the floor of both houses, as many times as necessary, bills to fund only a withdrawal of troops and nothing else. Of course, this would have been comical, given that the cost of withdrawing all troops and equipment from Iraq is pocket change to our bloated Pentagon. But it would have headed off the non-sensical attacks in the media that would have claimed that defunding a war was somehow an attack on the men and women sent to risk their lives in it. And this strategy would have made efforts to pass war funding over the heads of the leadership even less likely to gain traction.

Not only did millions of Americans, organized by United for Peace and Justice, Progressive Democrats of America, and many other groups, including those in the After Downing Street Coalition, lobby Congress to fund only withdrawal, but Congresswoman Barbara Lee introduced a bill and attempted to introduce an amendment to accomplish just that. At one point, ninety-one members of Congress signed onto a letter from the Progressive Caucus committing them to voting only to fund withdrawal. (Most of them went back on their word.) And, of course, Congressman Kucinich—a lone voice for peace in the wilderness—constantly hammered home the point that Congress simply had to refrain from bringing up a bill at all.

Congress has acted successfully in this manner before. The Vietnam War was de-funded by Congress (albeit after most troops were home). In 1970, Congress banned the use of funds to put US troops in Cambodia or to advise the Cambodian military. Then, in 1973, Congress set a date to cut off funds for combat activities in all of Southeast Asia. Congress had cut off the funding for the Contras in Nicaragua, and Reagan had secretly and illegally sold weapons to Iran and given the money to the Contras, leading to the Iran-Contra scandal during which Democrats carefully avoided impeachment in order to "focus on the elections" that they proceeded to lose, thus handing us the Bush dynasty. In 1994, Congress set a date to cut off funding for military operations in Somalia. In 1998, Congress set a date to cut off funding for military operations in Bosnia.

In January 2007, as the 110th Congress was just beginning, Senator Russ Feingold sought to remind his colleagues of all of this, chairing a Senate Judiciary Committee hearing on "Exercising Congress's Constitutional Power to End a War." Feingold said,

The Constitution gives Congress the explicit power "[to] declare War," "[t]o raise and support Armies," "[t]o provide and maintain a Navy," and "[t]o make Rules for the Government and Regulation of the land and naval Forces." In addition, under Article I, "No Money shall be drawn from the Treasury, but in Consequence of Appropriations made by Law." These are direct quotes from the Constitution of the United States. Yet to hear some in the Administration talk, it is as if these provisions were written in invisible ink. They were not. These powers are a clear and direct statement from the founders of our republic that Congress has authority to declare, to define, and ultimately, to end a war. Our founders wisely kept the power to fund a war separate from the power to conduct a war. In their brilliant design of our system of government, Congress got the power of the purse, and the President got the power of the sword. As James Madison wrote, "Those who are to conduct a war cannot in the nature of things, be proper or safe judges, whether a war ought to be commenced, continued, or concluded."[66]

The rest of the Senate and most of the House were not listening. I don't mean they disagreed. I mean they literally were not paying any attention. In October 2007, Senate Majority Leader Harry Reid was interviewed on the Ed Schultz radio program. Schultz asked Reid why he didn't just stop funding the war, and I got the impression that Reid had never seriously considered the idea:

> SCHULTZ: But Senator, don't you have the power to say you're not going to get the money even without sixty votes?

> REID: Sure we have the power on anything to stop the money, that's what it's all about, that's why we have three separate branches of government. But the thing we have to do is make sure we do it the right way. It's not a question of all or nothing, it's a question of making sure we do the right thing. What Feingold and I have pushed and we're going to continue to do that . . . get all the troops to start redeploying immediately, get all the

troops out of there by June except those needed for counterter-rorism, protecting our assets we have there, and a limited force for training Iraqis. That's what Feingold and I believe should happen, we're going to continue to push that. The majority of the Democrats support it, but not all the Democrats.

SCHULTZ: But you could say we're not bringing this to the floor, the funding's over, correct?

REID [very slowly, as if never having considered doing such a thing]: Yes, we could do that, yes.

SCHULTZ: Why don't you do that? The American people want you to do that.

REID: Ed, it's a situation where we have to do what is right . . . I say that Feingold and Reid are right. We say there should be imme-diate redeployment, set a deadline that everybody should be out except a limited number. That means they're gonna have to have some money . . . the troops there fighting counterterrorism, which we need, that is going to be some money, we have to do that.[67]

The complete obliviousness of the Senate Majority Leader and most other members of the Senate and House to the message that hundreds of thousands of activists were constantly e-mailing, phone calling, faxing, lobbying, and interrupting public events about was extremely frustrating. Even those who had begun pushing for an end to the war gave up hope. When asked in a public meeting to lead a filibuster of the next funding bill, Senator Feingold refused to attempt it.[68] Feingold, and the rest of us, were done in by a piece of childish nonsense repeated endlessly and unanimously by the univocal US corporate media: ending the funding would conflict with "supporting the troops." When we frame the debate over war money with the idea that funding war amounts to "supporting troops," the debate gets constrained: should we fund the war, or fund the war more and faster?

If, on the other hand, a debate over funding a war were framed by the idea that what you're funding is not troops, but a war, then one possible position in the debate would favor cutting off the funds. While you can cut off funds for war or Halliburton or Blackwater, you can never cut off funds for troops. I don't mean that you physically can't. I mean that politically it is impossible that any politician is going to support something understood to mean "cutting off funds for troops." But if we understood that the troops are going to have better living conditions and a higher chance of living, period, if we bring them home, and if we could talk about cutting off funds for profiteers, then cutting off the funds would become politically possible.

Attorney General Alberto Gonzales testified as follows before the Senate Judiciary Committee: "Be careful about criticizing the Department."[69] Gonzales suggested that criticizing him amounted to "attacking the career professionals [in the Justice Department]." Senator Dick Durbin responded to this by blurting out a bit of seldom-spoken truth: "That's like saying anyone who disagrees with the president's policy on the war is attacking the soldiers."

Yet Durbin and his colleagues were in the press every single day defensively promoting the idea that refusing to fund war amounts to not supporting soldiers. The troops would have been amazed and bewildered to learn that they might be receiving funding and that bringing them home would constitute an attack on them. The majority of those serving in Iraq had told pollsters in 2006 that they wanted the war ended that year.[70]

I tried to call the bluffs of all the "support the troopsers". Each time they passed another "supplemental" it amounted to approximately $1 million per troop in Iraq. I proposed actually giving the troops that money. If the money was for the troops, then give the troops the damn money, I said, a million dollars each. Put it right in their hands. The troops that wanted to give part or all of their share to the contractors and mercenaries and profiteers could do that. Those who wanted to fund a continued occupation could do that. Some would probably share a little with Iraqis. And those who chose to could buy a plane ticket home. After all, General David Petraeus had bragged to Congress about how the United States was selling commercial airplanes to Iraq. Somebody needed to use them. Alas, Congress ignored my proposal, as well as all serious proposals and bills that involved cutting off the flow of funds. In fact, if Congressman David Obey was at all typical, Congress members considered any proposals to stop funding the war to be ideas suited only to "idiot liberals."

Obey was a top Democrat in charge of drafting the bills to fund the wars. Tina Richards was the mother of an Iraq War veteran about to be deployed to Iraq for the third time. They spoke in the hallway of a congressional office building, and the encounter was captured on video:

RICHARDS: Hi, I'm Tina Richards. I had left a poem that my son had written [with one of your staffers]. I was wondering if he ever got it to you? He's a United States Marine, he's done two tours in Iraq. He's going to be deployed for a third tour.

OBEY: I honestly don't know, I'm so buried in appropriations bills, I only get back over here for about ten minutes a day. I've seen very little in my office.

RICHARDS: OK, because my son is suffering from PTSD, he's had several suicide attempts.

OBEY: I'm sorry to hear that.

RICHARDS: He tried to get help through the VA, and it took us six months to get his first appointment with the VA. In ten minutes they told him, "It sounds like you've got childhood issues." But he was able to do four years in the Marines, two deployments to Iraq, honorable discharge, presidential unit citation, and he was just fine for that, and now that he needs help from the VA he's been told that he's got childhood issues.

OBEY: We're holding hearings today and Wednesday. They're continually screwing those guys. The *Washington Post* is full of it.

RICHARDS: Well I've been talking about this for over a year now, and nobody seems to be paying much attention.

OBEY: Well, I guarantee what's happening at Walter Reed... [indecipherable]... whole damn thing...

RICHARDS: Well what about the, are you going to be voting against the supplemental?

OBEY: Absolutely not, I'm the sponsor of it for heaven's sake.

[NOTE: that didn't stop him from voting against the June 2008 supplemental after it was clear it would pass. Pelosi, too, voted No after orchestrating passage.]

RICHARDS: For the . . . uhh . . . to continue the war?

OBEY: It doesn't. The president wants to continue the war. We're trying to use the supplemental to end the war, but you can't end the war by going against the supplemental. It's time these idiot liberals understand that. There's a big difference between funding the troops and ending the war. I'm not gonna deny body armor. I'm not gonna deny funding for veterans' hospitals, defense hospitals, so you can help people with medical problems, that's what you're gonna do if you're going against that bill. [NOTE: You could of course fund veterans' care in a separate bill. You could do the same with body armor, except that it's not needed in most US neighborhoods, and you'd be bringing our men and women home.]

RICHARDS: There should be enough money already in the regular defense bills . . .

OBEY: (interrupting) Well there isn't.

RICHARDS: . . . without continuing the funding for the war.

OBEY: There isn't. There isn't. That's not the way it works. The money in the defense bill, it pays for a standing army, but it doesn't pay for these recurring costs. We're gonna add over a billion dollars more to what the president was asking for in that bill, so we can deal with exactly the type of problems you're talking about. How the hell do you get money to the hospitals if you don't provide the funding?

RICHARDS: Are you going to be in support of . . .

OBEY: I hate the war. I voted against it to start with. I was the first guy in Congress to call for Rumsfeld's resignation, but we don't have the votes to defund the war, we shouldn't because that also means defunding everything in that bill to help the guys who are the victims of war.

RICHARDS: Well there's an amendment to the supplemental that's being proposed to fully fund the withdrawal of the troops.

OBEY: That makes no sense. It doesn't work that way. The language we have in the resolution ends the authority for the war, it makes it illegal to proceed with the war. You don't have to defund something if the war doesn't exist. [NOTE: Obey's bill did no such thing, and in any case would not have meant that Richards' suggestion made no sense. Arguably, continuing to fund something that didn't exist would have made less sense than defunding it.]

RICHARDS: Oh, I didn't know that was in the supplemental.

OBEY: That's the problem, that's the problem. (Emphatic right arm gesturing.) The liberal groups are jumping around without knowing what the hell is in the bill! You don't have to cut off the funding for an activity that no longer is legal! [NOTE: Read that last sentence a few times.]

RICHARDS: Oh, and then approach it from that way.

OBEY: We're shutting it off.

At this point, Pete Perry, a peace activist who was with Richards, joined the conversation:

PERRY: What about the Church amendment that helped end the Vietnam war back in '72, '73?

OBEY: (Emphatically, voice raised) It took us thirty-one different efforts to get there, I was here for that.

PERRY: OK.

OBEY: I know what the hell I'm talking about.

PERRY: Did that end the ground war in Vietnam?

OBEY: No it didn't. The political pressure on the administration ended the war. The amendment that finally ended the funding was the [undecipherable] amendment, I was the sponsor of that amendment ...

PERRY: But if you pass the resolution, isn't he still the com-, mander in chief? Then ...

OBEY: [Voice raised.] We don't have the votes to pass it! We couldn't even get the votes to pass a nonbinding resolution one week ago! How the hell do you think we're gonna get the votes to cut off the war?

PERRY: By stopping the funding. [NOTE: Perry may have been suggesting the option of not bringing any funding bills to a vote. In any case, Obey was clearly stuck in the mindset of having to pass a bill in order to accomplish anything.]

OBEY: How, if you don't have the votes? It takes two hundred ...

PERRY: With a filibuster his supplemental request.

OBEY: There is no filibuster in the House.

PERRY: In the Senate they could do it, and all they need is forty-one votes. [NOTE: This was true, and Obey had no response to it.]

OBEY: I'm sorry. ... No, I'm not gonna vote for it [sic]. ... I'm the sponsor of the bill that's gonna be on the floor, and that bill ends the war ... if that isn't good enough for you, then you're smoking something that ain't legal! [Of course, funding wars of aggression is not legal, and Obey's bill did not in any way end any war and couldn't possibly have done so, because such a bill would have been vetoed if it made it through the Senate. Obey's bill actually contained a nonbinding suggestion to the president to eventually partially end the war, and even that was destined to be vetoed.]

PERRY: No I'm not, sir, no I'm not.

OBEY: You got your facts screwed up.

PERRY: It's nonbinding. How would it affect what he's doing on 1600 Pennsylvania Avenue?

OBEY: We don't have the votes! (He opens right side of suit jacket.) Do you see a magic wand in my pocket?

PERRY: No.

OBEY: How the hell are we gonna get the votes for it? We ain't got the votes! We do have the votes if you guys quit screwin' it up. We do have the votes to end the legal authority to end the war [sic], that's the same as defunding it. (At this point a staffer approaches Rep. Obey and taps him on the arm.)

PERRY: Tell us how we can help.

OBEY: I'm not going to debate it, you've got your facts wrong. (Obey then turns and walks away with his staffer to enter his office.)[71]

The corporate media was playing along with the notion that the Democrats were opposing a war by funding it. It's not surprising that Obey would not appreciate being confronted with the grotesqueness of this. Imagine if Obey or Pelosi had decided to mortgage their house, empty their bank accounts, max out their credit cards, and give all that money to Halliburton with a little gift card expressing their sincere opposition to everything Halliburton did. They would have looked no more foolish than they did, and I'd have preferred that scenario because they'd have been leaving the rest of us out of it.

In the spring of 2008, Democrats.com commissioned a poll from a corporate polling company asking questions that none of the other pollsters were asking. It found that a majority of Americans wanted Congress to cut off the funding and demand that the president end the war within six months.[72] That was a majority of the rightful sovereigns of this country, and they had heard more about Iraq than any other topic in the news over the preceding six years. If Obey wouldn't trust us on this one, what would he ever trust us on?

For those who understood how badly our military needed fewer troops, rather than more, there was also this alternative: for the same amount of money that each war funding bill wasted (including the 2008 supplemental that included a "GI Bill" amendment as cover for what it primarily did to GIs), we could have made college free for everyone, all veterans and all non-veterans. Doing so would have provided young people not from the overclass with the option of not entering the military unless they really wanted to.

To add insult to the injury Congress inflicted on itself with its excuses for inaction, in November 2008 lame duck President Bush agreed to a treaty (the so-called SOFA discussed above) that, at the insistence of the Iraqi government, set a firm date for withdrawal—exactly what Congress had been too cowardly to accomplish with the power of the purse. Bush left approval of the treaty up to the Iraqi Parliament and ignored the pathetic ghost of his own nation's government on Capitol Hill.

One of the better activist organizations that lobbies for peace is called Peace Action. It produces scorecards on Congress members each year based on their votes on a handful of selected occasions on topics related to peace and disarmament. Such documents are useful for identifying those Congress members who are doing a little bit better than the others. But the overall portrait suggested by such scorecards is what I hope to call into question. I was struck by this when in April 2009 I received an e-mail from Peace Action describing its scorecard report for 2008 and reading, in part,

> In the midst of an emerging sea change in American foreign policy thinking, 117 congressional leaders have recently demonstrated an especially strong record of leadership towards a more effective national security strategy. This is according to a peace and security performance report on the 2008 session of the 110th Congress, released jointly by Peace Action, the nation's largest grassroots peace organization, and its largest affiliate Peace Action West. . . . Fifty-eight members of Congress earned a perfect score in the report, including Senator Sherrod Brown (D-OH) and Representatives John Lewis (D-GA-5), George Miller (D-CA-7) and Raul Grijalva (D-AZ-7). Fifty-nine scored 90 percent.

On numerous occasions in 2007 and 2008, 117 No votes on funding bills, or Yes votes on amendments, or No votes on procedural votes to bring bills to the floor, or even a handful of votes in committees could have made a difference and saved lives or at least completely altered the story of what was happening in our government. Often large blocks of Republicans were voting the right way for the wrong reasons, and 117 Democrats joining them would have been decisive, or at least forced other members to change their votes or change the bills, for better or worse.

For the record, on March 23, 2007, in roll call 186 on HR 1591, the vote to fund the wars in Iraq and Afghanistan was 218–212, and only fourteen of the 212 were Democrats. (Apparently eight of the fourteen had the right motivation, as did one Republican and one Libertarian.) The rest of the 117 perfect Congress members? They voted to fund more war.

On April 25, 2007, in roll call 265 on HR 1591 the vote to fund the wars was 218–208, and only thirteen of the 208 were Democrats. On May 10, 2007, in roll call 336 on HR 2207 the vote to fund the wars was 302–120, and only five of the 120 were Democrats. On November 14, 2007, in roll call 1108 on HR 4156 the vote to fund the wars was 218–203, and only fifteen of the 203 were Democrats.

When they could vote against war funding but allow the funding to still pass, a lot of Democrats did the right thing. On May 24, 2007, in roll call 425 on HR 2206 the vote was 280–142, and 140 of the 142 were Democrats. The Democratic leadership had maneuvered a bill through with primarily Republican support. They did this again on June 19, 2008, when roll call 431 on HR 2642 funded the wars by a vote of 268–155, and 151 of the 155 were Democrats.

A month earlier, on May 15, 2008, in roll call 328 on HR 2642, a vote to fund the wars had failed by 141–149, with 147 of the 149 being Democrats. In this case 132 Republicans had voted "present." This made a lot of news, and is the only House war funding vote included in the grading system that got 108 House members such high marks on the 2008 scorecard, but the funding came through a month later because the Democratic "leadership" made the bill appeal to more Republicans.

The preceding evidence suggests that when a significant number of Democrats very rarely did the right thing, it didn't matter. But the above are only a small sample of key votes. On September 26, 2007, there was a vote in roll call 911 on HJ Res 52 to continue funding wars into 2008 at the same rate as in 2007. It passed by 404–14, with thirteen Democrats and one Libertarian voting no. There were numerous unheralded votes of this sort, votes on military budgets and overall budgets, and above all, procedural votes on whether to hold votes. Republicans and right-wing Democrats sometimes block procedural votes until bills are changed to satisfy them. I can't recall progressive Democrats ever having done so. It wouldn't be polite.

Nor would it be polite to filibuster a war funding bill in the Senate or to put a hold on such a bill. Even less well-mannered would be speaking out publicly against the leadership of one's own party. Those would be the actions of Congress members actually interested in blocking war funding, as opposed to the actions of those wanting to occasionally go on record with the proper votes. But can you imagine the change in the public discourse if 117 members of Congress had voted No on every war funding bill and every procedural vote to bring such bills to the floor, and if they had publicly chastised their colleagues who voted to fund war? What if those 117 had joined the peace movement or engaged in nonviolent resistance? Can you imagine? Could the Democratic leadership have withstood the pressure of 117 members of the House and Senate constantly demanding an end to any more funding bills? Dennis Kucinich actually did this, but he did it alone. It would have been difficult and considered very impolite. It would have tempted party leaders and campaign funders and media producers to take harsh actions. But unless someone does everything I can imagine them doing, I'm reluctant to call their performance "perfect," no matter how great their voting record may be on a handful of bills.[73]

With 2008 in the past, by 2009 the excuses were virtually gone, at least for the moment. Filibusters and vetoes cannot be seriously blamed for Congress's failure to represent us. And of course filibusters and vetoes did not deserve the blame to begin with. Congress members did. Cheney and Bush could not have done any of what they did without Congress. But, by the same token, Congress could not have done any of what it has done without us. It is our responsibility to make our demands clear and forceful, and to devise strategies that hold our representatives accountable if they fail to represent us.

III.

UNDOING THE IMPERIAL PRESIDENCY

13. A WORLD WITHOUT EMPIRE

Let's start with a quick survey of the current situation. Here's a test of your knowledge of the place of the United States in the world. Don't worry, I wouldn't get them all right either. Just try to get close, and then think about which ones you missed and why. Quick, go grab a pencil!

1. What percentage of the people in the world live in the United States of America? _____

2. Where does the United States rank on a list of nations with the largest gross domestic products (GDP)? (First? Second? Twenty-ninth? Eighty-fourth?) _____

3. Where does the United States rank on a list of nations with the largest GDP per capita? _____

4. What percentage of the US GDP per capita, adjusted for "purchasing power parity," is the median national GDP per capita? That is to say, for the nation right in the middle of the rankings, how much richer or poorer, at least by this crude measure, is someone with average income than someone with average income in the United States? For twice as rich, write 200 percent, for half as rich write 50 percent. _____

5. The United Nations uses the "Human Poverty Index" to measure deprivation (reduced lifespan, adult illiteracy, lack of clean water and health services, underweight children, etc.) within nineteen wealthy nations. With one being the least poverty and nineteen being the most, where does the United States rank? _____

6. Of all the nations in the world, where does Save the Children rank the United States on a list of the best nations in which to be a mother (in

terms of health, education, maternity leave, life expectancy, etc.)?
_____

7. Of all the nations in the world, where does the United States rank on the Environmental Performance Index developed by Yale University, Columbia University, the World Economic Forum, and the Joint Research Centre of the European Commission to measure environmental health, air pollution, water resources, biodiversity and habitat, productive natural resources, and climate change? _____

8. Can you name the top two nations on a list of the biggest producers of carbon dioxide, a major contributor to global warming? _____

9. Of all the nations in the world, where does the United States rank in press freedom, as measured by Reporters Without Borders?
_____

10. What percentage of the oil produced in the world is used by the United States? (Extra credit if you can name the single biggest US consumer of oil.) _____

11. In 1970, wealthy nations resolved, through the United Nations, that by the middle of the coming decade, they would each devote what percentage of their gross national product (GNP) to aid for less wealthy nations? _____

12. What percentage of gross national income (GNI) does the United States government now devote to foreign aid? _____

13. Where does that place the United States on a list of the nations contributing most generously to poor countries? _____

14. What does US aid increasingly consist of, instead of money? (Hint, it's also the biggest US export.) _____

15. Approximately how many military bases does the United States maintain within the United States and its territories? And how many in other people's countries? _____

16. Approximately what percentage of nations around the world have US troops stationed in them? _____

17. In what percentage of the years in which the United States has existed have US troops not been actively engaged in significant armed adventures on foreign shores? _____

18. Over the past two centuries, how many nations has the United States attacked, invaded, policed, overthrown, or occupied? _____

19. Can you list, in order, the two nations that Europeans said they considered the most dangerous in a 2006–2007 *Financial Times* survey?

_____

20. Where does the United States rank on a list of nations most deeply in financial debt to other nations? _____

21. How many deaths are there worldwide each year due to acts of terrorism? _____

22. How many deaths are there worldwide each year due to poverty and malnutrition? _____

ANSWERS:

1. 4.5 percent. (U.S. 306,323,675, World 6,776,781,205 as of 17:51 GMT (EST+5) Apr 30, 2009).[1]

2. First. (The United States is either first or second [with the European Union second or first, and Japan third], depending on which list you consult. But the European Union is not a single nation. This is the case, as well, if the GDP is calculated using a method called purchasing power parity).[2]

3. The United States comes in tenth, fifteenth, or seventeenth depending on which list you consult, and fourth, sixth, or eighth if calculated using PPP (European nations are listed individually, and nations ranking above the United States in at least one list include Qatar, Luxembourg, Norway, Singapore, Brunei, Liechtenstein, Bermuda, Kuwait, Jersey, Switzerland, Denmark, Ireland, Iceland, United Arab Emirates, Sweden, Netherlands, Finland, Austria, Australia, and Belgium.)[3]

4. 17 percent. (Of 180 nations in the International Monetary Fund's 2008 list, the nintieth ranked nation, Jamaica, has a per capita GDP of $7,766,

compared to $46,859 for the United States. Eighty-nine nations on the list have smaller per capita GDP than Jamaica.)

5. Seventeenth place. (Of nineteen nations, including Canada, Japan, Australia, the United States, and thirteen European nations, only Italy and Ireland fall below the United States.)[4]

6. Twenty-seventh place.[5]

7. Thirty-ninth place.[6]

8. China, United States. (Until recently the United States has been in first place, but various sources estimate that China has moved to the top of the list or predict that it soon will.)[7]

9. Forty-first place.[8]

10. 24 percent, significantly more than any other nation.[9] (The US military uses an estimated half million barrels of oil a day.[10])

11. 0.7 percent.[11]

12. 0.15 percent, plus another 0.16 percent in private contributions. (The United States gives more money than any other nation, but a smaller amount as a percentage of income or per capita than many other countries. While Americans believe their government devotes 15 to 20 percent of its budget to foreign aid, the truth is much less than 1 percent.[12])

13. Twenty-second among twenty-two wealthy nations, or fifteenth if including private contributions.[13]

14. Weapons.[14]

15. Approximately 6,000 in the United States and its territories, and approximately 1,000 in other countries.[15]

16. Approximately 77 percent.[16]

17. 14 percent.[17]

18. Sixty-two and rising.[18]

19. United States, China.[19]

20. First place.[20]

21. The US State Department reported there were more than 22,000 deaths from terrorism in 2007. Over half of those killed or injured were Muslims.[21]

22. About 9,125,000 people die every year of hunger or hunger-related causes, according to the United Nations.[22]

How did you do?

On March 6, 2007, the director of the Program on International Policy Attitudes (PIPA) at the University of Maryland, Steven Kull, began his address to a subcommittee of the House Foreign Affairs Committee by saying that he had bad news and good news.[23] The bad news was that opinions of the United States around the world had plummeted to abysmal record lows. The good news was that, "People around the world say that the problems they have with the US concern its policies, not its values." They hate our bombs, not our freedoms.

PIPA asked people in twenty-six countries whether the United States was having a positive or negative influence in the world. In only four countries did a majority think the United States was having a mostly positive influence. US State Department data from 1999 compared to recent polling by Pew found that favorable views of the United States had dropped from 83 to 56 percent in the UK, from 78 to 37 percent in Germany, from 77 to 49 percent in Morocco, from 75 to 30 percent in Indonesia, and so on. In his speech, Kull added a rather odd bit of analysis, saying, "These numbers are also not simply a reaction to the US decision to go to war in Iraq. Views of the US did go down sharply after the beginning of the Iraq war in 2003. But now, nearly four years later, they continue to move downward."

This was a strange thing to say, because the Iraq war had only worsened and not ended. It was continuing to worsen at the time Kull testified, and since 2003 it had come to include all sorts of additional news (Abu Ghraib, death counts, refugee crises, civilian massacres) that common sense would suggest people would disapprove of—not to mention the supposed "reelection" by the United States of the men who had launched the war, an event that itself had destroyed a lot of respect for the United States. Nor had the occupation of Iraq vanished from the world media the way it often had in the United States. People around the world continued to hear about the crimes in Iraq and sometimes to see images that would never be deemed appropriate for US "audiences." None of that proves that the numbers were simply a reaction to Iraq. Nothing like this is ever simple. But Kull's avoidance of blaming the Iraq war, while no doubt appreciated by Congress and the US media, was not justified by anything he said, and may have been an awkward attempt to avoid sounding like a leftist while still presenting honest information.

In fact, PIPA's poll asked about six different areas, and the one that met with the highest disapproval (75 percent) was US handling of the Iraq War. In comparison, 69 percent disapproved of US treatment of prisoners, 68 percent disapproved of how the United States handled the war between Israel and Hezbollah in Lebanon, 61 percent disapproved of US handling of Iran's nuclear program, 58 percent disapproved of US handling of global warming, and 55 percent disapproved of US handling of North Korea's nuclear program. Further suggesting the significance of Iraq, Kull went on to stress that, "The US military presence in the Middle East is exceedingly unpopular in virtually all countries. On average 69 percent believe the US military presence there 'provokes more conflict than it prevents' while just 16 percent see it as a stabilizing force."

The view around the world of the US invasion of Iraq was that the United States was placing itself outside of international law and giving itself the right to attack any nation it saw fit. "[I]n many countries around the world," Kull testified, "people express strong fears that the US will use military force against them. In virtually every country asked about this in polls done by Pew in 2003 and 2005, majorities perceived the US as a military threat to their country. This was even true of Turkey—our NATO ally—and Kuwait—a country the US has defended." And don't forget that quiz answer above: even Europeans see the United States as the most dangerous "rogue state." In March 2009 the US State Department criticized Algeria for human rights abuses, and in a typical rejection of the United States' right to any longer preach morality to others, the Algerian Interior Minister replied, "Americans should be telling us about what is going on at Guantánamo prison." Similarly, the United States would look silly if it asked Israel to stop contemplating an aggressive attack on Iran after threatening one ourselves for years.

While people around the world appreciated the eviction of Bush and Cheney's party from the White House in November 2008, actions carry more weight than personnel changes. The fact is, the rest of the world is looking at a much larger picture than most of us in the United States are seeing. The US military is not only in Iraq. It is in military bases all over the world. It is in the arming, funding, and training of oppressive regimes. It is in our threatening stance toward Iran and Pakistan. And overall, the way the world sees the United States is tied up in a long history of imperialist endeavors that have climaxed over the past eight years in the Middle East. This is not a new problem.[24]

Jackie Cabasso has written a paper called "StratCom in Context: The Hidden Architecture of US Militarism" that collects sources documenting the size of the US empire, which I've posted at www.afterdowningstreet/militarism. Cabasso cites Chalmers Johnson, who has written, "If there were an honest count, the actual size of our military empire would probably top 1,000 different bases in other people's countries."[25]

In a 2006 review of a Congressional Research Service study and two other surveys of US military interventions, journalist Gar Smith found that "in our country's 230 years of existence, there have been only thirty-one years in which US troops were not actively engaged in significant armed adventures on foreign shores. . . . The defining characteristic of our nation's foreign policy for 86 percent of our existence would appear to be a bellicose penchant for military intervention." According to Smith, over the past two centuries, the United States has attacked, invaded, policed, overthrown, or occupied sixty-two nations. A world map included with Cabasso's article makes clear how global the reach of these invasions has been. The graphic shows 156 countries with US troops, seventy with US bases, and forty-six outside the empire. Everyone knows about the major wars in places like Korea, Vietnam, and Iraq. Most people know something about the clandestine instigation of coups in South America. Probably fewer are aware that the United States' bad relationship with Iran began when CIA agent and grandson of Theodore Roosevelt, Kermit Roosevelt Jr., organized the overthrow of Iran's president, or that President Jimmy Carter armed Indonesia's attack on East Timor, or that the Bush-Cheney administration kidnapped and removed the elected president of Haiti. Many are aware of the anger generated by American military bases in places like Saudi Arabia, Yemen, Iraq, and Afghanistan. Fewer are aware of the fury with which ordinary people resent our bases in places like Korea and Europe, or of the resistance that has developed to Cold War structures like NATO that continue to exist in the absence of the Soviet Union. Almost no one in the United States spends time thinking about the fate of, for example, the people of Guam, which we have treated as a colony since World War II, turning the majority of the nation's land into a US military base and denying its people independence or full citizenship rights. Yet resistance—including organized nonviolent resistance—to our imperialist meddling is growing, and with it, awareness of what we have been doing.

People didn't organize suicide missions into the World Trade Center and the Pentagon because they disliked our freedoms. We have less freedom than various other nations they could have attacked. They disliked our policies. The hijackers may also have believed a bunch of religious nonsense and harbored religious hatred, but the apparent leader of the operation, Osama bin Laden, made clear that he wanted a change in US policies in Saudi Arabia and in Palestine. US "intelligence" agencies, even during the Bush-Cheney presidency, admitted that the occupation of Iraq is serving as a recruiting tool for terrorists. And that admission comes in the declassified summary of a National Intelligence Estimate (NIE). Past experience and anonymous reports both suggest that the classified version is more honest still. A *Washington Post* article based on comments from people who had seen the full NIE reports that:

> The war in Iraq has become a primary recruitment vehicle for violent Islamic extremists, motivating a new generation of potential terrorists around the world whose numbers may be increasing faster than the United States and its allies can reduce the threat, US intelligence analysts have concluded.[26]

People around the world are not generally opposing American empire so that they can have better lives and Americans have worse ones. There's not necessarily a zero-sum contest of that sort going on. We don't have to keep our empire going or give up our favorite luxuries (although there are plenty we should give up; we don't need them and they are doing other people harm). In fact, if we try to keep the empire going we will very likely lose everything: our rights, our economy, our environment as a habitable place, and quite possibly all of our lives in war. So shifting course is necessary for survival, but we don't have to see it as a setback. Author and journalist Helena Cobban argues that ending the British empire in Africa and Asia improved the lives of the people in Britain.[27]

Back to the good news. In his talk to the House Foreign Affairs Committee, Steven Kull also reported that people around the world express more fondness for the American people than they do for America as a nation. And it turns out they have good reason to. The American people may not be so much hypocrites as failures at self-governance. The hypocrisy is concentrated in Congress and the White House. That's the conclusion I draw from a March 2005 report by the Program on International Policy Attitudes (PIPA) on "The Federal Budget: the Public's Priorities."[28] PIPA told Americans the basic distribution of funds in a federal budget as proposed by President Bush and asked how they would rearrange the funding if they could. On average, Americans from across the political spectrum said they would cut the military budget by 31 percent, over twice the 15 percent cut that Congressman Dennis Kucinich had been proposing for years, earning himself the standing of a radical on Capitol Hill.

14. DETERRING REPETITION

"Well, it's about time!"
—Judge William Price in Iowa in July 2008, hearing the case of
citizens arrested for trying to make a citizens' arrest of Karl Rove.

By 2009, our failure in the United States to punish those guilty of war crimes was hurting our ability to persuade other nations not to engage in the same. A number of stories were reported, and probably more went unreported, of our State Department criticizing human rights abuses abroad and receiving essentially this reply: "Who the hell are you to talk?"

The first step in closing down an empire is bringing its emperors and oligarchs under the rule of law. While it may not be pleasant to stare recent crimes in the face and punish powerful people, failing to do so is very likely to lead to the repetition and expansion of the crimes and abuses that are thereby established as acceptable. Ceasing temporarily to engage in some of the crimes will not prevent those crimes from quickly coming back into use along with others not previously seen.

The purpose of prosecuting high officials for their crimes, or of prosecuting anyone for a crime, should not be revenge, retribution, or "justice" understood as revenge dressed up in a suit. We should rid ourselves of the notion of revenge, without which Bush and Cheney could never have persuaded so many people to cheer for their wars and abuses. Our purpose should be deterrence. As citizens, we must be clear about what is and is not acceptable from our leaders. Before we can move forward, lines must be drawn, including the very basic line establishing that laws will be enforced even against important individuals.

The possibilities of prosecution as a tool for holding Bush and Cheney accountable for their crimes are plentiful.[29] Nothing could have facilitated prosecution better than impeachment, and impeachment is still possible and appropriate, but prosecution can be conducted regardless of whether impeachment is ever attempted, fails, or succeeds. The new Justice Department under Attorney General Eric Holder, who supported the creation of an independent counsel for President Clinton, could create the same for Bush's and Cheney's far more serious violations. An Attorney General is supposed to place adherence to the law above obedience to the president. Congress could create an independent commission, independent of any desire to hide the complicity of members of either party in the crimes under investigation. But doing so should not become a substitute for criminal prosecution. State or local prosecutors, too, could prosecute Bush, Cheney, or their subordinates. There are also ways in which individuals can bring civil suits. Some of the crimes we're concerned with, including warrantless spying and torture, have statutes of limitations that will soon expire if not extended. Others, such as war crimes and murder, have no statutes of limitations. When the Justice Department finally prosecutes members of the Bush-Cheney White House, we will be able to think of our nation as governed by laws. In the meantime, some crimes can be tried at the state and local levels, and some can be tried by a foreign court or in the International Criminal Court.

By the spring of 2008, people were strategizing, not to mention fantasizing, about how a new president in 2009 would be able to hold the previous one accountable. But candidate Obama made clear he was not interested, telling the *Philadelphia Daily News*, "I would not want my first term consumed by what was perceived on the part of Republicans as a partisan witch hunt."[30]

As Obama campaigned he promised to cease engaging in crimes like warrantless spying and torture, but also maintained that he was unaware of any crimes that might require prosecution. This was the same contradiction that would be laid bare in February 2009 when the Obama administration would maintain both that Guantánamo needed to be closed in order to create a new policy in accordance with the law, and that everything at Guantánamo was, in fact, in accordance with the law.

During the 2008 campaign, vice presidential candidate Joe Biden let slip comments like this one: "In an Obama-Biden administration we will not have an attorney general who blatantly breaks the law." But the day after saying that, addressing a question from Fox News about "a report that if you guys are elected . . . you're actually going to pursue criminal charges against President Bush's administration and different people that served there," Biden replied,

> That's not true. I don't know where that report's coming from. What is true is the United States Congress is trying to preserve records on questions that relate to whether or not the law has been violated by anyone. Anybody should be doing that. . . . No one's talking about President Bush. . . . I've never heard anybody mention President Bush in that context. . . . No one's talking about pursuing President Bush criminally.[31]

Clearly Obama was opposed to the idea of prosecuting Bush or Cheney or their subordinates, even for crimes that he said he would cease committing as president. Some of those crimes might be things that he, his vice president, and members of his cabinet and of his party had been complicit in. Shortly after the election, Obama brought on advisers and proposed appointing to top positions people who had supported some of the crimes of the previous eight years. Even Attorney General nominee Eric Holder had, at times, supported violating the Geneva conventions and expanding the PATRIOT Act.[32] Obama's advisers told the media in November 2008 that he would not prosecute anyone high up for torture, even as Obama promised to end the practice. Obama did not, of course, promise to end the occupation of Iraq on his first day in office, and he had spent four years in the Senate voting to fund it. While Obama could never be accused of having launched that illegal war, his role in continuing it and other criminal policies would make prosecuting some of the crimes more difficult. The extent to which Obama stocked his cabinet with leading proponents of the war made the possibility of his Justice Department prosecuting any war crimes seem very slim.

The 109th Congress had already gone beyond ignoring presidential criminality and sought to provide immunity through legislation, particularly through the "McCain Amendment" to the Detainee Treatment

Act of 2005 and Section 7(e) of the Military Commissions Act of 2006. But even if we accept such legislation, which seems to mock the entire idea of the rule of law, there are, as Lawrence Velvel has pointed out,[33] many holes in the immunity granted, leaving many avenues to prosecution still available.

In May 2008, the National Lawyers Guild began urging Congress to appoint a special prosecutor, independent of the Justice Department, to "investigate and prosecute high Bush officials and lawyers including John Yoo for their role in the torture of prisoners in US custody." The Guild published a fourteen-page paper explaining how lawyers, including Yoo, Jay Bybee, David Addington, and William Haynes, counseled the White House on how to get away with war crimes. Guild President Marjorie Cohn had recently testified in Congress that it was "reasonably foreseeable" that the lawyers' advice "would result in great physical and mental harm or death to many detainees," and that more than 100 had died, many from torture. Torture—like genocide, slavery and wars of aggression—is absolutely prohibited at all times, Cohn pointed out. Torture is banned by the Convention Against Torture and other treaties, and is understood under the principle of jus cogens to be absolutely forbidden by international law. No country can ever pass a law that would allow torture. Cohn testified that Cheney, Rice, Rumsfeld, Powell, Tenet, Ashcroft, and Bush were liable under the War Crimes Act and the Torture Statute.[34]

In September 2008, I participated in a conference organized by Lawrence Velvel, dean of the Massachusetts School of Law. We formed a committee aimed at pursuing prosecutions and consisting of prominent lawyers, law professors, and activist agitators like myself. We called it the Steering Committee of the Justice Robert H. Jackson Conference on Planning for the Prosecution of High Level American War Criminals, or the Robert Jackson Steering Committee for short.[35]

Velvel drafted and released a memorandum on the role Bush administration lawyers had played in pretending to authorize torture. This powerful memo was published at about the same time that the Senate Armed Services Committee released a similar report. Both documents together were devastating to any claims of good intentions, and both were based on public information. In early March 2009, the Office of

Legal Counsel released previously secret memos making the case, if possible, even stronger.

And yet, the debate in the media at that time focused on the possibility of creating a "truth commission." So I drafted a brief statement on behalf of the Jackson Committee that read in its entirety:

> We urge Attorney General Eric Holder to appoint a non-partisan independent Special Counsel to immediately commence a prosecutorial investigation into the most serious alleged crimes of former President George W. Bush, former Vice President Richard B. Cheney, the attorneys formerly employed by the Department of Justice whose memos sought to justify torture, and other former top officials of the Bush Administration.
>
> Our laws, and treaties that under Article VI of our Constitution are the supreme law of the land, require the prosecution of crimes that strong evidence suggests these individuals have committed. Both the former president and the former vice president have confessed to authorizing a torture procedure that is illegal under our law and treaty obligations. The former president has confessed to violating the Foreign Intelligence Surveillance Act.
>
> We see no need for these prosecutions to be extraordinarily lengthy or costly, and no need to wait for the recommendations of a panel or "truth" commission when substantial evidence of the crimes is already in the public domain. We believe the most effective investigation can be conducted by a prosecutor, and we believe such an investigation should begin immediately.

This statement was signed by 142 organizations in the first two weeks after I wrote it (with help from colleagues), including the Center for Constitutional Rights, the National Lawyers Guild, the Society of American Law Teachers, Human Rights USA, After Downing Street, American Freedom Campaign, and many more.[36] And we were not alone. Other organizations were backing prosecutions too, including some that were nonetheless putting most of their efforts into creating a "truth commission." Members of Congress speaking at least somewhat in support of a special prosecutor included Nancy Pelosi, Jerrold Nadler, Jack Reed, Russ Feingold, Sheldon Whitehouse, John Conyers, and Carl Levin. Going back to the previous year, there were letters to Attorney General Mukasey asking for a special prosecutor or a criminal investigation from fifty-six members of Congress and from Senators Whitehouse and Dick Durbin. Retired Major General Antonio Taguba, who had reported on abuses in Iraq, favored prosecution. United Nations Special Rapporteur on Torture Manfred Nowak said that Obama was legally required to prosecute Bush and former Secretary of "Defense" Donald Rumsfeld.

A lot of commentators who had remained silent until that point, including former Attorney General Mukasey, the *New York Times*, and even defense lawyers for CIA officials involved in torture, suggested that prosecution would be hard to avoid after Eric Holder made certain statements during his Senate confirmation hearings. When Senator Patrick Leahy asked if waterboarding is torture and illegal, Holder agreed that it is. When Leahy then asked whether the President of the United States can immunize acts of torture, Holder said that he cannot. When Senator Diane Feinstein said that an Inspector General's report on politicized hiring, firing, and prosecuting at the Department of Justice is evidence that officials have lied to the Senate Judiciary Committee, and that doing so is illegal, Holder replied that he will review prosecutors' determination not to pursue criminal charges. When Senator Orrin Hatch asked if the president has the authority to engage in warrantless surveillance, Holder said no. When Senator Russ Feingold asked the same thing, Holder stammered and stuttered and called it a "hypothetical," but said no. When Feingold pointed out that lawyers at the Department of Justice, the White House, and the Office of the Vice President had written memos that clearly sought to sanction illegal actions, and asked "What is your view of the president's constitutional authority to authorize violations of the law?" Holder replied that the president does not have that authority.[37] Senator Levin may have put it best:

> I suggested to Eric Holder . . . that he select some people or hire an outside person who's got real credibility, perhaps a retired federal judge, to take all the available information, and there's

reams of it. Look, the Vice President, the former Vice President of the United States, acknowledged that they engaged in torture. He says that waterboarding's not torture, he's wrong. Waterboarding is torture, period. And this administration and Eric Holder has said so. It's torture and there's other forms that they engaged in, so what needs to be done, I believe, in addition to finishing the investigation, is for the Attorney General, the new Attorney General, to identify some people in his office to take the existing documentation. The acknowledgment, folks, this is not a very difficult—this is almost like a case in court with an agreed upon statement of facts, that the previous administration acknowledges that they engaged in waterboarding, period."[38]

When Senator Leahy held a committee hearing on March 4, 2009 on the question of whether to establish a "truth commission," witnesses chosen by the Democrats said yes. But witnesses chosen by the Republicans, and some of the Republican senators, argued (no doubt hypocritically, but perhaps accurately) that the appropriate forum for enforcing laws was through criminal prosecution, that creating a new forum outside of the legally sanctioned governmental structures would not be legal, and that in fact such a show trial would violate the rights of those investigated, who would not be permitted the same legal defense they would be entitled to in a court of law.

I used the website ProsecuteBushCheney.org as part of AfterDowningStreet.org to promote the above statement and to give people tools. We asked people to sign a petition to Holder and to collect signatures on it. We asked them to phone, e-mail, and fax the Office of the Attorney General.[39] We encouraged people to lobby their representatives and senators to ask Holder to appoint a special prosecutor, and to extend statutes of limitations.

We have also provided people with tools for other, non-federal approaches. Former Los Angeles prosecutor Vincent Bugliosi's 2008 book, *The Prosecution of George W. Bush for Murder*, argues that state and local prosecutors have the necessary jurisdiction to try Bush for murder and for conspiracy to commit murder. The book became a best seller without a single review in the corporate media or interview of the author. An enterprising citizen named Bob Alexander raised enough money to mail copies to fifty state attorney generals and 2,200 district prosecutors. We have provided people with tools to help persuade a prosecutor or elect one who doesn't need persuading.

Bugliosi's basic argument is as follows: by sending troops into war on false pretenses rather than in self-defense, Bush was knowingly and needlessly condemning some of them to death. The Iraqis who killed those soldiers in predictable and legally justifiable defense of their country fall into the legal category of "third-party innocent agent." This does not mean they are innocent, but rather that their actions do nothing to lessen Bush's guilt. In addition, Bugliosi argues, Bush could be found guilty of murder under the rule of "aiding and abetting," because he instigated the killing of American soldiers by ordering the invasion of Iraq.[40]

In November 2008, a district prosecutor in South Texas indicted Cheney and Gonzales on charges related to Cheney's financial investment in private prison companies and the influence they both had on contracts to those companies and investigations of crimes in the prisons. While that case went nowhere, it suggested that a zealous prosecutor might attempt to find local or state jurisdiction for others of the long list of possible crimes. Warrantless spying, for example, is banned by numerous state laws.

There are also a variety of ways in which citizens can file suit individually. My friend John Bonifaz served as attorney on a lawsuit against the president before the invasion of Iraq on behalf of Congress members and military families claiming an invasion would be unconstitutional without a proper congressional declaration of war. In 2007 John consulted with a professor at Rutgers University who worked up a case with his students for a full year, and filed it in 2008 in the Federal District Court in Newark, New Jersey. The complaint, filed on behalf of New Jersey Peace Action, seeks a declaratory judgment that the president's decision to launch a preemptive war against a sovereign nation in 2003 violated Article I, Section 8 of the United States Constitution, which assigns to Congress the power to declare war. Every peace and justice group in the country should be working with lawyers, choosing their favorite Cheney-Bush crime, and filing a suit, the point being to change the public conversation until we reach the point where a prosecutor will act.

There is also a procedure called "Qui Tam" found in the Federal False Claims Act that allows individual citizens to sue if the government spends money fraudulently, and to receive a percentage of any funds recovered. Such a suit could conceivably be filed, or perhaps hundreds of such suits could be filed, against government officials, including Dick Cheney, who set up illegal contracts with Halliburton and other corporations, including contracts to spend Iraq funding that had been legally appropriated for Afghanistan.

But the possibilities for prosecution do not end with Bush and Cheney. Citizens should hold accountable at least the top few dozen lawyers, cabinet members, and other top officials who conspired to violate laws on behalf of Bush and Cheney. Some of the lowest ranking torturers have already been held accountable. Our priority should be accountability for those who gave the illegal orders.

In May 2008 in Milano, Italy, twenty-five CIA agents and a US Air Force colonel went on trial in absentia for kidnapping a man on an Italian street and "rendering" him to Egypt to be tortured. The victim's wife testified for over six hours. A newspaper report read:

> Nabila at first rebuffed prosecutors' requests to describe the torture her husband had recounted, saying she didn't want to talk about it. Advised by prosecutors that she had no choice, she tearfully proceeded: "He was tied up like he was being crucified. He was beaten up, especially around his ears. He was subject to electroshocks to many body parts."
>
> "To his genitals?" the prosecutors asked.
>
> "Yes," she replied.[41]

The judge said that the current and immediate past prime ministers of Italy would be required to testify during the trial. But both of those individuals, Silvio Berlusconi and Romano Prodi argued, in a very Bush-Obama manner, that proceeding with the trial would reveal state secrets and jeopardize national security. (The security to have a foreign nation kidnap people from your nation's streets?) The judge suspended the trial in March 2009 until a higher court could rule on the "state secrets" claim.

A criminal investigation into rendition is also underway in Spain. The Center for Constitutional Rights, a US group, is working with attorneys abroad to develop more cases.

Foreign victims can also sue in US courts. In May 2008, an Iraqi sued US contractors for torture. Emad al-Janabi's federal lawsuit was filed in Los Angeles; he claimed that employees of CACI International Inc. and L-3 Communications punched him, slammed him into walls, hung him from a bed frame and kept him naked and handcuffed in his cell. In July 2008, three more Iraqis and a Jordanian who had been held and tortured in Abu Ghraib for years before being released without charges filed similar suits. Alleged methods of torture by the US contractors included electric shock, beatings, deprivation of food and sleep, being threatened with dogs, being stripped naked, being forcibly shaved, being choked, being forced to witness murder, having feces poured on them, being held down and sodomized (a fourteen-year-old boy) with toothbrushes, being paraded naked before other prisoners, being forced to consume water to the point of vomiting blood and fainting, and having a plastic line tied around their penises to prevent urination.[42]

On August 15, 2008, the Second Circuit Court of Appeals in New York announced that it would hear the case against the United States from Canadian victim of US torture Maher Arar. His suit named, among others, former Attorney General John Ashcroft, former Deputy Attorney General Larry Thompson, and former head of "Homeland Security" Tom Ridge.[43] The court heard arguments on December 9, 2008. Updates can be found on the website of the Center for Constitutional Rights (ccrjustice.org).

Even while Bush and Cheney were still in office, prosecutions were attempted in European courts against top officials, including Rumsfeld, Cheney, and US General Tommy Franks. In some cases these suits were dismissed on the grounds that there was not evidence the United States would not itself enforce the rule of law. So there is the possibility that if it becomes clear that the United States will not do the job, foreign courts will be more willing to allow cases under universal jurisdiction. However, we should be aware of the pressure the United States can bring against other countries.

In May 2003, an attorney in Belgium lodged a complaint on behalf of a number of Iraqi and Jordanian victims against US General Tommy Franks and members of his staff for war crimes in Iraq. The crimes included the bombing of civilian targets, the use of cluster bombs, and the targeting of the Palestine Hotel, which had been known to house journalists. The US Congress quickly passed a law allowing the US president to attack anyone (including Belgium) who would detain members of the US military. The White House also told Belgium to drop the case and change the law that permitted it ever to be brought, or the headquarters of NATO would be moved to another country, taking thousands of jobs with it. The law was changed and the case dropped before the US media ever mentioned it.[44]

Another possibility is prosecution by the International Criminal Court (ICC), which in March 2009 indicted the sitting president of Sudan, a nation that, like the United States, is not a member of the court. The ICC also planned in 2009 to decide on a measure that would allow it to prosecute the crime of aggressive war. Again there is the problem of dominant US influence over other nations and the United Nations, but the ICC remains a possibility; its decisions are not subject to Security Council veto, and it is a body the United States should join and support regardless of any action against the crimes of Bush-Cheney.

Prosecuting Bush and Cheney is a completely mainstream idea in Europe, including in England. But courts there are going to look first to the United States. If we seek to prosecute our former rulers here, even if we fail, our friends overseas will be more likely to pick up the ball. If we don't make a major effort, they still might. I would welcome their efforts with gratitude and shame. But if we manage to restore the rule of law ourselves it will have a strongly beneficial impact on the way the rest of the world views us.

One danger is that statutes of limitations will run out before domestic prosecutions begin. Most crimes must be prosecuted within five years. For torture, it's eight. For murder, there's no limitation. Some of us were working at the time I wrote this book on getting a bill introduced in Congress to extend the limitations on various crimes to ten years. While it's possible to argue that the clock doesn't start ticking on a criminal act until the last act of conspiracy to conceal the crime, I saw no point in taking the risk of having to win that argument, particularly with some of the worst crimes openly and proudly confessed to by the perpetrators.[45]

In April 2009, the British government began a criminal investigation of the role of Britain in US rendition, detention, and torture, and a Spanish judge pursued the indictment of six top Bush officials. The Obama White House pressured Spain to back off the case, and its future was uncertain at the time I wrote this. Also uncertain, but more likely to move forward, was a separate Spanish criminal investigation of Guantánamo, reportedly targeting Condoleezza Rice and Dick Cheney, among others, and begun on April 29, 2009. This foreign pressure, combined with the April 2009 release of four more memos from the Bush Justice Department purporting to authorize torture, helped move the debate forward. While numerous human rights groups proposed that the president create a commission to study the crimes of the previous president (raise your hand if you can spot the weakness in this), other groups joined the demand for a special prosecutor, including the ACLU and MoveOn.org.

As Attorney General Eric Holder left an appropriations subcommittee hearing on Thursday, April 23, 2009, I spoke up loudly from the third row, "We need a special prosecutor for torture, Mr. Attorney General. Americans like the rule of law. The rule of law for everybody."

He replied as he approached me and walked by, surrounded by bodyguards, "And you will be proud of your government."

I was joined by others in replying simultaneously, "Yes, we want to be proud of our government. We're ready. No need to wait."

Holder knew exactly what it would take for me to be proud of my government, and he told me directly that I would be.

Will I? Time will tell.

15. AMERICAN MILITARISM AROUND THE WORLD

Americans and communities all over the world would benefit greatly if we were to shut down our empire of bases, convert them into useful facilities, such as green energy producers or schools, and turn them over to the people of the lands they occupy, while bringing home the half million troops and 100,000 civilian employees we maintain overseas and training them for work in a reindustrialized, but green, America. The US Constitution sought to avoid a standing army, and necessarily did not even discuss the maintenance of a foreign empire, which would have required a standing army. Yet, now, many—perhaps most—people around the globe know the United States most directly through contact with our empire of bases.

US military bases have replaced taxes as one of life's two certainties. Chalmers Johnson has identified as many as 1,000. In fact the military admits to 865, but leaves many known bases (not to mention secret detention centers) out of that count, as well as over 100 bases in Iraq and over eighty in Afghanistan. You can call them enduring. You can call them lasting. You can call them substantial. You can even call them humanitarian aid missions. But the damn things are permanent, and there aren't too many corners of the globe in which you can hide from them.[46]

This is not normal. No other nation does this or has ever done it. US foreign bases account for 95 percent of the world's foreign bases.[47] And no other nations have bases in our country, which we would find shocking and dangerous. The United States has some 268 bases in Germany, 124 in Japan, 87 in South Korea, 83 in Italy, 45 in Britain, 21 in Portugal, 19 in Turkey. We have bases, for some strange reason, in Aruba, Australia, Bahrain, Bulgaria, Crete, Colombia, Denmark, Djibouti,

Egypt, Honduras, Israel, Jordan, Kuwait, Qatar, Romania, Singapore, Spain, Thailand, and the United Arab Emirates. We've held that notorious base at Guantánamo Bay since 1898, when we helped Cubans throw off Spanish rule only to smash their hopes for freedom by imposing US control.

These bases, large and small, do a lot more harm than good. They encourage resentment and anti-American activities, and they become targets for attack. They destabilize, rather than stabilize, regions and they encourage militarization and increased arms spending. In some nations they provide support for dictators and repressive regimes, adding to popular resentment. The bases are constantly expanding, seizing people's land and displacing them. Crimes and accidents accompany the bases, including high incidents of rape, sexual harassment, murder, and equipment-related disasters such as airplanes flying into ski lifts and less dramatic impacts that don't make the news. The bases tend to be extremely destructive of the natural environment and of the cultural environment, causing health hazards, social disruption, and increased prostitution. While America might benefit from millions of its citizens interacting with other people around the world, doing so from military bases does not make enriching cultural exchange easy. And the Americans' separation from their families and communities at home is an unnecessary sacrifice.

If we were to close our bases in other countries, we would still have 6,000 bases in the United States and its "territories." We could save perhaps $140 billion per year, not counting the even greater sum we could save just by leaving Iraq and Afghanistan, not counting the $600 million or so that could be saved by ceasing to fund NATO every year, and not counting the billions we could save by ceasing to provide other nations with weapons (roughly $4 billion per year, not counting discount sales of old weapons or sales of new ones, and of that roughly $1 billion is for Egypt and $2 billion for Israel, not counting nearly a billion now proposed to help repair the damage in Gaza done by the weapons we paid for). But to save all of that money from base closures would require demobilizing the troops rather than building new bases for them in the United States or fitting them into existing ones. The savings wouldn't come the first year, because there would be a cost involved simply in closing the bases and shipping everyone and everything home. And I'd prefer to see some investment in converting the abandoned bases to facilities that benefit the people who live near them. But even if not a penny was saved and the full $140 billion was spent every year training and employing people here at home in infrastructure creation, mass transportation, health care, green energy, and organic farming, the financial benefits to the US economy would be tremendous (nonmilitary investment creates more and better paying jobs than military investment even when that investment isn't overseas),[48] and the nonfinancial benefits of taking a different approach to our own nation and the world would be immeasurable.

There are organizations like the American Friends Service Committee and the Global Network Against Weapons and Nuclear Power in Space, as well as many other peace groups active in the no-bases movement. And there are groups like Veterans Green Jobs, Global Exchange, Green for All, and Farms Not Arms working to convert sword swingers into ploughshare pushers. But President Obama has proposed enlarging troop size, not shrinking it, and the military is proceeding with base expansion and construction all over the world.

I was an exchange student twenty years ago in Vicenza, Italy, and I have gone back several times, including a trip in 2007 to be part of a protest against a proposed new US military base. Vicenza is a UNESCO World Heritage site, a beautiful treasure of a town showcasing the Renaissance architecture of Andrea Palladio.

The US government has proposed to make Vicenza the largest US military site in Europe, but the people of Vicenza, and all of Italy, have sworn it will never happen. This story and others like it in the Czech Republic, South Korea, and other nations are unknown to Americans, despite the fact that these stories are all about the policies of the American government. In February 2007, approximately 200,000 people descended on Vicenza (population 100,000) to march in protest. Largely as a result, the Prime Minister of Italy was (temporarily) driven out of power. Meanwhile, just outside Vicenza, large tents now hold newly minted citizen activists keeping a 24/7 vigil and training senior citizens, children, and families in how to nonviolently stop bulldozers. The bulldozers they are waiting for are American.

The conflict, should it come about and should it be reported in the

United States, will be as surprising to American television viewers as were the attacks of 9/11, unless someone tells them ahead of time what is going on. In April 2007, a group of Italian Members of Parliament visited Washington, DC, attempting to do just that. In May, a group of citizens from Vicenza followed.

If you google "No Dal Molin" you'll find 546,000 results. Dal Molin is the name of the site of the proposed new military base. But the only US media link you'll find is Pacifica's radio program *Democracy Now!*, which interviewed one of the Italian activists in Washington in May 2007.

In Italy, the women leading the opposition to the base, women who were housewives and had never been activists until news of this proposal leaked, have appeared frequently in the media, even confronting the Prime Minister on stage at a public event. Vicenza has become a focus for peace activists in Europe, including Americans living abroad, and has been the site of numerous protests and acts of civil disobedience.

I spent a day in May 2007 with US peace activists Stephanie Westbrook and Medea Benjamin accompanying a delegation of four Italians to meetings with Congress members, senators, and their staffers. The Italians were led by two women, Cinzia Bottene and Thea Valentina Garbellin. The day before, the delegation had spoken with various Congress members, including Rep. Neil Abercrombie and Rep. Walter Jones. At these and many other meetings, the Italians dropped off materials, told their stories, and answered questions. The Congress members and staffers made no commitments but promised to look into the matter.

"The amazing thing," Cinzia said, "is that nobody in the United States, not even senators and Congress members, knows anything about it. But we found a great deal of interest." At the meetings I attended, this was the case too. Congress members and staffers knew nothing about it, and most declined to offer any help, with the exception of Rep. Kucinich, who proposed to write a "Dear colleague" letter and to visit Vicenza. The other exception was a meeting with three staffers on the Senate Armed Services Committee who had been to Vicenza to plan the new base years before any Italians had any hint it was happening.

The Senate staffers tried to be helpful, explaining as others had before them that what they needed to know about were potential impacts on water, traffic, power, pollution, and the environment. They also were very interested in learning about alternative locations for the base and accounts of the Italian government having offered other locations. But the danger brought to the people of Vicenza by making it a major military target was not a concern that had made it onto their radar screen. The damage to historic and artistic treasures was deemed "intangible." And the affront to the dignity of the people of Vicenza was unfortunate but insignificant.

The Italians explained that they had never protested the existing US base in Vicenza, which had been there for fifty years. In fact, there are a number of US military installations in and around Vicenza and throughout Italy, including facilities holding ninety atomic bombs, according to the Natural Resources Defense Council and Italian news reports.

"The people of Vicenza and the Americans have always been friends," Cinzia said. "But when you invite a friend to your house and give them a room, it changes when they demand to have the whole house."

As in much of the world, Vicenza is already overrun by American soldiers who drink too much, commit too many crimes, return from Iraq in mental anguish, and—since 9/11—remain ever more isolated from the Italians. It's the Vicentines' city, but they are second-class citizens. If an Italian is waiting in line in a hospital emergency room and a US soldier comes in, the soldier can go straight to the front. And the economic argument so cynically used all over the United States to keep our economy based on war does not work in Vicenza: Italian tax payers are paying a large portion of the cost of their own occupation.

American taxpayers, on the other hand, are completely oblivious to the fact that they are paying hundreds of millions of dollars for the construction of a base that has enraged the nation of Italy and serves no purpose that the people of the United States have ever debated or had any say in. While the State Department and the Pentagon make our decisions for us, the Congress approves the money without asking us about it. In fact, my impression is that most Congress members have no idea what is going on. The world is a very big place, after all, and the US Congress was only intended to be able to govern the United States.

The Vicentines handed in 10,000 signatures and requested a referendum, but were denied until October 2008, when 95 percent voted against the base proposal. The Italian government has said it will permit the base, but it has not actually issued the construction permits. Leaders of the opposition movement met with the Minister of Defense, who said that Italy was capable of saying No to the United States. But the US ambassador gave Italy a deadline of January 19, 2007, to accept the base, and the Prime Minister announced his acceptance of it on a trip abroad on January 16, 2007. While no permits have been issued, fiber-optic cables have been laid on the site, which activists have dug up and ripped out.

In September 2008, Italian police attacked and beat nonviolent protesters in Vicenza. The footage, viewable on the Internet, might have shocked Americans had they seen it, had they understood that the police were defending Americans' rights to spend billions of dollars on a base that would enrage Italians, and had the footage not looked so very similar to the recent footage of police in Denver and St. Paul attacking US citizens who escaped their "free speech cages" during the course of the Democratic and Republican conventions.

The first step in ending this approach to foreign bases should be holding hearings in Congress that present the costs and benefits of alternatives that include maintaining all the bases, closing some of them, and closing them all through a process that sees to the wellbeing of the troops and staff brought home, as well as the people left behind. Then legislation should be passed to do what makes sense rather than what the military industrial complex prefers.

16. **RESPECTING INTERNATIONAL TREATIES**

The United States was a leader during much of the twentieth century in the advancement of international law. Perhaps this was never without a degree of hypocrisy and various limitations, but it was also never the vicious destructiveness that characterized the approach to international law taken by Bush and Cheney.

A conference was held in Paris, France, in September 2005, organized by the Association for the Defense of International Humanitarian Law, France (ADIF) and the International Federation of Human Rights (FIDH). The remarks of a long list of outstanding expert speakers were updated, translated, and published in 2008.[49] It would be enlightening to many Americans to read this book, which documents the discussion of top proponents of human rights from around the world, including the United States, a discussion focusing on the single biggest impediment to establishing the international rule of law, to eliminating war as an instrument of policy, and to defending human rights around the world—the fierce opposition of the US government.

The United States had played a key role in creating the United Nations, in convening the tribunals in Nuremberg and Tokyo, and in developing and promoting the ideas of human rights and international law. And the United States favors, to this day, the concept of international law as applied to the crimes of any nation other than the United States (for example, the outrage voiced in opposition to Russia's flouting of international law in Georgia as I wrote this book in 2008). But this two-tiered system in which the United States operates with a set of rules completely unlike those for everyone else is eroding support for the entire idea of law as something applicable to the actions of nations, rulers, and militaries.

Better diplomacy and actual humanitarian foreign aid is essential because shifting our relationship with the rest of the world is not the same as fostering a good one. The United States should become a friend, rather than a bully, to the world by taking a lead in achieving the sort of goals set by the United Nations Development Program in its "Millennium Development Goals," which include eradicating extreme poverty and hunger; establishing universal primary education; gender equality and empowerment of women; reducing child mortality; improving maternal health; combating HIV/AIDS and malaria and other diseases; and ensuring environmental sustainability.

In a world without empire, the United States would need to begin treating its treaty obligations as seriously as the Constitution intended. Our Constitution makes treaties that the United States has ratified the supreme law of the land, but does not impose any penalty on presidents who violate them. Penalties could be imposed through legislation or amendment. The United States is currently failing to fulfill its obligation under all sorts of treaties to which the United States is nominally a party but in reality a scofflaw, such as the Nuclear Non-Proliferation Treaty, the Anti-Ballistic Missile Treaty, the Chemical Weapons Convention, the Biological Weapons Convention, and the United Nations Charter. The US could come into compliance with the Nuclear Non-Proliferation Treaty if it follows through with Russia on President Obama's proposal to reduce each nation's nuclear weapons to 1,000 and continue reductions from there.

The United States needs to comply with the UN Charter by paying the approximately $1 billion in past dues owed. While $1 billion is not much to the United States, the UN's entire annual budget is about $2 billion. If anybody doubts that the money is well spent, consider this: for $2 billion, the United Nations managed to be exactly right about invading Iraq, whereas for about $60 billion the US "intelligence community" managed to be exactly wrong. Of course, the United Nations needs its own systemic repairs, including a reorganization to democratize the world body and provide more equal representation to all nations. But our job is to support the institution and work for those changes.

We need to ratify and take part in many good treaties to which we are a national hold-out, such as the Kyoto Treaty on Global Climate Change (or a better update, which may come out of a conference in Copenhagen in December 2009), the International Criminal Court, the Biodiversity Treaty, the Forest Protection Treaty, the Comprehensive Test Ban Treaty, the Landmine Ban Treaty, the Cluster Munitions Treaty, and the treaty on Preventing an Arms Race in Outer Space (PAROS).

At the same time, we need to urge Congress and the president to end or reform treaties that are not serving the common good, including such monsters as NAFTA, the World Trade Organization, the International Monetary Fund, and the World Bank.

17. SPARE CHANGE FOR REAL CHANGE

One immediate and quantifiable benefit of becoming less militarized would be the vast financial savings—money that could be put to better use. Researchers have shown that investing public dollars in military jobs at home in the United States produces fewer and lower-paying jobs for the US economy than does public investment in health care, education, mass transit, or home construction.[50] Needless to say, the comparison must weigh more strongly against the military when its investment is overseas. And any benefit to the occupied nations with US bases has to be weighed against those nations' share of the cost of the bases. And that's all before considering the non-financial benefits of investing in living rather than in killing.

As usual, the people are ahead of their "leaders." In the study by PIPA cited above, 65 percent of Americans, when they saw how much money the military had, favored taking at least some of it away. In particular, majorities of Americans favored reducing spending on the capacity for conducting large-scale nuclear and conventional wars. Next on the list of cuts after the "defense" budget? The wars in Iraq and Afghanistan. Majorities of ordinary people taking this survey were also able to do what Congress members have declared impossible: distinguish between wars and soldiers. They favored slashing money for wars and the military while increasing funds for veterans and preserving funds for those on active duty. But the biggest increases went to education, job training, employment, and medical research. And the largest increase in percentage terms went to conserving and developing renewable energy: 70 percent of Americans favored an increase, and the proposed amounts of increase averaged 1,090 percent (yes, over 1,000 percent).

The Institute for Policy Studies (IPS) has found that the disparity in the US budget between military vs. nonmilitary foreign engagement is

197

18:1.[51] IPS has identified $61 billion that it recommends cutting from the military budget, including a $25 billion reduction in the nuclear arsenal combined with keeping "missile defense" in the research stage and stopping the weaponization of space, plus another $24 billion from scaling back or stopping research on unneeded weapons, $5 billion from unneeded conventional forces, and $7 billion in waste and pork. IPS proposes shifting these dollars to nonmilitary security.

Early in 2009, House Financial Services Committee Chairman Barney Frank published a plan to cut the budgets for wars and the military by 25 percent. This frequent star of television talk shows held a press conference about his plan that was completely ignored by the US corporate media. He proposed huge savings from de-escalating and eventually ending the occupation of Iraq, despite factoring in the costs of escalating the occupation of Afghanistan. Using his numbers, choosing to end both occupations would produce a savings of $162 billion per year.

Frank also drew on the work of IPS to propose cutting $60.7 billion per year from weapons systems that were not needed, didn't work, or were designed to fight nonexistent enemies. Many of the systems Frank and IPS proposed scaling back could be eliminated to save more money. If we were to eliminate rather than scale back the F/A-22 Raptor, "missile defense," Virginia-class submarines, the DDG-1000 destroyer, the V-22 Osprey, the expeditionary fighting vehicle, the F-35 Joint Strike Fighter, offensive space weapons, and Future Combat Systems, there would be a savings of $69.6 billion rather than $60.7 billion. Add that to the $162 billion from ending two wars, throw in roughly $100 billion more from closing bases around the world, gain another $4 billion by ceasing to give weapons to other nations, and pretty soon we're talking real money, in this case $335.6 billion.

The primary argument against such changes that you hear from Congress members is that our economy is awful and therefore we cannot cut anything that would eliminate jobs. (Nevermind that by shifting to a military-based economy and deindustrializing everything else we've ruined the country's economy during the past fifty years). The following responses are possible when your Congress member gives you that excuse:

1. Are you a socialist? If I were to propose government-funded jobs that didn't involve killing anyone you guys would reject it as socialism.

2. In fact, I do want to propose that instead of cutting anything we shift it to investment at home and investment in those areas most needed and which most benefit the rest of the economy. Imposing a nonworking fantasy weapon on the Czech Republic or Poland to protect against a nonexistent threat from Iran hardly creates as many US jobs as, say, funding that project your constituents keep asking for.

3. If this is really about fear, please bear in mind that weapons that don't work or that are designed to fight the Soviet Union or the Japanese fleet only make idiots feel safer.

Here's a sketch in the broadest terms of how undoing the imperial presidency might shift our public financial resources. This proposal uses, in some cases, very rough guesstimates at the costs of existing programs because the information is not publicly available.

Spare Change for Real Change

TAXES FOR TYRANNY
Warrantless and unjustified spying: $55 billion[52]
US military against US citizens (Northern Command): $2 billion[53]
Detentions, renditions, prison camps, torture, military commissions: $10 billion
Illegal propaganda: $0.5 billion

ENTITLEMENTS OF EMPIRE
Foreign bases: $100 billion[54]
Wars: $162 billion
Nondefensive weapons and military: $69.6 billion
Weapons gifts to other nations: $4 billion

WELFARE FOR THE WEALTHY
Paulson's Plunder and related giveaways and loans: $8,400 billion (that's $8.4 trillion)[55]

Failure to tax corporations: $500 billion[56]

Bush's tax cuts for the super-wealthy: $100 billion

Failure to collect Social Security tax on income above $97,500: $120 billion

Failure to tax financial transactions, investment income, and estates: $500 billion

Failure to restore truly progressive taxation on the highest incomes: $500 billion

Total financial cost of antidemocratic policies: $403.1 billion wasted on empire and tyranny, plus $1.72 trillion lost to the cause of making the rich richer, and another $8.4 trillion spent or loaned in an effort to "bail out" banks. That adds up to ten and a half trillion if you're counting. This shift we've made to talking in trillions instead of billions and inventing trillions of dollars out of thin air when bankers want it presents a new rhetorical hurdle when trying to persuade people that we can't find billions for health care and schools unless we cut billions from wasteful weapons. But rest assured that opponents of funding health care or schools or anything useful will denounce any proposed expense as impossible. One way around that would be to introduce legislation to take money from where we don't need it and to move it to where we do.

The possibilities for what could be done with the kind of annual public revenue increase and savings listed above are endless. They include, of course, eliminating deficits and paying off debts. But they also include everything presidential candidate Obama ever proposed and a great deal more. Priorities, I think, should include diplomacy, foreign aid, green energy, jobs, affordable housing, and education. Health care is, of course, a priority as well, but it is important to bear in mind when considering health care policy that we already spend, as private citizens and businesses, much more money than it would take to provide everyone, including the tens of millions who have no insurance and the hundreds of millions who have lousy insurance, with top-quality comprehensive private health care if we were to eliminate the private health insurance companies by instituting a single-payer system. That change would require significant public revenue (including, by one estimate, a 3 percent tax on employers) and expenditure, but would also involve major savings to individuals and companies that currently buy health insurance.

Progressive Democrats of America organized grassroots lobbying across the country in 2008 and 2009 for "health care not warfare," calling for an end to the wars in Iraq and Afghanistan and investment in single-payer health care, specifically Congressman John Conyers' bill, HR 676. Local groups of all sorts all over the country backed this effort, including a long list of city governments, local labor unions, Physicians for a National Health Program (PNHP), and the National Nurses Organizing Committee.

HR 676 would create single-payer health care. This would mean the elimination of all for-profit health insurance companies, along with their bureaucracies, advertising, and waste. (This tells you where the primary opposition to single-payer comes from.) With single-payer we wouldn't get government health care, just government insurance, so people would get complete choice of private health care; you could choose any doctor or hospital you want, not just the ones some company tells you to. It's Medicare, enhanced and expanded and covering everyone. As an added benefit, the plan in HR 676 would give us a net of 2.6 million new jobs.[57] In other words, it would be a more effective economic stimulus than much of what we have recently funded for that purpose.

Unlike most local labor unions, most national labor unions and coalitions joined a wide range of so-called progressive groups in taking their cue from politicians and proposing to invest huge amounts of money in health care, with much of it going to the health insurance companies that already waste so much of it. The question became whether such a plan would include a significant "public option," allowing people to choose public coverage if they wanted to (the myth being that most Americans truly adore their health insurance companies). In March 2009, President Obama invited 120 people to a health care summit to discuss the options. A major public outcry was required before he invited, at the last minute, two supporters of single-payer health care, Congressman Conyers and a doctor from PNHP. The president had already made clear to Congress at that point that he would model his health care reform efforts not on Clinton's failed bill, but on the banker bailouts; he wanted Congress to give him $600 billion, with which he would then decide what to do. Of course, what he proposed doing would resemble Clinton's failed plan in complexity and in seeking to both appease the health insurance companies and provide Americans with health care. The annoyance of having Congress approve the plan might just be, to some extent, avoided.

The larger question facing the American people today is whether we want to focus our resources on human needs, such as health care (whether or not we have to waste a large share on insurance companies to do so). Or are we content with spending more than half of every dollar of income tax on the military?[58] I'm confident in where my fellow citizens' priorities lie. I'm confident in our ability to resist fear, and in our willingness to make hard choices. The big question is whether we are willing to get organized, work, and sacrifice to compel our elected representatives to represent us.

IV.

FORMING A MORE PERFECT UNION

I think there is a proliferation of rights. I am often surprised by the virtual nobility that seems to be accorded those with grievances. . . . I have to admit that I am one of those people that still thinks a dishwasher is a miracle.

—Supreme Court Justice Clarence Thomas[1]

18. **RIGHTS WE'VE HAD**

According to the Declaration of Independence, "We hold these truths to be self-evident, that all men are created equal, that they are endowed by their Creator with certain unalienable Rights, that among these are Life, Liberty and the pursuit of Happiness."

The men who put their signatures to those words sought to endow each other with those rights, and those rights can be gained or lost. And since that day, people around the world have imagined, created, and struggled for a great many additional rights as well.

Our Constitution came very early in the history of the formal establishment of individual rights. It helped to inspire many other nations to develop the idea further, and to inspire international agreements. Our original Bill of Rights is no longer cutting edge, and yet it does a remarkably good job of providing many basic protections. The most glaring problem with it is not dated concepts or ambiguous wording, but our failure to enforce it. We have to make enforcement happen through Congress and the courts, or there will be no point in making improvements.

To restore and expand our rights, there are three basic steps we should take. The first is to enforce the rights already protected by the Constitution. The second is to ratify and enforce international agreements (some of which the United States has already ratified) providing additional rights. The third is to amend our Constitution to include a second Bill of Rights.

So, first things first: how are we doing on enforcing the rights that we are already supposed to have? Here are the basic rights provided by the US Constitution and its amendments, and a quick summary of the shape they're in today:

ARTICLE I, SECTION 9, habeas corpus:
The right not to be kidnapped and detained without charge or trial

205

has been eroded in the United States, its territories, and secret prisons. The Supreme Court has admirably insisted on the right, while Congress has been willing to toss it to the wind. Not a single individual has been held accountable for having violated it, and the violations have not ended. In 2001 and 2002, US Justice Department lawyers put down in "legal" opinions that the right to habeas corpus could be tossed aside. In 2007 Attorney General Alberto Gonzales testified before Congress that the right to habeas corpus that appears in the Constitution doesn't really exist. In 2009, the new Obama administration claimed the continued power to render and detain without charge.

ARTICLE I, SECTION 10, the right against ex post facto laws:

It is clearly unconstitutional to criminalize something that has already been done and then punish a crime that was not a crime when it happened. But what about taking actions that were crimes when they happened and immunizing the violators? This looks like Congress taking over the president's pardon power. If the ban on ex post facto laws is understood to include laws that grant retroactive immunity from prosecution, then Congress has been busy violating it by passing laws like the Military Commissions Act or the FISA Amendments Act, laws that claim to give immunity to past violators of crimes. We should consider whether to amend the Constitution to clarify that point.

FIRST AMENDMENT, freedom of religion, speech, press, and assembly, and the right to petition for redress of grievances:

President Bush punched quite a few holes in the wall of separation between church and state. He used agencies including the United States Department of Justice (DOJ), the Food and Drug Administration (FDA), the Park Service, the Department of Defense (DOD), the National Institutes of Health (NIH), the National Aeronautics and Space Administration (NASA), the Department of Education (DOE), the Department of Health and Human Services, and the Office of the Surgeon General to promote the establishment of a religion.[2] Freedom of the press has been severely curtailed by the establishment of a system that bars entry to ownership of effective media outlets to all but the very wealthiest. Pundits in the existing media outlets are often directly paid and told what to say by the Pentagon or the White House. Media outlets in occupied nations like Iraq are paid to publish false stories. Reporters on wars are "embedded" with the military, denied access, and banned from publishing important information and images. Independent reporters were preemptively detained but not charged with any crimes during the 2008 Republican National Convention. Freedom of speech and assembly have been radically curtailed to the point where we now have "free speech zones" consisting of walled-in cages outside and at a distance removed from political events. These freedoms are also absent in the workplace, where unionization is effectively blocked, and in "private" gathering places like shopping malls. While you can appeal to your government for a redress of grievances, you'd better do so by mail. People attempting to do so in person are usually prevented by security guards. A Justice Department memo on October 23, 2001, claimed the president could suspend First Amendment rights.[3]

SECOND AMENDMENT, the right to bear arms:

The Second Amendment was written to protect the Southern states' right to use armed militias to enforce slavery. We no longer have slavery, but we do have the National Guard, which is supposed to be under the control of state governors. We need to correct the current situation in which the US president controls the National Guard and sends its members to fight foreign wars for empire. If we read the Second Amendment as providing an individual right to bear arms, it is important to notice that it makes no distinction between the right to bear arms to violently protect oneself and the right to bear arms to easily slaughter masses of people, or the fact that some types of arms are much better suited to the latter than the former. Clearly, this is one right that needs to be limited by legislation or amendment to the extent that it conflicts with that "self-evident" right to "life."

THIRD AMENDMENT, the right not to have soldiers quartered in your house:

This is perhaps the only right we have that has not been threatened or eroded in any way in recent years. But, of course, that's because— counter to everything the framers of the Constitution intended—we are all paying significant portions of our income to the government in order to provide soldiers with their own homes on thousands of permanent military bases maintained in times of war and peace.

FOURTH AMENDMENT, the right against unreasonable searches and seizures without warrant, probable cause, and specificity:

That same memo that brushed aside the First Amendment, mentioned above, also claimed the president could toss out the Fourth Amendment. Our Fourth Amendment has been erased by legislation amending FISA, and should instead be protected by the repeal of FISA and the passage of new legislation. Rather than permitting the government to sidestep a rubber stamp court that routinely and even retroactively approves violations of the Fourth Amendment, such a procedure should be replaced by one that does not violate our rights. The Fourth Amendment requires a warrant describing specifically what is to be searched, and requires that the warrant be based on probable cause. FISA permits, and always permitted, retroactive warrants based on the flimsiest of evidence.[4]

FIFTH AMENDMENT, the right to grand jury, due process, and just compensation for property taken, and protection against double jeopardy and self-incrimination; SIXTH AMENDMENT, the right to a speedy and public trial by an impartial local jury, to be informed of the charges against you, to confront witnesses against you, to compel witnesses in your favor to appear, and to have the assistance of counsel; and SEVENTH AMENDMENT, the right to trial by jury:

These rights have been eroded by Bush and Cheney so that they now apply in some cases but not others. If the president calls you an "enemy combatant" you lose these rights. In June of 2002, Assistant Attorney General Jay Bybee and Deputy Assistant Attorney General John Yoo wrote a pair of secret memos denying an American citizen named Jose Padilla these rights on the grounds that he was guilty of various offenses. But the memos themselves served as his trial as well as his sentence; Padilla had never been charged with the crimes, much less found guilty. In 2009, the new Justice Department under Eric Holder sought to dismiss a case that Padilla brought against Yoo alleging that his memos had led to Padilla's detention and torture. Our due process rights must be restored to their intended state and then expanded to include protections unavailable in the eighteenth century, including the videotaping of all interrogations and confessions.

EIGHTH AMENDMENT, the right against excessive bail or fines or cruel and unusual punishment:

The cruelest punishments imaginable have been employed in violation of the Eighth Amendment, with the disgusting defense sometimes offered that "interrogation techniques" are not punishment at all. While torture and any degrading treatment are banned by numerous treaties and statutes, the Constitution would be improved by the clarification of the ban provided here.

THIRTEENTH AMENDMENT, the right against slavery except as punishment for crime:

Slavery is alive and well in US territories like the Marianas Islands and for immigrants held by force and compelled to work without compensation on farms in the United States;[5] slavery should be banned even as a punishment for crime, and that ban should be enforced.

FIFTEENTH AMENDMENT, the right to vote cannot be denied or abridged because of race:

Names are removed from registration rolls on the basis of race, and provisional ballots are rejected on the basis of race. If provisional ballots from African-Americans in Florida in 2000 had been rejected merely at the same rate as those for whites, President Al Gore's victory margin would have been substantial.

SIXTEENTH AMENDMENT, the right to vote cannot be denied or abridged because of sex:

This right cannot be protected for women any better than it can be for men. We do not have an individual right to vote, but only a guarantee that nobody be denied that right because of their race or sex. We require that everyone register, and then sometimes dump their names off the rolls. We hold elections on a weekday, when many people have to work.

We provide insufficient staff at polling places, so voting can take many hours out of someone's day. We insert the electoral college between the voters and the president. And we insert private corporations between the voters and the counting of the votes. We should create the right to directly elect the president and the right to have our votes publicly and verifiably counted on paper ballots at each polling place.

TWENTY-FOURTH AMENDMENT, the right to vote without paying a poll tax:

We no longer have poll taxes, but we have registration procedures, long lines, elections on a work day, voting rights denied as punishment for a crime, and a system so prone to errors that many voters are disenfranchised. Hollywood actor Tim Robbins had to spend a full day traveling around his city appealing to judges before he could get a glitch corrected and be able to vote in 2008; most people are not rich, white, famous movie actors with a full day to spare.

TWENTY-SIXTH AMENDMENT, the right to vote beginning at age eighteen:

This right cannot be protected for young people any better than for old. We should have universal registration when people reach eighteen. If we can register everyone for the military draft, why can't we register everyone to vote?

There you have it. We've got rights, but they are threatened. They need restoration and enforcement. They also need expansion and updates. But that's not the half of it. There's also the matter of rights we ought to have that were never imagined by the creators of our Bill of Rights.

19. RIGHTS WE NEED

In places where we are not already protected, or where we have been shown to be vulnerable over the last eight years or before, legislation and amendments can be used to expand our existing rights and establish entirely new ones. All of our rights, new and old, should be properly protected by placing violations of them in the criminal code.

1. The Right to Vote

Proposing a right to vote only surprises people who believe we already have it. Perhaps the most important as well as the least controversial right that we could create is one that Congressman Jesse Jackson Jr. has long advocated for: the individual national right to vote (allowing the creation of national uniform standards for elections).[6] I would add as well the right to directly elect the president, vice president, and all other elected officials, and to have one's vote publicly and locally counted in a manner that can be repeated and verified if questioned (effectively requiring hand-counted paper ballots), and the right to paid time off work to vote on election day, which would be made a national holiday or scheduled on a weekend. I would also propose establishing and enforcing serious criminal penalties for election fraud. I'll take up the issues of election fraud and voting rights at more length later in this book.

I think we should consider as well a less orthodox proposal, namely the right to be a candidate for elected office. Even if we all had the full and verifiable and unencumbered right to vote, our democracy would remain a weak one as long as only the extremely wealthy and those willing to take payments from the wealthy are able to credibly compete for elected office. We should have a right to know that the candidates in our elections are not corrupted by bribes (including the currently legal

211

bribes we euphemistically call "contributions"), and the right to ourselves be candidates in more than a nominal sense unless prevented by something other than our wealth and income. I'll take up below some of the policies that might be implemented to protect this right.

2. Right to Expanded Magna Carta Protections

We need to establish strict protection from arbitrary arrest, detention, exile, or enforced disappearance, and from all forms of slavery and forced labor, with criminal penalties for violators and compensation for victims. We need to strengthen our right against unreasonable search and seizure in this electronic age, amending the Constitution and/or replacing FISA with legislation that effectively protects us, creates criminal penalties for violators, and compensates victims. We should place in the Constitution new language to strictly ban all torture, all cruel, inhuman, or degrading treatment or punishment, rendition, medical or scientific experimentation on humans without their consent, and state executions. We should create criminal penalties for violators and compensation for victims.

We need to strengthen or create some additional rights for those who find themselves within our criminal justice system, including the right to presumption of innocence until proven guilty of a crime, the right to be told the charges against you at the time of your arrest, the right not to be detained without being arrested and charged, the right to obtain and to use in court a videotape of any relevant interrogations or confessions, the right of the accused to be detained separately from those already convicted, the right of juveniles to be detained separately from adults, the right not to be imprisoned for inability to fulfill a contract, the right to a penal system aimed at reformation and social rehabilitation, and the right to compensation for false conviction and punishment. The United States currently locks up a greater percentage of its citizens than any other nation, a heavy-handed and backward approach to social problems that mirrors our approach to foreign policy. Protecting innocents from the imprisonment onslaught and redirecting imprisonment to include rehabilitation, education, and preparation for civic participation are essential to undoing this damage.

I refer to all of the above as Magna Carta protections because I see them as part of that living tradition. Peter Linebaugh's recent book, *The Magna Carta Manifesto*, documents the meaning of the Magna Carta down through the centuries, prominent in that meaning being the tradition established by the Magna Carta that no man would be above the law, that no man would sit in judgment of himself, that no one would be tried or imprisoned without due process including judgment by a jury of peers.[7]

The Great Charter of Liberties was originally produced together with the Charter of the Forest, and these two documents were paired together for centuries before one of them was forgotten and the other was reinterpreted as the sacred text of private property, capitalism, God, and empire. The Charter of the Forest protects the rights of commoners to "commoning." That's a verb that encompasses the rights to use and maintain forests and wild places, to allow livestock to forage, and to gather wood, berries, mushrooms, and water. Linebaugh tells a global story of the loss of commons, of the enclosing of public spaces, of the creation of poverty and criminality, and of the Magna Carta as a manifesto against privatization. It strikes me as important right now that we recognize the power that the rule of law has had for good and its intimate ties to social as well as formal justice. Does Eric Holder—do the rest of us—want to oversee the demise of this tradition or its expansion and enhancement?

3. Equal Rights for All

We need, at long last, to place in our Constitution comprehensive equal rights for women, including the right to equal pay for equal work. We need comprehensive rights for all children, including the right to have their interests given primary consideration in public actions that concern them, and a ban on harmful child labor. We need a right to special care and assistance for mothers, fathers, and children, including paid maternal and family leave. We need these things much more than we need to hear anyone screaming about "family values"! And we need the Constitution to establish a right against any unfair discrimination on the basis of race, color, gender, sexual identity, language, religion or lack thereof, political or other opinion, national or social origin, property, birth, citizenship, or other status, including that of a migrant worker.

4. Environmental Rights

Our history is one of slowly expanding the group of people entitled to civil rights, breaking down barriers of wealth, race, sex, and age. But what about species? Although we've criminalized cruelty to animals in some cases, we've never dared to scandalize the philosophers by giving rights to nonhumans. I'm not proposing that we include dogs and pigs and insects in our Constitution as individuals. I don't think they have much more place there than do corporations, which have falsely claimed constitutional rights. But we might want to consider giving our environment as a whole a right to survive.

Of course we could simply give humans a right to a clean, safe and sustainable environment, and I think we probably should. But that's not the only possible solution. In September 2008, Ecuador created a new Constitution by a two-thirds public vote that included some changes that we might want to avoid (such as aggrandized executive power) and others we might want to consider, such as the recognition of legally enforceable rights of nature or ecosystem. The new Constitution provides nature the "right to exist, persist, maintain and regenerate its vital cycles, structure, functions and its processes in evolution" and mandates that the government take "precaution and restriction measures in all the activities that can lead to the extinction of species, the destruction of the ecosystems or the permanent alteration of the natural cycles."[8] Of course, an American document couldn't mention evolution until Americans were properly educated, but the rest of the language here might be useful. While an ecosystem can't sue on its own behalf over violation of its rights, people can do so for it.

5. Right to Education, Housing, and Health Care

To help give every child a chance and to foster young talent and innovation, America should guarantee the right to public education of equal high quality from preschool through college. We should have a right to decent, safe, sanitary and affordable housing. We should have a right to health care of equal high quality. These are things that ought not to be privileges for the wealthy but things to which we all have adequate access, in other words: rights.[9]

6. Worker Rights

We also need basic rights related to work and income established at the level of our Constitution. These should include the right to form and join a labor union and the right to strike, the right to employment (not to be confused with antilabor laws that go by the misleading name "right to work"), and the right to a living wage—that is to say, just and favorable remuneration for work ensuring for the worker and their family an existence worthy of human dignity, and supplemented, if necessary, by other means of social protection. We should have the right to a reasonable limitation of working hours and to periodic paid holidays. Not all of this will be acceptable to the US Chamber of Commerce, but most of it will make sense to most Americans.

7. Right to Basic Welfare

I would like to offer two additional proposals that might be somewhat controversial, one ensuring the basic welfare (food and shelter) of each individual whether or not employed and working, the other ensuring some limitation on the division of society into an overclass of super-wealthy families and everyone else.

The basic income guarantee, or BIG as it's known to the activists and academics who make up the US Basic Income Guarantee Network, is a government-ensured guarantee that no one's income will fall below the level necessary to meet their most basic needs for any reason, even if they are not working and earning the living wage that I (but not all supporters of a BIG) would also mandate.

How would a basic income guarantee work? Each month, every adult would receive a check from the government for the exact same amount. These checks, notes the Citizen Policies Institute, would be "large enough to meet basic costs of food and shelter . . . but not so large as to undermine incentives to work, earn, save, and invest." Some checks would be wasted on awesomely affluent Americans who have absolutely no financial worries. But there would be no need for a bureaucracy to determine who should receive the checks, and no stigma would attach to receiving them. That some small percentage of people would not work cannot be considered a fatal flaw in the BIG idea, not in a country where we already have a significant percentage of people not working, including those unable to work, those with no need to work and no desire to, those searching for work, those who have given up on searching for work, those who have calculated that they would spend more on childcare than they would earn if they took a job, those who are behind bars as a result of crimes that tend to increase with unemployment and poverty, and those working part-time who want full-time jobs. There are also many working full-time or more who would prefer to work part-time and train for other work if they could afford to. Surely anyone's displeasure with people receiving a basic income without working should not outweigh their displeasure with the current state of affairs in which tens of millions of Americans, including children, live in poverty. The Paulson's Plunder "bailouts" gave away, to some very wealthy people, far more money than would be required for a BIG, so perhaps it's best to think of a BIG as a real bailout for everyone, one that would actually stimulate the economy.

The past thirty years have seen tremendous growth in the United States in productivity and wealth, and yet we don't all seem very appreciative. In fact, as Yale political scientist Robert Lane has documented, surveys have found Americans' assessment of their level of happiness declining significantly.[10] The United States contains 4.5 percent of the world's population and spends 42 percent of the world's health care expenses, and yet Americans are less healthy than the residents of nearly every other wealthy nation and a few poor ones as well, as documented by Dr. Stephen Bezruchka of the University of Washington.[11] What's going on? We spend more on criminal justice and have more crime. How can that be? We're richer and have more poverty. Why is that?

Labor journalist Sam Pizzigati thinks he has a solution to these riddles.[12] In his recent book, *Greed and Good*, Pizzigati focuses on the extreme increase in inequality that the United States has seen over the past generation. The Federal Reserve Board has documented gains by America's wealthiest 1 percent of more than $2 trillion more than everyone in America's bottom 90 percent combined. We are now the most unequal wealthy nation on earth, and have reversed the relationship we had to Europe when the founders of this country rejected aristocracy. Today Europeans come to the United States to marvel at the excesses of wealth beside shameful poverty. Perhaps it's time for a right to some minimal level of equality.

Many of us would like to lift up those at the bottom. Few of us want to bring down those at the top. Pizzigati argues that you cannot do one without the other, because the super-wealthy will always have the political power to avoid contributing to bringing the bottom up. This will leave it to the middle class to assist those less fortunate, even as their own situations are slipping and their concept of success—based on the lifestyles of the CEO-barons—is being driven further out of reach. The middle class won't want to do this, and instead will support policies that benefit the super-wealthy.

But the existence of the super-wealthy, Pizzigati argues, has a long list of negative impacts on all of our lives. Get rid of vast concentrations of wealth, and all sorts of things happen, including lower murder rates, lower blood pressure, and lower housing prices. Research suggests that when people see their situations improving over time, and when they see their situations as acceptable by the standard of those around them, they tend to be happy. The United States had this in the 1950s and 1960s, a period when working families prospered and income over $200,000 was taxed at roughly 90 percent.

Developed societies with the healthiest and longest living people, extensive research shows, are not those with the highest average wealth, but those with the greatest equality of wealth.[13] Explanations for this fact vary from consideration of the levels of stress caused by economic insecurity to the focusing of health care on plastic surgery and other luxuries at the expense of treatment of actual illnesses. Research also shows that a country's murder rate varies with its inequality, not its overall wealth or its criminal justice spending.[14]

Pizzigati proposes a new system of income tax that would lower taxes on 99 percent of Americans and allow the wealthiest 1 percent to lower their taxes by lobbying to raise the minimum wage. This system would ensure a living wage and a maximum wage as well. If your household brought in less than the income of two full-time minimum wage workers, you would pay no income tax. Above that level you would pay 1 percent. Above twice the minimum wage you would pay 2 percent. And so on up to 10 percent. Any income above ten times the minimum would be taxed at 100 percent.[15] If those with high incomes wanted less of it taxed, all they would need to do would be to lobby Congress to raise the minimum wage.

This would mean significantly lower taxes on 99 percent of us. It would also mean an economy focused on products for a once-again expanding middle class, rather than our new aristocracy. The maximum wage proposal will almost certainly be attacked as being supposedly motivated by a desire to punish successful people (as if restricting someone to ten times the minimum wage is punishment, but the minimum wage itself is not). However, I favor a maximum wage for the simple reason that a democratic republic cannot survive with an aristocracy. My thought here is also a very American way of thinking and by no means new, but I'm afraid it is not nearly as widespread as is support for revenge and belief that revenge is everywhere.

8. Right to Be a Conscientious Objector

Here's another proposal that's sure to be controversial: we should create the right not to be made a participant in a war of aggression, as a soldier, contractor, or taxpayer. After all, wars of aggression are already illegal, so there ought not to be anything dangerous in giving individuals the right to obey the law. We should also update the Third Amendment to give us the right to live in towns and cities free from any public presence of military force. In fact, we should create the right to live in a nation either not armed for aggressive war or actively working toward disarmament and actively working toward global disarmament.

9. Freedom of the Press, and Freedom from War Lies

We should expand the First Amendment to require meaningful freedom of the press, and I will discuss later some policies that might make that a reality. But I think we might consider one strictly limited restriction on our First Amendment rights. This would involve the establishment of a right to protection from war propaganda, including any false, misleading, or fraudulent information intended to create support for war, with criminal penalties for violators. We should never underestimate the danger of restricting free speech or of opening up the possibility of further restricting free speech, but the clear fact is that war is much more destructive than any other human activity (with the possible exception of long term environmental destruction). It is already forbidden to falsely scream "Fire!" in a crowded building, so it might makes sense to forbid effectively drenching crowded buildings in lighter fluid. I would, however, expand the right to free speech to include the right to be a whistleblower and expose violations of the law by superiors, in public or private work places, without negative consequences.

10. Right to Know Your Rights

Finally, I think that we need enshrined in explicit terms in our Constitution, as well as perhaps elaborated in a book called "Self-Government for Dummies," the right to know what the laws are, and to have the laws applied equally to everyone.

20. CHANGES WE CAN MAKE

Fortunately, we do not have to start from scratch in constructing new human rights. Much work has already been done, some of it by that 95.5 percent of humans who are not Americans. Many of the rights proposed in the previous chapter I have taken word for word, or nearly word for word, from existing international treaties. Where we think it makes sense, we can ratify and enforce international treaties that establish rights for all human beings. Shouldn't Americans have, at a minimum, the rights that others around the world have or strive for? Shouldn't we provide those rights to foreigners visiting our country and expect those rights to be maintained for our citizens traveling abroad? Shouldn't we abide by those treaties that we have already signed, and join other nations in developing these rights, rather than standing in the way? Isn't there something fundamentally wrong with what we did to the people of New Orleans in 2005 and subsequent years that requires a reworking of the system that permitted it?

A major influence on the establishment of international rights was the work of President Franklin Delano Roosevelt and his wife Eleanor Roosevelt, who served as delegate to the UN General Assembly and chair of the committee that drafted the Universal Declaration of Human Rights. In his annual address to Congress in 1941, President Roosevelt said,

> In the future days, which we seek to make secure, we look forward to a world founded upon four essential human freedoms. The first is freedom of speech and expression—everywhere in the world. The second is freedom of every person to worship God in his own way—everywhere in the world. The third is freedom from want—which, translated into universal terms,

means economic understandings which will secure to every nation a healthy peacetime life for its inhabitants—everywhere in the world. The fourth is freedom from fear—which, translated into world terms, means a worldwide reduction of armaments to such a point and in such a thorough fashion that no nation will be in a position to commit an act of physical aggression against any neighbor—anywhere in the world. That is no vision of a distant millennium. It is a definite basis for a kind of world attainable in our own time and generation. That kind of world is the very antithesis of the so-called new order of tyranny which the dictators seek to create with the crash of a bomb.

That kind of world has still not been attained, but it is still attainable. Progress has been made here at home, although we've also taken significant steps backward. The same is true abroad. International rights and restrictions have developed over the decades, inspired by documents like the US Constitution and the Universal Declaration of Human Rights (UDHR). These new ideas have been incorporated into treaties to which the United States is, in some cases, already a party, treaties like the Geneva Conventions and the UDHR.[16] According to the US Constitution, those treaties and every other treaty to which the United States is a party are the law of the land:

> ... This Constitution, and the Laws of the United States which shall be made in Pursuance thereof; and all Treaties made, or which shall be made, under the Authority of the United States, shall be the supreme Law of the Land; and the Judges in every State shall be bound thereby, any Thing in the Constitution or Laws of any State to the Contrary notwithstanding.

In looking for ways to expand our Bill of Rights, we can turn to the International Bill of Rights,[17] which consists of three major treaties:

1. The Universal Declaration of Human Rights (UDHR), which the United States voted in favor of when it was unanimously passed by the United Nations in 1948;

2. The International Covenant on Economic, Social and Cultural Rights (ICESCR), which went into effect in 1976 and has been ratified by 159 nations but not the United States; and

3. The International Covenant on Civil and Political Rights (ICCPR), which went into effect in 1976 and has been ratified by 162 nations including the United States, although the US ratification included major exceptions and qualifications that rendered it toothless. There are also two additions to the International Covenant on Civil and Political Rights called optional protocols. The first has been ratified by 111 nations, but not the United States, the second by sixty-six nations but not the United States.

These three documents establish the sorts of rights we have been discussing, with the ICCPR focused more on legal and political rights, such as the due process rights that were found in the center of our US Bill of Rights at least prior to Bush-Cheney, and the ICESCR focused more on social rights such as health, education, and basic well-being. If the UDHR addresses life, and the ICCPR liberty, the ICESCR takes up the pursuit of happiness (or, if you prefer, the freedoms from want and fear). But the USA is being left behind. I encourage you to read these and many other treaties at http://www2.ohchr.org/english/law/index.htm.

We might begin to correct our deficiencies by considering the possibility of ratifying the second of these treaties and removing the exceptions to our ratification of the third, as well as ratifying the two optional protocols. Then we could legislate and enforce strict compliance with the entire package. There are seven additional major treaties aimed at protecting human rights:

1. The International Convention on the Elimination of All Forms of Racial Discrimination, which has been ratified by 173 nations, including the United States; however, the US ratification includes major exceptions.

2. The Convention on the Elimination of All Forms of Discrimination against Women, which is accompanied by an optional protocol. The United States is the only wealthy nation that has not ratified.

3. The Convention against Torture and Other Cruel, Inhuman or Degrading Treatment or Punishment, which is accompanied by an optional protocol. The United States has ratified the convention, but not the protocol, which creates enforcement.

4. The Convention on the Rights of the Child, which is accompanied by two optional protocols, one related to armed conflict, the other to slavery, prostitution, and pornography. The United States and Somalia are the only two nations that have not ratified this convention.

5. The International Convention on the Protection of the Rights of All Migrant Workers and Members of Their Families. No wealthy countries have ratified this convention, only poor ones.

6. The International Convention for the Protection of All Persons from Enforced Disappearance. This is a new treaty, not yet in force. Thus far seventy-three countries have signed, and four have ratified. The United States has done neither.

7. The Convention on the Rights of Persons with Disabilities, which is accompanied by an optional protocol. The United States is the only wealthy nation that has not ratified.

As you can see, of the above, the US has only ratified the International Convention on the Elimination of Racial Discrimination, which included major exceptions, and the Convention against Torture and Other Cruel, Inhuman or Degrading Treatment of Punishment, but only the convention, not the protocol. And, despite having signed the Convention Against Torture, we are violating it by failing to prosecute all acts of complicity in torture.

These treaties, combined with those above, would provide the United States, if enforced, with the vast majority of the rights I discussed in the previous chapter, and would do so in a way that united us with the rest of the world. We should abandon our rogue state status and join with the world community. In fact, we should lead the way by fully ratifying and aggressively legislating and enforcing all of these treaties. The United States would be obliged by the above treaties to accord equal rights to non-Americans, to work with other nations to eliminate world hunger, to report to the United Nations on its progress in providing all of the rights created by the treaties, and to take active steps in many areas, including by working to end racial discrimination, ensuring that the mass media disseminates material of social and cultural benefit to children, and ensuring access and lack of discrimination for people with disabilities.

There are other treaties that we should join and abide by, as well. The General Assembly resolution on "Permanent sovereignty over natural resources" and the "International Convention against the Recruitment, Use, Financing and Training of Mercenaries" both do what it sounds like they do, with obvious consequences for US behavior in Iraq and elsewhere. The same goes for the "Principles of Medical Ethics Relevant to the Role of Health Personnel, particularly Physicians, in the Protection of Prisoners and Detainees against Torture and Other Cruel, Inhuman or Degrading Treatment or Punishment." I've mentioned in a previous chapter the Rome Statute of the International Criminal Court, which Clinton signed and Bush unsigned. It should be signed, ratified, and enforced. So should the Convention on the Non-Applicability of Statutory Limitations to War Crimes and Crimes against Humanity, and the Principles of International Cooperation in the Detection, Arrest, Extradition and Punishment of Persons Guilty of War Crimes and Crimes Against Humanity.

Even if we were to ratify and enforce all of the above treaties, or most of them, and others like them, and new ones that we might originate, we would also need to place enforcement measures in our national code of law, and there would be an advantage to incorporating key rights and freedoms into the US Constitution, including some that are not established by the treaties above. Some of the changes we need can only be made by amending the Constitution. Constitutional amendments should not replace treaties, but can reinforce them. Our Constitution was designed to be amended. Article V reads:

> The Congress, whenever two thirds of both Houses shall deem it necessary, shall propose Amendments to this Constitution, or, on the Application of the Legislatures of two thirds of the several States, shall call a Convention for proposing Amendments,

which, in either Case, shall be valid to all Intents and Purposes, as part of this Constitution, when ratified by the Legislatures of three fourths of the several States, or by Conventions in three fourths thereof, as the one or the other Mode of Ratification may be proposed by the Congress . . .

Our original Constitution was not only written over two centuries ago, but it was written with the influence of a very antidemocratic spirit. We have amended the Constitution to include new groups of people within the umbrella of "we the people," and to make other improvements, but we have not amended the Constitution in the dramatic ways in which its authors certainly expected we would need to. We're dragging around with us a radically outdated structure of government. And, yes, even today we fail to live up to some of its better ideas, but that is in part because of the limitations imposed on us by some of its worse ones.

At this point of crisis, in the midst of economic and political turmoil, we are in need of serious change. I think we should seriously consider working to move two-thirds of the states, through their legislatures or through state conventions, to call a new constitutional convention as one of several approaches to reforming our government. It's about time we made the first use of a tool that has been sitting there gathering dust in Article V for over two centuries!

In fact, a group called Friends of the Article V Convention[18] has documented at least 754 applications already filed with Congress by the states (at least one from each of the fifty states) calling for a convention. But only four states have taken this action since the year 2000. Some combination of the following may be required to make a convention actually happen: new applications must be grouped within a short period of time from two-thirds of the fifty states, public pressure must be placed on Congress, or lawsuits must be brought against Congress by the states. The states' applications need not be identical in language or raise the same topics or propose the same amendments. But our goal should be to propose and pass at the convention a group of amendments that accomplishes comprehensive reform.

By proposing a coherent set of amendments, we can develop our vision of a better nation, facilitating the work that will win partial victories short of creating a constitutional convention—and perhaps victories at the state level as well. In order to work for a new national convention, we need not all agree on every goal, only on the need for major reform. From any individual's point of view, of course, opening up the Constitution to major changes will present the risk of making it worse. But if the convention itself is designed to include some of the reforms (public financing, public broadcasting, etc.) that we hope it will impose on the Constitution, the risk may pay off.

States could put the question of supporting a convention to a public vote or create requirements that must be met for citizens to force such an initiative to a vote. A more deliberative procedure might be tried as well. In 2004 and 2005, British Columbia, Canada, made use of a tool called a citizen assembly.[19] The government randomly selected 160 people: eighty women and eighty men representing each electoral district and native peoples. The assembly was assigned to review a single major issue, in this case the province's system of representative government. It heard from experts and held public hearings all over the province. It recommended policy changes that included shifting to a multi-seat proportional representation system. In 2005, 58 percent of the public voted for the proposal, but 60 percent was required for passage. However, the reform idea had gained momentum and appeared likely to eventually pass. The citizen assembly idea has now taken hold in Ontario, Quebec, and New Brunswick as well. In 2007, a citizen assembly in Ontario recommended changing the province's electoral system to allow for proportional representation, but the proposal was defeated in a public referendum.

A similar idea is "deliberative polling" as proposed by James Fishkin. A representative random sample of citizens are brought together in small groups to discuss their concerns. They are provided with factual information related to their concerns, and the groups are assembled for a three-day process of deliberation, during which they can consult with experts and policy makers. The more democratic the process is through which we create a constitutional convention, the more democratic will the outcome be.[20]

Many of the changes that most need to be made at the constitutional level could quite easily garner overwhelming popular support. These would begin with an appropriate second bill of rights. They would also include restrictions on abuses of power, as discussed in the first sections of this book.

Under a new and improved Constitution, the people should have the right to know the laws of the land and to have the laws applied equally to everyone. While I expressed reluctance above about amending the Constitution only to ban signing statements, a major revision of the Constitution should certainly establish that the president has no right to use signing statements or any other documents to encourage the violation of laws as passed by Congress and signed into law and no right to spend public (or private) funds on any activity authorized only by a signing statement, and that the Supreme Court has the exclusive power to rule on the constitutionality of laws.

The president and his or her subordinates should also be forbidden to create laws by (even if publicly) signing any document, be it an executive order, a memo, a determiniation, a finding, a directive, a proclamation, or any of the dozens of other labels applied to decrees from on high. Congress should give the president explicit and limited rule-making powers. All rules should be publicly available. And Congress should be understood to have the power to overrule them.

Government employees should have the right to expose violations of the law by superiors without negative consequences. The executive branch should be required to comply with oversight requests from Congress, a congressional committee, or the Supreme Court, and in order to claim any privilege from doing so should be required to present its case in closed session and abide by the decision of the Congress or the congressional committee or the courts. The vice president should be required to comply with all laws and rules applying to the legislative branch and to engage in no executive branch activity. The House, Senate, or any committee thereof should explicitly possess the power to hold noncompliant witnesses in contempt and to imprison them until the end of a two-year Congress in the case of the House or a House committee, or for a maximum of six years in the case of the Senate or a Senate committee. And so on.

Another important goal in revisiting the Constitution would be to deny the rights it conveys to corporations, while extending humans' rights into the workplace and into privately owned spaces such as shopping malls. Corporations are not mentioned in the Constitution, but at this point it is probably going to take a Supreme Court decision or a constitutional amendment to strip them of rights that should belong to us.

There has been progress on this front. Localities around the country, including Humboldt County, California, have denied corporations personhood and forbidden them from, for example, giving money to political campaigns, or from dumping sewage sludge on farms. We should follow these examples as well as legislating at the federal level a repeal of falsely claimed corporate power. We should repeal the anti-labor Taft-Hartley Act, which limits the right to form unions and to strike, and pass the Employee Free Choice Act, which enforces the right to form a union. We should bust up all corporate monopolies. We should not allow any corporation to become so dominant that when it goes broke the government claims an obligation to bail it out with our children's money for our own good. And we should prevent our government from engaging in such bailouts, particularly without the approval of Congress as required by the Constitution. But our hands will still be tied as long as corporations are considered constitutional persons.

On December 20, 1787, Thomas Jefferson wrote to James Madison, listing items he thought belonged in the Bill of Rights. He began with these: "freedom of religion, freedom of the press, protection against standing armies, restriction of monopolies, the eternal and unremitting force of the habeas corpus laws, and trials by jury in all matters of fact triable by the laws of the land ..." Yes, restriction of monopolies. Jefferson thought that was centrally important, and I think he was right.[21]

A great deal of useful information on the problem of corporate personhood is available from the Program on Corporations, Law and Democracy (POCLAD).[22] One result of the legal fiction that a corporation is a person is that the rights of real live people vanish on private property, making it hard to talk politics where people do their shopping or to talk union where we work. My friend Mike Ferner, a member of POCLAD, complained (in an e-mail to me),

> I can't walk up to a rail car sitting in a siding and try to measure the radiation coming from the decommissioned reactor vessel it's carrying (a real incident a few years ago outside Toledo,

Ohio) without getting arrested for trespass, but corporations can prohibit OSHA [the Occupational Safety and Health Administration] and other agencies from making inspections without a warrant. Citizens in Vermont can't pass an initiative that requires dairy product packaging to state if rBGH has been used, because the dairy industry has "negative free speech" rights, meaning they DON'T have to say something if they don't want to; just as utility companies can prohibit consumer groups from including conservation messages in utility bill mailings, because the companies have "negative free speech" rights. . . . Not to mention all the decisions local governments can't make (keeping out big box stores, refusing to site or expand a toxic waste dump, keeping out certain industries, etc. etc.) because of running afoul of the Commerce Clause and subsequent SCOTUS interpretations.

Congress recently stripped us of our Fourth Amendment rights when it "modernized" FISA. Maybe it can do the same for corporations. Maybe citizens can be given the positive right to include community messages in utility mailings. Until we can amend the Constitution, maybe we can strip corporations, piece by piece, of the rights they have usurped. And maybe we can restore the sort of death penalty that we can all agree on: the people's right, through our elected representatives, to end a corporation's charter.

One path to removing corporate personhood, without a constitutional convention, might be through the Supreme Court. In October 2008, Ralph Nader spoke with Supreme Court Justice Antonin Scalia about this question and reported on that conversation:

I asked him how the application of the Bill of Rights and related constitutional protections to the artificial creations known as corporations can be squared with a constitutional interpretation theory of "originalism." Justice Scalia said he had not put much thought into unconstitutional corporate personhood, but if a case was brought before him on the topic, he would be happy to delve into it. Unconstitutional corporate personhood is the central issue that prevents equal justice under the law and provides privileges and immunities to corporations completely outside of the framers' frame of reference in that large hot room in Philadelphia during the summer of 1787. The $700 billion blank check bailout of Wall Street is the latest manifestation of private corporate domination of our national government, a situation that Franklin Delano Roosevelt foresaw as "fascism" in a message to Congress in 1938.[23]

Another major reason for a constitutional convention is the pressing need for changes to the basic structure of our government, our system of elections and representation, the design of the three branches, and the need to limit the corrupting influences of media, money, and parties. While we've grown accustomed to "spreading democracy" abroad with bombs, we need to consider nonviolent approaches to producing more democracy here at home.

21. SPREADING DEMOCRACY TO WASHINGTON, DC

We all know that the problems we see in our government are not the work of one particular politician, no matter how mad we may be at him or her at the moment, or even the work of all of the top elected officials collectively. We know that there is something wrong with the system in which they all work, that only those willing to sell off parts of their souls can work within the current system, and that something would have to be fundamentally changed before people we know and respect could have the power to do the things we want. But exactly what changes would have to be made? What sort of system would allow us to start focusing on individuals and stop blaming the system? Below are the principal changes I think are necessary. I address in the following list the basic structures of our government and the corrupting influences of money and parties. While the corrupting influence of the media is touched on here, I address changes to our communications system more fully in the following section of the book.

1. Clean Campaign Financing

Our democracy is drowning in money, and most of the money is used to buy ads in the media. Most of the money comes from sources that expect and receive changes in public policy in return. Clearing out the money would eliminate undue influence and also free representatives, especially challengers, from spending a great deal of their time begging for money. A step in the right direction would be a voluntary system of public financing along the lines of what has now been set up in several states and a couple of cities. Under this system, a would-be candidate collects a very large number of very small donations and signatures in order to qualify, and then opts to take public financing in exchange for not raising any money privately. But making this work at the national level would require public funding the size of some small nation's budgets unless steps can be taken to reduce expenses.

The existing national system of optional public financing is not working. Obama committed to using it and then broke his promise and went outside it to raise more Wall Street money and more money overall than anyone before him. His campaign website continued to claim that he supported the idea of public financing:

> Obama supports public financing of campaigns combined with free television and radio time as a way to reduce the influence of moneyed special interests. In February 2007, Obama proposed a plan that requires major party candidates to agree on a fundraising truce, return excess money from donors, and stay within the public financing system for the General Election.[24]

Of course, supporting public financing with free television and radio time is a whole different thing from just supporting public financing. The bulk of political campaign money goes to buy television and radio ads. The Obama presidential campaign spent 23.2 percent of its money on administration of the campaign (salaries, travel, office rent, etc.) and 9.6 percent on all the other campaign expenses that might come to mind (events, polling, materials, mailings, consultants, get-out-the-vote work, etc.), but 47.9 percent on media, including $245 million on broadcast media, $27 million on the Internet, and $20 million on print advertising.[25] If we could eliminate the media expenses, we could afford to provide public financing that candidates would accept. So, rather than just trying to eliminate dirty revenue, we need to focus as well on eliminating dirty expenditures. This can also be described as creating clean resources.

And there's no reason we can't do it, since we already own the airwaves and give them away to the media companies. There's no reason we can't take a little back and give it to candidates. The airwaves—on the radio, on network television, and on the new digital television—and certainly a sufficient amount of satellite and cable television and radio and the Internet, all belong to the people. These are public resources, given away for free to giant corporations at huge financial loss to taxpayers. And, yet, outside of C-SPAN, coverage of election campaigns is extremely thin. The bulk of it is thirty-second paid advertisements that communicate very little, much of it dishonest, most of it negative, and a lot of it unimportant. When, in 2008, two presidential campaigns decided that Virginia was in play for the first time in decades, I got a glimpse of what swing states have to suffer through. If I turned on the television to watch athletes at the Olympics in China, I was also treated to Senator Obama claiming to have all the plans for new sustainable energy sources and Senator McCain swearing he'd fight big oil, big tobacco, corruption in Washington, and all the powers that be. Just going by these ads, I'd definitely have voted for McCain as the anti-corporate-power candidate (I suspect millions of people did), whereas in reality he was probably the more loyal to a corporate agenda.

Meanwhile, the mode we are supposed to get the facts from—our "free" media—is perhaps even more misleading. News coverage of elections is largely devoid of content, focusing on covering the advertisements, poll results, financial reports, scandals, and fluff. And even that coverage is slanted so that some candidates in the primaries receive literally hundreds of times the coverage of others. And it is all limited by what positions, topics, and debates are acceptable to the giant corporate conglomerates that own the media outlets to which we so generously give the air waves. Just prior to the 2008 election, viewers did get to see a thirty-minute statement from Obama, but it was an advertisement, for which he paid at least $2 million, and it was not matched by any similar statement from McCain. When Obama subsequently won the election, is it even possible that he credited his win entirely to voters and not at all to the people who supplied the $2 million or the other $700 million or so that he was given?

In a reformed and democratized system, candidates would qualify for public financing, public media coverage, and placement of their names on the ballot (without which no federal candidate would be permitted to compete) by collecting signatures and token donations. Legislation would require that basic means of communication, including any medium used by over half the people, be made available free of charge nationwide, that C-SPAN–style coverage of the federal government be made available year-round and around-the-clock everywhere, through each and every medium, and that—during limited election seasons— in addition to the governmental coverage, separate channels provide around-the-clock election coverage, free of advertising, inclusive of all qualified candidates, and immensely substantive, adding to debates and public forums in-depth interviews by diverse panels of interviewers, with all claims fact-checked and false statements so identified.

This would put C-SPAN on broadcast television, require network neutrality (equal access to all) on the Internet, and make the Internet available free everywhere. But the truly significant change would be the free substantive coverage of elections, allowing people to learn exactly what each candidate promised to do if elected. Each qualifying candidate who opted in would have equal access to appear in debates and forums, to be interviewed, etc. An equal amount of coverage would be provided of each candidate out on the campaign trail and speaking at public events. But there would be no campaign-produced ads or documentaries. And the amount of money awarded to candidates through public financing would not be sufficient to purchase massive television advertising, which would not look like a wise move anyway, because television coverage would always be available on the commercial-free E-SPAN (election channel). News reports on other channels and media would unavoidably call attention to what was being shown on E-SPAN, which would provide both national and local election news. The only reporting included on that channel would be fact-checking. If a candidate made a statement that was clearly factually false, that statement would be so labeled and explained on E-SPAN. Obviously such labeling would be prone to bias, but I think it would be preferable to broadcasting endless blatant lies unchallenged. Thousands of independent media outlets could offer their critiques of E-SPAN and as much substantive election coverage as they chose. The limited public financing needed for non-media expenses would be provided to candidates who qualified for public media coverage and opted to forego private fundraising in order to accept both.

Michael Moore made a somewhat similar proposal as one of his six proposals in *Mike's Election Guide 2008.* He proposed public financing, free air time, and spending limits, and wrote:

According to the International Institute for Democracy and
Electoral Assistance, in 72 countries around the world,
including 14 Western European countries ... political parties
are entitled to FREE MEDIA ACCESS. Same goes for Canada.
It's actually against the law for candidates in some of these
countries to purchase air time. In France, TV stations are
required to help the candidates produce their free and equal
commercial spots. In Ireland, political parties are entitled to
free three-minute broadcasts aired every evening after the
nightly news. Just three minutes? Wow, sounds like the rest of
the day's 1,440 minutes can then be spent in peace and quiet,
candidate-free. Any takers?"[26]

Moore misses the point in order to crack a joke. The point of any
package of reforms should be to make political discourse something we
want to engage in, not something we strive to avoid. And I'd rather see
airtime given simply to candidates, not parties. But this is the right
approach, and the United States is lagging behind.

If financial and other advantages of winning a party primary were
taken away (see below), and all candidates had an equal shot at collecting
the very large number of very small donations and signatures needed to
qualify for free coverage and public financing, we might see a greater
number of candidates in a general election. In order to reduce the
number of candidates sharing the public news coverage and to reduce
the risk of wasting votes on less popular candidates, it might make sense
to develop a process for holding a public primary, to be followed later
by a secondary or final election among the top two candidates or the top
five candidates. The advantage of reducing the field to two candidates
would be the assurance that the winner would have received votes from
a majority of those voting.

A voluntary and optional public financing system can be established
without a constitutional amendment or a Supreme Court ruling, but
such systems can be challenged in court. They can also be circumvented
by wealthy individuals and candidates who raise such huge amounts of
money that they prefer to forego the public funds and the free air time.
And such systems can be bypassed by third parties' issue ads and unof-

ficial propaganda, such as the fear-mongering, hate-mongering, anti-Muslim DVDs called *Obsession* that were mailed by the tens of thousands to the subscribers of corporate newspapers in swing states prior to the 2008 elections. Any system in which campaigns are largely determined by the spending of money is going to forever find loopholes to squeeze more money through, and is going to give advantages to those supported by moneyed interests, including those supported by major parties. We need free media and public financing, but ultimately we need something else as well. We need to ban private financing of public elections. The Supreme Court's definition of money as speech in *Buckley v. Valeo* must ultimately be overturned by a court reversal or a constitutional amendment. This was a ruling that said that limiting the spending of money on political campaigns is an unconstitutional limitation of "free speech." Just as we've given corporations the rights meant for people, we've given money itself the right to freedom of speech. In other words, spending money on a campaign is deemed to be protected by the First Amendment, even though that amendment was meant to protect speaking, not spending. That preposterous ruling must be overturned.

2. Reduced Power for Parties

Another major weakness in our current system of government is the strength of parties. Partisan thinking is so strong that to even say what I just did is usually interpreted as meaning that I want to build up a "third party" or at least knock down one of the two major parties to the benefit of the other. It's very difficult to imagine a government not dominated by parties, neither locked up by two parties nor overrun with dozens of parties, a system truly open to independent candidates.

Fact is, two platforms—in many cases practically the same—aren't gonna cut it. Whichever is leading at the moment dominates our government. The power of the two parties reduces 537 voices in Washington to two. It adds to the unfair advantage of incumbents, providing incumbents with all sorts of resources.[27] The power of parties, which are not mentioned anywhere in the Constitution, also removes critical tools from the Constitution. Congressman Jerrold Nadler in 2007 and 2008 said he believed impeachment could no longer be used unless two-thirds of the Senate belonged to a different party from the person impeached. I think he was wrong, that things were not yet that bad, but that they were moving in that direction. And, in fact, Nadler rightly abandoned this stance in 2009 by backing the impeachment of Judge Jay Bybee.

There are usually two views in Congress on any issue, and no more. Party leaderships decide, and almost every other member falls in line. And voters, and more importantly non-voters, know this. A candidate for Congress must almost of necessity gain the nomination of one party or the other, even as some eligible voters refuse to vote for any member of either. There are Republicans who would have spoken out against Bush and Cheney if not for party discipline. There are Democrats who would have done more than speak against Bush and Cheney if not for their party's discipline.

The growth of excessive party power goes hand in glove with the shift of power from Congress to the White House. Most Congress members now care much more whether the next president belongs to their party than they do whether Congress retains any power or whether government policies are changed. The most malicious influence of excessive party power, however, is in the relationship between Congress and activist organizations. Parties facilitate astroturfing as an alternative to grassroots organizing. Groups that purport to represent the views of citizens to Congress in reality represent the views of a political party in Congress to citizens. Activist organizations don't just compromise, they self-censor, and they lie. They, like members of Congress, follow a party line. It will be very interesting to see whether the groups that did this for the Democrats while Bush was president alter their behavior in any way now that the Democrats control the White House, the Senate, and the House. The early signs are not very encouraging.

To reduce the control of parties, we should ban "contributions" to parties except from candidates, and ban contributions to candidates from parties or from other candidates. When we provide free media (including the "debates") and public financing and ballot access, we should do so with no special privileges for parties. These sorts of changes, opening up elections, can—I think—clean up Congress better than term limits could. Term limits is a popular idea, but it would lead to the elimination of preferred representatives, and it would turn a great many representatives into lame ducks aware that they will no longer need to answer to voters.

Our highest ideal must not be "bipartisanship," but representation by people who listen to us rather than to the leadership of a party. The greatest creation of bipartisanship is the bipartisan gerrymandering of congressional districts that practically guarantees each district to a Democratic or Republican incumbent. And the opportunity to re-gerrymander to the particular advantage of one of those two parties has become the ultimate goal of our so-called representatives. In July 2008, House Speaker Nancy Pelosi told Katrina Vanden Heuvel, editor of *The Nation* magazine, that she had chosen not to impeach Bush or Cheney because her exclusive interest was in winning seats for Democrats in 2006, 2008, 2010, and especially 2012, at which point the Democrats could control redistricting.[28] This is the most powerful member of the House of Representatives telling us that not only can she not govern during an election year, or during an election pair of years, or during an election period of four years, but she can't focus on governing during a redistricting decade. The purpose of our people as a nation is now reduced to redistricting. Gerrymandering is the ultimate end of our existence. This is the depth of sleaze and emptiness we have sunk to, and this comment was made while Pelosi was on a book tour to promote her career as a model for girls and young women.

Pelosi's focus was not on pleasing her constituents and getting herself reelected. Her seat was very safe. A Republican would never win her district, and the powers of incumbency would help her ward off a challenge from Cindy Sheehan. Pelosi was not thinking of individual representation, but of party power. Her goal was to elect more Democrats, any Democrats, anywhere she could. The concern for elections is admirable. The distortions of factionalism are disturbing. And the reduction of each Congress to a period of endless campaigning instead of actual governance is disastrous.

People actually ask their Congress members "Should we lobby you for the stance we want, or would that embarrass you and risk offending the party leadership?" This amounts to flipping democracy upside-down. I don't want to see Congress members refuse to compromise. I want to see them compromise after they've pushed as hard as possible, alone or in coalition with others, for exactly what their constituents want. And they can only do that if their careers can survive giving offense to party leaders.

We need to require nonpartisan redistricting. One advantage of ending the gerrymandering is that districts would then be drawn with some sanity and resemble squares and other simple shapes more than dragons and scorpions. I agree with rightward leaning "centrist" Larry Sabato on this proposal, and with a proposal from David Wasserman that Sabato cites with approval.[29] Wasserman proposes minimum-split districting (MSD). This means that when drawing congressional districts every ten years, the boundary lines of localities are respected as much as possible. If it can be done, an entire town or city or county is included in a single district, rather than being split. According to Wasserman, MSD would not reduce representation of African Americans and other disadvantaged groups, but would better correspond to media "markets" and make partisan redistricting more difficult. Sabato favors making districts winnable by either of the two big parties, because he wants to see Congress very heavily dominated by one party or the other, thus facilitating passage of lots of laws (although the quality of the laws is presumably a different question from the quantity). I favor making districts winnable by candidates from any party or no party, so that each member of Congress better represents his or her constituents. This might mean fewer bills passing than in Sabato's scenario, but there is no reason to think it would lead to gridlock. Voters would still judge candidates based on both their ideals and their ability to compromise and get things done.[30] Americans reach strong majority opinion on lots of policy proposals, so our representatives ought to be able to do the same if they are properly representing us.[31]

3. Limited Election Seasons

There are a lot of reasons why citizens tend to see their main role as voting. Even many of the roughly half of eligible voters who do not vote do not participate in government in any other ways either. The corporate media constantly tells people that their role is to vote. Congress members tell them that too. When we do lobby and protest and otherwise try to influence representatives while they are in office, it sometimes has no impact and is simply ignored by the corporate media. And, of course, the media does not encourage citizen lobbying. It usually reports on legislation after it passes rather than before, and very often reports on the outcomes of proposals as certain even when there need be nothing certain about them. One way in which some space might be opened up for civic life in between and apart from elections would be to place some time limits on election seasons.

One way to shorten the eternal election season to a reasonable length would be to set a date before which there would be no free coverage, no public financing, and no spending of money on campaigns permitted, a solution that might require a constitutional amendment. I think six months is more than reasonable, allowing for a primary vote after four months if need be. Political parties that wanted to hold their own primaries and conventions prior to a public primary would need to do so within that four-month period, and sufficiently early to allow winners to benefit from the removal of losers from the coverage, assuming the losers chose to drop out. This would be a drastic reduction in the length of the election season, and it might be hard to persuade a corporate polling company to poll on it, but I strongly suspect such a change would be overwhelmingly supported by the American people. We're sick and tired of a bunch of vain, shallow, megalomaniacs making themselves and each other and the rest of us look really, really bad for over a year as we debate the subtle variations in their corporate-media-acceptable platforms. We'd vote to shorten elections if we could, even if it didn't mean more attention to governance instead. We'd prefer almost any other type of news to more election news. Even with legally limited election seasons, incumbents would go on making news year-round, but so might other notable citizens able to accomplish worthwhile projects benefitting society outside of public office—if, that is, we reformed the media. Here's President Barack Obama's opinion:

> Campaigns last too long and they cost too much money. And they're disproportionately influenced by Washington insiders, which is why it's not going to be enough just to change political

parties [in the presidency]. But we also have to make sure that we are mobilizing Americans across race and regions, if we're actually going to bring these changes about. Change doesn't happen from the top down, it happens from the bottom up. It's because millions of voices get mobilized and organized.[32]

Even if the party system and the media and the "financing" of elections were all unchanged, there would be a need to shorten the endless marathon of primaries and caucuses. There would also be a need to break the unfair and distorting hold that the two tiny, rural, mostly white states of Iowa and New Hampshire have on the nomination process. There are a number of ways that this could be done that I think most of us would agree would be fairer than the current system. One scheme would involve holding regional primaries. The nation could, for example, be divided into three regions, one of them voting at the end of the first month of campaigning, one after the second month, and the third after a three-month partisan primary season came to an end. And the order of the regions could be decided at the start of the season by lottery. One advantage of regional primaries is clear: candidates could focus their attention efficiently on campaigning in the appropriate region rather than jetting back and forth across the country.[33]

A disadvantage to a regional system is that it would cost a lot more money to compete in a whole region than in a few small states, setting the bar high for entry into the race. However, public financing could even the financial playing field, and the fact is that the candidate with the most money before Iowa almost always wins in the current system. Another disadvantage to a regional system is that a particular region might differ very strongly from the national consensus. However, combining the northeast and the southeast in a single region would likely cancel out the two strongest divergent regional views, and of course Iowa and New Hampshire differ drastically from the national consensus.

Another option is to go with randomly chosen groups of states in a series of primaries and beginning with a group of small states. But small states already have disproportionate power in our government. A scattered primary will have candidates spending much of their time traveling. And a sufficient number of primaries to make this workable will stretch the election season out longer than some of us would like to see it. A lot of political fanatics love nothing better than year-long or two-year-long election seasons, but those of us who see elections as getting in the way of the brief inter-election governance season would rather see the things shortened.[34]

But there's an additional twist if we decide to drop the idea that parties must remain central to the process. The same system of regional or random primaries could be used in a nonpartisan public presidential primary. We just need to balance the advantage of such a spaced-out primary, the advantage of allowing parties to precede such primaries with their own, and the need to keep the whole election season to a reasonable length. Ideally, to my mind, our ultimate goal should be replacing party primaries with public primaries open to all. Most Americans don't start paying serious attention to elections until after the primaries are over. A shorter primary season, and one open to all voters, might involve more, not less, public participation. And that is, above all else, what we want.

4. No More Electoral College

We need other electoral reforms as well. The time has come to eliminate the electoral college and elect presidents (and vice presidents) with the popular vote. In this I agree with public interest lawyer and director of the Brennan Center for Justice Michael Waldman, and disagree with Larry Sabato. While everyone sees problems with the electoral college, some want to keep it around and try to minimize its drawbacks, including the risk of electing a president who loses the popular vote. But the electoral college does not offer any benefits that, to my mind, outweigh the defects. Eliminating the electoral college and using the actual popular vote to elect a president would make every vote matter. That ideal solution requires amending the Constitution. A second-best solution would be for states to distribute their electoral votes proportionately. Maine and Nebraska already do so, and Hawaii, Illinois, Maryland, and New Jersey have passed laws committing to do so if enough states to provide an electoral college majority agree to do the same.

Because a presidential candidate currently wins all of a state's electoral votes or none (except in Maine and Nebraska), most candidates completely ignore states they are likely to win or lose and focus only on a handful of states that are considered uncertain. According to http://nationalpopularvote.com, which is seeking to change this procedure without eliminating the electoral college, "In 2004, candidates concentrated over two-thirds of their money and campaign visits in just five states; over 80 percent in nine states; and over 99 percent of their money in just 16 states." Critics of changing the system suggest that candidates might visit a lot more states but be inclined to focus on urban population centers. That might be true. But under the current system candidates ignore most rural areas and most urban areas alike. People are more likely to interact with a candidate if he or she visits a nearby city than they are if the candidate never enters their state at all.

The beauty of amending the Constitution, ideally in a convention, and tossing out antidemocratic relics like the electoral college, is that it opens our mind to other possibilities as well. We have the power to decide not just how we elect people, but to what positions we elect them. What, we must ask ourselves, should the House and Senate look like, and should both of them even exist?

5. A Bigger House, No More Senate

One clear problem with the House of Representatives is that it is too small. I know that sounds crazy. If something's not working, and already costs plenty of money, and already takes several months just to blow its nose, why in the world would we want to make it bigger? Well, consider this: each member of the House is expected to represent (on average, with variation from state to state) approximately 690,000 people.[35] The House is the same size it was in 1910, when the same 435 members were expected to represent approximately 213,000 people each. In 1860, 183 members represented about 100,000 constituents each. The original members of the House were sixty-five, and they represented about 60,000 people each. George Washington wanted each member to represent 30,000. Members of the House of Commons in London, even today, represent about 91,000 people each. The fact is that nobody, even if they were trying, could possibly represent 690,000 people. There is simply not enough time in the day to get to know even the most significant informal representatives of 690,000 individuals.

This issue is one on which I agree again with rightward-leaning "centrist" Larry Sabato, and right-wing columnist George Will. Sabato, author of *A More Perfect Constitution*, makes the case quite convincingly that the House should be enlarged from 435 to 1,000 members.[36] It is safe to assume, I think, that a larger House would also create larger committees. And, yes, everything would feel a bit more weighted down by numbers. But, let's face it, the problem with Congress has not been the volume of work but the failure of that work to reflect the concerns of the American people. Smaller districts would mean representation of the people from closer to them, and far better inclusion of local concerns in the creation of national legislation. A larger House with more members and more staffers could draft more legislation, rather than relying on lobbyists or the White House to do their work for them while they're off raising money. A larger Congress could work more closely with the various departments of the government and draw on their expertise in a different way than the White House does.

And what about the Senate? Can we have a larger House and still have the Senate too? And if we did not have the Senate, would anyone miss it? Steven Hill, director of the Political Reform Program of the New America Foundation, cofounder of Fair Vote/Center for Voting and Democracy and author of *Ten Steps to Repair American Democracy*, proposes that we simply abolish the Senate, and I believe he is correct.[37]

There are almost 34 million people in California. But California is given enough House members so that each one represents very roughly the same number of people as do representatives from any other state. Yet, California is given the exact same number of senators as Wyoming (two). A US senator from California is supposed to represent 17 million people, give or take, while a senator from Wyoming is only expected to represent 250,000 people. All else equal, which senator do you think is going to do a better job, and which is going to remain oblivious to the horrendous job that he or she is doing?

Thirty-nine states have more than two representatives in the House, meaning that in most states representation in the House is closer to the people than is representation in the Senate. Given our current system of financing election campaigns, this means that only candidates with access to greater amounts of money can compete for Senate seats. This is only part of the reason that it is almost always harder to pass decent legislation in the Senate than in the House. At least as big a part of the problem is the disproportionate influence in the Senate of the most lightly populated states. Senators representing 11.2 percent of the people of the United States, and very disproportionately white and rural people at that, can block any bill from passing the Senate, and therefore also render futile the passage of any bill in the House. That's the percentage of the population living in the twenty-one smallest states, which of course are represented by forty-two senators. It takes forty-one senators to sustain a filibuster. Senators representing only 7 percent of the people can block treaties or constitutional amendments. That's the percentage living in the seventeen least populated states, represented by thirty-four senators. That's one reason we should use a states-created convention, rather than Congress, to amend the Constitution and reform the congressional structure.

The electoral college and the Senate slightly distort our understanding of the extent to which the Republican and Democratic parties are supported in the country. McCain and Palin won 46 percent of the vote in 2008, if we can believe the official results, but only 32 percent of the electoral vote from states representing 31 percent of the nation's population. And a slight change in five states would have knocked McCain and Palin down to 17 percent of the electoral votes. In their top five states they only topped 55 percent in one, their fourth biggest state, Tennessee, where they picked up 57 percent. Their fifth biggest state, Missouri, was such a close contest that—given the state of our election system—nobody can really be sure who won it. Studies estimate that 51 percent of Americans lean toward Democrats and 38 percent toward Republicans. In the US House of Representatives, Republicans hold 40 percent of the seats and Democrats 60 percent. In the Senate, Republicans hold forty of 100 seats, but those senators represent only 37 percent of the population. The major distortion, of course, comes from the media pundits who look at all of this and declare the United States a "center-right nation."

When Thomas Jefferson returned from France and asked George Washington why the constitutional convention had added the Senate to the already discussed House during Jefferson's absence, Washington supposedly replied: "Why did you pour that coffee into your saucer?" Jefferson said, "To cool it." And Washington remarked, "Even so. We pour our legislation into the senatorial saucer to cool it."

Can you name one good thing the Senate has done in recent years that the House didn't do too and in most cases express a willingness to do better? If you can't, I would challenge you to explain what purpose the Senate serves. The Senate approves or rejects treaties and appointments, but the House would do a better job of it. The Senate holds hearings, but the House already does a better job of it. If no solid case can be made for the utility of the Senate, we can and must abolish it. The Senate is an idea whose time has passed. Restructuring our government to make it truly representative of our will requires amending the Constitution to eliminate the Senate.

The strongest argument for keeping the Senate is the extra representation that it provides for small states. And yet, I suspect that a majority of the people in our small states would prefer to be living under laws that the House could pass were it not for the Senate. The people of small states do not tend to favor campaign funding corruption, Wall Street bailouts, government secrecy, or even wars, torture, and illegal spying significantly more than the people in large states. But the people in the Senate tend to favor all such things significantly more than the people in the House. Senators also tend to favor, more than the House, measures that strip state governments of power on behalf of the federal government.

Rather than abolish it, Larry Sabato proposes a constitutional amendment to enlarge the Senate and create somewhat more equitable representation. Sabato proposes giving the ten most populous states two more seats each in the Senate, and one more seat each to the next fifteen most populous states.[38] This would mean 135 senators, or 137 if a new state were added or the District of Columbia were given two senators without becoming a state. This proposal would need to be tweaked, I think, to instead maintain an even number of Senators, thus preserving the vice president's role as tie-breaker if the full Senate votes and ties.

Instead of adding a senator to each of fifteen states, we could add one to each of fourteen or sixteen. If we're going to try to remove all of the vice president's unconstitutional and abusive powers, we might as well leave him the one power the Constitution gave him.

Short of abolishing the Senate, or enlarging it, we should at least make some serious reforms. The Constitution gave us the antidemocratic Senate, but it did not give us its most antidemocratic tool, the filibuster. The filibuster was created by accident when the Senate eliminated a seemingly redundant practice of voting on whether to vote. Senators then discovered, after a half-century of surviving just fine without the filibuster, that they could block votes by talking forever. In 1917 the Senate created a rule allowing a vote by two-thirds of those voting, to end a filibuster. In 1949 they changed the rule to require two-thirds of the entire Senate membership. In 1959 they changed it back. And in 1975 they changed the rule to allow three-fifths of the Senators sworn into office to end a filibuster and force a vote. Filibustering no longer requires giving long speeches. It only requires threatening to do so. The use of such threats has exploded over the past ten years, dominating the decision-making process of our government and effectively eliminating the possibility of truly populist or progressive legislation emerging from Congress. This has happened at the same time that the forces of money, media, and party have led the Democrats in both houses to view the filibuster as a convenient excuse, rather than as an impediment.

Were the Democrats serious about eliminating the filibuster excuse, they would either take every step possible to get sixty senators into their caucus (including by President Obama appointing Republican senators to his cabinet), or they would change the rule (Senate Rule 22) requiring sixty senators to break a filibuster. Changing the rule would only require fifty-one votes if done in the same manner in which it was in 1975. The rule could be changed to require fifty-five votes instead of sixty or, more democratically, to simply require 50 percent plus one.[39]

President Obama is aware of the antidemocratic function of the filibuster, and has mixed feelings about it. He wrote in *The Audacity of Hope*,

But throughout the Senate's modern history, the filibuster has remained a preciously guarded prerogative, one of the distinguishing features that separates the Senate from the House and serves as a firewall against the dangers of majority overreach.

There is another, grimmer history to the filibuster, though, one that carries special relevance for me. For almost a century, the filibuster was the South's weapon of choice in its efforts to protect Jim Crow from federal interference, the legal blockade that effectively gutted the Fourteenth and Fifteenth Amendments. Decade after decade, courtly, erudite men like Senator Richard B. Russell of Georgia used the filibuster to choke off any and every piece of civil rights legislation before the Senate, whether voting rights bills, or fair employment bills, or anti-lynching bills. With words, with rules, with procedures & precedents—with law— Southern senators had succeeded in perpetuating black subjugation in ways that mere violence never could. For many blacks in the South, the filibuster had snuffed out hope.[40]

I agree with Obama's concern but not with his initial praise for the firewall against "majority overreach." He's not talking about bans on discrimination against minorities. He's talking simply about forty-one very wealthy and powerful individuals deciding grave matters on behalf of the rest of the country despite the absence of even a pretense of representing a majority. Eight times, between 1800 and 1860, the House tried to ban slavery but could not win the support of the Senate, which only came after a bloody civil war. And even then, the Senate blocked basic rights for African Americans for a century. The Senate gives disproportionate representation to low-population states and provides those states with disproportionate public services. North Dakotans receive $2.03 in public services for every dollar they pay in taxes. And the extra money is drawn from the taxpayers of larger states with often greater needs. The Senators who confirmed Clarence Thomas's appointment to the Supreme Court represented fewer Americans than the Senators who tried to reject him.[41] In 2009, the Democrats chose not to change the filibuster rule and not to take available steps to seat one more Democrat in the Senate (they had fifty-nine in their caucus).

On April 28, 2009, after I'd written the preceding paragraphs, Republican Senator Arlen Specter of Pennsylvania put forward a series of bills to curtail presidential power and announced that he would now be a Democrat. These two steps in combination sent the Democrats in Congress a signal as to what was needed and denied them any excuse not to do it. That is, if the Democrats could manage to discipline Specter and fifty-nine others, they could—for the moment—avoid filibusters. While I'm fundamentally opposed to party discipline, I can't help thinking how potentially useful it might be, within the confines of our rotten system, for the party that claims to represent the people to no longer be able to blame the other party for its actions.

Steven Hill offers three other proposals regarding the current Senate.[42] Most governments with two legislative chambers place less power in the more aristocratic chamber and greater power in the more representative House. Hill proposes that as long as the Senate remains in its current state of unequal representation, it should not hold the power to approve appointments, at least not lifetime appointments to the Supreme Court, and at least not by a simple majority vote. Instead, that power should be given to the House of Representatives. I think it would make the most sense to give the power of approving all appointments and treaties to the House. In addition, the power to try impeachments—a power never mentioned by reformers like Hill, Sabato, Waldman, Jackson, et alia—is abused by the Senate, and the unlikelihood of a conviction in the Senate is used as an excuse by the House not to impeach. It would work much better, I think, for impeachment to be handled by a special, permanent House committee, and impeachment trials to be held by the full House.

One change certainly should be made to the House, and to the Senate as long as it exists. We should establish the constitutional right to be represented by voting members of Congress. Most glaringly, this right has been denied to the half million residents of Washington, DC, a major US city but also a territory over which the Constitution gave Congress control. More people live in DC than in Wyoming, which boasts two senators. DC needs to be represented, with or without becoming a state. But Congress does not view the people of DC as citizens. It views them as Democrats, or as including more Democrats than Republicans.

Therefore, Republicans in Congress favor taxation without representation for the people of DC. Whether or not we can rein in the plague of partisanship in Congress, the right of the people of DC to representation needs to be legislated and enshrined in the Constitution. So, I think, does the right of the people of DC to self-governance of the sort granted to each state.

In the Senate, Obama voted yes on granting DC a seat in the House, and on granting Utah a new seat in the House for purposes of partisan balance. The bill failed, and some opponents claimed to support DC voting rights but to believe a constitutional amendment was required. The same bill passed the Senate in February 2009, but with an amendment added to undo DC laws restricting gun use. At the time of this writing, the bill was stalled in the House by disapproval of the Senate's amendment.

Another reform was proposed in January 2009, when Senator Russ Feingold introduced a bill to create a constitutional amendment that would require special elections whenever a Senate seat became vacant and ban the practice of allowing governors to appoint replacement senators. This would indeed be a positive and democratic step, albeit one of tweaking an institution that ought to be eliminated.

6. No to IRV, Proportional Representation, and Term Limits

When we talk about reforming our governmental system, including through a constitutional convention, a lot of creative ideas emerge. Some appear strong even after close scrutiny. Others collapse or fail to work well in a package that includes comprehensive reform ideas. I want to explain briefly why I oppose some very noble sounding proposals. Many reform-minded activists whom I admire would recommend using instant runoff voting (IRV). Here's an explanation of IRV from Fair-Vote.org:

> Voters rank candidates in order of choice: 1, 2, 3 and so on. It takes a majority to win. If anyone receives a majority of the first choice votes, that candidate is elected. If not, the last place candidate is defeated, just as in a runoff election, and all ballots are

counted again, but this time each ballot cast for the defeated candidate counts for the next choice candidate listed on the ballot. The process of eliminating the last place candidate and recounting the ballots continues until one candidate receives a majority of the vote.... IRV acts like a series of runoff elections in which one candidate is eliminated each election. Each time a candidate is eliminated, all voters get to choose among the remaining candidates. This continues until one candidate receives a majority of the vote.

IRV is a brilliant and democratically motivated idea. It's heart is in the right place, and it's well designed. IRV goes a long way toward eliminating the need to compromise and vote for anyone other than your favorite candidate. You can mark your first-choice candidate as, just that, your first choice, and if he or she finishes last, your vote will go to your second choice candidate. Your vote is not wasted, and nobody accuses you of spoiling their election. IRV is of course faster and cheaper than holding actual runoffs. It also tends at times to favor candidates with strong first-choice support, at the expense of compromise candidates with stronger second-choice support. And, while IRV works well to create a record of protest votes for unlikely candidates, it does not always avoid the waste/spoiler effect when your first choice candidate is actually competitive. He or she can finish second, your second-choice candidate third, and your last-choice candidate can win. And when there are a great many candidates in a race, your vote can still be wasted on an unpopular candidate. Of course, voting without IRV has these same defects, but IRV adds a major defect that its benefits probably don't outweigh.

While IRV is a wonderful and well-intended idea, it accidentally conflicts with a more important one. The biggest weakness in our elections system is our inability to be certain our votes have been accurately counted. If we cannot count our votes in a public and verifiable manner at the level of each polling place, but must count them only at the district or state or national level, and if the entire counting process must begin again when a few lost votes are discovered late, we are tying two hands and a foot behind our backs. With ordinary voting, the totals for each candidate can be publicly tallied in front of diverse witnesses at a polling place and then forwarded to be added to the full district-, state-, or national-level count. With IRV voting, that isn't possible, and a tremendous amount of additional data has to be forwarded from each polling place without anyone having any idea what it means or whether it is accurately received and included. That's a recipe for disaster. Steven Hill argues in favor of IRV without addressing these drawbacks, and without explaining how it could work alongside another proposal he supports: voter verified paper trails.[43] The best compromise that would allow the use of IRV would be paper ballots counted by optical scan machines, with a requirement that the paper ballots be locally and immediately counted and the results announced. However, the results would be either insufficient or too complicated for anyone to judge whether what was forwarded to the district, state, or national processing center was accurate. So, I would regretfully forego IRV and begin reforming elections by repealing the Help America Vote Act (HAVA) and legislating verifiable elections with local hand-counting of paper ballots, whether we yet have a constitutional right to that or not.

Proportional representation is another idea for which Steven Hill, among others, makes a strong but ultimately unconvincing case.[44] Rather than electing one representative to Congress from each district, we could elect three of them all at once, granting a seat to each of the top three vote getters. While this would provide representation for minority positions, it would also fail to reflect the opinion of the majority, require either unmanageably large districts or an unmanageably large Congress or both, and allow a great deal of buck-passing. In Baltimore, the people threw out three-member districts by public initiative several years ago in favor of small single-member districts in which each representative could be closer to the people and would be unable to refer constituents to other representatives to have their concerns addressed.[45]

Term limits is an idea that Larry Sabato, among others, argues in favor of at least considering.[46] He sees the advantage as lying in removing from officials any concern about their reelection. I see that antidemocratic goal as exactly what we want to work against. The last thing we need is representatives who feel less accountable to the people. Term limits have tended, if anything, to strengthen the domination of a legislature by the leadership of a majority party, which also means reducing the accountability of each individual representative to the people he or she represents.

Sabato's book includes twenty-two other proposals, and there are several of them I cannot agree with. He proposes establishing rules for the continuity of government in the event of mass slaughter of elected officials, a proposal that strikes me as unnecessary fear mongering aimed at formalizing the obvious, namely that we should allow temporary replacements by governors if needed and quickly elect new representatives. Sabato would probably agree with me that secret presidential plans for transforming the government into a less representative body should be banned, but banning such plans does not require replacing them via constitutional amendment.

Sabato also favors longer terms for presidents and representatives and altered terms for senators. He wants to give the president the legal power of the signing statement in the form of an item veto. And he wants to tweak the electoral college but keep it around. It should already be clear why I find these proposals unpersuasive.

7. Limiting the Power of Supreme Court Justices

I've said a lot about reforming the legislative and executive branches of our government, but isn't there a third branch that every once in a while becomes extremely important? In fact, with four of nine Supreme Court justices willing to give the president unchecked power, the future of the court is critical. The judicial branch of our government gets the briefest discussion in the Constitution of any branch other than the Cheney Branch. While the powers of the judicial branch may be simple to establish, they are tremendous, and the terms of each justice, limited only by "good behavior," can be extensive, making the Supreme Court less democratic by far than even the Senate. Supreme Court justices are eternal lame ducks, never elected in the first place and never subject to reelection. They are, however, subject to impeachment, and five of them should have been impeached for halting the counting of presidential votes in Florida in 2000. The absurdly twisted ruling in the 2000 election case of *Bush v. Gore* did not claim to be based on any past precedents, and bizarrely claimed to itself not exist as a precedent for future cases. Two of the five justices voting in the majority had expressed a desire to retire under a Republican president and to do so soon. One of them did retire at the start of Bush's second term, and the other died. Another two had family connections to Bush or his legal team. All had been appointed or promoted by an administration containing either a Bush vice president or a Bush president.

In addition to overruling the public and picking presidents, the Supreme Court holds the more established—though nonconstitutional—powers of overruling Congress by determining a law to be unconstitutional, and of overruling the president by determining his actions to be unconstitutional. These powers have been used for good and ill. It was the Supreme Court that decided that money given to political campaigns constituted free speech. It is the Supreme Court that has allowed corporations to possess the same rights as human beings.

The Supreme Court has had its moments of true justice as well, mandating the racial integration of schools, denying President Truman the power to seize steel mills, and—as mentioned above—standing up to the elimination of habeas corpus. But the people have not had democratic control over these things.

There is a great concentration of antidemocratic power in the Supreme Court. Doing anything to solve that problem requires amending the Constitution. At the very least, we should give the approval power to the House instead of the Senate. But what can we do to limit the excessive power of Supreme Court justices? One thing we could certainly do would be to limit their terms. Both Steven Hill and Larry Sabato propose limiting them to fifteen years. Sabato also proposes expanding the court to include twelve justices, adding diversity, reducing individual power, and creating the possibility of a tie. A tie would uphold a lower court's ruling and set no precedent, reducing the influence of the Supreme Court.

Part of the power of the Supreme Court is found in the lesser known powers of the chief justice outside of the court, powers that are not found in the Constitution and some of which should be banned by it.[47] The chief justice oversees a massive bureaucracy, larger than many government departments, and decides who sits on the FISA Court and the

Alien Terrorist Removal Court. Most disturbingly, the chief justice chairs something called the Judicial Conference of the United States and appoints the director of the Administrative Office of the United States Courts. These bodies do not just administer courts, but they also lobby Congress on bills unrelated to the administration of courts. Such lobbying should be forbidden, and the administration of the courts should be opened to congressional oversight and public transparency.

8. Balancing the Budget

A major overhaul of the Constitution should probably also include the requirement of a balanced budget. In fact, we should probably go two steps further and require that as long as there is a national debt, it must be reduced every year, and once there is not a national debt, money should be put away into savings every year in case of emergencies. It is often assumed that a balanced budget amendment would prevent the government from spending in times of emergencies, but it needn't do so if money has been set aside. Some have proposed that a balanced budget amendment include exceptions for economic depressions or wars. I'm open to that idea as well, provided that it is restricted to defensive and legal wars. It is also often assumed that a balanced budget amendment would lead to cuts in useful programs that benefit the least well-off among us. Remember, military spending doesn't count as spending, and therefore most people can never imagine cutting it. If we limit the percentage of government spending that can go to the military, then useful services could not be cut without cutting the military, and would in fact have to be expanded in order to expand the military. But they could not be expanded without limit if the budget were required to balance. If a balanced budget really did have to hurt those most in need, then the debt crisis we are unleashing on our grandchildren would have to hurt those most in need in the future. By what right do we shift that pain onto those not yet born?[48]

Currently the lack of a balanced budget requirement and the lack of any congressional power is allowing the executive branch to borrow trillions of dollars for no good reason, burying our descendants in debt. We need to restore power to Congress and demand that Congress pass only balanced budgets every year, and in fact pay down the national debt every year, and that once it is paid down, Congress put money into savings for emergencies every year. Congress should also ban spending that occurs through so-called "earmarks" only vaguely related to the topic of the bill to which they are attached. In fact, bills should be restricted to single topics, limited in length, and required to pass a test of clarity. Our government has no business passing legislation that an educated citizen (and even many members of Congress) cannot remotely begin to comprehend.

9. Legislating by Initiative

One final reform to consider is establishing the right of the public to legislate by initiative, and the right of recall. We ought to be able to recall the president or the vice president or both, or a member of Congress. A constitutional amendment could establish a procedure for signature gathering to create a public recall election. Such a campaign would have to be funded by small donations from actual humans (not corporations), and the number of signatures needed would have to be quite high. Unlike impeachment, there would be no trial. Unlike impeachment, the people would have a guaranteed voice in the process.

Ideally we should have citizens also empowered to enact legislation. In twenty-four states, citizens do have the power of the public initiative, albeit sadly corrupted by corporate personhood and through it the influence of corporate money. Former US Senator from Alaska Mike Gravel has developed a proposal to give us the right to pass legislation by initiative at the national level.[49] State initiatives have earned a bad name in some quarters, but the cause of that seems largely to be the influence of money, including out-of-state money from corporate and religious power centers. As with elections of representatives, votes on initiatives cannot work as they should if corrupted by money, media, and party.

Kevin O'Leary has proposed a related idea, which Dana Nelson describes favorably as institutionalizing James Fishkin's deliberative polling plan discussed above. For each member of Congress, we would create a 100-person citizen assembly with the job of studying and deliberating on the important issues of the day. Members of the assembly would be chosen at random from citizens of a district not choosing to opt out. The 435 assemblies would create a 43,500-person National Assembly. The decisions of these bodies would, at the very least, inform Congress members. And many more citizens would become directly connected to government, as everyone would have a much greater chance of knowing an Assembly member than a Congress member. But it would also be possible, if we chose, to create a fourth branch of government, the People's Branch, giving the assemblies shared legislative duties with Congress, if only the power to send legislation to the floor or to veto it.

10. Additional Ideas

I've tossed quite a few reform proposals out there. Some of them could be achieved without amending the Constitution, while others could not. There may be other proposals as good or better that I have not mentioned or not even considered. The purpose of making the proposals I have is to further a conversation in which we think deeply about the ways we want to live and govern ourselves, whether and in what ways we support the concept of democracy about which we talk so often, and what we are willing to risk and sacrifice in order to actually advance by example that which our government so often claims to be supporting by slaughtering people around the globe.

V.

CITIZEN POWER

22. **THINKING**

The first thing to know and try our hardest never to forget about the American people is that we're a whole lot better than our televisions tell us we are. Our opinions are a whole lot better than the corporate media would have us believe, and a lot more of us are actually working for the betterment of our society than we know. We are a lot more active and courageous and less apathetic than those in power would have us believe or want us to be. And a lot more of us support progressive positions than call ourselves Democrats, much less progressives. But we could have much better opinions and be far more active, and we should be. I'm about to suggest ways to do this, and to offer lots of criticism of where we are right now. But please bear in mind that things are actually better in this regard than is commonly thought.

When I was writing this book, *Yes!* magazine helpfully published a collection of progressive policies favored by a majority of Americans in a variety of public opinion polls, according to which:[1]

➤ 67 percent favor public works projects to create jobs

➤ 73 percent say corporations don't pay a fair share of taxes

➤ 76 percent support tax cuts for lower- and middle-income people

➤ 80 percent support increasing the federal minimum wage

➤ 70 percent support habeas corpus rights for detainees at Guantánamo

➤ 58 percent believe a court warrant should be required to listen to telephone calls

➤ 68 percent believe a president should not act alone to fight terrorism without checks and balances of courts and Congress

➤ 79 percent favor mandatory controls on greenhouse gas emissions

➤ 90 percent favor higher auto fuel efficiency standards

➤ 75 percent favor clean electricity, even with higher rates

➤ 72 percent support more funding for mass transit

➤ 64 percent believe the government should provide national health insurance coverage for all, even if it would raise taxes

➤ 73 percent favor abolishing nuclear weapons, with verification

➤ 80 percent favor banning weapons in space

➤ 81 percent oppose torture and support following the Geneva conventions

➤ 85 percent say the United States should not initiate military action without support from allies

➤ 79 percent say the United Nations should be strengthened

➤ 63 percent wanted US forces home from Iraq within a year

➤ 7 percent [yes, 7 percent] favor military action against Iran

➤ 69 percent favor using diplomatic and economic means to fight terrorism, not the military

➤ 86 percent say big companies have too much power

➤ 74 percent favor voluntary public financing of campaigns

➤ 66 percent believe intentional acts are likely to cause significant voting machine errors

➤ 80 percent say ex-felons should have their voting rights restored

➤ 65 percent believe attacking social problems is a better cure for crime than more law enforcement

➤ 87 percent support rehabilitation rather than a "punishment-only" system

➤ 80 percent favor allowing undocumented immigrants living in the United States to stay and apply for citizenship if they have a job and pay back taxes

On September 15, 2008, the Associated Press reported on a poll it had conducted together with the National Constitution Center[2] which found that:

➤ by 54 percent to 38 percent, Americans favor upholding the rule of law over bending it in the name of public safety

➤ by 49 percent to 44 percent, Americans believe one branch of government has too much power; of those 49 percent, 46 percent say it is the president who has too much power, 34 percent say Congress, and 30 percent say the courts

➤ by 66 percent to 29 percent, Americans oppose giving the president more power in the name of improving the economy

➤ by 67 percent to 29 percent, Americans oppose giving the president more power in the name of improving national security, but Americans are split on giving Congress more power to improve the economy (49 percent against, 48 percent in support)

➤ by 50 percent to 45 percent, Americans oppose giving Congress more power in the name of national security; and by 73 percent to 22 percent Americans overwhelmingly believe Congress should have the power to force the president's closest advisors to testify

The most decisive result in the poll was in favor of restoring to the Congress the power of subpoena, and yet a significantly smaller percentage of respondents favored shifting power to Congress. This suggests that people were using their understanding of what powers the branches are supposed to have now, as opposed to what powers they actually have, as their baseline for answering the questions about power. Even so, Americans are clearly more reluctant to shift power to the president than to the Congress.

The area of activism I have been most recently involved with, that of the peace movement, has seen tremendous, widespread activism, sacrifice, and risk-taking. Again, it has not been nearly what it should be, and yet has been much more than most people realize. Millions of Americans have marched, rallied, e-mailed, phoned, faxed, visited their representatives, contacted the media, produced their own media, educated students about the lies of military recruiters, taken steps to keep students' information out of the hands of military recruiters, and spread the truth about the Iraq War to friends and neighbors. Opposition to the Iraq War has perhaps seen as many separate actions involving arrests for civil disobedience as any single past activist campaign in US history.[3] I know more people than I could list who have gone to jail, gone on starvation fasts, gone without sleep, given up time with their families, and otherwise sacrificed for others, without reward or recognition—but not without some successes, and not without building a movement beneath the media's radar that will almost certainly continue to grow. The American people not only mean well, but to a huge extent try their very hardest to do well by the world and by each other.

That being said, if we want to force the sort of changes we need, if we want to prevent the possibility of a slide into fascism and halt the ever increasing twin risks of global warming and nuclear war, we are going to have to do a whole lot better, which will have to begin by thinking and acting a whole lot better.

We are too isolated, often alone, cocooning, spending too little time with friends and strangers; drawing too sharp a line between friends and strangers; making friendships too seldom with people from backgrounds and in situations different from our own; traveling and commuting alone and for too many hours; dining alone; living in gated communities; living in largely segregated communities; living in communities that make a mockery of the name "community"; living where there are nothing but isolated houses; shopping where there are nothing but shops; working where there are nothing but workplaces; playing in isolated backyards; vacationing outside our communities; educating our children at home, in schools most people cannot afford, or in schools most people would not choose if they had a choice; placing too much trust in religion; and watching way too much television. Some of these problems require systemic fixes, some changes in our habits, and some both. We work too many hours, some because we have no choice, some because we want to acquire more consumer products than we need. We have too little contact with nature, some because we live in such a denatured environment, some because we can't seem to lift our rear ends off the sofa. We place too much importance on stupid and superficial analyses of public events, some because we're overworked, tired, or uneducated, most because we fail to turn off trash TV and radio (in which category I include the network nightly news shows) and because we fail to read enough books and websites.

We imagine that politics is an option. We say "well, I'm not a political person," as we would say "I'm not religious," or "I don't follow baseball." We suppose that politics does not affect us, that we shouldn't care how it affects others, or that we are powerless to have any control over it. I remember handing out DontAttackIran.org stickers with my friend Sarah Lanzman, and people kept telling her "No, thanks, I'm OK," until finally Sarah said, "Yeah? Well you might be OK, but will the Iranians be OK? Are the Iraqis OK?!" While most passersby did take and wear a sticker, and many signed a petition, some couldn't be bothered to view the question as anything larger than whether they themselves would be better off with a sticker on, what it would look like on their outfit, what the people they ran into might think of it. More than one person told me "I wouldn't want to offend anyone." But this comment ignores the most horrific offense—most of us don't imagine that when the bombs fall on a foreign country we ourselves are doing the killing. We are far too accepting of distant crimes where the victims are unlike us, far too unwilling to shake the boat, and too convinced that simple messages of peace and justice will offend real people the way they offend pundits on television who are paid to be offended. I wore "Impeach Bush and Cheney" T-shirts all over the country for years and received thousands of compliments and even favors and discounts in stores (and others told me they had the same experiences), and only three times (at least out loud within my hearing) did anyone have a negative reaction.

We like to retreat into personal endeavors, and individual creations, or at best into local and state activism. We think that "finding peace" in our hearts is as important as creating peace in the world. We think that planting a vegetable garden or buying organic is as important as taking the reins of power away from the oil barons, or that our cumulative small actions will lead to that result. Small actions can indeed lead to big results, and local and state successes can change national policy. They can even do so indirectly by organizing people into active citizens with the confidence to get things done. By no means should citizens refrain from local activism and creative small projects and businesses. It is quite valuable that, for example:[4]

➤ A housewife in Niagara Falls, NY, organized her community against local pollution in a campaign that led to the creation of the US EPA Superfund program.

➤ Over 100 towns in the United States have denied corporations legal personhood and constitutional rights in a campaign growing out of anger at the dumping of toxic sludge on farms.

➤ Residents of Norco, LA, poisoned by a Shell oil refinery and a Shell chemical plant, forced the company to pay the cost of residents relocating.

➤ A poor neighborhood in Chicago denied good grocery stores has done better by creating an organic urban farm and local market.

➤ North Dakota farmers defeated efforts by Monsanto to sell genetically engineered seeds.

➤ Loggers and environmentalists in a corner of Oregon have cooperated, resulting in better outcomes for both and new government policies for the whole Northwest.

➤ Residents of Tallulah, LA, and parents of juveniles imprisoned there have worked together to shut the Tallulah top-security juvenile prison down.

➤ Hundreds of towns and cities have passed resolutions against enforcement of unconstitutional sections of the USA PATRIOT Act.

➤ More than 400 US mayors have signed a pledge to reduce greenhouse gas emissions. Roanoke, VA, is among the cities leading the way.

➤ The Rosebud Sioux reservation in South Dakota is building community and prosperity by building windmills. Other Native Americans are doing the same, harnessing wind and sun.

➤ Local businesses in Utah, threatened by corporate big-box stores, have created a "Buy Local First" campaign with tremendous success.

➤ Trailing Europe but catching on, the United States now has about 300 worker-run businesses.

But there is no point in establishing policies for the EPA if we cannot compel the EPA to abide by them. There is no sense in passing laws at the local or state levels if the national government will overturn them, or if the same energy might have succeeded in passing a national law. The victories listed above should inspire us, and we should emulate them, but they should not distract us from placing a priority on national reform.

While Americans are not nearly as lazy and disengaged as we think, we certainly should be more active. But we should be more active while thinking of ourselves as humans, as citizens of the world, not just as Americans. We are far too accepting of the cartoon idea (literally instilled in us by childhood cartoons and permeating all of our culture) that some people are good guys and some bad guys. The essence of this idea is that there be no specific reason why anyone is a "good guy" or a "bad guy," that they just are those things. A lot of us do not value Iraqis less or hate Iraqis and want them killed for any particular reason, or because of anything they supposedly are or have done, or because of religious or racial bigotry, or petrolian greed, or anger at a mythical involvement in 9/11 or at the Iraqis' defense against our occupation of their country. Rather, some of those factors make it easier to see Iraqis as different from us, which allows us to accept the governmental dogma that they are "the bad guys." The new term for bad guys is, of course, terrorists, and it has evolved so thoroughly into this meaning, that suspects in the 2003 anthrax attacks in the United States cannot be called terrorists. It would make no sense to call them terrorists because they are Americans and white.

Those Americans who want to "defeat" Iraqis or Afghanis, those who view the "contest" in Iraq or Afghanistan as more than a sports event and harbor real animus for the Iraqis or Afghanis, primarily do so out of a desire for revenge. Among the shortcomings of Americans, support for revenge should be kept near the top of the list. It drives our foreign policy, our domestic criminal justice policy, our drug policy, our sports interests, our entertainment interests, and even our child raising techniques, without the slightest redeeming effect on the world. It is also the antithesis of the most creative, valuable, and wise contribution to human morals made by the man whose memory is daily disgraced by the nation that most loudly and obnoxiously proclaims its Christianity, namely Jesus of Nazareth.

Revenge is so common in our thinking that we tend to assume that everyone else is motivated by it as well. Urging the impeachment and prosecution of criminal presidents and vice presidents is often mischaracterized (though sometimes accurately characterized) as revenge, either for their misdeeds or for some past impeachment of somebody else. But if granting Bush and Cheney immunity for life, billion dollar pensions, and royal crowns would deter future presidents and vice presidents from wrongdoing, then that is exactly what I would propose we do. I oppose the death penalty, including for Bush and Cheney, precisely because it's been shown to encourage violence rather than to deter it.

Of course, violence and machismo are as much a part of our culture as revenge, and in order to satisfy these tendencies we're willing to make gods and heroes of the same people running our government whom we denounce as scoundrels whenever we're not convinced it's "war time."

The shift in understanding, and therefore in action, that we need as Americans will not come from a think tank, a political party, or any segment of the political punditry. Let me try to illustrate the gap between where we're headed and where we need to go by pointing to two documents, the 2008 Democratic Convention Party Platform[5] and a book by my friend, retired United States Army colonel and retired official of the US State Department, Ann Wright.

The Democratic platform opened by, admirably, noting that we faced crises of war, economic collapse, and environmental disaster. The first suggested solution was that we "abandon the politics of partisan division," as if the major issue before us was whether our elected officials spoke amicably or confrontationally, not the need for actual specific commitments to end war, create jobs, and protect the environment. Although the next sentence in the platform threw in the word "accountability," the platform made no mention of the governmental crimes of the Bush administration, no promises to punish the perpetrators, and no suggestion of ways to deter their repetition. Just vague plans to do better.

According to this platform, the Cheney-Bush gang didn't launch wars of aggression slaughtering over a million innocent people and ruining nations for human society. They made "mistakes," "failed," and "overextended our military." Not that they could have been expected to do much worthwhile, since "The American people do not want government to solve all our problems; we know that personal responsibility, character, imagination, diligence, hard work and faith ultimately determine individual achievement." This platform trips over itself sprinting backwards away from any assertion of power.

Someone should inform the Democratic Party that the top concern of the American public is neither turning a deficit into a surplus nor "competing in a global economy." It's seeing more people able to live a safe and happy and rewarding and sustainable life. We don't have to compete with other nations to do that. We just have to stop rigging the system against working people and against the environment.

Henry David Thoreau said "A very few serve the state with their consciences, and so necessarily resist it." These days it is more than a few, although their stories are not widely known. Ann Wright and her coauthor Susan Dixon, who teaches on the geography of peace and war at the University of Hawaii, have collected some of their stories in a book called *Dissent: Voices of Conscience: Government Insiders Speak Out Against the War in Iraq.*[6] Wright is herself one of the many heroes whose stories are told in the book. Many of us who follow the war and the peace movement know Ann and know that she resigned from the US diplomatic corps in protest of the invasion of Iraq. But can you name the other two US diplomats who had already done the same thing? Do you know their stories? This book includes dozens of stories of whistleblowers, courageous people responsible for much of what we know about what our government has done for the past eight years, people who in some cases saw their careers ruined as a result of speaking out.

Above all, *Dissent: Voices of Conscience* presents a sampling of the many stories of soldiers who have put down their weapons in this unjust war: Camilo Mejia, Pablo Paredes, Kevin Benderman, Stephen Funk, Abdullah Webster, Aidan Delgado, Katherine Jashinski, Melanie McPherson, Ehren Watada, Augustin Aguayo, Ricky Clousing, Mark Wilkerson, Jeremy Hinzman, Brandon Hughey, Joshua Key, Patrick Hart, Chris Magaoay, Darrell Anderson, Ivan Brobeck, Kyle Snyder, Ben Griffin, Malcolm Kendal-Smith, Mohisin Khan. There are many more, of course, who are not represented in the book.

All of these people have recognized that there was only one thing they could justly do, and they have done it. Perhaps it was illegal or disobedient, but it had to be done. Most of us are not in a position to leak information on unknown crimes or to refuse illegal orders. But we are in a position to help build a support fund for whistleblowers. We are in a position to recognize that nonviolent resistance is often our only moral choice. We will not create the necessary rebirth of American democracy by sending e-mails and making phone calls. We must do those things. We must educate. We must create new media. We must lobby. We must march. But the changes we need to create will be seen as a threat to those in power, and they will cling to power with more determination than they have ever had for anything else. Unless we creatively and nonviolently block the path the empire is headed down and redirect the nation, we will be increasingly ignored, repressed, manipulated, abused, and disappeared for the remaining days of this once bright and hopeful republic.

We need to organize, on a major scale, a fund to guarantee the safety and legal defense and financial well-being of whistleblowers. I'm inclined to think that this could be done in a way that would have far greater results than decades of congressional hearings.

But we also need to emulate the actions of whistleblowers in our own ways, breaking out of our comfortable routines and speaking truth to power. We need to work for concrete short-term goals while maintaining our long-term vision of a more democratic, peaceful, and just nation and world. And we need to work very hard to begin thinking of our nation as one among equals in the world.

Whistleblowers and the Democratic Party Platform fundamentally disagree over the question of whether things have gone drastically wrong, whether unusual actions are required to correct an unusually bad state of affairs. This disagreement may come down to the question of whether aggressive wars and everything they bring with them should be accepted as part of the normal course of events.

Our history books skip from war to war. On a video produced by RealNews.com, Gore Vidal recounts President John Kennedy saying to him (you have to imagine Vidal using an exaggerated Massachusetts accent): "What would Lincoln have been without the Civil War? Just another railroad lawyer!" In 2004, Russ Baker reported on interviews Mickey Herskowitz had conducted with George W. Bush in 1999 while writing his "autobiography" for him:

> "He was thinking about invading Iraq in 1999," said author and journalist Mickey Herskowitz. "It was on his mind. He said to me: 'One of the keys to being seen as a great leader is to be seen as a commander-in-chief.' And he said, 'My father had all this political capital built up when he drove the Iraqis out of Kuwait and he wasted it.' He said, 'If I have a chance to invade . . . if I had that much capital, I'm not going to waste it. I'm going to get everything passed that I want to get passed and I'm going to have a successful presidency.'"[7]

While we must most importantly deny presidents the power to launch wars, we should also rid them of the idea that launching or provoking a war is the key to success. We should rewrite our history books to celebrate those who avoided wars. We should improve our education system as our best insurance of decent policies in the future. We should impeach, prosecute, and condemn the memory of George W. Bush and Richard B. Cheney, as well as any future presidents who engage in unnecessary war. And we should get organized and get active on behalf of peace and justice, even when—especially when—the nation is not widely perceived to be going through a moment of crisis.

We should also stop thinking of the president as the focus of our democracy, and of democracy as something that involves heavy top-down leadership. We should think of ourselves as collectively the leaders of our democracy. And by "ourselves" we should include those we disagree with as well. While Washington, DC, needs more disagreement, debate, and discussion, and less chanting of "bipartisanship," it and the rest of us also need less bitter demonization of those we disagree with. Disagreement should be one of life's greatest pleasures, something that at least refines our own thinking and at best revolutionizes it. We should address with gratitude those who disagree with us and consider it our civic responsibility to speak out clearly when we disagree with them. We should all join together in switching off the TV pundits whose notion of disagreement is screaming names at each other.

23. THE TROUBLE WITH THE MEDIA

Even with all the reforms I've suggested in this book, laws and regulations cannot possibly close off every avenue for crime and abuse. There will always be crooked presidential lawyers who can find a way around the law. But they cannot always find a way around an informed and energized public, and that is created by democratic media. To be good citizens, we need to be informed. We need daily news that is not in the hands of the Pentagon and big business. The media we have now in the United States is guilty of war crimes and crimes against democracy, just as our leaders are.

Yes, media is a singular noun. It means the voice of the corporate news, a voice that comes through a variety of spokespeople controlled by a very small number of owners with common interests and a common understanding of what is news. The voice wavers at times, and debates with itself. "We should redeploy the troops to a different war in a couple of years," it says to itself. "No," itself replies to it, "we should wait a couple of years and then redeploy the troops to a different war." But 10 million people screaming at the top of their lungs "Bring them home now!" has the sound of absolute silence punctuated by the occasional burst of mocking laughter.

Our very politics are at stake when the media controls how different political affiliations and identifications are defined. While the media's own voices manipulatively denounce the media as "liberal," consumers of media content are presented with a dwarfed political spectrum: liberal or conservative. There is no recognition of other left political identities and the ideas they represent.

Imagine being angry that you couldn't find a job and that your food stamps had been cut back. Then, imagine that you were able to decide— as did a man in Tennessee in 2008 who murdered a handful of people at a performance of *Little Orphan Annie* at a progressive Unitarian

273

church—that the way to solve your problems was to attack "liberals," the people who support (albeit ineffectively) workers' rights, union rights, and fair trade; who oppose NAFTA, and tax breaks for shipping jobs overseas; who support investing in job creation at home; who want to tax corporations and the super-rich rather than small businesses and working people; and who want these protections for all races, genders, religions, and sexual orientations.

In a separate case, also in 2008, in Little Rock, Arkansas, a man barged into the state Democratic headquarters and shot and killed the state party chairman, then waved his gun at the building manager at the nearby Arkansas Baptist headquarters and said, "I lost my job." Clearly, we are not communicating our objectives to one another.

Speaking as a liberal or progressive who supports a sustainable full employment economy with guaranteed education, income, and health care, I'm sorry that we have failed these men so drastically, in fact failed so badly that they don't even have the slightest idea what we stand for. The first thing we need to do is not easy. We need to completely over-haul our communications system.

The timing couldn't be better, with television switching to digital, and so many digital channels being created that the corporations to whom we give them for free don't have the content to fill them. It would be very easy to put something useful to citizens of a democracy on some of those empty channels. But that won't happen without a massive pop-ular movement that forces it to happen. Our communications system is not suffering from a lack of technological breakthroughs, but from a lack of access for anyone but a small handful of mega-corporations being given special favors and a monopoly worth billions of dollars by our government with no strings attached and no requirement that they serve the public interest.

What we have in this country is a news media conglomerate that functions as a part of the executive branch of the federal government. Call it the United States Department of Media. Perhaps "branch" is not the right word, since, as we have seen, the executive branch is just about all that remains of our government. The number one excuse that pro-gressive Congress members and staffers give you for their hesitation to act on any issue is fear of the media.

It's very difficult to insert new voices into the media as long as it is a singular media. For media to become a plural noun would require breaking up monopolies, creating competition, and exercising some public control over the public's airwaves. Media critics Robert McChesney and John Nichols explain the current situation:

> Not only are media markets dominated by a handful of conglomerates with "barriers to entry," making it nearly impossible for newcomers to challenge their dominance, but they are also closely linked to each other in a manner that suggests almost a cartel-like arrangement. Some of the largest media firms own parts of the other giants; Liberty, for example, is the second largest shareholder in News Corporation and among the largest shareholders in AOL Time Warner. Moreover, the media giants employ equity joint ventures—where two competing firms share ownership in a single venture—to an extent unknown almost anywhere else in the economy.... By 2002, the nine largest media giants had an equity joint venture with six, on average, of the other eight giants.[8]

This cartel arrangement allows media outlets to misreport or not report at all on a significant story with the confidence that their colleagues will not interfere by producing accurate reporting. The most significant way in which the univocal US Department of Media controls public debate is not in how it presents a story or which of its two acceptable "positions" it stresses more than the other, but in the stories it chooses to present and those it chooses to completely ignore.

Often the whiteout of a story is not 100 percent complete. Often hugely important events are reported in the sixteenth paragraph of a single newspaper article and then forgotten, while other stories are repeated endlessly in print and on television. The lives of poor people at home and abroad are mysteries to media consumers (except when they shoot up a public gathering). The labor movement exists almost exclusively as something that appears out of nowhere to interrupt air travel or baseball games. Grassroots activism is almost nonexistent, and is dominated by goofy and frightening displays. The world outside the United

States is almost nonexistent and is dominated by scary threats. Important legislation is of interest to the public primarily the day after it passes, not when we could have done anything about it. A policy demanded by a majority of the public is of no news value at all if the president and the party leaders say it isn't. For example, there was never any movement to impeach Bush or Cheney. Corrections of media mistakes, including wars that could not have been launched without media complicity, don't merit much play. Corporate power is not a serious problem. Media ownership is not an issue at all. But scandals, celebrities, sex, violence, weather, sports, and financial news relevant to a tiny percentage of Americans are indispensible.

Endless accounts of torture by the United States are ignored or given the single-newspaper-article treatment, while an epic legislative battle between Senator John McCain and Vice President Dick Cheney becomes the primary story related to torture. In 2006, *Time* magazine recognized McCain's efforts to supposedly ban torture by naming him one of "America's 10 Best Senators."⁹ Time made no mention of the fact that torture had always been illegal, the fact that Bush had thrown out McCain's new law with a "signing statement," or the fact that the United States was continuing to torture people on a large scale.¹⁰ Thus McCain was able over the subsequent two years to talk about his torture victim status at every campaign stop without ever being asked about his silence on the signing statement; or his 2006 vote in favor of the Military Commissions Act, which purported to give the president the power to make decisions about torture; or his vote in February 2008 against a bill to (redundantly) ban torture and his applause for Bush's vetoing of that bill.

To the corporate media, sound bytes are more important than votes, words more meaningful than action. And this encourages Congress members to believe the same. After endless hours of depicting McCain as the crusader against torture, the media may have felt it would make itself look bad if it pointed out his support for torture. Or it may have decided that he was "really" against torture but had been compelled to start voting for it for some obscure reasons, just as Pelosi was "really" against the Iraq War and warrantless spying, but was compelled to support them by wise political calculations that could not be questioned.

The best example I've seen of forcing a topic into the corporate media against the media's will fell far short of the sort of coverage that would be needed to support a healthy democracy. In May 2005, Steve Cobble, John Bonifaz, Bob Fertik, Tim Carpenter, and I formed After Downing Street, a nonpartisan coalition of over 200 veterans groups, peace groups, and political activist groups that began to pressure both Congress and the media to investigate whether President Bush had committed impeachable offenses in connection with the Iraq War. The coalition took its name from several documents that emerged in May and June of 2005, the Downing Street Memos, which revealed that George W. Bush had decided to overthrow Saddam Hussein in the summer of 2002. We thought that exposing the fraudulent basis for the Iraq War might help to end it and to prevent new wars.

After Downing Street worked closely with the peace movement in the United States and abroad, organizing national days on which events were held in hundreds of cities; lobbying in Congress for investigations (especially during the 109th Congress, when impeachment was understood to be beyond reach, and some of Bush and Cheney's crimes were still unknown), for censure,[11] and for impeachment; introducing and passing pro-impeachment resolutions at the local and state levels; and organizing the peace movement to address the issue of accountability for the war. In the process, we saw the percentage of Americans who believed the war was based on lies climb and the percentage of Americans who wanted the troops brought home rise right behind it.

In November 2005, the *Christian Science Monitor* published an article with the headline "Why Iraq War Support Fell So Fast," which speaks to how the work that After Downing Street was doing to expose the lies and demand accountability was key to ending support for the war:

> John Mueller, an expert on war and public opinion at Ohio State University, links today's lower tolerance of casualties to a weaker public commitment to the cause than was felt during the two previous, Cold War–era conflicts. The discounting of the main justifications for the Iraq war—alleged weapons of mass destruction and support for international terrorism—has left many Americans skeptical of the entire enterprise.[12]

A state-by-state analysis suggested that the work that After Downing Street promoted, including town and city impeachment resolutions, was effective in lowering Bush's approval rating and raising his disapproval rating. That is to say, we were educating the public about the president's performance and about the acceptability of public criticism.

After Downing Street began in May 2005, when cofounder John Bonifaz sent a memo to Congressman John Conyers and the coalition released a statement to the press. Bonifaz's memo included this: "In light of the emergence of the Downing Street Memo, Members of Congress should introduce a Resolution of Inquiry directing the House Judiciary Committee to launch a formal investigation into whether sufficient grounds exist for the House of Representatives to exercise its constitutional power to impeach George W. Bush, President of the United States."

Within weeks, After Downing Street developed a highly trafficked website and a community of hundreds of bloggers and thousands of real world activists. By mid-June 2005, the pressure had made the Downing Street Memos a front page story and a topic of conversation on the cable news shows. Numerous media outlets printed lists of excuses for their belated coverage. The *USA Today*'s Mark Memmott wrote this in a front-page story on June 8, 2005:

> *USA Today* chose not to publish anything about the memo before today for several reasons, says Jim Cox, the newspaper's senior assignment editor for foreign news. "We could not obtain the memo or a copy of it from a reliable source," Cox says. "There was no explicit confirmation of its authenticity from (Blair's office). And it was disclosed four days before the British elections, raising concerns about the timing."

Others began coverage as if they had been covering the matter for weeks; an NBC talk show referred to "the now-famous Downing Street Memo" in that network's first mention of the matter.[13] Pundits cited this phenomenon as the first clear example of the public's ability to appeal to the blogosphere to overrule editors' and producers' decisions not to cover an important story.[14] Those pundits had it half right. It was the combined communications of the blogosphere and progressive radio shows on Air America, Pacifica, and other stations that overruled the corporate media.

On June 16, 2005, Congressman John Conyers and dozens of other Congress members held an unofficial hearing on the Downing Street Memos in the basement of the US Capitol. After Downing Street assisted in recruiting witnesses, alerting the media, organizing a rally at the White House, and (with other groups helping) collecting over 500,000 citizens' signatures and 120 Congress members' signatures on a letter to the President. Witnesses at the hearing were Joe Wilson, Ray McGovern, John Bonifaz, and then-little-known Cindy Sheehan.

Congress members joined a crowd of activists outside the White House following the hearing and delivered the letter and signatures to the gate. This day of events galvanized a national community of activists and became a model for future rallies and hearings. Thousands of house parties were built around viewing videos produced on this day. In late June, *Newsday* published this account of the After Downing Street movement:

> An online movement of bloggers and political activist groups is trying to keep the Downing Street memos in the public eye and stoking support for a congressional investigation. The memos, sent among top British foreign intelligence officials, state that President George W. Bush was predisposed to going to war with Iraq and "intelligence and facts were being fixed around the policy." The After Downing Street movement wants Congress to examine whether Bush's path to war is grounds for impeachment.[15]

But this breakthrough victory for the public's right to insist that the media cover a substantive story unpopular with those in power and with the media itself was extremely limited. By July, the Downing Street Memos were largely forgotten by the media, almost never to be heard of again. The weeks during which the story did exist in the media consisted mostly of passing references and misleading accounts. The evidence was generally reported as a "claim" by peace activists (despite being the official minutes of a government meeting planning a war), and—as if that wasn't enough—the content of the Downing Street Minutes was reported as "old news" that everybody supposedly already knew about. The trouble with that line, of course, was that there had never been a time when Bush and Cheney lying us into the war had been treated as new news. The story was "old news" when first broached. Yet the story had not been publicly known before.

The *Washington Post* first earned the nickname "Pentagon Post," and other outlets similar labels, not because we thought the corporate media was actually secretly taking orders from the Pentagon, but because it always reported the news more or less as if it were. This was clearly the way to please advertisers. This was also the way to please media owners with ties to the weapons, "reconstruction," and oil industries. This was the way to please those in power to whom the media wanted "access." And this was the way to do "professional," "objective" reporting that proved it had no point of view by adopting the point of view of the White House.

Only after the occupation of Iraq had been underway for five years did we learn that many voices in the media were actually on the Pentagon payroll and taking their orders in a direct and literal sense.[16] Of course, we already knew that Fox News and the *Washington Times* were taking direction from Karl Rove, but there was still a widespread belief in the relative purity of most other outlets.[17]

It was revealed that the Pentagon engaged in a years-long secret domestic propaganda campaign to promote the invasion and occupation of Iraq, and the media cooperated in full. Secretary of "Defense" Donald Rumsfeld had recruited seventy-five retired military officers and had given them talking points to deliver on Fox, CNN, ABC, NBC, CBS, and MSNBC, and according to the *New York Times* report on April 20, 2008, which has not been disputed by the Pentagon or the White House, "Participants were instructed not to quote their briefers directly or otherwise describe their contacts with the Pentagon." According to the Pentagon's own internal documents, the military analysts were considered "message force multipliers" or "surrogates" who would deliver administration "themes and messages" to millions of Americans "in the form of their own opinions."[18] In fact, they did deliver the themes and the messages and did not reveal that the Pentagon had provided them with their talking points. Robert S. Bevelacqua, a retired Green Beret and Fox News military analyst, described this as follows: "It was them saying, 'We need to stick our hands up your back and move your mouth for you.'"[19]

When the story came out, the White House press secretary defended the blatantly illegal program, which of course had fallen within the area of activity managed by the White House Iraq Group (WHIG), a White House taskforce formed in August 2002 to market the war. During the ensuing months and years, US television networks continued to use as talking heads the same pundits who had been exposed as Pentagon propagandists, not to mention such figures as Karl Rove and Alberto Gonzales, who had left office under clouds of scandal and were under investigation for wrongdoing.

After our limited success in forcing the Downing Street Minutes into the corporate media, each time a new "smoking gun" was added to the arsenal of evidence over the ensuing months and years, we tried to mobilize the same level of media activism, always with less success than each previous effort. The reason was not that the evidence was weaker or less dramatic, but that people no longer believed exposing the evidence would motivate the Congress to act.[20] People tend to engage in activism when success seems likely, which is another way of saying when the activism is least needed. We had already forced conclusive documentary evidence into the media, the media had reported it, and then the whole thing had been forgotten and impeachment dumped "off the table." So, what would have been the point of forcing the media to mention another piece of evidence? That was how people thought about it.

Until the early twentieth century in the United States there was much more media diversity, and "balanced" or "objective" journalism had not yet been heard of. It was perfectly normal for everyone to be aware that each newspaper represented the viewpoint of its owner, and for labor unions and political parties to publish newspapers representing their viewpoints. When the markets became dominated by a small number of papers, the fact that they reflected the interests of their owners had to be disguised, or people could have objected to the lack of freedom of the press. The solution was found in making journalism "professional" by training reporters to pretend (and to believe) that they had no points of view at all, that they had no influence on readers at all, that they simply recorded reality or presented "both sides" without bias. Of course, the owners of the newspapers continued right along refusing to publish anything that might threaten their interests—anything not "fit to print."

Some of the most heroic and dramatic tales coming out of the wars in Iraq and Afghanistan were inventions of the military and the White House. In 2004, the Cheney-Bush gang knowingly promoted a false account of the death of a former football star, Specialist Pat Tillman, stating that he had died in a hostile exchange and delaying release of the information that he had died from friendly fire; he was shot in the forehead three times in a manner that led investigating doctors to believe he had been shot at close range.[21]

On April 24, 2007, Specialist Bryan O'Neal, the last soldier to see Specialist Pat Tillman alive, testified before the House Oversight and Government Reform Committee that he was warned by superiors not to divulge information that a fellow soldier killed Specialist Tillman, especially to the Tillman family. The White House refused to provide requested documents to the committee, citing "executive branch confidentiality interests."

The same crowd of much-desired sources for the media also created a false account of the injury of a US soldier named Jessica Dawn Lynch, reporting that she had been captured in a hostile exchange and had been dramatically rescued. On April 2, 2003, the Pentagon released a video of the supposed rescue and falsely claimed that Lynch suffered stab and bullet wounds, and that she had been slapped about on her hospital bed and interrogated. Lynch said that the Pentagon "used me to symbolize all this stuff. It's wrong. I don't know why they filmed [my rescue] or why they say these things. . . . I did not shoot, not a round, nothing. I went down praying to my knees. And that's the last I remember." She reported receiving excellent treatment from Iraqis, and that one person in the hospital even sang to her to help her feel at home.

When regular old White House lies didn't work out so well, the same gang of liars had better luck by illegally purchasing the news it wanted. In his impeachment articles, Congressman Kucinich provides some of the ways in which the government did so, including the hiring of the Lincoln Group to place misleading articles in Iraqi newspapers, the production of video "news" releases by various governmental departments, and the bribing of columnists to praise Bush's proposals.[22]

All of this, including the production of videos that pretended to be independent news reporting, was unnoticeable until discovered and publicized by the Center for Media and Democracy.[23] The news produced by the White House looked exactly like the news produced by the so-called independent media. Completely unqualified reporters planted in presidential briefings who could be turned to for guaranteed softball questions did not stand out as particularly different from all the other reporters. Columns pushing outrageous nonsense in exchange for public dollars looked more or less like most of the other columns being printed in large US newspapers. Video news clips produced by the government looked like video news clips produced by corporations to subtly market their products, and those looked pretty much like the "legitimate" news produced by the media. All of this suggests that there is a larger media problem to be addressed even if we can bring the White House back under the rule of law.

Perhaps more pressing than the illegality of these propaganda tactics is the fact that the "free" press in America went along with it. And worse, the coverage not planted only echoed the same mantras and misinformation as the planted material. The fact is, we do not have a free media in America because our media is run by corporate interests. We can see the negative impacts in this everywhere we look. Americans are not only uninformed and distracted with useless content, we are actually misinformed, and it shows.

Part and parcel of the problem with the media is the problem with polling. Important topics to the American people, but not our rulers, are not polled on, or the results are not reported, or they are misleadingly reported. In 2006, *Newsweek* reported the shocking news that a majority of Americans favored impeaching the president. But read how *Newsweek* reported this:

> Other parts of a potential Democratic agenda receive less support, especially calls to impeach Bush: 47 percent of Democrats say that should be a "top priority," but only 28 percent of all Americans say it should be, 23 percent say it should be a lower

priority and nearly half, 44 percent, say it should not be done. (Five percent of Republicans say it should be a top priority and 15 percent of Republicans say it should be a lower priority; 78 percent oppose impeachment.)[24]

When 44 percent of Americans do not want something done, but 51 percent want it to be either a top priority or a lower priority, another way to report that is: a majority of Americans want it done.

In the weeks leading up to the 2008 elections, the *Washington Post* labeled any state in which McCain was ahead by even 2 percent as "leaning Republican," but they labeled states where Obama was ahead, even by 14 percent, as "battlegrounds." Many pollsters accurately forecast a decisive electoral-college victory for Obama, but the big corporate media outlets did not.

Then there's the overreporting of polls, especially election polls, at the expense of better news. And the use of pollsters as supposedly expert pundits. I watched CNN's polling guru declare impeachment unpopular without ever having conducted (or at least reported on) any poll. And let's not forget the use of polls to reflect bad reporting. When media outlets report something over and over again, they are almost always able to poll on it and discover that a lot of the public agrees with what it's been hearing.

Media outlets and polling companies should not be allowed to be one and the same. Media outlets might report more honestly on all polls if their aim wasn't to promote their own, and polling companies might poll better if not purely trying to please media outlets. While we, at least halfheartedly, fund public media, we do not fund public polling. I think we should.

What is the answer? First and foremost, we need to create alternatives that will deliver truthful news. We need to use the web, the airwaves, and print publishing to get the truth out there and allow Americans a chance to see things clearly, and make the right decisions.

The task of reforming the media would benefit from constitutional amendment, but could also be accomplished in great measure without it. We need antitrust laws and prosecution to break up the existing monopolies, and a law to severely restrict media ownership in the future, so that no company or individual can own more than one or two media outlets.

We need to repeal the Telecommunications Act of 1996 that has allowed a company like Clear Channel to buy up every radio station in sight. We need the same restrictions applied to polling companies as to news outlets, and a ban on owning both a news outlet and a polling company.

Other media reforms are possible through legislation. We should provide a tax credit that each tax payer can donate to a nonprofit media outlet. We should create and fairly distribute more licenses for low-power, noncommercial radio stations, and for digital TV channels. We should require certain hours of commercial-free news reporting (including local, national, and foreign news) from stations that we have given a section of our public airwaves. And we should take back from each station certain hours to be used for public news and children's programming, to be funded at the expense of the stations, which are, as I've said, the companies benefitting from the gift of our airwaves.

We should subsidize print media in order to encourage the production of more newspapers. And we should provide extra-low mailing costs to nonprofit and noncommercial publications. We should create truly public TV, radio, and Internet media, nationally and locally, including public access, and also independent community stations, all of it completely free of commercials and "grants" and "sponsors," with locally elected boards for local outlets, and with funding that is national and guaranteed. We should protect the reporters' right to keep sources confidential, with only one exception—cases in which the information provided by a source was false and has damaged the public. We should ban all advertising aimed at children.

It is common in lists of media reform proposals to include reinstatement of the Fairness Doctrine, which used to require equal time on media outlets for opposing political points of view. I would like to see that doctrine reinstated for public media, although I consider it a weak and minor piece in a reform agenda. But I would like to see such a proliferation of other nonprofit and for-profit media outlets that there would be no need to apply any fairness doctrine to them. I would like to see a return to an awareness that legitimate news sources have points of view, and to see that awareness develop to the point where it would strike most people as absurd to propose a fairness doctrine.

Amending the Constitution would open up huge possibilities for reforming our communications system.[25] Many other nations' constitutions have built on what ours began over two centuries ago. The Constitution of East Timor develops each freedom in greater detail than does that of the United States, including the freedom of the press. It includes this clause: "The monopoly on the mass media shall be prohibited." We, too, need to ban media monopolies, public or private. We need to ensure at the level of the Constitution that all Americans have a right to diverse and nonprofit, noncommercial media. This is nothing other than the freedom of the press articulated in the economic and technological world we actually inhabit.

We need also to guarantee the presence in every community of truly public media, free of commercial pressures and inclusive of diverse viewpoints. Trillions of our tax dollars are given away in the form of broadcast licenses to local public media outlets with locally elected boards who do nothing to represent local interests. Flip through the channels and just try to find something you would have chosen to put on there if it had been up to you.

We also need an amendment requiring that any medium used by over half the people be made available free of charge nationwide, so that everyone will have equal access to satellite television, the Internet, and whatever medium comes next.

We need to prosecute Bush, Cheney, and their gang for the illegal propaganda described above, but that is only a first step. We need to focus on busting the media monopolies maintained by our government against our interests. We need to legislate major changes in how the media is owned and controlled, and to establish our right to meaningful freedom of the press through constitutional amendment.

Hand-in-hand with governmental reform, we need to begin, to the extent that we are able, building democratic media right now. We should start supporting media outlets that support us, and stop supporting the other ones. For the money that peace and justice groups dump into corporate media for advertisements, we could give major support to truly independent media. For the money that we funnel into corporate media advertisements through political campaigns, we could remake our communications system.

We should be urgently devoting our attention and our resources to creating and supporting media outlets that report the news in a non-corporate manner. We should also support investigative journalists independent of any outlets. We should support reporting that challenges authorities and that turns to people other than authorities to include their voices. We should strive for a communications system in which incumbent politicians lose a little bit of their reelection advantage because there are more stories being written about admirable people outside of politics who could choose to run for office and serve as temporary representatives before returning to other pursuits.

We should stop having anything to do with destructive, dishonest media outlets, no matter how prestigious. We shouldn't talk to them and then promote them by bragging about the few words they misquoted in a "balanced" article. We shouldn't appear on their shows and then send the video to all our friends. We shouldn't fund them with our advertisements. And we shouldn't watch them, listen to them, or subscribe to them. (Yes, I'm guilty of all of these things, but I am trying to mend my ways.) We should focus on funding and promoting media outlets that are moving in the right direction. Nothing will better persuade corporate media outlets to improve their own reporting.

Among the media outlets we should support are bookstores and publishers. Our democratic newspaper today is not a newspaper at all, but rather a stack of books. Most insights into what our government has been doing over the past several years have appeared first in books, and often only in books. The story of illegal spying appeared in the *New York Times* after a year's delay because the reporter James Risen was about to publish it in a book—titled *State of War*—a book containing a half dozen other big stories that have yet to make it into newsprint. Books are critical because stories that truly give us new ways of looking at the world often need the space of a book to be properly told.

24. **VOTING**

We've looked at the topic of aggressive war, which the Nuremberg tribunal deemed "the supreme international crime differing only from other war crimes in that it contains within itself the accumulated evil of the whole." Election fraud is the supreme domestic crime differing only from other governmental crimes in that it contains within itself the accumulated evil of the whole, sometimes even including the supreme international crime. We should not have to take it on faith that our votes are counted. Doing so virtually guarantees that they sometimes will not be. And there is strong evidence that in many cases in recent years they have not been.

Of course we need media reform if we are to have election reform, since the corporate media maintains that election fraud does not and cannot exist. Or, rather, it could exist in the future. With each passing election we are told that the system worked flawlessly again, and at the same time we are told that it is full of weaknesses that might cause trouble in the future. Tampering with electronic voting machines, in particular, is the most unmentionable of topics in the corporate media. The suppression of votes through tampering with voter rolls is slightly more acceptable as a topic for fleeting and misleading news reporting. The variety of election fraud techniques employed in recent years is never reported as a totality.

The Constitution is one level at which we should reform our electoral system. The topic of elections is the most amended topic in the Constitution, and it is in dire need of further improvement. Individuals must have the right to vote, to vote with only a reasonable investment of time, and to have all votes publicly and locally counted in a manner that can be repeated and verified if questioned. No private companies should oversee any vote counting. Individuals convicted in court of attempting to fraudulently alter election outcomes should be imprisoned for a minimum of ten years.

Congressman Jesse Jackson Jr. has said, "The United States stands virtually alone on denying constitutional protection of the right to vote. 108 of the 119 democratic nations in the world have a right to vote in their Constitution—including the Afghan Constitution and the interim Iraqi Constitution."[26] A constitutional amendment would allow the federal government to create a universal system to ensure that no citizen's right to vote was infringed upon, rather than allowing fifty states, 3,000 counties, and 12,000 different election jurisdictions to all set their own policies, design ballots, purchase machines, decide what hours the polls are open, and determine who is eligible to vote and whether they must bring ID with them. This system has not been working very well.[27] As Congressman Jackson points out,

> [M]ore than a million votes in the 2004 election were discarded. In one instance, 4,500 votes were lost forever when a touch screen voting machine malfunctioned in North Carolina and there was no backup. In Florida and Pennsylvania—two of the most important battleground states in the presidential contest— more than half of the provisional ballots cast were not counted. Election officials claim most of those were from unregistered voters. The question remains, why weren't they registered? Did the local officials make mistakes when preparing voter rolls, a partisan organization simply not mail in their registration forms, or were these voters simply not registered?"[28]

The individual right to vote would facilitate the creation of what many other democracies have, namely universal registration. If you are of voting age, if you can be entered into a Social Security database; if you can be sent thousands of miles away to use billion-dollar weapons to kill and die for a pack of lies, there is no reason you cannot be entered into a national voters database. There is no reason we cannot remove the pointless hurdle of requiring people to register, and to reregister if they move. A constitutional duty to protect our right to vote would mean a database maintained by the federal government and not shared with—much less managed by—a private company unaccountable to the people.

The individual right to vote should not be taken away, as voting privileges now are in several states for millions of Americans, because they were once convicted of a felony. Bill Clinton's former speech writer and director of the Brennan Center Michael Waldman does not advocate a constitutional right to vote, but does recommend universal voter registration, or, as a second choice, election-day registration.[29] He also recommends re-enfranchising people who have been convicted of crimes and fulfilled their punishments, pointing out the Jim Crow origins of felon disenfranchisement, including in my home state of Virginia:

> Carter Glass, later a prominent Democratic US senator, assured Virginia's constitutional convention in 1901 that felony disenfranchisement would "eliminate the darkey as a political factor in this state in less than five years." Virginia's law is still in effect. Today, one in four black men there is barred from voting.[30]

I agree with Waldman. If someone has finished the punishment imposed by a court, no further punishment should be imposed by the rest of us. Steven Hill, the author of *10 Steps to Repair American Democracy*, agrees and pushes this thinking a step further:

> At the very least, those who have finished their jail time should be reenfranchised automatically via a simple and straightforward procedure. But one has to ask, what is the point of disenfranchising prisoners while serving time in jail? Many prisoners come from the poorest and most vulnerable communities, and while they are in jail is a good time to instill in them the good habits of citizenship, including voting. Like Maine and Vermont, most European democracies allow prisoners to vote because voting is considered a human right.[31]

Creating a constitutional right to vote would enfranchise other people, as well, who have been shut out of the system, including children of American families living abroad, and American citizens living in Puerto Rico, Guam, and the Virgin Islands.

Waldman opposes voter ID laws, proposes a national registration list, and suggests making election day into two days over a weekend. Michael Moore's six proposals in *Mike's Election Guide 2008*, also include weekend elections and universal registration. These are all ideas pointing in the right direction, I think. We want to make it easier to vote, not harder. We must have a very different approach from that of President Richard Nixon, who said, "You got people voting now—blacks, whites, Mexicans and the rest—that shouldn't have anything to say about government; mainly because they don't have the brains to know."[32]

While electronic voting machines have made large-scale election fraud and/or error an increasing part of election day USA, very few cases of individual "voter fraud" have actually been recorded. It is already a major felony for a voter to attempt to vote illegally or vote twice. Very few people will ever be inclined to take that risk for no apparent benefit. US attorneys may be hired and fired based on their willingness to prosecute such chimeras, and the media may play it up endlessly, but "voter fraud" is an excuse to impose requirements on voters, discourage voters, remove voters from registration rolls, and deny voters the right that should be, but isn't, in our Constitution.[33] Election fraud, on the other hand, in which significant numbers of votes are avoided, suppressed, altered, or erased, is a crime with obvious beneficiaries, clear means, and little detection or accountability. This is why I would expand on Jackson's idea of a right to vote to include the right to have your vote publicly and locally counted in a manner that can be repeated and verified if questioned, although also in a manner that does not reveal which individual cast which vote. This requirement would be satisfied, for example, by anonymous paper ballots being publicly collected and hand-counted before a group of witnesses including representatives of each campaign. The requirement would not be satisfied by a vote count performed within a machine, or by the counting of paper ballots that identified the voters who had cast them.[34]

But wait! What about all those shiny expensive machines that can do the tedious counting of votes for us?

They're not up to the job. In the past few elections, and in the 2008 party primaries, we've seen such problems as: precincts turning out more voters than exist (is 110 percent voter turnout an achievement in some people's minds?), huge percentages of people voting in minor races but supposedly failing to vote at all in key contests, results that vary from unadjusted exit polls by unheard of margins, major candidates receiving large percentages of the vote in one precinct and zero votes in the next, voters observing their vote being switched to a different candidate before their eyes, varied results that correlate better with the types of machines used in various jurisdictions than with any other factor that might explain them, and no way in the world to go back and meaningfully recount any of these troubling elections. After bloggers and activists and authors and filmmakers had pounded this issue for years, on August 1, 2008, the *New York Times* finally published a column by Adam Cohen admitting that DRE (direct recording electronic) voting machines do not count votes in a way that can ever be verified.[35]

Of course, not all of the problems that we've seen in recent years have involved machines. We've also seen people forced to wait twelve hours to vote, people turned away in the general election who voted in the same location in the primaries, flyers advising Democrats to vote the day after the election, and all the usual array of abuses and tools of suppression and intimidation. We saw them all again in 2008. Universal rules and standards, and a national database, would go a long way toward reducing these problems, including the most serious: the elimination of voters from the rolls.

The story of recent electile dysfunction is very well told in a film called *Uncounted: The New Math of American Elections* by David Earnhardt.[36] Viewers come away from this film understanding that the Democratic Party landslide in 2006 likely fell far short of what voters actually voted for, that George Bush was never once elected president, and that the solution to the 2000 Florida debacle (the solution of buying electronic voting machines) took a relatively small problem and made it enormous.

Uncounted is a nonpartisan take on the issue and concludes with a very tame list of things you can do: Contact your Congress member. Ask for election day to be a national holiday. Write a letter to the editor. Be an observer at the polls. Et cetera. But, as Brad Friedman of Brad-Blog.com points out in the film, if the cheating is happening inside a computer, it will make no difference how many people are observing it.

We need to be pushing for fundamental—probably constitutional—change!

A collection of essays edited by Mark Crispin Miller called *Loser Take All: Election Fraud and the Subversion of Democracy, 2000–2008* tells the story better than any other single source I've seen. It conveys many compelling points, most crucially that the Supreme Court stopped a recount in Florida in 2000 that would have made Al Gore president. This is not speculation. The recount was later done in April 2001. The *Miami Herald* determined that Gore had won, as did the National Opinion Research Center (NORC) at the University of Chicago, which counted every countable vote. This was not a determination based on speculating what would have happened had people not been removed from the rolls or turned away from the polls. This was simply a recount of votes that had been cast. It was not based on someone's interpretation of how much a chad had to be punched through. It did, however, include "write-in overvotes," that is, ballots on which someone has selected a candidate and also written that same candidate's name on the ballot. These were clear attempts by voters to make doubly sure their votes counted, and yet these ballots had been excluded by tabulating machines. The media reported extensively on the NORC results, even noting that by any reasonable interpretation Gore won Florida's electoral votes and therefore the presidency. But this was noted in a paragraph toward the end of most articles while headlines trumpeted the false report that Bush's victory had been confirmed. This was managed in part by reporting that recounting only those counties that Gore had asked to have recounted would have resulted in Bush winning, even though recounting the entire state, by any of several methods, would have given the win to Gore.[37]

Numerous elections were quite possibly stolen in 2002 in Colorado, New Hampshire, Minnesota, and elsewhere, including Senate, Governor, and House races in Georgia that were practically openly swiped by Diebold's elections unit president flying in at the last minute and altering the election machines. The theft of Don Siegelman's 2002 election as governor of Alabama was even clearer. One county reported a set of results from electronic machines that made Siegelman governor, then recalculated and reported a different set of results. The new results were statistically impossible, and the pair of reports strongly suggested exactly how the machines were rigged, first mistakenly and later as intended.[38]

John Kerry and John Edwards almost certainly won the presidential election in 2004.[39] The evidence of specific fraud and vote suppression in Ohio and elsewhere is overwhelming,[40] but so is the evidence of the exit polls, which does not even account for the suppression of votes. The argument that the exit polls were probably right and the official results wrong, rather than the other way around, is best told in *Was the 2004 Presidential Election Stolen?* by Steven F. Freeman and Joel Bleifuss.[41]

Evidence of election fraud and suppression was not limited to Ohio or to the presidential race in 2004, but was widespread and systematic. This was also true in 2006. In many cases, Democratic turnout apparently overwhelmed Republican fraud in 2006, and the Democrats picked up thirty new seats in Congress. But some of those victories were probably by larger margins than people believe. In other races, Republican fraud appeared successful. I highly recommend reading the evidence in *Loser Take All*, and then thinking about how the 110th Congress might have been different with forty or fifty new Democrats rather than thirty. The 2008 primaries and elections saw a wide variety of suppression techniques reported, as well as visible vote-flipping by DREs, leaving us to wonder, of course, about the invisible variety. The preelection polls showed a significant margin for Obama in the presidential race, and the official results maintained it, but there was never any explanation offered of how pollsters had improved their trade. We were left to assume they had just gotten lucky.

We shouldn't have to assume or guess or worry. We should be able to know and to double check to the satisfaction of everyone. We need to repair our elections. We should completely repeal the Help America Vote Act (HAVA), and require hand-counted paper ballots of a uniform design with uniform procedures (with appropriate exceptions and provisions to allow the disabled who cannot vote on paper by themselves the greatest likelihood of having their votes made anonymously and verifiably counted). If this cannot be done legislatively, it should be done by constitutional amendment. We should ban corporations from having anything to do with counting our votes, and create a public exit-polling system. Everyone should be registered to vote on their eighteenth birthday. Election officials should be banned from participating in political campaigns, and election fraud should be made a major felony.

States should be banned from requiring ID cards from voters at the polls unless that requirement is part of a larger package of reforms. The fact is that poor people are more likely to not have a driver's license or certified copies of birth certificates or other acceptable IDs. Voter fraud is almost unheard of, but probably more likely to occur by absentee ballot or by voting in more than one state, offenses that are not prevented by requiring IDs at the polls. ID requirements in many states today serve primarily to disenfranchise and intimidate voters while instilling in everyone's mind the myth of voter fraud. Universal registration, combined with a universal, free, and easily obtainable ID card, would allow me to support ID requirements, but would not be acceptable to the Republican partisans currently pushing that idea for partisan gain.

Michael Waldman, like Adam Cohen, wants to fix DRE voting machines by requiring that they spit out paper receipts for each voter, but the idea that voters would reliably check those receipts for accuracy is, as far as I know, completely speculative. And requiring that the paper receipts be counted to verify the electronic count would be an endless struggle. The needs that Waldman recognizes for checks and controls on such a system are extensive, and the financial cost would be ongoing.[42] In the long run, we have no choice but to get rid of electronic machines incapable of transparency. In the short run we have no choice but to pressure candidates to challenge any questionable election results and to organize ourselves to challenge such results with or without assistance from candidates.

Obama and his presidential election campaign avoided commenting on DREs. But he did speak up against suppression. Obama sponsored a bill in the Senate that would have criminalized deceptive information about elections, such as flyers telling people to vote in the wrong place or at the wrong time, or warning them not to vote if they have an unpaid parking ticket. Obama sponsored another bill that would have increased the penalties for voter intimidation, and yet another that would have banned preventing anyone from voting as a result of voter "caging." (Caging is the practice of sending mail to select lists of voters, and if it is not delivered and received, removing them from the rolls.) Obama also sponsored a resolution that would have rhetorically opposed photo ID requirements. None of these admirable efforts went anywhere, and the verifiability of elections was not one of the main topics of discussion in the early months of the 111th Congress and the Obama presidency. This should be at the top of the list, and we are the ones who will have to put it there.

25. TAKING ACTION

How exactly do we compel our government to give us what we want, to create appropriate laws and obey them, to establish appropriate rights and respect them, to follow our lead in actually creating transformational change that we don't have to believe in because we can see it? One thing is clear: voting is the least of our tools and responsibilities. A democratic and honest system of elections is essential, but even with such a thing in place, most of our work should begin the day after election day.

Many of us are struggling, financially and otherwise. We have immediate problems and short-term goals. But we need to be strategic about using our immediate struggles to build organizations and patterns of behavior that can win larger victories down the road, including seemingly esoteric victories in redesigning the structure of our government. When the Paulson's Plunder bailout was originally proposed in 2008, the public outrage was tremendous. Congress and the media were flooded with calls and e-mails, and 90 percent were against the thing. Momentarily, we won. The House voted No. But that victory did not last. The influences of money, media, and party quickly regrouped and overpowered us. We did not have the strength to withstand the assault. If we are ever to have that strength, we will need to limit the influence of money, create truly independent media, and bust up the monopolies on political power and decision making now headquartered in parties. And we will have to be active and organized.

Community organizations like ACORN build groups of active, engaged people willing to use any combination of creative nonviolent techniques to achieve their goals. Watching the successes of such efforts reveals how amazingly little is needed, how close people doing nothing on their sofas are to seizing power over their cities, states, and country. It doesn't take as much as most people imagine. Labor unions have tremendous potential. A Department of Labor worthy of the name, a

National Labor Relations Board worthy of respect, and the effective legalization of the right to organize may be about to usher in a new era of organizing. We should all be part of making sure that happens. Campaigns and coalitions organized around major issues, like the peace movement, are absolutely essential, too, as is the growing independent media online and off. The ability to be truly independent of political corruption, and not merely of Republican political corruption, will be decisive. So will our ability to prioritize the big things and work together with those we do not agree with on everything.

Issues that we think of as domestic, including employment and the environment, increasingly require global solutions. Issues that we think of as international, including diplomacy and war, have a greater impact on our domestic affairs than anything else, impacting our rights, our finances, our safety, and in some cases our lives. To assert that you only work on domestic issues makes as much sense as claiming not to be a political person. Equally misguided, however, is asking people to focus on international issues when they are facing life-threatening injustices at home. We need to find ways to unite our movements for peace and justice, and to think clearly about our relationship to government.

While we need to cease worshipping our government in the area of international affairs, waving flags and singing war songs, we also need to stop hating the entire idea of government when it comes to domestic affair—meaning the useful things that a government, and only a government, can do. Rather than looking at how our tax and legal systems have been made to benefit corporations and the super-wealthy, rather than looking at military expenses, rather than looking at the good done by the government and the intentional sabotaging of good government departments by the same people who want us to hate "big government," we often do the job of the robber barons for them and demand that, for better or worse, the nonmilitary wing of the government shrink. Because we can't seem to distinguish bad government from all government, enemies of the government like Grover Norquist can delight in creating bad government and promoting awareness of it.[43] Sadly, there's a significant side effect. Bad government generates more than just hatred of government. It leads to crashes on Wall Street, mortgage crises, foreclosures, unemployment, unpreparedness for natural disasters, unsafe food, unsafe workplaces, the exacerbation of global warming, and the proliferation of weapons, hatred, ignorant media, and insufficient education. Ultimately, it generates revolution.

We are a nation of growing class division, with the unique trait of a great many in the lower class identifying emotionally with those in the upper class. The class divisions in the United States shock visitors from more egalitarian countries, including those of "old" Europe, but fail to shock Americans. The respect, if not worship, bestowed on corporate pirates, heirs and heiresses, celebrities, and supposed authorities of all sorts ill befits an educated people capable of critical thought. And yet, many of us continue to vote and agitate against our own economic interests by choosing candidates on the bases of religious bigotry, racism, and xenophobia, as well as the simple habit of having "been a Republican" up until now. Others of us assume that Democrats will naturally oppose destructive corporate-driven policies despite being funded by the same corporations and having long since adopted the flawed strategy of trying to win Republican votes rather than educating, inspiring, and registering new voters.

We often hesitate to question elected officials if they belong to a particular party; we resist cooperating with people in one activist campaign because on another topic we oppose them; we try to keep veterans out of the peace movement; or we insist that only veterans should lead a peace movement; and while we struggle with oppressive racism and sexism and other forms of discrimination in our own minds and in the structure of our society, we also throw around false charges of bigotry as an all too easy way to claim superiority over each other. We need more self-respect, respect for others, tolerance of differences, and a willingness to question, challenge, disagree, debate, and demand explanation, treating all assertions on their own merit, not the status of those asserting them.

We need to face up to the fact that no matter how angelic a manner in which someone may have acquired tens of billions of dollars, by hoarding that money they are depriving others of life and recklessly distorting our political system. There is a great shame in hoarding riches no matter where they came from. And there is likewise a shame in not joining with other working people in an effort to build and maintain a union strong enough to speak for all of us. We may not all think we are laborers. Perhaps we view labor as something beneath us or we secretly fantasize about joining the ranks of the gazillionaires. But unless we own large businesses and make all of our own decisions about what we will work on, when, and how, then we are workers and we need a working people's union, or our chances of bettering ourselves will continue to shrink. There are unions that can now be joined by units of workers in every field and by individuals regardless of where we work, whom we work with, and whether our workplace is unionized.[44]

We have reached a critical moment, at great expense, but with great possibility. Things have gotten bad enough in the minds of enough Americans that there is an opening for creating a mass movement for real change, and that movement is already growing all around us. We've been aided in this growing opportunity not just by the crimes and abuses of Bush-Cheney and the US Congress, but by the arrogance and directness of them.

In order to build a movement to compel our government to do great things, we have to restore in people's minds the idea that a government can do anything useful at all. We have to expose, as Thomas Frank does in *The Wrecking Crew*, how intentionally the critics of bad government have worked to make the government bad. We have to expose the horrible failure of corporations to do the job of government when asked to fill that role. We have to expose as baseless and harmful the pseudoscientific theories that claim to show that helping people actually hurts them, that charity is cruelty, that a higher minimum wage hurts workers, that health coverage leads to poor habits and bad health, that altruism doesn't "really" exist and therefore should not be engaged in, and so on. Most of us do not fully accept this sort of thinking, and yet its effects float around in the backs of our heads and the corners of our culture.

In her book, *The Samaritan's Dilemma: Should Government Help Your Neighbor?*, Deborah Stone addresses the problem that many Americans do not think of government as a way to help anyone or do any good in the world. Those who want to do good often choose to do so privately, and are often then frustrated by the much greater harm done by the government they've ignored. Stone traces dismissal of government to claims of the past few decades that government aid goes to parasites who would actually be better off if forced to shape up and take care of themselves.

Stone agrees that there are many cases in which people are best served by showing them how to help themselves. But, she points out,

> The problems that get people pumped up about politics are ones that are beyond the capacity of individuals to solve themselves, no matter how smart or skilled they are or could become and no matter how hard they try. Among these problems: health insurance; much if not most illness and injury; safe and affordable housing; steady work with sufficient pay and benefits to take care of a family; adequate retirement income; affordable higher education and effective primary education; broken, violent neighborhoods; transportation between where people live and where they work; and all the various forms of discrimination, in which people are treated on the basis of stereotypes, no matter what their merits.[45]

Stone even blames the help-is-harmful ethos for the diminishment of community in the United States and the rise of bowling alone. Disagreeing somewhat with Robert Putnam, she writes,

> I trace this withdrawal to a deeper moral source: People who think of themselves as kind and compassionate hesitate to belong to a club of meanies. When people are told not to reach out to other people because help is harmful, they have to harden themselves and act mean when they would rather be kind. If citizens don't join groups, cooperate with each other, or participate in politics as much as we used to, it's likely because we can't get along with OURSELVES. The contradiction between our private and public moralities is too hard to bear. (emphasis in original)[46]

Arguments against helping people, Stone shows, tend to be based on sleights of hand that occur prior to the supposed arguments. Those in need of help are depicted from the start as not needy, not hungry, not suffering in any way. And help is defined from the start as a reward, not as alleviation of any sort of suffering. "To believe help is harmful," she writes, "you have to think of it as something people can do without. You have to have already decided that they don't really need it. And that is the big deception, the invidious moral claim at the heart of conservative logic." Nonetheless, as Stone points out, polls show that most Americans want their government to take some of their money and give it to those in need. Most Americans are altruistic and want to be more so. And people are often most altruistic if you tell them that they already are, give them credit for it, and give them responsibility for it. The best way to give people responsibility is often to ask them to help someone else. The best programs and organizations for developing active citizens are not those that refrain from helping, but those that show people how they can help others. It's not "Teach a man to fish" so much as "Teach a man to teach others to fish."

Ronald Reagan made "I'm from the government and I'm here to help you" sound like a line out of a horror movie just before an axe comes through a wall. "Together we are the government and we help each other," is an attitude that cannot be given the prominence it deserves without a movement that thinks very differently from Democratic Party strategists. We need what Bob Fertik at Democrats.com (an activist group I work for, not the Democratic Party) calls "aggressive progressives."

Being an aggressive progressive means putting your populist policy choices first and your friendship with a political party second. In March 2007, the peace movement was split in two, because some groups supported Congresswoman Barbara Lee's proposal to fund only a withdrawal from Iraq, and some groups backed Speaker Nancy Pelosi's plan to keep funding the war—something they never would have done had it been a Republican plan to keep funding the war. Some of those same groups later refused to oppose President Obama's plan to escalate the war in Afghanistan, something they would have denounced loudly had it been Bush's plan. Numerous groups claiming to mobilize people's voices in the debate over health care actually impose the voice of the president and his health care plan on people inclined to demand a single-payer solution. More than anything else, we need well-organized and powerful activist organizations and media outlets that are truly independent. Groups on the right do a better job of this than do those on the left. Republicans are pulled by voices further to the right than their own, but leftist groups begin by demanding whatever the Democrats have already committed to.

It's true that demanding what neither party has committed to can seem hopeless. But it can improve the immediate outcomes and have a larger impact down the road. The Cheney-Bush impeachment movement that grew up during their terms in office may have failed to impeach (well, never say never, and impeachment would still be best), but it educated, it influenced public opinion, it helped build the peace movement, it trained new activists and built new connections across interest areas, groups, and international borders, it exposed the Iraq war lies so well that it became very difficult to get Americans to believe Iran war lies, it impacted elections, and it laid the groundwork for criminal prosecution of the men our Congress refused to impeach. Perhaps it even laid the groundwork for a future impeachment of a new president by a re-empowered Congress.

The peace movement did not prevent the invasion of Iraq or immediately end the occupation, but it brought the likely end closer. The lion's share of credit for reducing or ending the occupation of Iraq, when and if that comes, should go to the Iraqi people, but a significant portion would belong to the US peace and justice movement, from which continued pressure to end the occupation more quickly and more completely is needed. Yet the peace movement was floundering at the dawn of the 111th Congress and had been shut down for six to eight months in deference to the 2008 elections.

What is needed in US civil society is a revolution. But one way in which we will not succeed is violently. No amount of violence or strategic placement of violence could possibly create a more democratic republic. In our struggle for peace and justice we must not only avoid violence, but reject it so completely that no use of it can be plausibly attributed to us.

Well then, someone who had watched too much television might ask, aren't we pretty much out of luck?

Only if the Indians had no choice but to submit to British rule, only if the Poles had no choice but to bow down to Soviet power, only if the

Danes and the Dutch and the Norwegians could take no actions against
Nazi policies, only if the people of El Salvador or Guatemala had to
suffer dictatorship in silence, only if the citizens of Argentina and Chile
had no recourse when their rights were removed, only if the people of
the Philippines could never restore democracy (or shut down US bases!),
only if a French military coup in Algeria was irreversible, only if rights
simply could not belong to farm workers, only if the Czech and Slovak
people had to suffer occupation for eternity, only if abused workers in
Namibia had no possible recourse, only if the people of Latvia and
Russia and Thailand and Serbia could only throw bombs or cower in
fear, only if Apartheid was permanent in South Africa, only if Jim Crow
was never to leave the American South, only if the eight hour day and
the weekend were still futuristic fantasies (rather than nostalgic memo-
ries), only if women would never vote.

The fact is that much more has been accomplished in the past 100
years by nonviolence than by violence, and the potential for victories
through violence is diminishing, while the potential for nonviolent victories is on the rise. The weaponry of those in power weighs against the
chances of violent success, but the spread of human knowledge weighs
in favor of nonviolent achievement. Most of the victories that have been
achieved by nonviolence have happened without extensive study, planning, training, or strategic decision making, and they have succeeded
against far greater powers of violence by rendering the use of violence
counterproductive. Handled properly, and drawing on lessons of the
past, a nonviolent campaign could probably do more than most people
imagine, and more than has ever been done before.

If you haven't already, you should consider reading a pair of books:
A Force More Powerful: A Century of Nonviolent Conflict by Peter
Ackerman and Jack Duvall (also available as a video),[47] and *Waging
Nonviolent Struggle: 20th Century Practice and 21st Century Potential*
by Gene Sharp.[48] And it wouldn't hurt to throw in *A Testament of Hope:
The Essential Writings and Speeches of Martin Luther King, Jr.*[49]

During the recent years of activist efforts aimed at ending the occupation of Iraq, a peace movement led by leftists attracted many from the
center and right. Some of those on the right, greatly enamored of the
military and used to operating in well-funded organizations, but dis-

gusted by this particular war, offered their advice to the peace movement. We should be more strategic, more like war planners, they said. (Because the war had, of course, been so well planned!) There was actually great wisdom in this advice, but most of those offering it, including former UN weapons inspector Scott Ritter, who had bravely spoken out against the war lies, seemed unaware that the framework for strategically planning nonviolent campaigns had been well worked out by people like Gene Sharp. There's no need to draw simplistic lessons from war theorists in order to make the peace movement more efficient. A peace movement is far more complicated than a war, and the thinking is already far advanced.

We need to plan carefully and to be prepared. Any initial success in our efforts will bring repression that will be easy to mistake for defeat rather than for what it is, a tribute to our power. Throughout history, the most powerful movements have had to meet the most powerful suppressive reactions. We must be disciplined, resolved, and fearless. Victory in a nonviolent campaign comes—if it comes—following repression and a refusal to be frightened by it or to back down. People are usually hurt. Often people are killed. But casualties are lower than in a violent conflict, and probably lower in the long run than what would result from passivity. Through "political jujitsu" repression can be made to weaken the repressors, just as dogs and fire hoses in the South hurt the defenders of Jim Crow. Violent attacks on the nonviolent are very difficult to speak in support of.

A nonviolent movement does not need to bother with secrecy, and can be far more effective without it. It cannot tolerate tactics that include destruction of property or sabotage, which tend to work counter to the larger goals of the movement, to require secrecy, and to risk violence. A nonviolent movement needs a great deal of discipline and organization. Leadership is usually helpful, but dependency on too few leaders can be risky. Understanding of the movement's strategy should be dispersed among many leaders. The movement should take the initiative with a plan for action while at the same time being prepared to react to events and adjust accordingly. What will we do in the face of an apparently stolen election or a new war, for example? What about a refusal to end an old war or a decision to escalate another one?

How can we make best use of nonviolent protest and persuasion? What can be gained by spreading public identity with a movement, for example by encouraging everyone in the country to wear orange in support?[50] What can be gained through disruption of events in Washington and elsewhere, as most prominently practiced by CODEPINK: Women for Peace? What forms of targeted noncooperation with war and abusive government can be developed to the point of having a serious impact? Can military tax resistance be built into something more than a small club? The National Campaign for Nonviolent Resistance and other organizations have begun training activists in civil disobedience and civil resistance. No War, No Warming is another excellent group with a message in its name that has great and growing potential. Port Militarization Resistance is a group in Washington State that has shown how to block war supplies from leaving US ports. The International Longshoreman's and Warehouse Workers' Union has shut down West Coast ports in opposition to the occupation of Iraq. Can such actions be sustained? Can a broader organization support those workers and keep out scabs? Can other transportation workers refuse to cooperate with aggressive war?

In March 2009, environmental advocates organized a well-designed and massively funded weekend conference and Monday nonviolent direct action on Capitol Hill aimed at demanding the closure of the coal-burning Capitol power plant and at passing legislation to combat global warming. The larger success remains to be seen and will certainly require more work, but the initial impact was inspiring. The news generated by plans for the action led to Congress announcing an end to the burning of coal on Capitol Hill prior to the event. The willingness of various well-known figures to risk arrest helped to make civil resistance look mainstream. And college students turned out in huge numbers, energized and ready to act. Will other movements learn from this example? Will movements join together for the greater good?

Gene Sharp's advice to anyone planning a nonviolent campaign is to draw up a strategic estimate. Part of that involves identifying our opponent's "pillars of support," as well as our own strengths and resources. If our opponent is a militarized empire intent on war, its sources of support probably include the corporate media, corporate funding, political parties (both of them), military recruiters and advertising, members of the military, mercenaries, weapons makers, government employees, lobbyists, international allies, police, prisons, and spies. By calling these groups opponents I do not mean that they should be viewed as enemies or with prejudice, but that we should recognize their opposition and seek to undo it. Which of these groups are the weakest and most vulnerable to influence? As corporate power has sought to "defund the left" by busting unions in government departments, are there ways in which we can defund the right? I don't mean can we shift more of the corruption of money to the Democrats; I mean can we take any money away from the cause of war and empire entirely? Can we make mercenaries more trouble than they are worth? Can our cause put on the mantle of the "rule of law"? Can we gain the support of the police? Can we slow recruitment until a draft is the only way to keep wars going, but prevent a draft?[51]

Our own power and potential for greater power lies in the coalition we can build of activist groups focused on domestic and international issues, in organizing and training, in funding, in media of our own creation, in leaders, in sympathetic and organized government employees, in protection we can offer to whistleblowers and resisters, in our international allies, in local and state governments, and possibly even in the Congress or the Supreme Court resisting the abuses of the White House in the interests of a balance of powers.

John R. MacArthur, author of *You Can't Be President: The Outrageous Barriers to Democracy in America*, manages to point out a number of instances in our history when moments of crisis have allowed popular campaigns for progressive legislation and positive changes in government to succeed, notably including the Homestead Act and the Morrill Land-Grant Colleges Act of 1862 passed during the Civil War during a burst of activity by Radical Republicans that saw legislation freeing slaves, prohibiting the return of slaves, abolishing slavery in Washington DC and territories, and passage of the Thirteenth, Fourteenth, and Fifteenth Amendments, which had their full impact during a later positive shock: the Civil Rights Movement. "It's fair to say," MacArthur says, "that most of the other outstandingly popular congressional legislation in American history took place during times of national upheaval, when the normal political order could not resist change."[52]

As you probably recall, Dick Cheney and several other top members of the Bush administration had wished to invade Iraq for years. They had made their goals public through a think tank called the Project for a New American Century (PNAC). They had stated that their mission would be difficult, "absent some catastrophic and catalyzing event—like a new Pearl Harbor." They found that event in the attacks of September 11, 2001. We can find our catastrophic and catalyzing event in the attacks between 2001 and 2008. I propose that we use the Bush-Cheney copresidency as our "new Pearl Harbor," and that we take the opportunity of the coming years not only to undo the damage, but to democratize our republic far beyond the brilliant cutting edge system the founders gave us over two centuries ago, which is long overdue for an update.

Turn to almost any page in this book and you will find an issue to work on. Work on what moves you, what would make a difference in your life and your family's life. Mobilize your community, your school, your clubs and organizations. I can't provide a complete list of useful organizations that you might want to join to work for the cause of peace and justice, but hundreds of good ones are listed at http://afterdowningstreet.org/coalition, and material related to this book is available at http://davidswanson.org.

If we fail to strategically and creatively work, sacrifice, and take risks for peace, justice, and the future of the United States and the planet on which it has such decisive impact, there is a very good chance that our future will take us from bad to worse, that we will not be able to control global warming, nuclear weapons, or fascist tendencies in our government. To understand the benefits of holding Bush, Cheney, and other government officials responsible for their crimes and limiting their power, we need only examine the growing list of actions taken by President Obama that he would not have taken had Bush and Cheney already been held accountable for the same or similar actions. These include firing missile strikes into foreign nations; detaining people without charge, due process, rights, or limitation; declaring the power of rendition; writing signing statements; and making claims of near absolute power (to classify evidence, to declare things state secrets, and to declare things executive privileged) in order to keep secret the illegal activities of the Bush-Cheney years. As the Obama presidency advances, and the ones after it as well, we will see each abuse and distortion of power that has gone uncorrected further entrenched and established, and quite possibly abused and expanded upon, unless we act.

Peace and justice organizations saw their funding dry up when Obama became president, revealing the poor education of funders. The change of an elected official can provide an opportunity to accomplish real change, but not if that opportunity is not seized and acted upon. If we fail, we face the certainty that someone in Washington will eventually assume all of the powers that Cheney collected and piled up in the executive branch of the government, abuse those powers, and add to them further.

"Power concedes nothing without a demand. It never did and it never will," said Frederick Douglass. The power Cheney amassed to pass on to future presidents and vice presidents is a ticking time bomb. To put out the fuse, we don't need to torture anyone. We just need to stand up, lock arms, abandon all fear, form a more perfect Union, establish Justice, ensure domestic Tranquility, provide for the common defence, promote the general Welfare, and secure the Blessings of Liberty to ourselves and our Posterity.

It may take us more than a generation or two to accomplish these goals. We may have to be willing to fight for our whole lifetimes without fully succeeding. But we have no choice in the matter. We must change the structure of our government if we are to transform its policies, and we must transform its policies if we are to survive and prosper.

Can we have justice if our laws only apply to some of us and if the treaties our nation signs only apply to other nations but not our own? Can we achieve domestic tranquility if whole cities are abandoned to hurricanes and whole segments of our population are unable to find living-wage jobs, while our elected leaders focus on ginning up hatred of immigrants? Can we provide for the common defense if warnings of terrorist attacks are ignored while we increase hostility all over the world by imposing military bases on other people's countries? Can we promote the general welfare while rigging the economy to benefit the wealthiest and handing trillions of dollars in foreign debt to our descendants? Can we secure the blessings of liberty from inside chain-link free-speech zones?

Our rights are not secondary to or a distraction from the economy or any other important issue. They are the basis of our ability to impose our collective will through a representative government. We can allow the presidency to continue becoming an imperial throne, or we can create democratic representation. We can allow our government to continue becoming an arm of the military, or we can create peace, justice, and happiness in greater measure than previously imagined. The choice belongs to all of us together.

To Do List

1. Enforce laws at every level, but especially at the federal level, and especially for the highest officials. Deter the crimes of waging aggressive wars, misleading Congress, defrauding Congress, misspending funds, war crimes, murder, warrantless spying, torture, domestic propaganda, violating the Hatch Act and the Voting Rights Act, obstruction of justice, misprision of felony, retaliating against whistleblowers, etc. Find petitions to sign, coalitions to join, suits to file, and local and state resolutions to pass. Pursue legislation to extend statutes of limitations. Learn how to make a citizen's arrest, and the means of filing complaints with bar associations, judicial councils, and universities. Check out resources to organize nonviolent resistance at http://prosecutebushcheney.org.

2. Restore to Congress the power to legislate, the power to begin and end wars, raise and spend money, approve or reject treaties and appointments, and oversee the functioning of the federal government (including through the power of impeachment and the power of inherent contempt). Find steps to take at http://afterdowningstreet.org. One good initial step would be to impeach Jay Bybee. Support bills already introduced that would help restrain the imperial presidency. Support the creation of a House Select Committee to study means of restraining presidential power.

Here are some more specific steps:

➤ Demand that Congress ban the use of funds for any activities created in violation of the law by presidential signing statements.

➤ Amend the Constitution to clearly ban the use of presidential pardons to pardon crimes authorized by the president.

➤ Amend the War Powers Act and the Constitution to include the requirement that congressional authorizations of war include time limits of no more than twelve months, after which Congress must vote again to extend the war or end it, to disallow the unconstitutional initiation of wars without congressional approval, and to make the law enforceable.

➤ Make war profiteering by any war maker a major felony. This would apply to any employee of the federal government or anyone who had within the past decade been an employee of the federal government.

➤ Legislate a requirement that, in any war, the military-aged children and grandchildren of the president, the vice president, all cabinet officials, and all Congress members serve on the front lines in the most dangerous combat positions—no exceptions, no exemptions.

➤ Prohibit the use of mercenaries or any armed contractors, as well as the use of any military force on American soil except when directly engaged in defensive war against a foreign nation.

➤ Repeal the Detainee Treatment Act of 2005, the Military Commissions Act of 2006, the 2008 FISA Amendments Act, the Protect America Act, the original Foreign Intelligence Surveillance Act, and the PATRIOT Act.

➤ Ban secret budgets, secret laws, and secret agencies.

➤ Change the Senate rules to eliminate the filibuster.

➤ Amend the Constitution to eliminate the Senate.

➤ End all rendition, as distinct from extradition.

➤ Amend the Constitution to make the ban on ex post facto laws include any laws that would retroactively grant immunity for crimes.

➤ Amend the Constitution to bar the vice president from exercising executive power.

➤ Amend the Constitution to clarify the congressional power of inherent contempt.

➤ Amend the Constitution to include the right to vote and to have one's vote counted publicly at the polling place.

➤ Give Washington, DC, full voting representation in Congress.

➤ Amend the Constitution to ban private financing of campaigns, create public financing, and provide free airtime to candidates.

➤ Sign and ratify the Rome treaty to join the International Criminal Court.

3. Expose more information and educate. Urge the president to release more classified information and support organizations suing in court for the release of documents, photographs, videos, etc. Ask Congress to update and reissue the subpoenas that were refused during the 110th Congress, and to enforce them through inherent contempt. Support media reform and independent media outlets. Be the media, be a media activist, and be an activist for peace and justice. Report on your work at http://afterdowningstreet.org. Join and support After Downing Street, Democrats.com, Progressive Democrats of America, the National Accountability Network, the Peace Team, the World Can't Wait, CODE PINK: Women for Peace, Veterans for Peace, High Road for Human Rights, the American Freedom Campaign, the Center for Constitutional Rights, the National Lawyers Guild, and the American Civil Liberties Union. Establish and support a fund for whistleblowers and support groups like the National Security Whistleblowers Coalition. Counter military recruitment, and support groups like National Network Opposing Militarization of Youth and groups supporting soldiers in their duty to refuse illegal orders, such as Courage to Resist.

4. Advance a long-term vision in which the corrupting influences of money, media, and party are restrained, and our rights are restored, enforced, and expanded. Those rights include equal rights for all; the right to vote and to have our votes counted publicly and locally; environmental rights; the right to education and healthcare, worker rights,

and basic welfare; freedom of press and freedom from war lies; and the right to know your rights. Push for approval, ratification, and enforcement of international human rights treaties. Build toward constitutional amendments or a convention with a plan to establish whistleblower protection, inherent contempt, and a ban on signing statements. Strip corporations of human rights, restrict monopolies, reduce the power of parties, eliminate the electoral college and the appointment of senators, and limit terms for judges. Promote clean campaign money, nonpartisan (not bipartisan) redistricting, limited election seasons, a bigger House with no Senate, a balanced budget. Limit bills to single topics and require clarity, allow legislation by public initiative, allow recall elections, create citizen assemblies, and develop a fourth (people's) branch of government.

NOTES

Introduction

1. The US Constitution, written in 1787 and effective 1788, is available in full for no charge on numerous websites. You can request a free copy from your Congress member or senators. I recommend the fold-up wallet version, which can be purchased from the National Constitution Center at (215) 409-6700 or http://constitutioncenter.org/constitutionday/Pocket_Constitution.aspx (accessed April 16, 2009).

2. Interview by Martha Raddatz aired by ABC's *Good Morning America* on March 19, 2008; video and transcript posted by Amanda Terkel of Think Progress, http://thinkprogress.org/2008/03/19/cheney-poll-iraq (accessed April 16, 2009).

3. The first ten amendments to the US Constitution, collectively known as the Bill of Rights, became part of the Constitution in 1791. The Constitution now has twenty-seven amendments, all of which are included in most, if not all, online and printed versions of the Constitution.

4. Surveys on approval of Congress as a whole do not necessarily parallel approval of each separate congress member or senator by their constituents. Approval of Congress as a whole hit record lows in the summer of 2008 (13 percent approval according to NBC/*Wall Street Journal*, 14 percent according to Gallup, 23 percent according to AP/Ipsos). Congress's popularity had taken a leap at the beginning of the 110th Congress in January 2007, the Congress having new Democratic majorities (43 percent according to ABC/*Washington Post*, 35 percent according to Gallup, 34 percent according to AP/Ipsos). These and other polls are collected by PollingReport.com, http://www.pollingreport.com/CongJob.htm (accessed April 16, 2009). Approval of both Congress and the president had soared immediately following the attacks of September 11, 2001 (84 percent for Congress according to Gallup). During previous decades Congress's popularity rarely broke 50 percent but hit relative peaks around the times of the impeachments of Nixon and Clinton. For data on those years see Gallup News Service, "Congress Approval Rating Matches Historical Low," http://www.gallup.com/poll/28456/Congress-Approval-Rating-Matches-Historical-Low.aspx (accessed April 16, 2009).

5. For an account of Congress's failure to take on its responsibilities, please see Part II of this book on "Congressional Collapse." For a list of surveys finding majority opinion on a wide range of issues in opposition to the actions of Congress, see the chapter of this book on "Thinking."

6. Michael Goldfarb, "Senator George Mitchell on Iraq, Congress, and the Constitution," The Weekly Standard Blog, http://www.weeklystandard.com/weblogs/TWSFP/2007/04/senator_george_mitchell_on_ira.asp (accessed April 16, 2009). Goldfarb hyperlinked his words "near dictatorial" to a website containing a paper from 1788 by Alexander Hamilton, in which Hamilton argues more strongly than most of the nation's founders ever did for an "energetic" executive. Hamilton even stresses that an executive needs "unity," which may sound familiar from Bush-Cheney era talk of a "unitary executive," but one of the chief reasons that Hamilton

314

writes that he wanted a single executive was so that we would know whom to hold accountable for crimes and abuses, something one does not picture being done to a near-dictator. See: Alexander Hamilton, "The Federalist Papers: No. 70, The Executive Department Further Considered," Yale Law School, http://avalon.law.yale.edu/18th_century/fed70.asp (accessed April 16, 2009).

7. ABC News Blogs, "Biden to Supporters: 'Gird Your Loins,' For the Next President 'It's Like Cleaning Augean Stables,'" *The Radar*, October 20, 2008, http://blogs.abcnews.com/political-radar/2008/10/biden-to-suppor.html (accessed April 16, 2009).

8. In February of 2002, the voters of New Orleans approved the first-ever citywide minimum wage increase by a margin of 63 percent to 37 percent. The city's new minimum wage was pegged to always be one dollar higher than the federal minimum wage, which was then $6.15 per hour. Businesses with fewer than $500,000 in revenues, as well as the city government, were exempt. The increase was ultimately overturned by the Louisiana Supreme Court in September 2002. For more on this and similar campaigns see ACORN's Living Wage Resource Center, http://www.livingwagecampaign.org (accessed April 16, 2009).

9. If you worry about the "tyranny of the majority" or the rule of incompetent commoners, or if you know someone who does, an understanding of the wisdom of majority rule can be found in: Richard D. Parker, *Here the People Rule: A Constitutional Populist Manifesto* (Cambridge, Mass.: Harvard University Press, 1994).

10. Ron Suskind, "Why Are These Men Laughing?" *Esquire*, January 2003.

11. Kjell Aleklett, "Dick Cheney, Peak Oil and the Final Count Down," *Energy Bulletin*, http://www.energybulletin.net/node/349 (accessed April 16, 2009).

12. "Cheney's energy plan focuses on production," *USA Today*, May 1, 2001.

13. Dick Cheney, "Remarks by the Vice President at the Air National Guard Senior Leadership Conference at the Adams Mark Hotel, Denver, Colorado," The White House, http://georgewbush-whitehouse.archives.gov/news/releases/2002/12/20021202-4.html (accessed April 16, 2009).

14. Interview with Vice President Dick Cheney, *Meet the Press*, NBC, Transcript for March 16, 2003, http://www.mtholyoke.edu/acad/intrel/bush/cheneymeetthepress.htm (accessed April 16, 2009).

15. Ibid.

16. "Iraq insurgency in 'last throes,' Cheney says," CNN, http://www.cnn.com/2005/US/05/30/cheney.iraq (accessed April 16, 2009).

17. "Constitution of the Commonwealth of Massachusetts," 1780, http://www.mass.gov/legis/const.htm (accessed April 16, 2009).

18. Thomas Paine published "Common Sense" anonymously, first in two printings by Robert Bell and then in 1776 in an expanded version published by W. & T. Bradford of Philadelphia. The section quoted was in all three printings. For full text free online, see Thomas Paine, "Common Sense," Archiving Early America, http://www.earlyamerica.com/earlyamerica/milestones/commonsense/text.html (accessed April 16, 2009).

19. Beyond the usual revolving-door corruption scheme in which Cheney worked in the government to benefit Halliburton, left to work for Halliburton to benefit himself, and returned to government where he worked to benefit Halliburton, for at least two years of his vice presidency, Cheney received hundreds of thousands of dollars in "deferred compensation" from his employer. See: "Cheney's Halliburton Ties Remain," CBS News, September 26, 2003, http://www.cbsnews.com/stories/2003/09/26/politics/main575356.shtml (accessed April 16, 2009).

I. Presidential Power Grab: Damage Done and Repairs Needed

1. When Bush signed an order on February 7, 2002, sanctioning torture, he was violating the 1996 War Crimes Act, the 1994 Torture Statute, and the Torture Act of 2000, as well as the Eighth Amendment, the Fifth Amendment, and numerous treaties which—under Article VI of the U.S. Constitution—are the law in the United States, including the Universal Declaration of Human Rights, the Convention Against Torture, the International Covenant on Civil and Political Rights, the Inter-American Declaration on the Rights and Duties of Man, and the Third and Fourth Geneva Conventions.

2. Among the laws violated by Bush's warrantless spying programs were the Foreign Intelligence Surveillance Act, the Stored Communications Act of 1986, and the Fourth Amendment. To watch a video of Bush admitting to these crimes go to the archived White House website and watch the December 19, 2005, press conference. Bush claimed he began these crimes only after September 11, 2001, which was not true; he began them earlier. Bush claimed to have legal justification for violating the law, but those claims completely collapsed. He also claimed the spying was limited in ways that it was not. And when asked why he didn't try to change the law rather than violating it, he said he just didn't have to because he was the president.

3. In the case of torture, the first Detainee Treatment Act was contained in HR 2863, the "Department of Defense, Emergency Supplemental Appropriations to Address Hurricanes in the Gulf of Mexico, and Pandemic Influenza Act, 2006." The signing statement is dated December 30, 2005. The second Detainee Treatment Act was part of HR 1815, the "National Defense Authorization Act for Fiscal Year 2006." The signing statement is dated January 6, 2006. In the case of warrantless spying, see the Defense Appropriations Bills for 2005 and 2006 and accompanying signing statements. Here are two databases of Bush's signing statements: http://acslaw.org/node/5309 and http://coherentbabble.com/signingstatements/TOCindex .htm (accessed April 28, 2009).

4. Charlie Savage, "Scalia's Dissent Gives 'Signing Statements' More Heft," *Boston Globe*, July 15, 2006.

5. T. J. Halstead, "Presidential Signing Statements: Constitutional & Institutional Implications, CRS Report for Congress," updated September 17, 2007, http://www.fas.org/sgp/crs/natsec/RL33667.pdf (accessed April 28, 2009).

6. Joyce Green, "Presidential Signing Statements," http://www.coherentbabble.com/faqs.htm.

7. Government Accountability Office Report to Senator Robert Byrd and Congressman John Conyers, June 18, 2007, on Presidential Signing Statements Accompanying the Fiscal Year 2006 Appropriations Acts, http://rawstory.com/other/GAOLegalopinionB-308603.pdf (accessed April 28, 2009).

8. Deputy Assistant Attorney General John Elwood made this claim before the House Judiciary Committee on January 31, 2007. I was there and blogged the hearing at http://afterdowningstreet.org/signing (accessed April 28, 2009).

9. Title 18 of the US Code, our national laws, our red-white-and-blue tough-on-crime book of books has a little section called 2441 that prescribes a fine or prison or death to any American who commits or conspires to commit a war crime, including torture or cruel or inhuman treatment. This was what caused then White House counsel Alberto Gonzales to warn the president and others in a January 25, 2002 memo that they should play word games as the best defense of their own necks. Title 18 also contains section 2340, which, like 2441, defines torture with clarity and sanity, and prescribes prison or death for those who engage in it, and prison for those who conspire to commit it. These laws were in place long before the Bush-era charade of Congress pretending to ban torture and Bush pretending he could legalize it with a signing statement. The United States had also already signed and ratified the Convention Against Torture, which requires criminal prosecution of "an act by any person which consti-

tutes complicity or participation in torture." These laws could be enforced without the death penalty, which I oppose.

10. David Swanson, "McCain, Torture Supporter," September 12, 2008, http://davidswanson.org/node/1429 (accessed April 28, 2009).

11. The FISA Amendments Act of 2008.

12. Jeff Stein, "Wiretap Recorded Rep. Harman Discussing Aid for AIPAC Defendants," *Congressional Quarterly*, April 19, 2009.

13. Government Accountability Office Report to Senator Robert Byrd and Congressman John Conyers, June 18, 2007, on Presidential Signing Statements Accompanying the Fiscal Year 2006 Appropriations Acts, http://rawstory.com/other/GAOLegalopinionB-308603.pdf (accessed April 28, 2009).

14. Charlie Savage, "Bush Challenges Hundreds of Laws: President Cites Powers of His Office," *Boston Globe*, April 30, 2006, http://www.boston.com/news/nation/articles/2006/04/30/bush_challenges_hundreds_of_laws (accessed April 28, 2009).

15. John Dean, "The Controversy over Curtailing Habeas Corpus Rights: Why It Is a Bad Day For The Constitution Whenever Attorney General Alberto Gonzales Testifies," *FindLaw*, January 26, 2007, http://writ.lp.findlaw.com/dean/20070126.html (accessed April 28, 2009).

16. Michael Roston, "Bush Signing Statement on US-India Nuclear Deal Erases Congressional Restrictions," *Raw Story*, December 19, 2006, http://www.rawstory.com/news/2006/Bush_signing_statement_seeks_to_erase_1219.html (accessed April 28, 2009).

17. "Senator Asks Bush to Explain Signing Statement That Gives President Authority to Open Mail Without Warrant," *Raw Story*, January 8, 2007, http://www.rawstory.com/ news/2007/Senator_asks_Bush_to_explain_signing_0108.html (accessed April 28, 2009).

18. "CRS Report for Congress: Presidential Signing Statements: Constitutional and Institutional Implications," Updated September 17, 2007, by TJ Halstead, Legislative Attorney, American Law Division: ftp.fas.org/sgp/crs/natsec/RL33667.pdf (accessed April 28, 2009).

19. American Bar Association Task Force on Presidential Signing Statements and the Separation of Powers Doctrine Report with Recommendations, August 2006, http://abanet.org/op/signingstatements (accessed April 28, 2009).

20. David H. Remes, Gerard J. Waldron, and Shannon A. Lang, "Presidential Signing Statements: Will Congress Pick Up The Gauntlet?" June 26, 2006, http://constitutionproject.org/pdf/Signing_Statements_Memo_from_Covington_&_Burling.pdf (accessed April 28, 2009).

21. Congressional Record: July 25, 2006 (Senate) Page S8189-S8190: http://www.fas.org/irp/congress/2006_cr/s072506.html (accessed April 28, 2009).

22. On April 30, 2008, the Subcommittee on the Constitution of the Senate Judiciary Committee held a hearing on "Secret Law and the Threat to Democratic and Accountable Government," which of course identified a clear threat and then did nothing about it. See http://www.fas.org/sgp/congress/2008/043008aftergood.pdf (accessed April 28, 2009) for the testimony of one of the witnesses, Steven Aftergood.

23. Dennis Kucinich, David Swanson, and Elizabeth de la Vega, *The 35 Articles of Impeachment and the Case for Prosecuting George W. Bush* (Port Townsend, WA: Feral House, 2008) Article XXII, http://afterdowningstreet.org/busharticles (accessed April 28, 2009).

24. Ibid., Article XXVI.

25. Brian C. Kalt, "The Constitutional Case for the Impeachability of Former Federal Officials: An Analysis of the Law, History, and Practice of Late Impeachment," June 26, 2006, http://afterdowningstreet.org/node/37834 (accessed April 28, 2009).

26. I blogged the hearing here: http://afterdowningstreet.org/node/35043 (accessed April 28, 2009).

27. *Boston Globe* Questionnaire on Executive Power, December 20–22, 2007, http://www.ontheissues.org/2007_Exec_Power.htm (accessed April 28, 2009).

28. Statement on Signing the American Recovery and Reinvestment Act of 2009, February 17, 2009, http://www.coherentbabble.com/ss2009.htm#a200901 (accessed April 28, 2009).

29. Barack Obama, Memorandum for the Heads of Executive Departments and Agencies, Subject: Presidential Signing Statements, March 9, 2009, http://www.whitehouse.gov/the_press_office/Memorandum-on-Presidential-Signing-Statements (accessed April 28, 2009).

30. Ceci Connolly and R. Jeffrey Smith, "Obama Positioned to Quickly Reverse Bush Actions," *Washington Post*, November 9, 2008, p. A-16.

31. Stephen Kinzer, *Overthrow: America's Century of Regime Change From Hawaii to Iraq* (New York: Henry Holt and Co., 2006).

32. Murray Polner and Thomas E. Woods Jr., *We Who Dared to Say No to War: American Antiwar Writing from 1812 to Now* (Philadelphia: Basic Books, 2008).

33. Ibid.

34. US House Judiciary Democratic Staff, *George W. Bush versus the U.S. Constitution: The Downing Street Memos and Deception, Manipulation, Torture, Retribution, and Coverups in the Iraq War and Illegal Domestic Spying* (Chicago: Academy Chicago Publishers, 2006), http://afterdowningstreet.org/constitutionincrisis (accessed April 28, 2009); Elizabeth de la Vega, *United States v. George W. Bush et al* (New York: Seven Stories Press, 2006); Dennis Kucinich, David Swanson, and Elizabeth de la Vega, *The 35 Articles of Impeachment and the Case for Prosecuting George W. Bush* (Port Townsend, WA: Feral House, 2008) Articles I-IV, http://afterdowningstreet.org/busharticles (accessed April 28, 2009); David Swanson, "Bush Lied, Knew He Was Lying, Thought It Was Funny, and Killed Over a Million People," After Downing Street, July 21, 2008, http://afterdowningstreet.org/node/34952 (accessed April 28, 2009); Key Documents, After Downing Street, http://afterdowningstreet.org/keydocuments (accessed April 28, 2009).

35. Project for a New American Century, "Rebuilding America's Defenses," September 2000, http://www.scribd.com/doc/9651/Rebuilding-Americas-Defenses-PNAC (accessed April 28, 2009).

36. Ibid.

37. Russ Baker, "Bush Wanted To Invade Iraq If Elected in 2000," Guerrilla News Network, October 27, 2004, http://www.gnn.tv/articles/article.php?id=761 (accessed April 28, 2009).

38. Project for a New American Century, Letter to President Bush, September 20, 2001, http://zfacts.com/p/165.html (accessed April 28, 2009).

39. The following two quotes from Rice and Powell were read by Ray McGovern during the June 16, 2005, Downing Street Minutes basement hearings in the U.S. Capitol. Video of Powell and Rice making these statements, with narration from Australian journalist John Pilger, is here: http://www.thememoryhole.org/war/powell-rice-wmd.wmv (accessed April 28, 2009).

40. Vincent Bugliosi, *The Prosecution of George W. Bush for Murder* (Cambridge, MA: Vanguard Press, 2008).

41. Murray Waas, "What Bush Was Told About Iraq," *National Journal*, March 2, 2006, http://nationaljournal.com/about/njweekly/stories/2006/0302nj1.htm (accessed April 28, 2009).

42. See http://georgewbush-whitehouse.archives.gov/news/releases/2003/01 (accessed April 28, 2009) for the video.

43. This memo did make the news, at least briefly and outside the United States. See http://afterdowningstreet.org/whitehousememo (accessed April 28, 2009). I always called it the White House Memo. It is the same document that Vincent Bugliosi calls the Manning Memo. It was first reported on by Phillipe Sands in *Lawless World: America and the Making and Breaking of Global Rules* (Viking Adult, 2005). Part of the conversation recorded in the memo is recreated in Crawford, Texas, rather than the White House, in Oliver Stone's 2008 film *W*.

44. "US Plan To Bug Security Council: The Text," *The Guardian*, March 2, 2003, http://www.guardian.co.uk/world/2003/mar/02/iraq.unitednations1 (accessed April 28, 2009).

45. Jonathan Schwarz, "Will We Create a Pretext for War With Iran?" A Tiny Revolution, January 12, 2007, http://tinyrevolution.com/mt/archives/001271.html (accessed April 28, 2009). Michael Isikoff and David Corn, *Hubris: The Inside Story of Spin, Scandal, and the Selling of the Iraq War* (Crown, 2006).

46. Faiz Shakir, "To Provoke War, Cheney Considered Proposal To Dress Up Navy Seals As Iranians And Shoot At Them," Think Progress, July 31, 2008, http://thinkprogress.org/2008/07/31/cheney-proposal-for-iran-war.

47. ABC News, December 16, 2003.

48. Iraqi deaths as a result of the invasion and occupation, measured above the high death rate under international sanctions preceding the attack, are estimated at 1.2 million by two independent sources (Just Foreign Policy's updated figure based on the Johns Hopkins/Lancet report, and the British polling company Opinion Research Business's estimate as of August 2007). According to the United Nations High Commissioner for Refugees (UNHCR), the number of Iraqis who have fled their homes has reached 4.7 million. If these estimates are accurate, a total of nearly 6 million human beings have been displaced from their homes or killed, as of August 2008. Many times that many have certainly been injured, traumatized, impoverished, and deprived of clean water and other basic needs.

49. See http://youtube.com/watch?v=09EbssUgHj4 (accessed April 28, 2009).

50. Ron Suskind, *The Way of the World: A Story of Truth and Hope in an Age of Extremism* (Harper, 2008).

51. "'Way Of The World' Sees Fabricated Case For War," National Public Radio, *Morning Edition*, August 5, 2008, http://www.npr.org/templates/story/story.php?storyId=93293353 (accessed April 28, 2009).

52. "Iraqi diplomat gave U.S. prewar WMD details," *NBC Nightly News*, March 20, 2006, http://www.msnbc.msn.com/id/11927856 (accessed April 28, 2009).

53. James Risen, *State of War: The Secret History of the C.I.A. and the Bush Administration* (Free Press, 2006).

54. "Saddam Hussein's Son-In-Law Says Torture Common In Iraq," CNN, September 21, 1995, http://cnn.com/WORLD/9509/iraq_defector/index.html (accessed April 28, 2009).

55. Jonathan Schwarz suggested I ask Powell about this, and I tried to do so at an event in Washington in 2004, but the moderator, Gwen Ifill, only allowed questions to be asked to her prior to Powell taking the stage. I asked her this question. People applauded. Ifill never brought it up.

56. Bob Wodward, *Plan of Attack* (Simon & Schuster, 2004).

57. David Swanson, "Colin Powell, Liar Extraordinaire," January 12, 2006, http://davidswanson.org/node/435 (accessed April 29, 2009).

58. Peter Eisner and Knut Royce, *The Italian Letter: How the Bush Administration Used a Fake Letter to Build the Case for War in Iraq* (Rodale Books, 2007).

59. Ibid.

60. James Bamford, *A Pretext for War: 9/11, Iraq, and the Abuse of America's Intelligence Agencies* (Anchor, 2005); Lindsay Moran, *Blowing My Cover: My Life As a CIA Spy* (Berkley Trade, 2005).

61. Dick Cheney, Remarks at the American Enterprise Institute in Washington, DC, on April 15, 1994, http://www.youtube.com/watch?v=6BEsZMvrq-I (accessed April 29, 2009).

62. Joel Roberts, "Bush Vows To Fire Leak Criminals: President Shifts Language On CIA Leaks; Still No Comment On Rove," CBS/AP, July 18, 2005, http://www.cbsnews.com/stories/2005/07/18/politics/main709678.shtml (accessed April 29, 2009).

63. David Swanson, "Bush's Four Anti-Terror Successes All Fictional," January 27, 2007, http://davidswanson.org/node/710 (accessed April 29, 2009).

64. "Video shows Bush got explicit Katrina warning: President, Chertoff were clearly told of storm's dangers numerous times," Associated Press, March 2, 2006. Video: http://msnbc.msn.com/id/11627394 (accessed April 29, 2009).

65. James Risen broke this story in his book *State of War* after failing to get the *New York Times*, for which he worked to publish it for over a year.

66. International Committee of the Red Cross, "ICRC Report On The Treatment Of Fourteen 'High Value Detainees' In CIA Custody," February 2007, http://www.nybooks.com/icrc-report.pdf (accessed April 29, 2009).

67. Ron Suskind, *The Way of the World: A Story of Truth and Hope in an Age of Extremism* (Harper, 2008).

68. Marcy Wheeler, "Habbush's Freedom Fries Forgeries," FireDogLake, August 11, 2008, http://emptywheel.firedoglake.com/2008/08/11/habbushs-freedom-fry-forgeries (accessed April 29, 2009).

69. Dennis Kucinich, David Swanson, and Elizabeth de la Vega, *The 35 Articles of Impeachment and the Case for Prosecuting George W. Bush* (Port Townsend, WA: Feral House, 2008) Article VII, http://afterdowningstreet.org/busharticles (accessed April 29, 2009).

70. John Bonifaz, *Warrior King: The Case for Impeaching George Bush* (Nation Books, 2003).

71. Presidential Letter, March 19, 2003, http://afterdowningstreet.org/node/611 (accessed April 29, 2009); Report In Connection With Presidential Determination Under Public Law 107-243, http://afterdowningstreet.org/downloads/3-18-03report.pdf (accessed April 29, 2009).

72. Dennis Kucinich, David Swanson, and Elizabeth de la Vega, *The 35 Articles of Impeachment and the Case for Prosecuting George W. Bush* (Port Townsend, WA: Feral House, 2008) Article VI, http://afterdowningstreet.org/busharticles (accessed April 29, 2009).

73. In May 2005, when a particularly strong (at least at that point) piece of evidence emerged, known as the Downing Street Minutes, attorney John Bonifaz wrote a letter about the crimes of fraud and false statements to Congressman John Conyers, and we launched a campaign for accountability called After Downing Street. Memorandum re the President's Impeachable Offenses to Rep. John Conyers, Jr., from John C. Bonifaz, May 22, 2005, http://afterdowningstreet.org/node/5 (accessed April 29, 2009).

74. Dennis Kucinich, David Swanson, and Elizabeth de la Vega, *The 35 Articles of Impeachment and the Case for Prosecuting George W. Bush* (Port Townsend, WA: Feral House, 2008) Articles I-IV, http://afterdowningstreet.org/busharticles (accessed April 29, 2009).

75. Phyllis Bennis, *Challenging Empire: How People, Governments, and the UN Defy US Power* (Olive Branch Press, 2005).

76. "President George Bush Discusses Iraq in National Press Conference," the White House, March 6, 2003, http://georgewbush-whitehouse.archives.gov/news/releases/2003/03/20030306-8.html (accessed April 29, 2009).

77. Dennis Kucinich, David Swanson, and Elizabeth de la Vega, *The 35 Articles of Impeachment and the Case for Prosecuting George W. Bush* (Port Townsend, WA: Feral House, 2008) Article VIII, http://afterdowningstreet.org/busharticles (accessed April 29, 2009).

78. Michael A. Lundberg, "The Plunder of Natural Resources During War: a War Crime," Georgetown Journal of International Law, March 22, 2008.

79. Marjorie Cohn, "Aggressive War: Supreme International Crime," Truthout, November 9, 2004, http://web.archive.org/web/20041110060613/http://www.truthout.org/docs_04/110904A.shtml (accessed April 29, 2009).

80. Michael Haas, George W. Bush, *War Criminal?: The Bush Administration's Liability for 269 War Crimes* (Praeger Publishers, 2008). War crimes in Iraq have also been extensively reported on at http://afterdowningstreet.org and in some cases described by US veterans in events organized by Iraq Veterans Against the War, http://ivaw.org/wintersoldier (accessed April 29, 2009). War crimes are the norm in every war. The aggressive war that stole our southwestern states from Mexico was no exception to the rule. General Zachary Taylor told the War Department: "I deeply regret to report that many of the twelve months' volunteers, in their route hence of the lower Rio Grande, have committed extensive outrages and depredations upon the peaceable inhabitants. There is scarcely any form of crime that has not been reported to me as committed by them." Murray Polner and Thomas E. Woods Jr., *We Who Dared to Say No to War: American Antiwar Writing from 1812 to Now* (Philadelphia: Basic Books, 2008).

81. Dennis Kucinich and David Swanson and Elizabeth de la Vega, *The 35 Articles of Impeachment and the Case for Prosecuting George W. Bush* (Port Townsend, WA: Feral House, 2008) Article XVI, http://afterdowningstreet.org/busharticles (accessed April 29, 2009).

82. Ibid., Article XIII.

83. Ibid., Article XIV.

84. Ibid., Article XV.

85. Ibid., Articles XVII-XX.

86. Ibid., Article XXI.

87. Ibid., Article XXIII.

88. American Civil Liberties Union, "U.S. Operatives Killed Detainees During Interrogations in Afghanistan and Iraq," October 24, 2005, http://www.aclu.org/intlhumanrights/gen/21236prs20051024.html (accessed April 29, 2009).

89. Daniel Dombey and Stanley Pignal, "Europeans See US as Threat to Peace," *Financial Times,* July 1, 2007, http://www.ft.com/cms/s/0/70046760-27f0-11dc-80da-000b5df10621 .html?nclick_check=1 (accessed April 29, 2009).

90. "Karzai Says Air Strike in Afghanistan Kills 37," Associated Press, November 5, 2008, http://www.msnbc.msn.com/id/27556113 (accessed April 29, 2009).

91. Karen DeYoung, "Spy Agencies Say Iraq War Hurting U.S. Terror Fight," *Washington Post,* September 24, 2006, Page A-1.

92. Jonathan S. Landay, "U.S. Eliminates Annual Terrorism Report," Knight Ridder Newspapers, April 16, 2005, http://seattletimes.nwsource.com/html/nationworld/2002243262_terror16 .html (accessed April 29, 2009).

93. See http://www.youtube.com/watch?v=QSVfwDwrlBE (accessed April 29, 2009).

94. James Madison, "Political Observations," April 20, 1795. *Letters and Other Writings of James Madison, Volume IV,* page 491. When president in 1812, Madison was all too eager to push the nation into unnecessary war, but he did not do so without the approval of Congress.

95. Evan Derkacz, Republican Calls For Hanging Of Those Who Oppose President, Alternet, February 15, 2007, http://alternet.org/blogs/video/#48101 (accessed April 29, 2009).

96. Abraham Lincoln, letter to his law partner William Herndon, quoted in "The Genius of Impeachment," by John Nichols, *The Genius of Impeachment: The Founders' Cure for Royalism* (New Press, 2006).

97. Abraham Lincoln, speech on floor of House of Representatives, January 12, 1848; Murray Polner and Thomas E. Woods, Jr., *We Who Dared to Say No to War: American Antiwar Writing from 1812 to Now* (Philadelphia: Basic Books, 2008).

98. President Polk's descendant William Polk authored a book with former Senator George McGovern outlining a plan to end the Iraq War. Now there's improvement of a sort that some prominent families can't compare to! A full account of Lincoln's spot resolution can be found in John Nichols' masterful book *The Genius of Impeachment: The Founders' Cure for Royalism.* However, it is worth noting that when Lincoln himself was president, he was all too eager to go to war, declared blockades without congressional approval, enlarged the army without congressional approval, spied without warrants on telegrams, suspended habeas corpus, and drove the nation into debt.

99. David Michael Green, "A Government of People, After All," OpEdNews, July 17, 2008, http://www.opednews.com/articles/A-Government-of-People—Af-by-David-Michael-Gree-080717-199.html (accessed April 29, 2009).

100. "National War Powers Commission Recommends War Powers Consultation Act of 2009," Miller Center of Public Affairs, University of Virginia, July 8, 2008, http://www.virginia.edu/uva-today/newsRelease.php?id=5680 (accessed April 29, 2009).

101. Larry J. Sabato, *A More Perfect Constitution: 23 Proposals to Revitalize Our Constitution and Make America a Fairer Country* (New York: Walker Publishing Company, 2007).

102. Center for Constitutional Rights, "Restore. Protect. Expand. Amend the War Powers Resolution," April 2009, http://ccrjustice.org/get-involved/action/take-action-repeal-aumf-iraq (accessed April 29, 2009).

103. I recommend a book that attempts to list every law, agreement, signing statement, status of forces aggreement, and department or commission regulation put in place between 2001 and 2008 that violates the Constitution and treaties to which the United States is party: Ann Fagan

Ginger, *Undoing the Bush/Cheney Legacy: A Tool Kit for Congress and Activists* (Meiklejohn Civil Liberties Institute, 2009).

104. 31 USC§ 1301: "[A]ppropriations shall be applied only to the objects for which the appropriations were made except as otherwise provided by law." The illegal use of funds would cause an automatic diminution in funds available to the guilty agency.

105. For fiscal year 2009, our government has budgeted $653 billion for the Pentagon, and $150 billion for the military portion of other departments. But this budget includes a ludicrously low $38 billion for the wars in Iraq and Afghanistan, so that those military occupations have had to be once again funded with an "emergency" supplemental to the tune of $162 billion. The War Resisters League has added the cost of veterans' benefits, and included 80 percent of the cost of interest on the national debt, to arrive at a total of $1.449 trillion. That compares to $1.210 trillion in nonmilitary US spending. These figures do not include trust funds, such as Social Security, which are not part of the federal budget. In February 2008, the Center for Arms Control and Non-Proliferation calculated that US military expenses were 48 percent of world military expenses, but the figure they used for the United States was only $0.711 trillion, failing to take into consideration the cost of the interest that will have to be paid by our descendants.

106. Conyers's staff had written a book on Bush and Cheney's impeachable offenses prior to spending two years refusing to impeach them, during which time they, in fact, wrote a second book on the same topic. *US House Judiciary Democratic Staff, George W. Bush versus the U.S. Constitution: The Downing Street Memos and Deception, Manipulation, Torture, Retribution, and Coverups in the Iraq War and Illegal Domestic Spying* (Chicago: Academy Chicago Publishers, 2006), http://afterdowningstreet.org/constitutionincrisis (accessed April 28, 2009); "Reining In The Imperial Presidency: Lessons and Recommendations Relating to the Presidency of George W. Bush," House Committee on the Judiciary Majority Staff Report to Chairman John Conyers Jr., January 13, 2009, http://afterdowningstreet.org/downloads/conyers09.pdf (accessed April 29, 2009).

107. Dennis Kucinich, David Swanson, and Elizabeth de la Vega, *The 35 Articles of Impeachment and the Case for Prosecuting George W. Bush* (Port Townsend, WA: Feral House, 2008) Article V, http://afterdowningstreet.org/busharticles (accessed April 29, 2009).

108. I blogged the hearing until the committee staff insisted that only members of the corporate media were permitted to use computers during a hearing; my friends held up signs protesting the war, and the Capitol Police started hauling them out and roughing people up in the hallway. See http://afterdowningstreet.org/node/26632.

109. Calculating the military portion of the tax to be paid would involve multiplying the total tax to be paid by 54 percent, or whatever the correct figure was in a given year. Military expenses would include expenses for military operations by any departments of the government, wars funded through "emergency supplementals," veterans' care, and interest on that portion of the national debt resulting from past military expenses. Or, perhaps better, tax tables could be used to calculate one's nonmilitary tax, which could then be multiplied by 1.174, or whatever the correct figure was in a given year, to generate one's military tax. Then the two could be totaled.

110. 8.4 trillion divided by 303 million equals 27,722.

111. "Fed Defies Transparency Aim in Refusal to Disclose," by Mark Pittman, Bob Ivry and Alison Fitzgerald, Bloomberg.com, November 10, 2008.

112. "Support for Bank Bailouts at 6%," Zogby International, March 31, 2009, http://www.zogby .com/blog/loader.cfm?p=/2009/03/31/support-for-bank-bailouts-at-6 (accessed April 29, 2009).

113. David Enrich and Marshall Eckblad, "Bailed-Out Banks Face Probe Over Fee Hikes," *Wall Street Journal*, April 13, 2009.

114. Bryan Bender, "Pentagon Board Says Cuts Essential," *Boston Globe*, November 10, 2008, http://www.boston.com/news/nation/articles/2008/11/10/pentagon_board_says_cuts_essential (accessed April 29, 2009).

115. *This Week*, ABC, February 1, 2009.

116. Dave Lindorff points out that a capitalist solution would involve breaking up monopolies, and a socialist solution would involve government ownership or joint ownership, whereas a "bailout" for monopolies is just the temporary fix of a kleptocracy. Dave Lindorff, "'Too Big To Fail' Has an Easy Answer: Anti-Trust or Public Control," November 11, 2008, http://afterdowningstreet.org/node/37601 (accessed April 29, 2009).

117. "An Investigation into the Removal of Nine U.S. Attorneys in 2006," US Department of Justice Office of the Inspector General and Office of Professional Responsibility, September 2008, http://www.usdoj.gov/oig/special/s0809a/final.pdf (accessed April 29, 2009).

118. Charlie Savage, "Obama's War on Terror May Resemble Bush's in Some Areas," New York Times, February 17, 2009, http://www.nytimes.com/2009/02/18/us/politics/18policy.html?_r=1&ref=politics&pagewanted=all (accessed April 29, 2009).

119. For an example of a declassified NSA document from December 2000, see http://www.gwu.edu/~nsarchiv/NSAEBB/NSAEBB24/nsa25.pdf (accessed April 29, 2009); Jason Leopold, "Bush Authorized Domestic Spying Before 9/11," Truthout, January 13, 2006, http://www.truthout.org/article/jason-leopold-bush-authorized-domestic-spying-before-911 (accessed April 29, 2009).

120. Dan Eggen and Paul Kane, "Gonzales Hospital Episode Detailed: Ailing Ashcroft Pressured on Spy Program, Former Deputy Says," Washington Post, May 16, 2007.

121. "Press Conference of the President," the White House, December 19, 2005, http://georgewbush-whitehouse.archives.gov/news/releases/2005/12/20051219-2.html (accessed April 29, 2009).

122. "Press Briefing by Attorney General Alberto Gonzales and General Michael Hayden, Principal Deputy Director for National Intelligence," the White House, December 19, 2005, http://georgewbush-whitehouse.archives.gov/news/releases/2005/12/20051219-1.html (accessed April 29, 2009).

123. "Whistle-Blower Outs NSA Spy Room," Wired News, April 7, 2006.

124. Lesley Cauley, "NSA Has Massive Database Of Americans' Phone Calls," USA Today, May 11, 2006.

125. Shane Harris, "NSA Sought Data Before 9/11," National Journal, November 2, 2007.

126. Dan Eggen, "NSA Spying Part of Broader Effort," Washington Post, August 1, 2007.

127. David Swanson, "New NSA Whistleblower Speaks," July 1, 2007, http://afterdowningstreet.org/node/24183 (accessed April 29, 2009).

128. David Swanson, "New NSA Whistleblower Tells of Faulty WMD Evidence," May 19, 2008, http://afterdowningstreet.org/node/33525 (accessed April 29, 2009).

129. Brian Ross, Vic Walter, and Anna Schechter, "Exclusive: Inside Account on U.S. Eavesdropping on Americans," ABC, October 9, 2008, http://abcnews.go.com/Blotter/Story?id=5987804&page=1 (accessed April 29, 2009). ABC was prompted in this by its former employee James Bamford, who wrote about both Kinne and Faulk in a book that came out at the same time: James Bamford, The Shadow Factory: The Ultra-Secret NSA from 9/11 to the Eavesdropping on America (New York: Doubleday, 2008).

130. Dennis Kucinich, David Swanson, and Elizabeth de la Vega, The 35 Articles of Impeachment and the Case for Prosecuting George W. Bush (Port Townsend, WA: Feral House, 2008) Articles XXIV–XXV, http://afterdowningstreet.org/busharticles (accessed April 29, 2009).

131. "Obama Backs Bill Giving Immunity To Telecoms," Huffington Post, June 20, 2008, http://www.huffingtonpost.com/2008/06/20/obama-backs-bill-giving-i_n_108370.html (accessed April 29, 2009).

132. Dennis Kucinich, David Swanson, and Elizabeth de la Vega, The 35 Articles of Impeachment and the Case for Prosecuting George W. Bush (Port Townsend, WA: Feral House, 2008), http://afterdowningstreet.org/busharticles (accessed April 29, 2009).

133. Memorandum RE: Standards of Conduct For Interrogation Under 18 USC ßß 2340-2340A, from Assistant Attorney General Jay S. Bybee to White House Counsel Alberto R. Gonzales,

August 1, 2002, http://www.washingtonpost.com/wp-srv/nation/documents/dojinterroga-tionmemo20020801.pdf (accessed April 29, 2009).

134. John Yoo, Public debate with Doug Cassel in Chicago Illinois, December 1, 2005, http://youtube.com/watch?v=Vt1-eWU2Iio (accessed April 29, 2009).

135. American Civil Liberties Union, "U.S. Operatives Killed Detainees During Interrogations in Afghanistan and Iraq," October 24, 2005, http://www.aclu.org/intlhumanrights/gen/21236prs20051024.html (accessed April 29, 2009).

136. "Bush's State of the Union Speech," CNN, January 29, 2003, http://www.cnn.com/2003/ALLPOL-ITICS/01/28/sotu.transcript (accessed April 29, 2009).

137. *Boston Globe* Questionnaire on Executive Power, December 20–22, 2007, http://www.ontheis-sues.org/2007_Exec_Power.htm (accessed April 28, 2009).

138. Ibid.

139. "Smart on Crime: Recommendations for the Next Administration and Congress," The Con-stitution Project, November 5, 2008, http://2009transition.org (accessed April 29, 2009).

140. The statement and signers are posted at http://prosecutebushcheney.org.

141. Erna Paris, *The Sun Climbs Slow: The International Criminal Court and the Struggle for Jus-tice* (New York: Seven Stories Press, 2008).

142. "Treaties," United States Senate, http://www.senate.gov/artandhistory/history/common/briefing/Treaties.htm (accessed April 29, 2009).

143. Ruth Conniff, "Et Tu, Feingold? Senator Russ Feingold supports confirmation of John Ashcroft as Attorney General," *The Progressive*, March 2001.

144. Dennis Kucinich, David Swanson, and Elizabeth de la Vega, *The 35 Articles of Impeachment and the Case for Prosecuting George W. Bush* (Port Townsend, WA: Feral House, 2008) Article XXXIII, http://afterdowningstreet.org/busharticles (accessed April 29, 2009).

145. "Bush Pleads for 'Spirit of 9/11'," BBC, September 10, 2005, http://news.bbc.co.uk/2/hi/amer-icas/4233266.stm (accessed April 29, 2009).

146. Elizabeth Holtzman and Cynthia L. Cooper, *The Impeachment of George W. Bush: A Prac-tical Guide for Concerned Citizens* (New York: Nation Books, 2006).

147. This disaster "killed at least 1,282 people, with 2 million more displaced. 302,000 housing units were destroyed or damaged by the hurricane, 71 percent of these were low-income units. More than 500 sewage plants were destroyed, more than 170 point-source leakages of gasoline, oil, or natural gas, more than 2,000 gas stations submerged, several chemical plants, eight oil refineries, and a superfund site was submerged. Eight million gallons of oil were spilled. Toxic materials seeped into floodwaters and spread through much of the city and surrounding areas." Dennis Kucinich, David Swanson, and Elizabeth de la Vega, *The 35 Articles of Impeachment and the Case for Prosecuting George W. Bush* (Port Townsend, WA: Feral House, 2008) Article XXXI, http://afterdowningstreet.org/busharticles. (accessed April 28, 2009).

148. See Dennis Loo and Peter Phillips, *Impeach the President: The Case Against Bush and Cheney* (New York: Seven Stories Press, 2006).

149. I opposed the war and do not want to see wars better run or more efficient. I believe every sol-dier who took part was taking part in a crime, and I wouldn't have preferred to see more Iraqis killed than Americans saved. But none of that justifies the injuries and deaths inflicted on those soldiers by Bush's unconstitutional negligence.

150. David Swanson, "What Protection?" *The Humanist*, September/October 2008.

151. Robert Winnett, "President George Bush: 'Goodbye from the World's Biggest Polluter,'" *Telegraph*, July 10, 2008, http://www.telegraph.co.uk/news/worldnews/2277298/ President-George-Bush-Goodbye-from-the-worlds-biggest-polluter.html (accessed April 29, 2009).

152. Amanda Terkel, "Ex-EPA Official: White House Lied To Hide Cheney's Role In Eviscerating Global Warming Testimony," Think Progress, July 8, 2008, http://thinkprogress.org/2008/07/08/burnett-cheney (accessed April 29, 2009).

153. On May 9, 2007, President Bush released "National Security Presidential Directive/NSPD 51," which effectively gives the president unchecked power to control the entire government

and to define that government in time of an emergency, as well as the power to determine whether there is an emergency. The document also contains "classified Continuity Annexes." In July 2007 and again in August 2007 Rep. Peter DeFazio, a senior member of the House Homeland Security Committee, sought access to the classified annexes. DeFazio and other leaders of the Homeland Security Committee, including Chairman Bennie Thompson, were denied a review of the Continuity of Government classified annexes.

154. Eugene Jarecki, *The American Way of War: Guided Missiles, Misguided Men, and a Republic in Peril* (Free Press, 2008).

155. *Boston Globe* Questionnaire on Executive Power, December 20–22, 2007, http://www.ontheissues.org/2007_Exec_Power.htm (accessed April 28, 2009).

156. See http://www.propublica.org/special/missing-memos.

157. Tim Shipman and Melissa Kite, "UK Government Suppressed Evidence On Binyam Mohamed Torture Because MI6 Helped His Interrogators," *Telegraph*, February 7, 2009, http://www.telegraph.co.uk/news/newstopics/politics/defence/4551441/UK-government-suppressed-evidence-on-Binyam-Mohamed-torture-because-MI6-helped-his-interrogators.html (accessed April 29, 2009).

158. Jason Lewis, "Food Writer's Online Guide To Building An H-Bomb . . . The 'Evidence' That Put This Man In Guantánamo," *Daily Mail*, February 8, 2009, http://www.dailymail.co.uk/news/article-1138845/Food-writers-online-guide-building-H-bomb-evidence-man-Guantanamo.html (accessed April 29, 2009).

159. Glenn Greenwald, "New And Worse Secrecy And Immunity Claims From The Obama DOJ," Salon.com, April 6, 2009, http://www.salon.com/opinion/greenwald/2009/04/06/obama (accessed April 29, 2009).

160. Commuting a sentence leaves a criminal record but removes any punishment, and the president's power to grant reprieves and pardons has been interpreted to include this power as well.

161. Marcy Wheeler, "George Bush Authorized the Leak of Valerie Wilson's Identity," FireDogLake, May 29, 2008, http://emptywheel.firedoglake.com/2008/05/29/george-bush-authorized-the-leak-of-valerie-wilsons-identity (accessed April 29, 2009).

162. John Yoo, Public debate with Doug Cassel in Chicago Illinois, December 1, 2005, http://youtube.com/watch?v=Vti-eWU2Iio (accessed April 29, 2009).

163. Lawrence Velvel, "Attempted Statutory Immunity For The Executive's War Crimes," After Downing Street, September 8, 2008, http://afterdowningstreet.org/node/35878 (accessed April 29, 2009).

164. James Madison, "The Federalist No. 10, The Utility of the Union as a Safeguard Against Domestic Faction and Insurrection," November 22, 1787, http://www.constitution.org/fed/federa10.htm (accessed April 29, 2009).

165. The House Judiciary Committee Subcommittee on the Constitution discussed this topic on February 28, 2001, and Congressman Barney Frank promoted his proposal to end pardon power as of October 1st of a president's final year in office. "Presidential Pardon Power Hearing Before The Subcommittee On The Constitution Of The Committee On The Judiciary," House Of Representatives, One Hundred Seventh Congress, First Session, February 28, 2001, http://commdocs.house.gov/committees/judiciary/hju71180.000/hju71180_of.htm (accessed April 29, 2009).

166. Dana Nelson, *Bad for Democracy: How the Presidency Undermines the Power of the People* (University Of Minnesota Press, 2008).

167. Michael Duffy, "The Cheney Branch of Government," *Time*, June 22, 2007, http://www.time.com/time/nation/article/0,8599,1636435,00.html (accessed April 29, 2009).

168. John Dean, *Worse Than Watergate: The Secret Presidency of George W. Bush* (New York: Little, Brown and Company, 2004).

169. Jonathan Mahler, "After the Imperial Presidency," *New York Times Magazine*, November 2008.

170. Glenn Harlan Reynolds, "Where Does the Vice President Belong?" *New York Times* op-ed, October 27, 2008.
171. "Vice President's Remarks to the Traveling Press," White House, December 20, 2005, http://georgewbush-whitehouse.archives.gov/news/releases/2005/12/20051220-9.html (accessed April 29, 2009).
172. Cheney's offenses are collected at http://impeachcheney.org.

II. Congressional Collapse

1. Camp Hope: Countdown to Change, http://camphope2009.org (accessed April 29, 2009).
2. Jonathan Mahler, "After the Imperial Presidency," *New York Times Magazine*, November 2008.
3. David Ignatius, "An Opening for the Democrats," *Washington Post*, January 12, 2007, Page A-19.
4. John Walsh, "How Rahm Emanuel Has Rigged a Pro-War Congress," *Counterpunch*, October 14-15, 2006, http://www.counterpunch.org/walsh10142006.html (accessed April 29, 2009).
5. Here's a good place to find polls: http://www.pollingreport.com/issues.htm. Also see the chapter on "Thinking" below.
6. Polls on impeachment are collected at http://afterdowningstreet.org/polling, and here is polling on using the power of the purse: http://democrats.com/iraq-poll-2.
7. Robert Parry, "Bush's New War Lies," *Consortium News*, September 10, 2003, http://www.consortiumnews.com/2003/091003a.html (accessed April 29, 2009); "Misperceptions, the Media and the Iraq War: Study Finds Widespread Misperceptions on Iraq Highly Related to Support for War," Program on International Policy (PIPA) at the University of Maryland and Knowledge Networks, October 2, 2003, http://www.worldpublicopinion.org/pipa/articles/international_security_bt/102.php?nid=&id=&pnt=102&lb=brusc (accessed April 29, 2009).
8. Congressional approval trends are discussed in the Introduction to this book and in a footnote there.
9. "Senate Judiciary Committee Hearing for Nomination of Judge Mukasey as Attorney General, Day Two," CQ Transcripts Wire, October 18, 2007, http://www.washingtonpost.com/wp-srv/politics/documents/transcript_mukasey_hearing_day_two_101807.html (accessed April 29, 2009).
10. Impeachment is assigned to the House in Article I, Section 2, and the power to hold trials for those impeached to the Senate in Article I, Section 3. Article II has three mentions of impeachment, including a reference to "Removal of the President from Office" in Section 1 which has been altered by amendment, as well as the stipulation in Section 2 that the president cannot pardon an impeachment, and the listing in Section 4 of who can be impeached. Article III, Section 2 makes impeachment trials the only non-jury trials.
11. Richard J. Ellis, *Founding the American Presidency* (Rowman & Littlefield Publishers, 1999) page 243, http://books.google.com/books?id=ybmeEcpEvlsC (accessed April 29, 2009).
12. John Nichols, *The Genius of Impeachment: The Founders' Cure for Royalism* (New York: New Press, 2006).
13. At the start of the 110th Congress in early 2007, new House Judiciary Committee Chairman John Conyers shouted on a stage on the national mall to hundreds of thousands of activists "We Can Fire Him!" as the crowd, which had been shouting "impeach!", cheered in support. Then Conyers got off the stage and explained to a reporter that he only meant that we could elect someone new in November 2008. Of course, some wiser souls than most of the rest of us began pushing for Bush's impeachment during his first term, including Bob Fertik of Democrats.com who began in 2000. When I began working for Bob in 2005 I proposed trying to end the war and he suggested that trying to impeach the president was more realistic.

14. I don't often use the word "comity," but I distinctly recall meeting with a staffer for the new House Intelligence Committee Chairman in early 2007, because when she told me they wouldn't investigate the war lies in order to preserve comity, I thought at first that she'd said comedy. And it would have been funny if only . . .

15. Jeanne Cummings, "Impeachment Proves Risky Political Issue: Some Democratic Activists Push Removing Bush From Office, But Mainstream Steers Clear," *Wall Street Journal*, March 6, 2006, Page A-4, http://afterdowningstreet.org/node/8583 (accessed April 29, 2009).

16. Here's that poll: see http://afterdowningstreet.org/node/4421 and here are all the polls ever done on impeaching Bush and/or Cheney: http://afterdowningstreet.org/polling (accessed April 29, 2009).

17. David Swanson, "Congresswoman Cynthia McKinney Makes the Case for Impeachment," January 5, 2007, http://afterdowningstreet.org/node/16976 (accessed April 29, 2009).

18. See http://afterdowningstreet.org/cheney (accessed April 29, 2009).

19. See http://afterdowningstreet.org/bush (accessed April 29, 2009).

20. Jodin Morey, "Conyers: Obama's More Important Than Justice, Impeach Later," *Impeach for Peace*, March 19, 2008, http://impeachforpeace.org/impeach_bush_blog/?p=5012 (accessed April 29, 2009).

21. US House Judiciary Democratic Staff, *George W. Bush versus the U.S. Constitution: The Downing Street Memos and Deception, Manipulation, Torture, Retribution, and Coverups in the Iraq War and Illegal Domestic Spying* (Chicago: Academy Chicago Publishers, 2006), http://afterdowningstreet.org/constitutionincrisis (accessed April 28, 2009); "Reining In The Imperial Presidency: Lessons and Recommendations Relating to the Presidency of George W. Bush," House Committee on the Judiciary Majority Staff Report to Chairman John Conyers Jr. January 13, 2009, http://afterdowningstreet.org/downloads/conyers09.pdf (accessed April 29, 2009).

22. Dennis Kucinich, David Swanson, and Elizabeth de la Vega, *The 35 Articles of Impeachment and the Case for Prosecuting George W. Bush* (Port Townsend, WA: Feral House, 2008), http://afterdowningstreet.org/busharticles (accessed April 29, 2009).

23. See Further Reading at the back of this book.

24. Brian C. Kalt, "The Constitutional Case for the Impeachability of Former Federal Officials: An Analysis of the Law, History, and Practice of Late Impeachment," June 26, 2006, http://afterdowningstreet.org/node/37834 (accessed April 28, 2009).

25. "U.S. Public Widely Distrusts Its Leaders," Zogby International, May 23, 2006, http://zogby.com/news/readnews.cfm?ID=1116 (accessed April 30, 2009).

26. NB: President Gerald Ford testified before Congress while Dick Cheney was working for him. "George Stephanopoulos' Interview With Vice President Dick Cheney," ABC, *This Week*, November 5, 2006, http://abcnews.go.com/ThisWeek/Story?id=2629168&page=1 (accessed April 29, 2009).

27. He made this claim at a July 25, 2008, hearing on impeachable offenses that was very carefully designed not to be a real impeachment hearing and not to have any possible consequences, no matter what was heard.

28. Here is an index of outstanding subpoenas from the 110th Congress: http://democrats.com/subpoenas (accessed April 29, 2009).

29. An index of House Judiciary Committee hearing transcripts can be found here: http://judiciary.house.gov/hearings/legislation.html (accessed April 29, 2009).

30. David Swanson and Jonathan Schwarz, "Tomgram: Swanson and Schwarz, The New Investigation Season," Tom Dispatch, February 2, 2007, http://tomdispatch.com/post/161913/swanson_and_schwarz_the_new_investigation_season (accessed April 30, 2009).

31. Document 7, "Report on Whether Public Statements Regarding Iraq by U.S. Government Officials Were Substantiated by Intelligence Information, Together With Additional and Minority Views," Select Committee on Intelligence, United States Senate, June 2008, http://intelligence.senate.gov/080605/phase2a.pdf (accessed April 30, 2009).

32. Satyam Khanna, "Leahy And Cornyn: White House Trying To 'Eliminate' FOIA Office," Think Progress, January 26, 2008, http://thinkprogress.org/2008/01/26/leahy-foia (accessed April 30, 2009).

33. Michael Waldman has proposed allowing the minority party in Congress to issue subpoenas. But parties are not Constitutional elements of our government, and checks and balances between two parties (and what if there are more than two?) do nothing to further representation of the people. Without the power of impeachment a minority party could not enforce compliance with its subpoenas anyway, and while the minority Democrats up through 2006 talked a good line, a review of their performance from 2007 to 2008 suggests that they would have accomplished very little with a minority subpoena power.

34. See http://democrats.com/subpoenas for a collection of subpoenas not complied with.

35. Nancy Pelosi had made this commitment in May 2006, months before becoming speaker, in response to a bluff by the Republican National Committee claiming that talk of impeachment would benefit Republicans. She did say that new information might change her position, but with indisputable evidence of the gravest offenses imaginable already public knowledge, her final position was crystal clear.

36. David Swanson, "How to Put Rove Behind Bars for Years," *Let's Try Democracy*, August 6, 2008, http://davidswanson.org/node/1416 (accessed April 30, 2009).

37. Marcy Winograd, "Waxman Says He Will Keep an Open Mind on Impeachment," After Downing Street, August 8, 2007, http://afterdowningstreet.org/node/25571 (accessed April 30, 2009).

38. "Contempt of the Senate," *New York Times*, May 16, 1897, http://query.nytimes.com/gst/abstract.html?res=9A00E1DC1630E132A25755C1A9639C94669ED7CF (accessed April 30, 2009); "Order of the Senate," *Time*, February 26, 1934, http://time.com/time/magazine/article/0,9171,747022,00.html?promoid=googlep (accessed April 30, 2009).

39. Among many other impeachable offenses, a majority of Americans knew Bush had misled the public about the reasons for war. Here are polls: http://democrats.com/bush-lied-polls.

40. Dennis Kucinich, David Swanson, and Elizabeth de la Vega, *The 35 Articles of Impeachment and the Case for Prosecuting George W. Bush* (Port Townsend, WA: Feral House, 2008) Article XXVII, http://afterdowningstreet.org/busharticles (accessed April 29, 2009).

41. Ibid., Article XXVI.

42. "Press Conference of the President," White House, December 19, 2005, http://georgewbush-whitehouse.archives.gov/news/releases/2005/12/# (accessed April 30, 2009).

43. "Video Shows Bush Got Explicit Katrina Warning: President, Chertoff Were Clearly Told Of Storm's Dangers Numerous Times," Associated Press, March 2, 2006, video: http://msnbc.msn.com/id/11627394 (accessed April 30, 2009).

44. This charge formed the basis for one of three articles of impeachment introduced by Congressman Dennis Kucinich against Dick Cheney in April 2007: http://impeachcheney.org.

45. In *Rosul v. George W. Bush* the Supreme Court ruled that detainees were being wrongfully imprisoned at Guantánamo Bay Detention Center in Cuba. The Bush administration's detainment policies and actions were ruled unconstitutional and illegal, in violation of the Fifth, Sixth, and Seventh Amendments. Again in June 2008 in the case of *Boumediene et al v. Bush et al.*, the Supreme Court struck down part of the Military Commissions Act restoring the right to habeas corpus, or at least trying to; see http://www.scotusblog.com/wp/wp-content/uploads/2008/06/06-1195.pdf. And in *Hamdan v. Donald Rumsfeld, George W. Bush, et al.*, the Supremes ruled that the Military Commissions instituted by the Bush Administration violated the Universal Code of Military Justice and the Geneva Conventions, which are U.S. law under Article VI of the Constitution. The Bush administration's actions were found to be illegal and unconstitutional, violating the Fifth, Sixth, and Seventh Amendments.

46. Jan Crawford Greenburg, Howard L. Rosenberg, and Ariane de Vogue, "Bush Aware of Advisers' Interrogation Talks," *ABC World News With Charles Gibson*, April 11, 2008, http://abcnews.go.com/TheLaw/LawPolitics/Story?id=4635175&page=1 (accessed April 30,

2009); Ali Frick, "Bush: I Personally Authorized Torture Of Khalid Sheikh Mohammed," Think Progress, January 11, 2009, http://thinkprogress.org/2009/01/11/bush-authorized-torture (accessed April 30, 2009); "Transcript: Cheney Defends Hard Line Tactics," ABC, *Good Morning America*, December 15, 2008, http://abcnews.go.com/Politics/story?id=6464697&page =1 (accessed April 30, 2009).

47. International Committee of the Red Cross, "ICRC Report On The Treatment Of Fourteen 'High Value Detainees' In CIA Custody," February 2007, http://www.nybooks.com/icrc-report.pdf (accessed April 29, 2009).

48. David Swanson, "Live Blogging Hearing on Impeachment (Not Yet Impeachment Hearing)," After Downing Street, July 25, 2008, http://afterdowningstreet.org/node/35043 (accessed April 30, 2009).

49. See http://democrats.com/subpoenas for the list.

50. Will Bunch, "Obama would ask his AG to 'immediately review' potential of crimes in Bush White House," *Philadelphia Daily News*, April 14, 2008, http://www.philly.com/philly/blogs/attytood/Barack_on_torture.html (accessed April 30, 2009).

51. Jonathan Schwarz, "Looking Forward To It," A Tiny Revolution, November 5, 2008, http://tinyrevolution.com/mt/archives/002677.html (accessed April 30, 2009).

52. "Rep. Baldwin Introduces Bill to Undo and Prosecute Bush-Cheney Crimes," After Downing Street, September 26, 2008, http://afterdowningstreet.org/baldwinbill (accessed April 30, 2009).

53. See http://www.youtube.com/watch?v=HaG9d_4zij8 (accessed April 30, 2009) for video.

54. David Swanson, "Party Leaders Crack Down on Rep. Sherman for Reporting Threat of Martial Law," After Downing Street, October 24, 2008, http://afterdowningstreet.org/node/37101 (accessed April 30, 2009); David Swanson, "Rep. Brad Sherman Makes Further Non-Retraction of Report on Threats of Martial Law," After Downing Street, October 27, 2008, http://afterdowningstreet.org/node/37162 (accessed April 30, 2009).

55. The 110th Congress passed in 2007 the "John Warner National Defense Authorization Act for Fiscal Year 2007," which included measures making it easy for the president to institute martial law if he or she chose. Congress repealed those measures in 2008 in the "National Defense Authorization Act for Fiscal Year 2008."

56. Charlie Savage, "Obama's War on Terror May Resemble Bush's in Some Areas," *New York Times*, February 17, 2009, http://www.nytimes.com/2009/02/18/us/politics/18policy.html?_r=1&ref=politics&pagewanted=all (accessed April 29, 2009).

57. "Agreement Concerning Accomodation," Committee on the Judiciary, *U.S. House of Representatives v. Harriet Miers et al.*, http://www.talkingpointsmemo.com/documents/2009/03/congress-bush-administration-agreement-on-rovemiers-testimony-3409.php?page=1 (accessed April 30, 2009).

58. "Reining In The Imperial Presidency: Lessons and Recommendations Relating to the Presidency of George W. Bush," House Committee on the Judiciary Majority Staff Report to Chairman John Conyers Jr., January 13, 2009, http://afterdowningstreet.org/downloads/conyers09.pdf (accessed April 29, 2009).

59. Jan Crawford Greenburg and Howard L. Rosenberg and Ariane de Vogue, "Bush Aware of Advisers' Interrogation Talks," *ABC World News With Charles Gibson*, April 11, 2008, http://abcnews.go.com/TheLaw/LawPolitics/Story?id=4635175&page=1 (accessed April 30, 2009); Ali Frick, "Bush: I Personally Authorized Torture Of Khalid Sheikh Mohammed," Think Progress, January 11, 2009, http://thinkprogress.org/2009/01/11/bush-authorized-torture (accessed April 30, 2009); "Transcript: Cheney Defends Hard Line Tactics," ABC: *Good Morning America*, December 15, 2008, http://abcnews.go.com/Politics/story?id =6464697&page=1 (accessed April 30, 2009).

60. David Swanson, "John Yoo Writes That Bush Authorized Torture," After Downing Street, January 29, 2009, http://afterdowningstreet.org/node/39407 (accessed April 30, 2009).

61. "Tortured 9/11 Suspect May Never Be Prosecuted: Pentagon Official," Agence France Press, January 15, 2009, http://afterdowningstreet.org/node/39003 (accessed April 30, 2009).

62. Jill Lawrence, "Poll: Most Want Inquiry Into Anti-Terror Tactics," *USA Today*, February 12, 2009, http://www.usatoday.com/news/washington/2009-02-11-investigation-poll_N.htm (accessed April 30, 2009).

63. Marc Ambinder, "Why They Kept Secret," *The Atlantic*, February 10, 2009, http://politics.theatlantic.com/2009/02/considered_in_light_of_the.php (accessed April 30, 2009).

64. Patrick Leahy, "A Truth Commission to Investigate Bush-Cheney Administration Abuses Hotlist," Daily Kos, February 12, 2009, http://www.dailykos.com/story/2009/2/12/1350/08709/262/696385 (accessed April 30, 2009).

65. Bob Fertik, "Victory! House Judiciary Democrats Want Special Prosecutor for Torture," Democrats.com, April 28, 2009, http://democrats.com/victory-house-judiciary-democrats-want-special-prosecutor-for-torture (accessed April 30, 2009).

66. Russ Feingold, "Opening Statement of U.S. Senator Russ Feingold, Senate Judiciary Committee Hearing, Exercising Congress's Constitutional Power to End a War," January 30, 2007, http://feingold.senate.gov/statements/07/01/20070130.htm (accessed April 30, 2009).

67. Bob Fertik, "Reid Admits He COULD Block Iraq Funds—But He WON'T," Democrats.com, October 30, 2007, http://democrats.com/harry-reid-admits-he-could-block-iraq-funds-but-he-wont (accessed April 30, 2009).

68. While I consider the filibuster an antidemocratic tool that we'd be better off without, I did want to see it used by a minority of senators on behalf of the majority of Americans who opposed the Iraq war. No such luck. See "VIDEO: Senator Russ Feingold Is Urged to Filibuster Occupation Funding, and Refuses," After Downing Street, February 20, 2008, http://afterdowningstreet.org/node/31205 (accessed April 30, 2009).

69. Tim Grieve, "The Attorney General Takes Cover," *Salon*, April 19, 2007, http://mobile.salon.com/politics/war_room/2007/04/19/gonzales6/index.html (accessed April 30, 2009).

70. Leo Shane III, "Poll of Troops In Iraq Sees 72% Support For Withdrawal Within A Year," *Stars and Stripes*, Mideast edition, March 1, 2006, http://stripes.com/article.asp?section=104&article=34538&archive=true (accessed April 30, 2009).

71. Here's a video that I posted and sent to CNN and MSNBC, who aired it while missing the point: http://www.youtube.com/watch?v=mS4wHMCc57k (accessed April 30, 2009). Here's the full transcript: http://afterdowningstreet.org/node/19420 (accessed April 30, 2009).

72. Bob Fertik, "Democrats.com Poll: 68% Want Our Troops Safely Home in 6 Months," Democrats.com, May 5, 2008, http://democrats.com/iraq-poll-2 (accessed April 30, 2009).

73. "Congressional Scorecard for the 110th Congress, 2008," Peace Action and Peace Action West, http://www.peace-action.org/scorecard08 (accessed April 30, 2009).

III. Undoing The Imperial Presidency

1. "U.S. and World Population Clocks," US Census Bureau, http://www.census.gov/main/www/popclock.html (accessed April 30, 2009).

2. A 2007 World Bank list places the United States first. A 2008 International Monetary Fund list places the United States second behind the European Union, as does the *2008 CIA World Fact Book*. All three lists are available at http://en.wikipedia.org/wiki/List_of_countries_by_GDP_(nominal) (accessed April 30, 2009).

3. All the lists cited are posted at http://en.wikipedia.org/wiki/List_of_countries_by_GDP_(nominal)_per_capita and http://en.wikipedia.org/wiki/List_of_countries_by_GDP_(PPP)_per_capita (accessed April 30, 2009).

4. The Human Poverty Index is posted at http://en.wikipedia.org/wiki/Human_Poverty_Index#The_human_poverty_index_for_selected_OECD_countries_.28HPI-2.29 (accessed April 30, 2009).

5. "Mother's Day Report Card: The Best and Worst Countries to Be a Mother," Save the Children, May 6, 2008, http://www.savethechildren.org/newsroom/2008/best-worst-countries-mother .html (accessed April 30, 2009).

6. "Environmental Performance Index 2008," Yale University, http://epi.yale.edu (accessed April 30, 2009).

7. "List of countries by carbon dioxide emissions," Wikipedia, http://en.wikipedia.org/wiki/List_of_countries_by_carbon_dioxide_emissions (accessed April 30, 2009).

8. "2008 Worldwide Press Freedom Index," Reporters Without Borders, http://www.rsf.org/article.php3?id_article=29011 (accessed April 30, 2009).

9. "Energy Statistics > Oil > Consumption (most recent) by country," Nation Master, http://www.nationmaster.com/graph/ene_oil_con-energy-oil-consumption (accessed April 30, 2009).

10. Nick Turse, *The Complex: Mapping America's Military Industrial Technological Entertainment Academic Media Corporate Matrix* (New York: Metropolitan Books 2008).

11. Pete Engardio, "Bush Balks at Pact to Fight Poverty," *Business Week*, September 2, 2005.

12. Steven Radelet, "Think Again: U.S. Foreign Aid," *Foreign Policy*, February 2005, http://www.foreignpolicy.com/story/cms.php?story_id=2773 (accessed April 30, 2009); Anup Shah, "US and Foreign Aid Assistance," Global Issues, April 13, 2009, http://www.globalissues.org/article/35/us-and-foreign-aid-assistance#Almostallrichnationsfailthisobligation (accessed April 30, 2009).

13. Steven Radelet, "Think Again: U.S. Foreign Aid," *Foreign Policy*, February 2005, http://www.foreignpolicy.com/story/cms.php?story_id=2773 (accessed April 30, 2009).

14. Israel and Egypt are the leading recipients of billions of US dollars every year in military "aid."

15. Jacqueline Cabasso, "StratCom in Context: The Hidden Architecture of U.S. Militarism," After Downing Street, April 23, 2008, http://afterdowningstreet.org/militarism (accessed April 30, 2009).

16. Ibid.

17. Ibid.

18. Ibid.

19. Daniel Dombey and Stanley Pignal, "Europeans See US as Threat to Peace," *Financial Times*, July 1, 2007, http://www.ft.com/cms/s/0/70046760-27f0-11dc-80da-000b5df10621 .html?nclick_check=1 (accessed April 29, 2009).

20. "U.S. Is The Biggest Debtor And It's Recovery In This Recession Is Limited By It's Debt," Investment Watch, October 19, 2008, http://investment-blog.net/us-is-the-biggest-debtor-and-its-recovery-in-this-recession-is-limited-by-its-debt (accessed April 30, 2009).

21. "Terrorism Deaths Rose in 2007," *Voice of America*, May 2, 2008.

22. I've borrowed questions 21 and 22 from an article I read while revising this book: Bill Quigley, "Twenty Questions: Social Justice Quiz 2008," Truthout, September, 12, 2008.

23. "Global Polling Data On Opinion of American Policies, Values And People, Hearing Before the Subcommittee On International Organizations, Human Rights, And Oversight of the Committee On Foreign Affairs, House Of Representatives One Hundred Tenth Congress, First Session, March 6, 2007, Serial No. 110-4," http://www.internationalrelations.house.gov/110/33821.pdf (accessed April 30, 2009).

24. Jackie Cabasso wrote a paper called "StratCom in Context: The Hidden Architecture of US Militarism" that collects sources documenting the size of the US empire, and I've posted it at http://afterdowningstreet.org/militarism. Cabasso cites Chalmers Johnson, who wrote, "If there were an honest count, the actual size of our military empire would probably top 1,000 different bases in other people's countries." Jacqueline Cabasso, "StratCom in Context: The Hidden Architecture of US Militarism," After Downing Street, April 23, 2008, http://afterdowningstreet.org/militarism (accessed April 30, 2009).

25. Ibid.

26. Karen DeYoung, "Spy Agencies Say Iraq War Hurting U.S. Terror Fight," *Washington Post*, September 24, 2006, Page A-1.

27. Helena Cobban, *Re-Engage: America and the World After Bush* (Boulder, CO: Paradigm Publishers, 2008).

28. "PIPA-Knowledge Networks Poll: The Federal Budget: The Public's Priorities," February 18-25, 2005, http://www.pipa.org/OnlineReports/DefenseSpending/FedBudget_Mar05/FedBudget_Mar05_quaire.pdf (accessed April 30, 2009).

29. AfterDowningStreet.org began pushing for prosecution in December of 2005; see http://prosecutebushcheney.org.

30. Will Bunch, "Obama would ask his AG to "immediately review" potential of crimes in Bush White House," *Philadelphia Daily News*, April 14, 2008, http://www.philly.com/philly/blogs/attytood/Barack_on_torture.html (accessed April 30, 2009).

31. David Edwards and Muriel Kane, "Biden Denies Report: 'No One's Talking About Pursuing Bush Criminally,'" Raw Story, September 4, 2008, http://www.rawstory.com/news/2008/Biden_would_prosecute_Bush_officials_if_0904.html (accessed April 30, 2009).

32. David Swanson, "What to Ask Eric Holder," After Downing Street, January 11, 2009, http://afterdowningstreet.org/node/38889 (accessed April 30, 2009).

33. Lawrence Velvel, "Attempted Statutory Immunity For The Executive's War Crimes," After Downing Street, September 8, 2008, http://afterdowningstreet.org/node/35878 (accessed April 30, 2009).

34. "National Lawyers Guild Calls For Special Prosecutor To Investigate Bush Administration Officials And Lawyers Who Wrote Torture Memos," May 12, 2008, http://www.nlg.org/news/index.php?entry=entry080512-145553 (accessed April 30, 2009).

35. Papers of the Robert Jackson Steering Committee are posted at http://afterdowningstreet.org/robertjackson (accessed April 30, 2009).

36. See http://prosecutebushcheney.org for the full list.

37. "Senate Confirmation Hearings: Eric Holder, Day One," *New York Times*, January 16, 2009, http://www.nytimes.com/2009/01/16/us/politics/16text-holder.html (accessed April 30, 2009).

38. Jason Leopold, "Senate Report to Reveal New Details of Bush Officials' Role in Torture," *The Public Record*, March 27, 2009, http://www.pubrecord.org/torture/797-senate-report-to-reveal-new-details-of-bush-officials-role-in-torture-.html (accessed April 30, 2009).

39. His contact information is 202-514-2001; AskDOJ@usdoj.gov; fax: 202-307-6777.

40. Vince Bugliosi, *The Prosecution of George W. Bush for Murder* (New York: Vanguard Press, 2008).

41. Elisabeth Rosenthal, "Woman Speaks Of Husband's Torture At CIA Abduction Trial In Italy," *International Herald Tribune*, May 14, 2008.

42. David Dishneau, "Abu Ghraib Inmates Sue Contractors, Claim Torture," Associated Press, July 1, 2008.

43. For a fictionalized story somewhat like that of Arar, see the Hollywood movie *Rendition*.

44. Nils Andersson and Daniel Lagolnitzer and Diana G. Collier, *International Justice and Impunity: The Case of the United States* (Atlanta, GA: Clarity Press, 2008).

45. Here is an extensive list of crimes and their statutes of limitations: http://afterdowningstreet.org/sites/afterdowningstreet.org/files/crimesandstatutes.pdf (accessed April 30, 2009).

46. "Department Of Defense Base Structure Report Fiscal Year 2007 Baseline (A Summary Of DOD's real Property Inventory)," Office Of The Deputy Under Secretary Of Defense (Installations & Environment), http://www.defenselink.mil/pubs/BSR_2007_Baseline.pdf (accessed April 30, 2009).

47. Hugh Gusterson, "Empire of Bases," *Bulletin of the Atomic Scientists*, March 10, 2009, http://www.thebulletin.org/web-edition/columnists/hugh-gusterson/empire-of-bases (accessed April 30, 2009).

48. Robert Pollin and Heidi Garrett-Peltier, "The U.S. Employment Effects of Military and Domestic Spending Priorities," Political Economy Research Institute at University of Massachusetts, Amherst, October 2007.

49. Nils Andersson and Daniel Lagolnitzer and Diana G. Collier, *International Justice and Impunity: The Case of the United States* (Atlanta, GA: Clarity Press, 2008).

50. Robert Pollin and Heidi Garrett-Peltier, "The U.S. Employment Effects of Military and Domestic Spending Priorities," Political Economy Research Institute at University of Massachusetts, Amherst, October 2007.

51. "Report of the Task Force on A Unified Security Budget for the United States, FY 2009," Institute for Policy Studies, 2009.

52. This is the $47 billion spying budget, plus $13 billion for military spying, minus $5 billion that I'm guesstimating might be defensible.

53. This is the US military using US troops on US soil with a mission that includes, at least as initially announced, "crowd control."

54. I'm using $100 B here instead of $142 because some of the cost of bases in Afghanistan is contained in the figure saved by ending those wars.

55. I hope this is not an annual expense!

56. Amy Weiss, "GAO Finding: Majority Of Corporations Pay No Taxes. Sen. Levin Decries 'Tax Trickery,'" BuzzFlash, August 12, 2008, http://blog.buzzflash.com/alerts/451 (accessed April 30, 2009).

57. "First-of-Its Kind Study: Medicare for All (Single-Payer) Reform Would Be Major Stimulus for Economy with 2.6 Million New Jobs, $317 Billion in Business Revenue, $100 Billion in Wages," California Nurses Association, http://tinyurl.com/hcarestimulus (accessed April 30, 2009).

58. "Where Your Income Tax Money Really Goes," War Resisters League, http://www.warresisters.org/pages/piechart.htm (accessed April 30, 2009).

IV. Forming a More Perfect Union

1. "A Reticent Justice Opens Up to a Group of Students," *New York Times*, April 14, 2009.

2. David Swanson, "Imagine There's No Heaven," Let's Try Democracy, September 6, 2008, http://davidswanson.org/node/1422 (accessed May 1, 2009).

3. John C. Yoo and Robert J. Delahunty, "Memorandum for Alberto R. Gonzales, Counsel to the President Re: Authority for Use of Military Force to Combat Terrorist Activities Within the United States," October 23, 2001, http://www.usdoj.gov/opa/documents/memomilitaryforce-combatus10232001.pdf (accessed May 1, 2009).

4. See also the chapter on "The Power of the Judiciary" in this book.

5. John Bowe, *Nobodies: Modern American Slave Labor and the Dark Side of the New Global Economy* (New York: Random House, 2007).

6. Jesse Jackson Jr., *A More Perfect Union: Advancing New American Rights* (New York: Welcome Rain Publishers, 2001).

7. Peter Linebaugh, *The Magna Carta Manifesto: Liberties and Commons for All* (Berkeley, CA: University of California Press, 2008).

8. Cyril Mychalejko, "Ecuador's Constitution Gives Rights to Nature," Znet, September 27, 2008, http://www.zmag.org/znet/viewArticle/18934 (accessed May 1, 2009).

9. For excellent discussions of the rights to health care, housing, education, the environment, and equal rights for women, see Jesse Jackson Jr., *A More Perfect Union: Advancing New American Rights* (New York: Welcome Rain Publishers, 2001).

10. Dorie Baker, "Professor Lane Explains The Economics Of Happiness," *Yale Bulletin and Calendar*, March 16, 2001, http://yale.edu/opa/arc-ybc/v29.n22/story5.html (accessed May 1, 2009).

11. Stephen Bezruchka, "Health and Poverty in the U.S.," *Z Space*, December 9, 2003, http://zmag.org/znet/viewArticle/9413 (accessed May 1, 2009).

12. Sam Pizzigati, *Greed and Good: Understanding and Overcoming the Inequality that Limits Our Lives* (New York: Apex Press, 2006) available free online at http://www.greedandgood.org/New-ToRead.html (accessed May 1, 2009).

13. Ibid.

14. Ibid.

15. This would need to include all personal income, even that not worked for. A similar system could be figured out for the taxation of businesses' income, as well as for the taxation of estates.

16. The United States is a party to and should uphold: the Convention on the Prevention and Punishment of the Crime of Genocide; the Geneva Convention relative to the Treatment of Prisoners of War; the Geneva Convention relative to the Protection of Civilian Persons in Time of War; the Protocol Additional to the Geneva Conventions of August 12, 1949, and relating to the Protection of Victims of International Armed Conflicts (Protocol I); and the Protocol Additional to the Geneva Conventions of August 12, 1949, and relating to the Protection of Victims of Non-International Armed Conflicts (Protocol II).

17. "The International Bill of Human Rights," Office of the United Nations High Commissioner for Human Rights, http://www2.ohchr.org/english/law/index.htm (accessed May 1, 2009).

18. See http://article-5.org.

19. Steven Hill, *10 Steps to Repair American Democracy* (PoliPointPress, 2006).

20. Discussed by Dana D. Nelson. See Further Reading at the end of this book, *Bad for Democracy: How the Presidency Undermines the Power of the People* (Minneapolis: University of Minnesota Press, 2008).

21. Francis Newton Thorpe, *The Constitutional History of the United States*, Volume II (Chicago: Callaghan & Company, 1901) page 212, available free online at http://books.google.com (accessed May 1, 2009).

22. See www.poclad.org.

23. "Nader: Time To Challenge Corporate Personhood In Court," *Undernews*, October 27, 2008, http://prorev.com/2008/10/nader-time-to-challenge-corporate.html (accessed May 1, 2009).

24. "Resource Flyers," BarackObama.com, Aug 26, 2007.

25. "Barack Obama, Expenditures Breakdown," Center for Responsive Politics, http://www.opensecrets.org/pres08/expend.php?cycle=2008&cid=N00009638 (accessed May 1, 2009).

26. Michael Moore, *Mike's Election Guide 2008* (New York/Boston: Grand Central Publishing, 2008).

27. One of the few commentators I know of who places an appropriate emphasis on the damage done by empowering parties is John R. MacArthur, publisher of *Harper's* and author of *You Can't Be President: The Outrageous Barriers to Democracy in America* (Brooklyn, NY: Melville House, 2008).

28. Katrina Vanden Heuvel, "Woman in the House: A Conversation With Nancy Pelosi," *The Nation*, July 29, 2008, http://www.thenation.com/doc/20080804/kvh (accessed May 1, 2009).

29. Also in agreement on the need for nonpartisan redistricting is Michael Waldman. Waldman is a former Bill Clinton speechwriter and the current director of the Brennan Center. His 2008 book is called *A Return to Common Sense: 7 Bold Ways to Revitalize Our Democracy* (Naperville, IL: Sourcebooks, Inc., 2008).

30. Larry J. Sabato, *A More Perfect Constitution: 23 Proposals to Revitalize Our Constitution and Make America a Fairer Country* (New York: Walker & Company, 2007).

31. Steven Hill argues that the root problem is actually partisan residential patterns, and that even nonpartisan commissions could not create competitive districts in most states without splitting up localities and communities of interest through bizarre gerrymandering of a different sort. Hill supports nonpartisan redistricting, but believes other solutions are needed as well. Hill puts most of his hope in proportional representation and instant runoff voting (IRV), ideas that I think have a lot of merit but ultimately more drawbacks than advantages. I put more of my hope in smaller districts, reduced advantages for parties, public financing, and better media. But I agree with Hill that a coherent package of solutions is needed, none amounting to a mir-

acle cure on its own. Later in this book I discuss how we might get smaller districts and what I think is wrong with proportional representation and IRV. Steven Hill, *10 Steps to Repair American Democracy* (Sausalito, CA: PoliPointPress, 2006).

32. 2007 AFL-CIO Democratic Primary Forum, Aug 8, 2007.

33. Michael Moore proposes four regional primaries as one of his six proposals. Moore is also one of the few commentators, at least that I happen to have found, who is willing to propose a shortened election season. He suggests four months for primaries and two months for a general election. Michael Moore, *Mike's Election Guide 2008* (New York/Boston: Grand Central Publishing, 2008).

34 Fair Vote describes and compares various proposals for primaries at http://fairvote.org/?page=871. Pick the scheme you like best; they're all better than what we've got.

35. "Congressional Apportionment," United States Census Bureau, http://www.census.gov/population/www/censusdata/apportionment.html (accessed May 1, 2009).

36. Larry J. Sabato, *A More Perfect Constitution: 23 Proposals to Revitalize Our Constitution and Make America a Fairer Country* (New York: Walker & Company, 2007).

37. Steven Hill, *10 Steps to Repair American Democracy* (Sausalito, CA: PoliPointPress, 2006).

38. Larry J. Sabato, *A More Perfect Constitution: 23 Proposals to Revitalize Our Constitution and Make America a Fairer Country* (New York: Walker & Company, 2007).

39. William Greider, "Stop Senator No," *The Nation*, December 10, 2008, http://www.thenation.com/doc/20081229/greider (accessed May 1, 2009).

40. Barack Obama, *The Audacity of Hope: Thoughts on Reclaiming the American Dream* (New York: Crown, 2006), page 81.

41. Steven Hill, *10 Steps to Repair American Democracy* (Sausalito, CA: PoliPointPress, 2006).

42. Ibid.

43. See Further Reading at the end of this book.

44. See Further Reading at the end of this book.

45. The reform effort in Baltimore would have been more effective with nonpartisan redistricting. The Mayor redrew the map with districts aimed at keeping incumbents in office. One of the districts he drew resembled an eagle.

46. Larry J. Sabato, *A More Perfect Constitution: 23 Proposals to Revitalize Our Constitution and Make America a Fairer Country* (New York: Walker & Company, 2007).

47. Judith Resnik and Theodore Ruger, "One Robe, Two Hats," *New York Times*, July 17, 2005, http://query.nytimes.com/gst/fullpage.html?res=9E06E4DE1130F934A25754C0A9639C8B63&p agewanted=2 (accessed May 1, 2009); Steven Hill, *10 Steps to Repair American Democracy* (Sausalito, CA: PoliPointPress, 2006).

48. After I'd begun writing this book, I remembered that a professor at the University of Virginia here in Charlottesville, Larry Sabato, had recently published a book called *A More Perfect Constitution: 23 Proposals to Revitalize Our Constitution and Make America a Fairer Country* (New York: Walker & Company, 2007). I picked up a copy and am greatly indebted to Sabato for a wealth of information. While I oppose most of his twenty-three proposals and much of his general outlook on the world, his support for a balanced-budget amendment is one point on which I very much agree with him.

49. See http://nationalinitiative.org.

V. Citizen Power

1. Sarah van Gelder, "Our Own Agenda: 10 Policies For a Better America," *Yes!*, Fall 2008, http://yesmagazine.org/purpleagenda (accessed May 1, 2009).

2. AP polls can be found at http://surveys.ap.org (accessed May 1, 2009); "AP/ABT SRBI—August 22-August 29, 2008 National Constitution Center Poll, Final Data—September 2, 2008,"

http://surveys.ap.org/data/SRBI/AP-National%20Constitution%20Center%20Poll.pdf (accessed May 1, 2009).

3. For some of the actions around the country in 2007, see http://afterdowningstreet.org/node/29133; for those in 2008, see http://afterdowningstreet.org/node/34589. Of course, the total count of arrestees does not match that of the movement against the Vietnam War, and the incidents are less numerous than those found in the historic labor movement or the civil rights movement as a whole, but the amount of activity in contrast to public knowledge that it exists puts this movement in a league of its own.

4. These examples are taken from Kevin Danaher, Shannon Biggs, and Jason Mark, *Building the Green Economy: Success Stories from the Grass Roots* (Sausalito, CA: PoliPointPress, 2007).

5. The 2008 Democratic National Platform, http://www.democrats.org/a/party/platform.html (accessed May 1, 2009).

6. Ann Wright, *Dissent: Voices of Conscience: Government Insiders Speak Out Against the War in Iraq* (Koa Books, 2008), http://voicesofconscience.com (accessed May 1, 2009).

7. Russ Baker, "Bush Wanted To Invade Iraq If Elected in 2000," Guerrilla News Network, October 27, 2004, http://www.gnn.tv/articles/article.php?id=761 (accessed April 28, 2009).

8. Robert W. McChesney and John Nichols, *Our Media, Not Theirs: The Democratic Struggle Against Corporate Media* (New York: Seven Stories Press, 2002); Edward S. Herman and Noam Chomsky, *Manufacturing Consent: The Political Economy of the Mass Media* (New York: Pantheon, 2002); Robert W. McChesney, Rich Media, *Poor Democracy: Communication Politics in Dubious Times* (New York: New Press, 2000).

9. Massimo Calabresi and Perry Bacon Jr., "America's 10 Best Senators," *Time*, April 16, 2006, http://www.time.com/time/magazine/article/0,9171,1184028,00.html (accessed May 1, 2009).

10. David Swanson, "McCain, Torture Supporter," *Let's Try Democracy*, September 12, 2008, http://davidswanson.org/node/1429 (accessed May 1, 2009).

11. Censure is just a reprimand with no actual penalty. It does not exist in the Constitution and probably shouldn't.

12. "Why Iraq War Support Fell So Fast," *Christian Science Monitor*, November 21, 2005, http://www.csmonitor.com/2005/1121/p01s02-usfp.html (accessed May 1, 2009).

13. "Transcript for June 5," NBC's *Meet the Press With David Gregory*, June 5, 2005, http://www.msnbc.msn.com/id/8062380 (accessed May 1, 2009).

14. Jay Rosen, "The Downing Street Memo and the Court of Appeal in News Judgment," Huffington Post, June 20, 2005, http://www.huffingtonpost.com/jay-rosen/the-downing-street-memo-a_b_2902.html (accessed May 1, 2009).

15. India Autry, "Movement Takes Bush to Task," *Newsday*, June 23, 2005.

16. David Barstow, "Behind Analysts, the Pentagon's Hidden Hand," *New York Times*, April 20, 2008.

17. For in-depth coverage see "Investigating the Pentagon's Pundits," *Source Watch*, http://www.sourcewatch.org/index.php?title=Investigating_the_Pentagon%27s_pundits#_note-analyst (accessed May 1, 2009).

18. David Barstow, "Behind Analysts, the Pentagon's Hidden Hand," *New York Times*, April 20, 2008.

19. Ibid.

20. For a look at some of the evidence that emerged, see http://afterdowningstreet.org/keydocuments.

21. Dennis Kucinich, David Swanson, and Elizabeth de la Vega, *The 35 Articles of Impeachment and the Case for Prosecuting George W. Bush* (Port Townsend, WA: Feral House, 2008) Article X, http://afterdowningstreet.org/busharticles (accessed April 28, 2009).

22. Ibid., Article I.

23. Video News Releases, Center for Media and Democracy, http://www.sourcewatch.org/index.php?title=Video_news_releases (accessed May 1, 2009).

24. David Swanson, "*Newsweek* Poll Shows Majority Supports Impeachment," After Downing Street, October 24, 2006, http://afterdowningstreet.org/node/14897 (accessed May 1, 2009).
25. While I have not seen any media reformers propose constitutional amendments, some of the following proposals are heavily influenced by various authors and activists, especially Robert McChesney, John Nichols, and http://FreePress.net.
26. A statement by Jesse Jackson Jr. released in March 2005.
27. Steven Hill, too, supports establishing a right to vote. Steven Hill, *10 Steps to Repair American Democracy* (Sausalito, CA: PoliPointPress, 2006).
28. A statement by Jesse Jackson Jr. released in March 2005.
29. Waldman is a former Bill Clinton speechwriter and the current director of the Brennan Center. His 2008 book is called *A Return to Common Sense: 7 Bold Ways to Revitalize Our Democracy* (Naperville, IL: Sourcebooks, Inc., 2008).
30. Ibid.
31. Steven Hill, *10 Steps to Repair American Democracy* (Sausalito, CA: PoliPointPress, 2006).
32. Steven Hill cites this comment, which was tape-recorded by Nixon in the Oval Office, and printed in James Warren, "Some Vintage Nixon Saves the Day," *Chicago Tribune*, August 19, 2001.
33. Dennis Kucinich, David Swanson, and Elizabeth de la Vega, *The 35 Articles of Impeachment and the Case for Prosecuting George W. Bush* (Port Townsend, WA: Feral House, 2008) Article XXVIII, http://afterdowningstreet.org/busharticles (accessed April 28, 2009).
34. Michael Moore gets this one right too, making paper ballots one of his six proposals in *Mike's Election Guide 2008*. He does so even while drastically understating the problems with electronic machines and maintaining that while such machines could swing an election, he is able to know that they have never done so yet.
35. Adam Cohen, "A Tale of Three (Electronic Voting) Elections," *New York Times*, August 1, 2008.
36. David Earnhardt, *Uncounted: The New Math of American Elections*, http://uncountedthemovie.com.
37. Mark Crispin Miller, *Loser Take All: Election Fraud and the Subversion of Democracy, 2000–2008* (Brooklyn, NY: Ig Publishing, 2008).
38. Ibid.
39. And presumably impeachment would have been restored to Congress if Kerry and Edwards had been awarded what they won, because—as later emerged—Edwards had had an extramarital sexual affair, which everyone in Washington understands to be the gravest threat possible to our system of government.
40. Dennis Kucinich, David Swanson, and Elizabeth de la Vega, *The 35 Articles of Impeachment and the Case for Prosecuting George W. Bush* (Port Townsend, WA: Feral House, 2008) Article XXIX, http://afterdowningstreet.org/busharticles (accessed April 28, 2009).
41. Steven F. Freeman and Joel Bleifuss, *Was the 2004 Presidential Election Stolen? Exit Polls, Election Fraud, and the Official Count* (New York: Seven Stories Press, 2006).
42. Steven Hill, too, advocates for machines with a voter verified paper trail, but does not address the problems with that solution or explain how it is compatible with his proposal for instant runoff voting. Steven Hill, *10 Steps to Repair American Democracy* (Sausalito, CA: PoliPointPress, 2006).
43. Norquist told Thomas Frank that conservatives should welcome blatantly corrupt earmarks on legislation because, like any other unpopular act of government, they help turn people against the government. See Thomas Frank, *The Wrecking Crew: How Conservatives Rule* (New York: Metropolitan Books, 2008).
44. See http://workingamerica.org/join.
45. Deborah Stone, *The Samaritan's Dilemma: Should Government Help Your Neighbor?* (New York: Nation Books, 2008).
46. Ibid.

47. Peter Ackerman and Jack Duvall, *A Force More Powerful: A Century of Nonviolent Conflict* (New York: St. Martin's Press, 2000).

48. Gene Sharp, *Waging Nonviolent Struggle: 20th Century Practice and 21st Century Potential* (Manchester, NH: Extending Horizons Books, 2005).

49. Martin Luther King Jr., *A Testament of Hope: The Essential Writings and Speeches of Martin Luther King, Jr.* (New York: HarperOne, 1990).

50. Orange is a color that was used in the Ukraine and has been used in the United States, in part because it was the color of prison uniforms used in Guantánamo.

51. See the National Network Opposing Militarization of Youth: http://nnomy.org.

52. John R. MacArthur, *You Can't Be President: The Outrageous Barriers to Democracy in America* (Brooklyn, NY: Melville House, 2008).

Acknowledgments

I wrote the initial draft of this book between August 8 and September 8, 2008, during which time I avoided blogging. (In some chapters I've drawn on pieces of writing that I had previously blogged.) I revised the book in the weeks following September 8, and following the November 4 elections, and again in March and April 2009. For years prior to that radically unusual month in 2008, I had written so much on the Internet that I was often asked about my "books" and had to reply that I'd never written any. Now I have, and I have many thank-yous to hand out for having had the privilege to do so and for having had the past few years of activism and discussion to draw on for inspiration and motivation.

Above all I thank the Internet, and especially all the people who post comments beneath articles I write, correcting and disputing things. You work for free. When you're not helpful I can ignore you. And not much gets past you.

Once I'd written a book, I was quickly able to find a wonderful publisher. I want to thank Crystal Yakacki, Dan Simon, and Seven Stories Press. Crystal encouraged me to completely reorganize what I had originally drafted, resulting in a far more useful presentation, and then proposed good edits of that.

I also want to thank all the people who read a draft of the book (or part of one) in September 2008 and offered helpful comments. They are: Jeff Cohen, Jonathan Schwarz, Bob Fertik, Steve Cobble, and Mike Ferner. And in April 2009 those people who read small or large sections of the book and offered helpful comments: William Greider, Richard Cook, John Bonifaz, Jason Leopold, and Jeff Cohen. I am, of course, solely to blame for failing to benefit from any good advice that I have not heeded and for any other flaws in the book.

I got involved in documenting the crimes and abuses of our government in May of 2005, when some friends and I set up a website and an activist coalition called AfterDowningStreet.org. Bob Fertik, who runs Democrats.com, has provided a large part of my income for over four years as I've worked on that project, and to him I am forever indebted.

Steve Cobble, John Bonifaz, and Tim Carpenter were also among those who launched AfterDowningStreet.org, and I've benefitted tremendously from working with each of them. Thanks also goes to May First for hosting the site and to Velvet Revolution for paying the hosting fees.

I've benefitted as well from my contact with many activists, writers, and volunteers including Jonathan Schwarz, David Waldman, Sophie De Vries, Pris Sears, Maura Yost, Bill Moyer, Ray McGovern, Elizabeth de la Vega, Marjorie Cohn, John Nichols, Dennis Loo, Debra Sweet, Elizabeth Holtzman, Medea Benjamin, Glen Ford, Gael Murphy, Desiree Fairooz, Jodie Evans, Shahid Buttar, Ann Wright, Elliott Adams, Michael McPhearson, Bill Perry, Cindy Sheehan, Dede Miller, Tiffany Burns, Adam Kokesh, Dave Lindorff, John Kaminski, Geoff Millard, Tim Goodrich, Mike Kim, Lennox Yearwood, Kevin Zeese, Mike Ferner, Charlie Anderson, Phyllis Bennis, Karen Dolan, Richard Bell, Karen Bradley, Zool, Dan DeWalt, Richard Matthews, Phil Burk, Larry Everest, Carlos Arredondo, Melida Arredondo, Mike Hersh, Diane Wittner, Brad Friedman, Brett Kimberlin, Ilene Proctor, Marcy Winograd, Michael Jay, Robert Fitrakis, David Earnhardt, Mark Crispin Miller, Peter Phillips, Ellen Taylor, Leslie Angeline, Jes Richardson, Pete Perry, Leslie Cagan, Sue Udry, Linda Weiner, Elaine Brower, Linda Boyd, Cynthia Papermaster, Vincent Bugliosi, Sherwood Ross, Bruce Fein, Michael Ratner, Aaron Rubin, Tom Engelhardt, Bruce Gagnon, Rain Burroughs, Chris Dorsey, Jodin Morey, Mikael Rudolph, Kathleen Gabel, Alex Zeese, Chris Belcher, Sandra Marshall, Bill Hughes, Barry Student, Tyler Westbrook, Kevin Behrends, Marsha Coleman-Adebayo, Barbara Cummings, Michael Eisenscher, Denice Lombard, Travis Morales, George Ripley, Vicenta Montoya, Pat Elder, Suz Krueger, Jay Kohn, Sibel Edmonds, Jacob Park, Geoff King, Charlie Jenks, Joan Wile, Linda Schade, Nick Mottern, Dinah Mason, Cynthia McKinney, Tina Richards, Norman Solomon, Laura Flanders, Sam Husseini, Eric Oemig, Dave Meserve, Stacy Bannerman, Mimi Kennedy, Rocky Anderson, Patricia Foulkrod, Daniel Ellsberg, Osagyefo Uhuru Sekou, Raed Jarrar, John Judge, Nadir, Michael Zmolek, Peter Gamble, Verna Avery Brown, Matthew Cardinale, Jennifer Van Bergen, Katie Heald, Lori Perdue, Peter B. Collins, Clark Kissinger, Will Covert, Carrie Biggs-Adams, Jose Rodriguez, Virginia Rodino, Amy Branham, Joan

Stallard, Ted Glick, Granny D, Andrew Burgin, Charlie Imes, Ellen Tenney, Sunsara Taylor, Alfredo Lopez, Jamie McLelland, Eleanore Eveleth, Tim Rinne, Harry Lonsdale, Nadia McCaffrey, Michael Smith, Karen Meredith, Gene Bruskin, Kelly Dougherty, Charlie Anderson, Stephen Lendman, Phil Restino, Ann Wilcox, Trevor Phillips, Stephanie Westbrook, Cinzia Bottene, Dana Balicki, David Rubinson, Jamilla El-Shafei, Karen Bernal, Joia Jefferson-Nuri, Dahr Jamail, Ralph Miller, Malachy Kilbride, Brad Newsham, Dahlia Wasfi, Francis Boyle, John Bruhns, Daniel Fearn, Larisa Alexandrovna, Frank Mandanici, Bill Lackemacher, Lawrence Velvel, David Michael Green, Garda Ghista, Mark Karlin, Scott Galindez, Rob Kall, Cindy Piester, Dave Allsopp, Steve Bhaerman, Carly Miller, Matthew Gerbasi, Bill Mitchell, Robert Greenwald, Karen Kwiatowski, Antonia Juhasz, Stephen Zunes, Brendan Smith, Jeremy Brecher, Sheldon Rampton, Gareth Porter, John Stauber, Danny Schechter, J. E. McNeil, Allison Hantschel, Jeff Cohen, Jonathan Tasini, Howard Zinn, Keith Murphy, Thom Hartmann, Jeeni Criscenzo, Bill Scheurer, Luke Ryland, Moya Atkinson, the late David Cline, Marietta Elaine Hedges, Kevin Murray, Jack Gilhooley, Amy Baxter, Adrienne Kinne, David Murfee Faulk, Jason Leopold, Mike Hearington, Susan Harman, Andy Worthington, Ben Davis, Peter Weiss, Kristina Borjesson, Colleen Costello, and thousands more whom I will list at http://davidswanson.org and to whom I apologize for not including here. Of course, none of the people listed above necessarily agree with all or any of the opinions in this book.

I especially want to thank those activists and writers with whom I've worked in Charlottesville, Virginia, including Sarah Lanzman, Sue Chase, Susan Oberman, Shallel, Iela, Sean McCord, Virginia Rovnyak, Tamar Goodale, Linda Lisanti, Bob Hoffman, Mike Johnson, Bill Anderson, Helena Cobban, Ken Zelin, Jeff Winder, Lorrie Delahanty, Chip Tucker, Dave Norris, Donna Goings, and hundreds more whom I will list at http://davidswanson.org, and none of whom necessarily agree with everything in this book.

I also want to acknowledge Congressman Dennis Kucinich who went further than any other member of the House or Senate to try to hold Dick Cheney and George W. Bush accountable for their crimes while they were in office, and Congressman Robert Wexler who greatly advanced that agenda together with his terrific staff people, including Eric Johnson, Brian Franklin, Ellen McLaren, and Joshua Rogin.

I want to thank all of my family, and extended family, including Ralph, Suzzanne, Matt, Kelly, Mark, Hallie, Travis, and my friends, especially those with whom I don't see eye to eye on all things political. I am forever grateful to my parents, Neil Swanson and Linda Swanson, for everything they have taught me and done for me.

Nothing in my life would be possible without the most loving, inspiring, amazing, wise, and generous woman ever born, my wife Anna Catherine Naylor Swanson.

This book is dedicated to my son, Wesley Neil Swanson, age three.

INDEX

International Convention on the
Elimination of All Forms of Racial
Discrimination, 222, 223
International Convention on the
Protection of the Rights of All
Migrant Workers and Members of
Their Families, 223
International Covenant on Civil and
Political Rights (ICCPR), 74, 222
violation of, 316n1
International Covenant on Economic,
Social and Cultural Rights
(ICESCR), 222
International Criminal Court (ICC), 81,
85, 186, 196, 224, 312
International Federation of Human
Rights (FIDH), 194
International Longshoreman's and
Warehouse Workers' Union, 306
Internet, 234
interrogation techniques, 209
IPS. *See* Institute for Policy Studies
Iran, 29, 109, 173
Cheney triggering war in, 35
Iran-Contra scandal, 153
Iraq, 29, 173, 174
bombing runs, 34
building military bases in, 55
death in, 319n48
displaced people in, 319n48
ending occupation of, 52
Inspector General in, creation of, 18
National Intelligence Estimate on, 95
permanent military presence in, 83
United Nations authorization for
attacking, 33
United States democracy v., 83–84
war crimes in, 320n80
withdrawal cost, 153
Iraqi National Congress, 70
Iraq treaty, 44, 82–83
as advisory, 85–86
resistance to, 82–83
Iraq Veterans Against the War, 320n80
Iraq War
body/vehicle armor for, 90

Cheney responding to opinions on, 1,
4
creation of excuses for, 34
de-funding, 119, 153–64
disapproval of, 172
Feingold on ending, 153–54
international law violated by, 43
legality of, 40–44
misspending of funds in, 56
preparation for, 34
protests, 41
as recruiting tool for terrorists, 174
supporting troops in, 155
IRV. *See* voting, instant runoff
Isikoff, Michael, 23, 34–35
Israel, 189
The Italian Letter (Eiser & Royce), 37–38
Italy
military bases in, US, 188, 190–93
rendition trial in, 184

Jackson, Andrew, 14
Jackson, Jesse, Jr., 289, 334n9
jail, 138–39. *See also specific jails*
al-Janabi, Emad, 185
Jane's, 63
Japan, 188
Jarecki, Eugene, 94
Jefferson, Thomas, ix, x, 228
on creation of Senate, 246
on elected despotism, 124
Jennings, J. Scott, 133
Jeppesen DataPlan, 96
Jewel v. NSA, 97
Jim Crow, 248, 290
Johnson, Andrew, 125, 128
Johnson, Chalmers, 173, 188, 332n24
Johnson, Stephen, 91
John Warner National Defense
Authorization Act for Fiscal Year
2007, 51, 329n55
Jones, Walter, 191
journalists, investigative, 287

Progressive Democrats of America, 153
Project for a New American Century
    (PNAC), 31, 32, 51, 308
proportional representation, 252, 335n31
ProsecuteBushCheney.org, 182, 310
*The Prosecution of George W. Bush for
    Murder* (Bugliosi), 33, 182–83
public relations (PR), 5
publishers, 287
Puerto Rico, 29
Putnam, Robert, 301

al Qaeda
    Cheney on, 6
    Hussein and, forged letter between, 40
Qatar, 189
Qui Tam, 184
Qwest, 69

Rasul v. Bush, 75, 328n45
Reagan, Ronald, 302
    signing statements by, 14
RealNews.com, 271
recall, right of, 256
redistricting, 238. *See also* minimum-split
    districting
    non-partisan, 239, 335n29, 335n45
redress of grievances, right to petition
    for, 206–7
Reed, Jack, 151, 181
regime change, 29. *See also* war; *specific
    regime changes*
    accountability for, 29
Reid, Harry, 152
    Schultz interviewing, 154–55
religion, freedom of, 206–7
rendition, extraordinary, 64, 73
    banning, 311
    Jeppesen DataPlan role in, 96
    Obama claiming, 78

trial in Milano, Italy, 184
    trial in Spain, 185
Reporters Without Borders, 168
Republican Party
    election fraud, 294
    impeachment benefiting, 328n35
    Justice Department hiring/firing
        based on loyalty to, 65
    party loyalty ahead of institutional
        loyalty in, 106
"Restore. Protect. Expand. Amend the
    War Powers Resolution," 49–50
revenge, 268
revolution, 303–4
Reyes, Silvestre, 134
Reynolds, Glenn Harlan, 106–7
Rice, Condoleezza
    on Hussein, 32
    punishing, 9
    subpoena refusal of, 134
Rich, Marc, 100
Richards, Tina, 157–61
Richardson, Elliot, 121
Ridge, Tom, 185
rights. *See specific rights*
rights, knowing, 219
Risen, James, 39, 67, 287
Ritter, Halsted, 128
Ritter, Scott, 305
Robbins, Tim, 210
Robert Jackson Steering Committee, 179
Roberts, John, 87
Rockefeller, Jay, 134–35
Romania, 189
Roosevelt, Eleanor, 220–21
Roosevelt, Franklin Delano, 220–21
Roosevelt, Kermit, Jr., 174
Roosevelt, Theodore, 117
Rove, Karl, 65, 66, 106, 133, 280
    citizens' arrest of, 176
    executive privilege claimed by, 140–41
    private testimony, 146
Royce, Knut, 37–38
rule of law, abandoning, 8
Rumsfeld, Donald, 185
    Soviet weaponry claims of, 31

About the Author

David Swanson is a writer, an activist, and an online organizer who writes about our representative government as one with experience attempting to compel our government to represent us.

Swanson holds a master's degree in philosophy from the University of Virginia. He has worked as a newspaper reporter and as a communications director, with jobs including press secretary for Dennis Kucinich's 2004 presidential campaign, media coordinator for the International Labor Communications Association, and three years as communications coordinator for ACORN, the Association of Community Organizations for Reform Now. Swanson is cofounder of AfterDowningStreet.org; Washington director of Democrats.com; and a board member of Progressive Democrats of America, the Backbone Campaign, and Voters for Peace. Swanson lives in Charlottesville, Virginia, with his wife Anna and son Wesley. His website is http://davidswanson.org.

Swanson wrote the introduction for *The 35 Articles of Impeachment and the Case for Prosecuting George W. Bush* by Dennis Kucinich with additional material by Elizabeth de la Vega. *Daybreak: Undoing the Imperial Presidency and Forming a More Perfect Union* is his first book.

About Seven Stories Press

SEVEN STORIES PRESS is an independent book publisher based in New York City, with distribution throughout the United States, Canada, England, and Australia. We publish works of the imagination by such writers as Nelson Algren, Russell Banks, Octavia E. Butler, Ani DiFranco, Assia Djebar, Ariel Dorfman, Coco Fusco, Barry Gifford, Hwang Sok-yong, Lee Stringer, and Kurt Vonnegut, to name a few, together with political titles by voices of conscience, including the Boston Women's Health Collective, Noam Chomsky, Angela Y. Davis, Human Rights Watch, Derrick Jensen, Ralph Nader, Gary Null, Project Censored, Barbara Seaman, Gary Webb, and Howard Zinn, among many others. Seven Stories Press believes publishers have a special responsibility to defend free speech and human rights, and to celebrate the gifts of the human imagination, wherever we can. For additional information, visit www.sevenstories.com.